DOMINATION, LEGITIMATION, AND RESISTANCE

Contributions in Labor History
SERIES EDITORS: MILTON CANTOR AND BRUCE LAURIE

Class, Sex, and the Woman Worker
Milton Cantor and Bruce Laurie, editors

When Workers Fight: The Politics of Industrial Relations in the Progressive
Era, 1898-1916
Bruno Ramirez

DOMINATION, LEGITIMATION, AND RESISTANCE

THE INCORPORATION OF THE NINETEENTH-CENTURY ENGLISH WORKING CLASS

FRANCIS HEARN

Contributions in Labor History, Number 3

GREENWOOD PRESS
WESTPORT, CONNECTICUT • LONDON, ENGLAND

Library of Congress Cataloging in Publication Data

Hearn, Francis.
   Domination, legitimation, and resistance.

   (Contributions in labor history ; no. 3
ISSN 0146-3608)
   Bibliography: p.
   Includes index.
   1. Labor and laboring classes—Great Britain—
History. 2. Industrial sociology. I. Title.
II. Series.
HD6957.G7H4   301.44'42'0941   77-84753
ISBN 0-8371-9847-X

Library of Congress Catalog Card Number: 77-84753
ISBN: 0-8371-9847-X
ISSN: 0146-3608

First published in 1978

Greenwood Press, Inc.
51 Riverside Avenue, Westport, Connecticut 06880

Printed in the United States of America

10 9 8 7 6 5 4 3 2 1

To FRANK *and* CATHERINE HEARN, *with love.*

Contents

Acknowledgments

In preparing this book, I have had the good fortune to be able to work closely with and learn much from many people. Especially important to me are Bill Harrell, Jim McKelvey, and Ken Neubeck. Each read several drafts of the manuscript and gave generously of his time, his knowledge and encouragement, his scholarship and humor. Milton Cantor and Bruce Laurie also provided many valuable suggestions for improving the manuscript. I am indebted as well to Volker Meja and Zvi Namerwirth. Neither has read the manuscript, but without them as teachers I would have no manuscript to be read. These people have enabled me to make my book better than it was; that it isn't better than it is, is entirely my fault.

Finally, I would like to thank Priscilla for her help, her understanding, and her smile. She makes life pleasant and writing books like this enjoyable.

Francis Hearn

DOMINATION, LEGITIMATION, AND RESISTANCE

Introduction

Four equally important and related goals guide the present study. These are:

First, a clarification, modification, and extension of the categories and insights of Critical Theory as they have been developed especially by Herbert Marcuse and Jürgen Habermas. While this dialectical theory can be neither proved nor disproved by the logic of empirical investigation, when translated into research questions the categories it contains can be extended and enriched.

Second, a critique of the Marxian dialectic. The premise underlying the evaluation of Marx's theoretical formulations is that the Marxian account of nineteenth-century English society—especially in its emphasis on the category of labor as the only mode of human self-realization—was an accurate one. This judgment permits an analysis of this society to be partially effected by an immanent criticism of Marx's work, and permits a reconsideration of the extent to which the Marxian categories were bounded by the categories of the society to which they were applied.

Third, an explanation and understanding of the events and processes which led to the incorporation of the English working class into the larger society by the 1850s. By focusing on England in this period, the impact of industrialism and capitalism on legitimacy and domination—a major concern of Marx and the Critical Theorists—can be clearly assessed.

Fourth, an account of the specific conditions under which the legitimacy of prevailing institutional arrangements will be seriously challenged by those who benefit least from them.

In pursuit of these goals, historical and sociological approaches to data analysis and explanation are employed. For the historian, explanation entails not prediction but description. The task of historical study is not to generate testable hypotheses but to identify the forces which contributed to a given state of affairs. Corresponding to this conception of historical study as a descriptive endeavor is the development of explanation by context. As Gordon Leff suggests, historical explanation is always contextual, for the conditions on which it rests only obtain for particular times and particular places. Moreover, since contexts are never identical, it follows "that history is a body of knowledge, not a store of axioms or laws which can be applied to events of the same nature."[1] According to this position, all the historical approach can do is provide a chronological narrative detailing how a particular outcome originated and was maintained.

Where historical problems tend to be delimited with reference to specific empirical contexts, sociological problems "tend to be rooted in and . . . generated by some conceptual apparatus . . ."[2] In contrast to the historian, the sociologist seeks to make his knowledge capable of explaining more than particular historical facts by approaching these facts as an illustrative case of a formal, conceptual model. While analytic models can enhance the generalizability of acquired knowledge, they often promote the neglect of the human element in social relationships.

If sociohistorical critique is to be successful it must overcome the tendency toward abstract generalization associated with the empirical-analytic approach and the kind of contextual determinism (which neglects significant historical trends) we find employed in the historical-interpretive approach. To do this is to resolve the tension between the unique and the general in a way that the resulting method does not abridge the flexibility and cumulative insight inherent in the historian's position, but does allow for the acquisition of knowledge which has applicability beyond and which makes intelligible the particular facts scrutinized. In resolving the tension, the strategy will be to see the general as manifested in the unique or the concrete. By compelling us to search for the general in the concrete, this strategy reduces the danger of reifying the historical situation. At the same time, this procedure alerts us to the seeds of future development contained in the unique and, in so doing, enables us to locate historical events as a sequence occurring within a range of possible variation, not as a mere random occurrence. Thus, by translating the general into the concrete, an analysis is possible whereby "the creativity of human interpretations and actions are linked with the structural milieu in which they operate."[3]

In any sociological study of relatively wide scope it is impossible for a single worker to master all the relevant primary sources that are available. It becomes necessary, accordingly, to rely extensively on secondary sources. Unable in these instances to assume the historian's concern with facts, the sociological investigator must depend upon what appear to be adequate assessments by accepted authorities. A number of difficulties, including the problem of selectivity, are associated with the use of secondary accounts. The potential severity of these problems, however, can be reduced if the sociological investigator acquires a full acquaintance with the historical research which has bearing on his problem and, as well, familiarizes himself with the points of controversy which continue to prevail among historians of the period in question.

As an interpretative study which aims to organize previously collected data in terms of a new analytical perspective, this study should not be assessed in accordance with the standards of historiography. Rather, the study should be judged (1) by the adequacy of the information gathered: Has contrary evidence been overlooked? Has the best evidence been used? (2) by the heuristic value of the categories: Are new, suggestive, and significant questions raised by the analysis? and (3) by the contribution the analysis makes to the improvement of social theory (Critical or Marxian theory in particular), to the study of social change, social movements and problems of legitimacy and authority, and to the understanding of the human condition.

NOTES

1. Gordon Leff, *History and Social Theory* (New York, 1971), p. 67.

2. Neil Smelser, *Essays in Sociological Explanation* (Englewood Cliffs, 1968), p. 35.

3. David Sallach, "Critical Theory and Critical Sociology: The Second Synthesis," *Sociological Inquiry* 43, 2 (1973): 137. Also see Barrington Moore, "Strategy in Social Science," *Political Power and Social Theory* (New York, 1958), pp. 111-159.

CHAPTER 1
Critical Theory and Social Incorporation

Max Horkheimer and Theodor Adorno, perhaps the two most influential figures in the development of Critical Theory, introduce a collection of their essays in 1944 by writing, "we had set ourselves nothing less than the discovery of why mankind, instead of entering into a truly human condition, is sinking into a new kind of barbarism."[1] The barbarism to which Horkheimer and Adorno refer is expressed in the visibly brutal atrocities committed in the name of Fascism; but more importantly, this uncivilization and irrationality is found also in the new forms of domination emerging in the midst of civilization and rationality. In both contemporary capitalist and socialist societies, domination has fused with a rationality of technique and technical control which enters into the realm of conscious reflection to absorb its negative and critical functions. Totalitarianism in modern civilization rests more on the impoverishment of culture and consciousness than on material impoverishment, and its dynamics are more subtle, its consequences more insidious, than previous forms of domination. Reason, the critical theorists claim, has been reduced to an instrument, severed from human content.[2] Formalized and instrumentalized, the rationality of civilization is used increasingly to manage and manipulate, to administer and control, to impose an identity between the individual and society, between actuality and potentiality. Instrumental reason obliterates discrepancies, gaps, and contradictions; it swallows up negation, and so betrays the truly human condition.

The modern form of totalitarianism, brought about by the false identity of opposites engineered by the spread of instrumental reason, receives the primary attention of Critical Theory, and is most forcefully characterized by Herbert Marcuse's category of one-dimensionality. The productive apparatus of technological civilization is totalitarian, Marcuse suggests, in that "it determines not only the socially needed occupations, skills, and attitudes, but also individual needs and aspirations."[3] The opposition between individual and social needs is thus obliterated, and the immediate identification or unification of the individual with the society is the result. "In this process, the 'inner' dimension of the mind in which opposition to [and negation of] the status quo can take root is whittled down."[4] The contrast between the given and the possible is cancelled as society acquires the capacity to repulse all alternatives. In this setting

> emerges a pattern of *one-dimensional thought and behavior* in which ideas, aspirations, and objectives that, by their content, transcend the established universe of discourse and action are either repelled or reduced to terms of this universe. They are redefined by the rationality of the given system and of its quantitative extension.[5]

In short, one-dimensional society emerges from the suppression of culture and consciousness and of the capacity for critical transcendence which they sustain. By eliminating the transcendent goals of culture, technological civilization "thereby eliminates or reduces those factors and elements of culture which were antagonistic and alien to the given forms of civilization."[6] In this way, culture is integrated into society and the negative integrated into positive.

One-dimensional society, then, rests on a rationalization of technique which permits the expression of only those needs and aspirations which can be satisfied by the established arrangements. By flattening out culture and consciousness, technological rationality has engendered "the closing of a vital space for the development of autonomy and opposition, the destruction of a refuge, of a barrier to totalitarianism."[7] Thus, as long as the system continues to employ technology to deliver the goods which satisfy the needs it has shaped, a critical subjective awareness of the liberating potentialities of technology will not emerge. Under these circumstances, fundamental emancipatory social change is blocked; for such social change, Marcuse writes, "presupposes the vital *need* for it, the experience of intolerable conditions and of their alternatives—and it is this need and this experience which are barred from developing in the established culture."[8]

Marcuse's category of one-dimensionality, by suggesting the constriction of culture and consciousness to the constraints of instrumental reason, affords the beginnings of an explanation of the social cohesion of advanced industrial society and, more specifically, of the integration of the working class into its structures. To fully develop such an explanation, as Michael Mann notes, "we must look back to the historical incorporation of working-class political and industrial movements in the nineteenth and twentieth centuries within existing structures."[9] Only by reconstructing the manner in which the universe of discourse has been closed, and the transcendent goals of culture blocked, will it be possible to apprehend—to know and to change—the existing forms of cultural domination. What is required, in short, is a search for the historical roots of one-dimensionality.

In large measure, the present study is conceived as part of this search. By reconstructing the conditions which lead to the depoliticization and eventual incorporation of the English working class during the industrial revolution, this study seeks to locate the historical origins of one-dimensionality in the early development of industrial capitalism. As it developed in these initial stages, one-dimensionality does not receive expression as, to use Marcuse's term, *mimesis* or the complete identification of the individual with his society. Rather, the one-dimensionality which took root in mid-nineteenth century England rested on the systematic blockage of the capacities found in culture and consciousness, capacities which enable the formulation of alternatives in terms of which people anticipate the future and discredit the present. It was with the suppression of these capacities and in the absence of alternatives that the English working class lost its rebellious disposition and entered into the institutions of industrial capitalism.[10] The analysis of these developments will be guided by the theoretical framework contained in Jürgen Habermas' recently developed 'work and interaction' dialectic.

THE RECONSTRUCTED DIALECTIC

Much of Habermas' work is geared to the formulation of a social theory of knowledge; that is, a theory of knowledge with epistemological categories grounded in basic socio-historical processes. In this formulation, Habermas reflects well the appreciation and critique of Marxian social theory that has characterized Critical Theory from the start.

The one-dimensionality or collapse of dimensions which Marcuse observes in advanced industrial society, Habermas discerns in Marxism. Although Marx viewed the making of history as a practical activity involving will and consciousness, there is in his writings a 'latent positivism' which directly contributed to the more objectivistic interpretation of social change formulated by his followers.[11] Briefly, Habermas argues that by identifying reality with man's productive activity and by replacing Hegel's abstract life-forms with the 'means of production,' Marx confines the dynamics of the dialectic to the category of labor, and thereby "reduces the process of reflection as such as a motive force of history. . . ."[12] Reflection, especially in Marx's later work, is conceptualized in terms supplied by the model of production, and the result is a blurring of the distinction between the logical status of natural science and that of critique. This, Habermas suggests, made it easy for the Marxian analysis of social change to eventually incorporate the natural scientific method, and, by so doing, to surrender the concern with practical activity and with the active process of reflection it embodies. The practical or cultural moment of the dialectic is reduced to a function of the technical moment, and a passive materialism is the consequence.[13]

If the practical moment is to be restored to the dialectic, it is necessary to undermine the latent positivism inherent in Marx's use of the category of labor. According to Habermas, productive activity is a self-generative process which, by contributing to the development of the forces of the production, extends man's mastery over nature, and thereby frees society from the external forces of nature. By advancing the level of productive forces, productive activity may mitigate hunger and toil, but it cannot directly effect human emancipation. In other words, human emancipation is a practical activity, and is not directly connected with the technical problem-solving orientation of productive activity. Once this is recognized, it is necessary to incorporate alongside labor a second mode of self-realization, one which, as a self-formative process, complements productive activity by seeking freedom from the internal forces of compulsion.

By rooting the dialectic in the category of labor, Marx not only sets the groundwork for the de-emphasis of the practical moment and the disavowal of methodological self-reflection, but also relativizes the field to which key concepts ('ideology' and 'class') are applied. The assumptions of historical materialism, Habermas contends, hold for only a limited set of sociohistorical conditions. For instance, in advanced industrial society, where domination rests more on the satisfaction of privatized needs than it does on collective repression, the emphasis on class interests is misplaced. Accordingly, the dialectic must be reformulated so that it can be used for initiating reflection that penetrates "beyond the level of particular historical class interests to disclose the fundamental interests of mankind as such, engaged in the process of self-constitution."[14] The stress on class interests, in other words, must be replaced by an emphasis on human interests.

Habermas proposes to reformulate the dialectic by replacing the relation of forces and relations of production with the more general and analogous relation of work (as a system of purposive-rational action) and interaction (as a system of symbolic interaction). The work and interaction dialectic is developed in accordance with the epistemological assumptions underlying Habermas' theory of cognitive interests. According to the theory of cognitive interests, the acquisition of knowledge is guided by basic orientations inherent in the specific conditions of social labor (work) and the institutional and normative framework (interaction), which together regulate the way the human species secures its existence. Rooted in the interest structure of the species, these basic orientations allow reality to be apprehended (i.e., to be known and acted upon). Work is guided by a cognitive interest in certainty and technical control; and, as a system of purposive-rational action, it enhances man's mastery over nature. Directed by a practical interest in the extension of intersubjective understanding, interaction as a system of communicative behavior enables the practical understanding of life situations. Thus, where the system of work orients action on the basis of technical rules which can be conditionally predicted, the system of symbolic interaction orients action on the basis of social norms and reciprocal expectations.

Mediating the technical and practical interests, is an interest in the emancipation of consciousness from its dependence on reified controls. On the level of social organization, work and interaction are mediated by self-reflective knowledge which, by analyzing the historically variable constraints imposed by the system of work and the system of symbolic interaction, defines or redefines the objects of possible knowledge.[15] In other words, the technical viewpoint (productive knowledge) and the practical viewpoint (reflective knowledge) are synthesized by an emancipatory consciousness (self-reflective knowledge) which enhances the power of the species to shape its future.[16]

Reconstructed in this way, the dialectic becomes capable of accounting for the practical moment, focusing on human interests, and initiating methodological self-reflection. Beyond this, the reconstructed dialectic reformulates the relationship between theory and practice so that the logical status of natural science is now clearly distinguished from the logical status of critique. As distinct form natural science, critique involves both reconstruction and self-reflection. By reconstructing the dialectical course of history with reference to what has suppressed mankind's evolution toward autonomy and freedom, critique intends to "restore missing parts of the historical self-formation process to man, and, in this way, to release a self-positing comprehension which enables him to see through socially unnecessary authority and control systems."[17] On the basis of critique, then, the unity of knowledge and interest—and, in turn, the necessary correlation between transcendental perspectives of inquiry and knowledge-constitutive interests—are comprehended.

By relating knowledge so directly to the social processes of work, interaction, and power, Habermas' epistemology is at the same time a social theory. The work and interaction dialectic can be used, as Schroyer observes, for conceptualizing the history of mankind and the development of societies in terms of the ongoing interaction of two action systems,

> purposive rational action that secures the human capacity to satisfy human needs, and symbolic interaction systems which form the institutional framework of society based upon grammatical rules and societal norms that enable men to engage in communication and interaction.[18]

These systems of social action imply not fixed or stable social conditions and relationships, but the need for societies to change and undergo progressive historical development.

The work and interaction dialectic restores what Marx calls "superstructure" to a dimension of the dialectic, and thus disclaims the primacy of either culture or productive activity. In an important divergence from Marx, Habermas suggests that class struggle as the agent of progressive historical development requires not only structural antagonisms generated by productive relationships but also an analysis of societal constraints in terms of the reflective comprehension of the ideological content contained in cultural traditions. In other words, false consciousness does not dissolve merely in response to changes in the material base. A cultural revolution expressive of human potentiality must accompany, not follow, the technical revolution of substructure which expresses societal potentiality.

Habermas' work and interaction dialectic promises a valuable approach to study of the creation, maintenance, and transformation of the social order. However, before a serious effort is made to execute the kind of analysis he proposes, it is necessary to add substance to Habermas' formalistic treatment of categories and relationships. This task is taken up below in a manner which involves an extension of and, on occasion, a departure from Habermas' basic theory. The end result, hopefully, will be a sociological perspective that enables an explanation and understanding of legitimacy and domination, rebellion and revolt.

Work Dimension

The subsystem of work is characterized by instrumental action and rational choice. Instrumental action is shaped by technical rules (as distinct from social norms) rooted in empirical knowledge constituted by conditional predictions about observable events. Accordingly, "instrumental action organizes means that are appropriate or inappropriate according to criteria of an *effective* control of reality."[19] The possible alternative choices, established by the instrumental organization of means, set the framework for strategic action which rests on rational calculation. Instrumental and strategic action are directed toward technical problem-solving endeavors, and have as their goal the extension of man's mastery over nature in as precise and formalized a way as possible.

As the organization of work becomes increasingly reliant upon technology, a greater emphasis is placed upon exact calculation and computation. This emphasis is reflected in the extension of formal rationality which Max Weber describes as "the extent of quantitative calculation or accounting which is technically possible and which is actually applied."[20] As action more closely approximates the standards of formal rationality, it becomes detached from goals and values independent of the system in which it occurs. In this way, the system becomes self-legitimating as the criteria—the ends and values— used to assess the prevailing institutions are supplied by the system itself.[21]

As a result, the further growth of productive forces is expedited and, in turn, the technical control over nature is enhanced. Under these circumstances, however, the technical achievements of the advancing productive forces need not contribute to human liberation, material or otherwise. Indeed, it is entirely possible that the improved productive apparatus will be employed to strengthen social and political domination.

In summary, the productive forces include the tools and techniques of production, the scientific and technical knowledge, the manpower, and the system of labor at the disposal of society. The progressive development of the productive forces occurs within the subsystem of instrumental action; it is furthered by, and it furthers, the extension of formal rationality. "The more industrialized a society is and the more advanced its division of labor and organization," writes Karl Mannheim, "the greater will be the number of spheres of human activity which will be functionally rational and hence also calculable in advance."[22] Such calculation promotes the advancement of technical control which establishes two contending possibilities—one, the amelioration of the struggle for existence; the other, the penetration of formalized domination to all areas of social life. In this context, the productive force is "the term designating the sum-total of the resources for liberation available to a given society."[23] As suggested earlier, however, this *potential* for libration can only be actualized as a dialectical synthesis of work and interaction.

Interaction Dimension

Interaction, or the system of symbolic interaction, is the social medium through which the practical interest develops toward mutual understanding. Only on the basis of shared understandings do people give coherence and meaning to the experiences they encounter in the institutions they have created and in the structures in which they live. Habermas discusses the interaction dimension largely in terms of language or communicative practice. Here, however, the system of symbolic interaction will be examined in terms of the more generic concept of culture.

Culture, of course, has more than a communicative function. Rooted in the sentimental bases of social interaction, culture, "the bestowal of symbolic meaning on things, acts, events, and persons, . . . transforms the instrumental and the impersonal . . . into a realm of evocative, expressive, person-centered meanings."[24] Expressive and consummatory, created by people engaged in activities pursued for their own sake, culture has its origins in the nonrational elements of social life. Given its nonrational basis, the cultural realm is not subject to the same degree of control, manipulation, and predictability applied to the system of instrumental action.

With this conception of culture, the work and interaction dialectic becomes a dialectic of the rational and nonrational aspects of social life. In this context, symbolic or ideological representations are to be understood not as functions of a given historical situation—as the Marxian dialectic would have it—but as "integral and defining part[s] of the situation. These representations do not simply 'reflect' material constraints; indeed they can anticipate, some would say, create, new material possibilities in historical situations."[25] Culture, then, has a transcendent, potentially critical, dynamic aspect; and its creation expresses the recognition, in Bauman's words, "that the real, tangible, sentient existence . . . is neither the only object nor the most authoritative; much less is it the only object of interested knowledge."[26] The idealized, meaningful, and human future social order, anticipated by culture at times, enters into tension with the formalized, impersonal, and technical future which is anticipated—or, more accurately, predicted—by instrumental action. From such tensions, crises of legitimacy, transformations of systems of domination, and, on occasion, rebellion and revolt emerge.

By according a central place to the nonrational in the system of symbolic interaction, I depart significantly from Habermas' formulation. Such a departure is necessary, however, since Habermas' reconstructed dialectic—while perfectly capable of identifying the conditions under which a repudiation of the prevailing arrangements is likely—is unable to account for the formulation of future alternatives to these arrangements. Habermas' critical theory, Schroyer remarks, "remains too narrow because it has . . . avoided a systematic development of its own formalistic utopian moment. Critical theory cannot ignore the utopian anticipation of the objectively possible. To its tradition of negative critique there must be restored the systematic anticipation of socially emergent alternatives."[27] Injected with a concern for the nonrational processes of culture-creation, the work and the inter-action dialectic becomes capable of accounting for the formulation of social alternatives or images of the future. Although nonrational in origin, these images of the future, by affording a standpoint from which the present can be evaluated, facilitate a critical or practical rationality which, unlike the formal rationality of instrumental action, promotes emancipatory self-reflection. Indispensable to this nonrational mode of anticipating the future is a playful attachment to the past.

In the pages that follow, I shall argue that meaningful images of the future are created and sustained in the interaction of past and play, receiving content from the past and context, or form, from play. In this interaction, the past is playfully or imaginatively reconstructed, portrayed not as it actually was, but as it ought to have been. Thus the future is anticipated with reference to a past that never was. More concretely, this argument suggests that tradition and play give a person both contact with and distance from his situation, thus providing a basis for evaluating that situation and, if desirable, for acting to change it. A sense of continuity, both rooted and changeable, emerges from the interaction of past and play and supplies the organizing principle around which novel aspects of reality are incorporated into prevailing structures of meaning. Without this sense of continuity the future would frighten, not stimulate; and future-oriented social change would be resisted, not furthered.

Past and Future   Meaningful anticipations of the future, be they personal or collective in nature, have strong roots in the past. Bernot and Blancard, in their study of a small French village, observe that peasants sustained a longer, more meaningful perspective of the future than did workers who had recently migrated to the community. In contrast to the workers who anxiously regarded the future as uncertain and threatening, the peasants possessed a "memory of the future"; with a deeper attachment to traditional structures and value orientations, they perceived the future in more promising terms as a continuation of the past.[28] Similarly, personal anticipations of the future, as Cottle and Klineberg find, are "primarily created out of the implications of the past experience, of the sense of continuity and of orderly predictable change that it may provide."[29] This point is supported generally in the literature on revitalization and millennial movements, and more specifically in Lifton's examination of time imagery among activist Japanese youth.[30]

Lifton's analysis suggests three primary modes of anticipating the future—transformation, restoration, and accommodation. Each has the capacity to bridge inner emotional experience with existing social currents; and, by neutralizing the prevailing sense of historical dislocation, each facilitiates participation in social change. Also common to these modes of anticipating the future was a concern with recapturing the past. The mode of transformation, although tracing present evils to the past and demanding a comprehensive restructuring of social existence, exhibited a "profound underlying nostalgia for old cultural symbols." More specifically,

> the transformationist youth embraces a vision of the future intimately related to, if not indeed a part of, his longing for a return to an imagined golden age of the past. . . . [This] longing for a golden age of the past—a longing intensified during periods of inner dislocation caused by rapid historical change—supplies a basic stimulus for his future-oriented utopian quest.[31]

The symbolism of the future expressed in the mode of transformation (and this appears even more clearly in the modes of restoration and accommodation) derives from the past—not the historically factual past, but the imaginatively conceived "golden age" of the past.

Recently, Peter Marris has attempted to place this process of anticipating the future with reference to the past in broader theoretical perspective. Marris focuses on the 'conservative impulse' which he describes as the tendency of individuals and collectivities to assimilate reality and to interpret new experiences in terms of their prevailing structures of meaning. The conservative impulse defends, not prejudice and ignorance, but the predictability of life and the continuity of meaning, and thus "is an aspect of our ability to survive in any situation: for without continuity we cannot interpret what events mean to us, nor explore new kinds of experience with confidence."[32] When structures of social meaning disintegrate, Marris finds, people experience a deep-seated sense of loss, and "try at once to reassert the past and escape into an idealized, detached vision of the future."[33] In short, an image of the future emerges from the reaffirmation of the past. While lamenting the betrayal of tradition, the conservative impulse simultaneously supplies a justification for participation in social change. The traditions betrayed in the present must be retrieved in the future.

Growing from a concern with conserving the past, these images of the future aim for reintegration, not disruption. Reintegrative aims, however, often prompt rebellious and revolutionary practices. Indeed, the participants in modern peasant wars, in the early American labor movement, and in the direct action riots in eighteenth-century western Europe, legitimated their rejeciton of the present and anticipated their future goals with reference to traditional values and beliefs.[34] Although couched in terms of a restoration of the past, the demands issued by the participants in these uprisings were future oriented. The past they sought to restore was not a past that was; it was a past that should have been and that could be in future-time. It was a playfully reconstructed past, and in play the past comes to be regarded as both superior to the present and the goal of the future.

Past and Play[35]   Typically, the connection between past and play is examined in its most routinized forms, namely, myth and ritual. Although constituted in part by past experiences and pre-established elements, play also initiates exploration, a search for novelty. In play the past is not merely preserved; it is relived in such a way that a positive response to novelty is made possible. By minimizing the uncertainties of the future, play bridges new experiences and prevailing structures of meaning. Inclusive of both completed and non-completed time, play contributes to the conceptualization of the future as a fulfillment of the past. In play, time is continuous yet reversible, and is experienced "not as a precipitate rush of successive moments, but rather as the one full moment that is, so to speak, a glimpse of eternity."[36] In this context, memory is transformed into a vision of "ultimate unity" as the playfully reconstructed past informs the image of the future.[37]

Play is vital to the maintenance of continuity; and it shares with the conservative impulse the tendency to assimilate and accommodate, as well as the capacity to carry and sustain the past.[38] Indeed, by enlarging existing structures of meaning, play enhances experiential continuity. As Eric Klinger writes,

> Play permits the accommodative stretching of available schemas so as to provide an experiential bridge between an established cognitive repertory and a strange new set of circumstances. Play thus gradually invests the new events with meaning and promotes the cultivation of new cognitive, verbal, and motor skills.[39]

Thus, play simultaneously strengthens and transforms the conservative impulse, fortifying its roots in the past while stimulating it to embrace the new.

Several features of play combine to transform the past into a "golden age" which appears as both superior to the present and a worthy model of the future. Play does not conceal nor deny the social reality; rather, it reorders and represents this reality, making it more manageable and more meaningful.[40] Just as play enables the child to represent and transcend himself, so it also permits the collectivity to represent and transcend itself, to establish a set of criteria which allows a reflective assessment of the present order. As Richard Sennett suggests, play encourages people "to objectify the law, to look at it, to weigh it, to judge it, by having stepped beyond its terms." Play guides people "beyond the existing rules so that they might become fully conscious of what those rules" are.[41] In this way, play can initiate a tension between what is and what can be, a dialectic between the real and the possible. The 'possible' projected in play is not confined by realistic considerations; instead it is a 'possible' that promises freedom from compulsion, hierarchy, inequality, and injustice.[42] In the possible social order created in play, rules are not abandoned—they are self-imposed; control does not disappear—it becomes more relaxed and human. In short, as Richard Burke notes, play gives rise to a "free, intrinsically satisfying [world] governed by rules of man's own making, . . . [a] meaningful world that man can call his own."[43] The social order experienced in play often proves more satisfying than the prevailing social arrangements; it enables the individual to acquire an awareness of the self as a cause of activity and as a participant in a cause, and thus invites transgression of conventional constraints.[44] Imaginatively recalled and given shape in these terms, the past offers the symbols which constitute the image of a better society of the future.

The Playful Reconstruction of the Past   Participation in future-oriented social change presupposes the availability of a set of standards which enable people to discredit, to legitimate opposition against, and to anticipate future alternatives to the present social arrangements. I have suggested that such critically evaluative standards emerge meaningfully from the playful reconsideration of the past. *By itself,* the past (or the conservative impulse) is only capable of guiding conservative or retrogressive social change; *alone,* play encourages participation in the creation of artifice, not actuality, and thus serves to stabilize the present order by fostering the pretense of freedom in reality.[45] With the interaction of past and play, the past social arrangements appear as emancipating and just; they constitute a social order that both was and can be. The playfully transmitted past, then, generates the symbolic prerequisites for participation in progressive social change. The professed aims of this participation, while stated in terms of a restoration of the past, anticipate the future—a future conceptualized and experienced as a past that never was, a future defined as a past that ought to have been.

Efforts to revitalize the past usually reflect a concern with constructing a more humanly satisfying culture, and they often revolve around and are furthered by an experience of "communitas" in which the instrumental requirements of structure and differentiation are subordinated to the human needs for expressiveness and wholeness.[46] The evocation of the past as a guide to a desirable future is typically stimulated by psychological stress resulting from cultural disintegration or structural dislocation. When present conditions force the abridgement of traditional expectations, or they deteriorate to the extent that the existing arrangements can no longer fulfill the claims that have been made for them, efforts to sustain continuity become directed toward the past. Structural-cultural dislocation, however, not only prompts an orientation toward the past but, by diminishing the force of existing constraints, also permits greater spontaneity and playfulness. As a result, the past often is revitalized in festival, standing as an object of reaffirmation and collective celebration. During these liminal periods, or times out of structure, new cultural forms are generated from the playful, imaginative and fantastic attachments to the past.[47] Recaptured in festival, the past transcends the present and points to the future. Thus when playful access to the past is possible sociocultural disintegration produces not *anomie* but fantastic visions of a more desirable society.

By incorporating the categories of remembrance and play into the system of symbolic interaction, emphasis is placed on its noninstrumental—and critical and transcendent—elements. In this way, the work and interaction dialectic becomes a dialectic between the instrumental and the noninstrumental, a two-dimensional dialectic wherein the noninstrumental supplies the criteria with which the instrumental is critically evaluated and regulated. Emancipatory consciousness emerges from this dialectic.

Emancipatory Consciousness and the Norm of Reciprocity

In Habermas' social theory of knowledge the technical and practical interests of work and interaction are mediated by an emancipatory interest. A specific emancipatory interest is required by Habermas' scheme to account for movements of human liberation, since such activity is not explicable merely in terms of the advancement generated by the development of the productive forces. Expressed as critical self-reflection, the emancipatory interest is an interest in emancipation from illegitimate authority relations in the social world. Emancipatory consciousness, or critical reason, seeks to reconcile the ideals embodied in culture (what 'ought' to be) with that which is made objectively possible (what 'can' be) by the existing system of work—and, in this way, to pressure authority relations to become more responsive and responsible.

The question still remains as to what determines whether critical reflection promotes activities and symbolic forms which are oppositional, rather than integrative, in orientation. The answer proposed here is derived from Alvin Gouldner's discussion of the norm of reciprocity. Reciprocity entails a situation of mutual dependence wherein both parties to the relationship, to the extent that each has rights and duties, require and receive from one another reciprocal services. Gouldner emphasizes, however, that each party fulfills its obligations, not simply as a response to the constraints emanating from the diviision of labor, but also because each shares a higher-level moral norm. That is, existing beyond reciprocity as a pattern of exchange rooted in a structurally determined mutual dependence, there is "a generalized moral norm of reciprocity which defines certain actions and *obligations* as repayments for benefits received. . . . In sum, the norm of reciprocity requires that if others have been fulfilling their status duties to you, you in turn have an additional or second-order obligation (repayment) to fulfill your status duties to them."[48]

Although the norm of reciprocity universally underlies all social relationships, for the purposes at hand attention is concentrated on its impact on those relationships concerned with the distribution of socially produced goods. The exchange and repayment of benefits regulated by the norm of reciprocity need not result in an exchange of equivalences. More important than equivalence of response is *adequacy* of response. The standards employed to evaluate whether or not, and to what degree, the responses are adequate derive from a reflective stance which measures potentiality against actuality. In terms of such reflection, legitimacy is either granted to or withheld from the distributive process of society and its accompanying forms of domination. Accordingly, the norm of reciprocity bridges the economic and political spheres of society, such that economic or instrumental activity becomes subject to political principles of legitimacy.

All societies, because of the demands imposed by the division of labor and the necessity to structure material provisions, are organized so as to assure the sustained provision of those products required for the subsistence of its members. The norm of reciprocity facilitates the development of these necessary distributive institutions through a process Karl Polanyi refers to as redistribution. In Polanyi's scheme redistribution, which contributes political power to society's central agencies, consists of the "obligatory payments to central political or religious authority, which uses the receipt for its own maintenance, to provide community services, and as emergency stock in case of individual or community disaster."[49] As a normative prescription, redistribution provides society with a degree of centricity by assuring that a certain amount of socially produced resources is expended and stored for protective purposes. These resources which eventually become used as the basis of political power are, of course, made available by the productive forces of society. However, this 'norm of redistribution,' like the norm of reciprocity, is a transactional mode expressive of underlying social obligations; and as such it requires that power relationships be evaluated in terms of adequacy of response. Should the use of power not be in accordance with the prevailing normative prescriptions, legitimacy will be withheld. This factor accounts for efforts on the part of the superordinate party (or class) to make power relationships effective and adequate. There are, then, certain restrictive limits to the amount of imbalance or exploitation that occurs in the relationship.

The norm of reciprocity serves as both a stabilizing and disrupting force. Although the moral requirements generated by the norm of reciprocity do not in themselves constitute clear-cut directives for action, they do provide a basis upon which critical value orientations and standards of evaluation are made explicit. As a generalized norm it stipulates that all parties to a relationship have both rights and duties; and as a specific obligation it embodies concrete expectations which are incorporated into notions of 'right' and 'just' (and, in this way, it is closely connected with substantive rationality). As a result, power and justice are linked together. Through the norm of reciprocity it becomes possible to define what constitutes an acceptable and meaningful response and, in turn, to determine which activities and policies warrant legitimacy. Thus, in a superordinate-subordinate relationship, while the superordinate group doubtlessly possesses a wider scope of freedom of action, its actions cannot be arbitrary: for any activity on the part of this group which fails to meet the standards of adequacy of response, or contradicts the moral requirements of the norm of reciprocity, will be opposed by the subordinate group. Although initially responding to the abridgment of or nonresponsiveness to the reciprocal expectations expressed in cultural traditions, this opposition need not result in a conservative attempt to recapture the past or maintain the status quo: for through the process of reflection (comprehension as radical practice) the goals of the conflict can be couched in terms of the anticipatory content embodied in the prevailing structures and consciousness. When this occurs, social protest assumes a future orientation which seeks to transcend the established social relationships for ones more emancipatory in nature.

TWO-DIMENSIONAL AND ONE-DIMENSIONAL SOCIETY

The relationship between systems of instrumental action and systems of symbolic interaction is historically variable. At this point, it is necessary to distinguish the properties of and identify the conditions favorable to two-dimensional and one-dimensional society. For our purposes, it is sufficient to distinguish the relation between work and interaction as it exists in what Habermas calls "traditional societies" (what we will call preindustrial capitalist societies) on the one hand, and industrial capitalist societies on the other.

In Shapiro's words, two-dimensional society is based "on the external quality of the confrontation of man and nature, form and matter, and on the corresponding irreducibility of the lower level to the higher, of the individual to the universal."[50] It is a politicized society wherein questions of instrumental action, such as the allocation of natural resources and labor, the distribution of products, and the organization of work, are expressive of underlying social obligations and relationships. These features of two-dimensional society are found in traditional or preindustrial capitalist forms of societal organization.

Traditional societies differ from primitive societies in that social and political obligations are not expressed as nor given legitimacy in terms of kinship relations. More particularly, Habermas suggests three traits which distinguish the traditional from more primitive social forms: (1) a centralized ruling power (state organization of political power in contrast to tribal organization); (2) the division of society into socioeconomic classes (distribution to individuals of social obligations and rewards according to class membership and not according to kinship status); and (3) the prevalence of a central world-view (myth, complex religion) to the end of legitimating political power (thus converting power into authority).[51]

Beyond this, traditional societies possess a relatively advanced technology and specialized division of labor which make possible the creation of surplus. The most important feature of traditional society, however, is that the number, kind, and extent of structural changes generated by the economy and the surplus it creates are regulated by the prevailing institutional framework. More specifically, the political order, which receives its legitimacy from the institutional framework, governs the productive forces in accordance with particular cultural standards.

Traditional society exists as long as changes in the system of instrumental action are shaped by the intersubjectively shared traditions which provide legitimations to the political order. However, in societies where the convergence of the capitalist mode of production with industrialization has taken place the economic system is equipped "with a self-propelled mechanism that ensures long-term continuous growth (despite crises) in the productivity of labor. . . . [such that it] guarantees the *permanent* expansion of subsystems of purposive-rational action and thereby overturns the traditionalist 'superiority' of the institutional framework to the forces of production.''[52]

By allowing for the permanent extension of productive forces, industrial capitalism develops a basis which not only frees structural changes generated by the economic system from the guidance of cultural traditions, but also enables the economic system to provide its own legitimation. In Habermas' words, "it provides a legitimation which is no longer called down from the lofty heights of cultural tradition but instead summoned up from the base of social labor.''[53] In short, the convergence of industrialization and capitalism sets the stage for the minimization and, later, the abrogation of the interaction dimension. We find in these circumstances what Marcuse refers to as 'one-dimensionality.'

In one-dimensional society culture becomes instrumentalized. The nonrational element of human intervention and creation is masked as the "system of symbols, of consciousness, of sensibility of preconscious and unconsciousness meanings, [becomes] assimilated to the imperatives of machine production, market organization, and bureaucratic power.''[54] The system of symbolic interaction is now adaptive to, rather than transcendent of the instrumental sphere of economic, industrial, and technological growth. The result is an integration of the two dimensions, not through dialetical synthesis, but through the collapse of the interaction dimension into the work dimension—a collapse of the negative into the positive, as it were. This integration by collapse has serious consequences both for the nature of political domination and the form of social protest. In the first place, the power system is no longer reliant upon the institutional framework for its legitimacy. Rather, power now receives its legitimacy on the basis of its immediate connection with the system of labor which is constantly reproduced as an ordered and regulated form. Under these conditions, "the property order can change from a *political relation* to a *production relation* because it legitimates itself through the rationality of the market, the ideology of exchange society, and no longer through a legitimate power structure. It is now the political system which is justified in terms of the legitimate relations of production.''[55] In this way, instrumental standards of rational calculation penetrate through society, and principles of legitimacy are gradually emptied of their moral content.

The historical roots of one-dimensional society can be traced partially to the emergence of the liberal concept of society, which contends that the achievement of social or public benefits derives from the private pursuit of economic interests unhampered by political interference. In practice, this identification of society with economy encourages a devaluation of political action. Under these conditions, as John O'Neill notes, freedom and equality come to be interpreted in purely economic terms "rather than as political action about the nature and conditions of production and consumption.''[56]

Thus the political or reflective mode as an avenue of self-realization comes to be minimized. The power of reflection and the negativity inherent in human time and space—"whose synthetic unity is constituted by human presence, through memory of the past and the projection of a future"— become reified as they "are absorbed into a single economy whose rhythms are linear and mechanical."[57] Arising from this destruction of the sense of human space and time is, on the level of the individual, the incapacity to coherently express subjectively felt needs and, on the class level, the inability to adequately locate oneself in history and society.[58]

The mechanism perfected under the conditions of industrial capitalism, and which made possible the permanent growth of productive forces and the pursuant one-dimensionality, was the self-regulating market. Prior to the end of the eighteenth century—while industrial production was at best an accessory to commerce, and the machine was an inexpensive and non-specific tool—a viable self-regulating market did not exist. The central elements of industry—land, labor and capital—were brought into the market with the convergence of the factory system and commercial system, and with the consequent weakening of the system of symbolic interaction.[59] Detached from social obligations and political relationships, land and labor were converted to commodities subject to regulation in accordance with the formal rationality of the market mechanism. Through this transformation, money emerged as the predominant means of exchange.

The development of industrialization, and the increasing reliance on money as the primary means of exchange, facilitated the application of the major features of formal rationality, namely, quantification and calculation. With the spread of formal rationality, domination shifted from a political and status relation to an exchange relation. "This signifies," Habermas writes, "a depoliticization of the class relationship and an anomization of class domination."[60] Domination determined by the objective laws of the market economy is not susceptible to political pressure.

Underlying this shift in domination is the transformation of the norm of reciprocity. With industrial capitalism it becomes possible to express exchange relations in a precise and quantifiable manner. This marks an important shift from earlier situations where social obligations, because they were qualitative, were largely unspecified and therefore contingent upon the establishment of trust. In industrial capitalism, exchange is regulated in accordance with a quantitative principle of equality, and obligations are specified in terms of the exchange of equivalents. In short, unspecifiable *social* obligations are replaced with specifiable *economic* obligations, such that prescriptions of reciprocity are satisfiable on purely economic grounds. Where once the 'higher' social orders were responsible for the well-being of the 'lower' orders, now the individual capitalist was merely responsible for paying the individual worker a 'fair day's wage' in return for a 'fair day's work.' In a society where domination is quantified and privatized, it becomes increasingly difficult to generate a critical image of society.[61]

In one-dimensional society there is a devaluation of the cultural validity of man's senses and perceptions. The decision-making process is more and more circumscribed by a self-regulating market adjoined to a self-expanding technology. The emerging one-dimensionality—the elimination of the institutional framework as a source of legitimacy, the distortion of reflection, the transformation of political relations into exchange relations, and the consequent expansion of instrumental action and formal rationality—conceals the liberating potential of industrial and technical achievements. As the capacities for political reflection and developing critical categories are suppressed, as the past is forgotten and play is blocked, rebellion and revolution—as concrete expressions of the need for a more responsive social order—decline in occurrence and intensity.

CRITICAL THEORY AND THE ENGLISH WORKING CLASS

> The great English working class, this titanic social force which seemed to be unchained by the rapid development of English capitalism in the first half of the century did not finally emerge to dominate and remake English society. . . . Instead, after the 1840s it quickly turned into an apparently docile class. It embraced one species of moderate reformism after another, became a consciously subordinate part of bourgeois society, and has remained wedded to the narrowest and greyest of bourgeois ideologies in its principal movements.[62]

I will attempt to explain this transformation by demonstrating that the suppression of the practical interest and the corresponding suppression of culturally meaningful frameworks—by preventing the worker from locating himself in history and in society—had the effect of circumscribing the worker's capacity to challenge the legitimacy and authority of prevailing power structures. In order to carry out such a demonstration it is necessary to first indicate the prior existence of these critical capacities and, in turn, to relate these capacities to working class social protest. This will be done by carefully examining (in terms of the categories associated with the work and interaction dialectic) the dramatic shifts which occurred in the association between power and authority relationships and working class social protest in the period between the mid-eighteenth and mid-nineteenth centuries.

This period will be classified into three phases, each distinguished by the kind and degree of working class opposition it witnessed. The preindustrial capitalist phase covers the years between 1750 and 1790. During this time, social protest on the part of the oppressed was frequent and usually spontaneous in origin. Opposition generally arose in response to unfulfilled obligations and took the form of direct action riots. Organized along the principles of mercantile capitalism, the system of work was characterized by household production, small-scale manufacturing, and an imperfect market for both produce goods and labor. At this time, the system of work was neither self-regulating nor self-expanding: changes in the productive apparatus were regulated by institutional values and norms in such a way that they did not infringe upon the reciprocal rights and duties embedded in the status system of society. When these obligations were not adequately met, the authority of the established order was challenged.

With the intensified industrial expansion which began to occur at the end of the eighteenth century, adequacy of response as defined by traditional normative prescriptions was precluded. At this point—the 'crisis of power and authority' phase—we confront the major contradiction between work and interaction dimensions, between the burgeoning productive forces and the institutional framework. Out of this contradiction emerged, during the first quarter of the nineteenth century, the most intense working class radicalism in English history. It is during these years of increasing disaffection and social bifurcation that E. P. Thompson locates the growth of class consciousness and the development of working class political and industrial organizations.[63]

Beginning in this phase and extending throughout the third or 'industrial capitalist' phase, we find a number of indicators of the increasing adaptation of the institutional framework to the productive forces. From the early 1800s on, the dismantling of economic controls and restrictions on industrial changes, and their replacement with more flexible legal policies, proceeded steadily. All these changes can be taken as measures of the increasing adaptation of the system of symbolic interaction to the system of instrumental action. The convergence of industrialization and capitalism made necessary the establishment of national markets for consumer goods and labor, the creation of a stable monetary and credit system, the concentration of capital, the elaboration of flexible investment policies, and the development of a mobile labor force. The changes in the legal system were effected to facilitate the acceptance of these factors and, by so doing, to facilitate industrial expansion.

The changes in working-class social protest—from spontaneous, direct action riots and mobs in the 'preindustrialist capitalist' phase to the more organized and intense actions in the 'crisis of power and authority' phase, and finally to the infrequent, often unguided opposition put forth in the 'industrial capitalist' phase—will be explicated with reference to the corresponding shifts in the relationship between work and interaction. More specifically, an attempt will be made to account for the 'deradicalization' of the working class by reference to those occurrences which made the practical interest ineffectual; that is, in terms of 'one-dimensionality.' This analysis will proceed in a necessarily general fashion. A more specific application of the English working class by reference to those occurrences which made the practicurred in the 'industrial capitalist' phase. Here, an effort will be made to demonstrate a positive relationship between radical political activity (Chartism, in particular) and those segments of the working class which, in the face of industrial capitalism, retained an institutional framework non-adaptive to the system of work. Historical case studies will provide another means of gaining partial support for the proposed explanation. Here the focus will be on the Cooperative Movement and Trade Unionism, and an effort will be made to trace the impact of industrial capitalism on the shift in demands, organization, and social composition experienced by these two largely working-class associations. More specifically, the concern is to explain why this movement and these trade organizations lost their rebellious disposition and became integrated into the established order, by investigating whether or not and to what extent the capacity to formulate critical, transcendent alternatives—a capacity once sustained by working-class culture—was suppressed.

NOTES

1. Max Horkheimer and Theodor Adorno, *Dialectic of Enlightenment* (New York, 1972), p. xi. On the early development of Critical Theory see Martin Jay, *The Dialectical Imagination* (Boston, 1973).
2. Max Horkheimer, *Eclipse of Reason* (New York, 1974), pp. 3-57.
3. Herbert Marcuse, *One-Dimensional Man* (Boston, 1964), p. xv.
4. Ibid., p. 10.
5. Ibid., p. 12.
6. Herbert Marcuse, "Remarks on a Redefinition of Culture," *Daedalus* 94, 1 (1965): 193. The broad influence of the "Culture and Civilization" distinction on Critical Theory is examined in Francis Hearn, "The Implications of Critical Theory for Critical Sociology," *Berkeley Journal of Sociology* 18 (1973): 127-158. Also, Frankfurt Institute of Social Research, *Aspects of Sociology* (Boston, 1973), pp. 89-100.
7. Marcuse, "Remarks on a Redefinition of Culture," p. 194.
8. Ibid., p. 198.
9. Michael Mann, "The Social Cohesion of Liberal Democracy," in *Contemporary Analytical Theory* (New York, 1972), p. 227.
10. Other attempts at explaining the incorporation of the nineteenth-century English working class are discussed in J.M. Cousins and R.L. Davis, " 'Working Class Incorporation'—A Historical Approach with Reference to the Mining Communities of S.E. Northumberland 1840-1890," in *The Social Analysis of Class Structure* (London, 1974), pp. 275-297.

11. For Habermas' critique of the latent positivism in Marxian theory see Jürgen Habermas, *Knowledge and Human Interests* (Boston, 1971), pp. 43-63; Albrecht Wellmer, *Critical Theory of Society* (New York, 1971), pp. 67-119; and Trent Schroyer, "The Dialectical Foundations of Critical Theory: Jürgen Habermas' Metatheoretical Investigations," *Telos* 12 (Summer, 1972): 93-114.

12. Habermas, *Knowledge and Human Interests,* pp. 44.

13. A summary discussion of the technical and the practical moments is presented by Schroyer, "The Dialectical Foundations of Critical Theory," p. 95.

14. Jürgen Habermas, "Technology and Science as 'Ideology,' " in *Toward a Rational Society* (Boston, 1970), p. 113.

15. See Kurt Jürgen Huch, "Interest in Emancipation," *Continuum* 8 (Spring Summer, 1970): 30.

16. Habermas' theory of cognitive interests, treated only briefly here, has aroused an ongoing discussion in sociology and in the philosophy of social science. See the special issues of *Continuum* 8 (Spring Summer, 1970) and *Philosophy of the Social Sciences* 2, 3 (1972). A critical introduction to this discussion is found in Guttörn Floistad, "Social Concepts of Action," *Inquiry* 13 (Summer, 1970): 175-198.

17. Trent Schroyer, *The Critique of Domination* (New York, 1973), p. 31.

18. Schroyer, "The Dialectical Foundations of Critical Theory," p. 103.

19. Habermas, "Technology and Science as 'Ideology,' " p. 92.

20. Max Weber as quoted in Joachim Israel, *Alienation: From Marx to Modern Sociology* (Boston, 1970), p. 100.

21. For a treatment of formal rationality in terms of Habermas' theory of cognitive interests, see Zygmunt Bauman, *Towards a Critical Sociology* (Boston, 1976), pp. 78-79.

22. Karl Mannheim, *Man and Society in an Age of Reconstruction* (New York, 1940), p. 55.

23. Herbert Marcuse, *Studies in Critical Philosophy* (Boston, 1973), p. 213.

24. Gertrude Jaeger and Philip Selzmick, "A Normative Theory of Culture," in *The Study of Society* (New York, 1970), pp. 103-105.

25. Norman Birnbaum, "The Crisis in Marxist Sociology," in *Recent Sociology,* 1 (New York, 1969), pp. 30-31.

26. Zygmunt Bauman, *Culture As Praxis* (Boston, 1973), p. 173.

27. Schroyer, *The Critique of Domination,* p. 34.

28. Lucien Bernot and Rene Blançard, *Nouville, Un Village Francais* (Paris, 1953).

29. Thomas Cottle and Stephen Klineberg, *The Present of Things Future* (New York, 1974), p. 34.

30. The literature on revitalization and millenial movements express a central concern with religion as a point of convergence between past and play. See Anthony Wallace, "Revitalization Movements," *American Anthropologist* 58 (April, 1956): 264-281. Also, Yonina Talmon, "Pursuit of the Millennium: The Relation Between Religious and Social Change," *The European Journal of Sociology* 2 (1962): 130-144.

31. Robert Lifton, "Individual Patterns in Historical Change: Imagery of Japanese Youth," *Comparative Studies in Society and History* 6 (Winter, 1964): 372.

32. Peter Marris, *Loss and Change* (New York, 1974), p. 2.

33. Ibid., p. 166.

34. The peasant uprisings are examined in Eric Wolf, *Peasant Wars of the Twentieth Century,* (New York, 1969); the early American labor movement in Herbert Gutman, "Work, Culture, and Society in Industrializing America," *American Historical Review* 78 (June, 1973): 531-588; the 18th century direct-action riots in George Rudé, *The Crowd in History* (New York, 1964) and E. P. Thompson, "The Moral Economy of the English Crowd in the Eighteenth Century," *Past and Present* 50 (February, 1971): 76-136.

35. I offer the following as a tentative definition of play: Play is a context, a set of principles for organizing experience, constituted by any activity that is voluntary and open-ended (i.e., free from both external and internal compulsions), noninstrumental (in the sense that it is pursued for its own sake and has, as its center of interest, process rather than goal), and transcendent of ordinary states of being and consciousness. This conception of play, to be rounded out below, borrows from previous ones offered by Richard Burke, " 'Work' and 'Play,' " *Ethics* 82, 1 (1971): 33-47; Stephen Miller, "Ends, Means, and Galumphing: Some Leitmotifs of Play," *American Anthropologist* 75 (1973): 87-98; and, Anthony Giddens, "Notes on the Concepts of Play and Leisure," *The Sociological Review* 12 (1964): 73-89.

36. Eugen Fink, "The Oasis of Happiness: Toward an Ontology of Play," in *Game, Play, and Literature* (Boston, 1968), p. 21.

37. As Lifton finds in "Individual Patterns in Historical Change," p. 381, the quest for the 'ultimate future' is simultaneously a quest for the 'ultimate past.'

38. See Edward Norbeck, "Man at Play," *Natural History* 80 (December, 1971): 48-53; Jean Piaget, *Play, Dreams, and Imitation in Childhood* (New York, 1962); and Robert White, "Motivation Reconsidered: The Concept of Competence," *Psychological Review* 66 (September, 1959): 297-334.

39. Eric Klinger, "Development of Imaginative Behavior: Implications of Play for a Theory of Fantasy," *Psychological Bulletin* 72 (Fall, 1969): 293.

40. See Georg Simmel, *The Sociology of Georg Simmel* (New York, 1950), p. 43.

41. Richard Sennett, "Charismatic De-Legitimation: A Case Study," *Theory and Society* 2 (Summer, 1975): 180.

42. See Burke, " 'Work' and 'Play' "; Miller, "Ends, Means, and Galumphing"; Harvey Cox, *The Feast of Fools* (Cambridge, 1969); Don Browning, *Generative Man* (New York, 1975); Hugh Duncan, *Communication and Social Order* (New York, 1962); and Johan Huizinga, *Homo Ludens* (Boston, 1950).

43. Burke, " 'Work' and 'Play,' " p. 42.

44. See Robert Neal, *In Praise of Play* (New York, 1969), p. 41.

45. In the counter-culture that blossomed in the United States in the 1960s, play provided an avenue of escape, not a mode of confronting reality. The playful communities of 'freaks' and 'flower children' gave the appearance of freedom *within* the prevailing institutional arrangements. See Barbara Myerhoff, "Organization and Ecstasy: Deliberate and Accidental Communitas among Huichol Indians and American Youth," *Symbol and Politics in Communal Ideology* (Ithaca, 1975), pp. 33-67.

46. See Wallace, "Revitalization Movements," p. 265. The notion of communitas is presented by Victor Turner, *The Ritual Process* (Chicago, 1969).

47. See Sherry Turkle, "Symbol and Festival in the French Student Uprising," *Symbol and Politics in Communal Ideology* (Ithaca, 1975), pp. 68-100.

48. Alvin Gouldner, "The Norm of Reciprocity: A Preliminary Statement," *American Sociological Review* 25 (April, 1960): 170, 176.

49. George Dalton, "Introduction," to *Primitive, Archaic, and Modern Economies: Essays of Karl Polanyi* (New York, 1968), p. xiv.

50. Jeremy Shapiro, "One-Dimensionality: The Universal Semiotic of Technological Experience," in *Critical Interruptions* (New York, 1970), p. 153.

51. Habermas, "Technology and Science as 'Ideology,'" p. 94.

52. Ibid., pp. 95-96.

53. Ibid., p. 97.

54. Norman Birnbaum, *The Crisis of Industrial Society* (New York, 1969), p. 113.

55. Habermas, "Technology and Science as 'Ideology,'" p. 97. Also see Jürgen Habermas, *Legitimation Crisis* (Boston, 1975), pp. 20-31.

56. John O'Neill, *Sociology as a Skin Trade* (New York, 1972), p. 33.

57. Ibid., p. 23, 243.

58. See Claus Mueller, "Notes on the Repression of Communicative Behavior," in *Recent Sociology*, 2nd ed. (New York, 1970), pp. 101-113.

59. See Karl Polanyi, *The Great Transformation* (Boston, 1944), Chapter 6.

60. Habermas, *Legitimation Crisis*, p. 21.

61. We have argued previously that when the norm of reciprocity is violated protest is likely to ensue. However, in some situations it is possible to conceal violations by redefining the norm of reciprocity. In industrial capitalism, the norm of reciprocity was defined in terms of exchange of equivalents, labor power for wages. This 'exchange of equivalents,' however, concealed the imbalance or exploitation actually occurring. In this sense, Marx's critique of capitalism can be regarded as an attempt to illustrate and explain the concealment of the violations of the moral requirements of reciprocity. See Chapters 4 and 6.

62. Tom Nairn, "The English Working Class," *Ideology in Social Science* (New York, 1973), p. 188.

63. E. P. Thompson, *The Making of the English Working Class* (New York, 1963).

CHAPTER 2

Legitimacy and Social Protest in Preindustrial England, 1750-1790

Throughout most of the eighteenth century, English society was similar in its structural and institutional outline to Habermas' description of "traditional society." The social circumscribed the economic; or, as Polanyi notes, "the economic system was submerged in general social relations; markets were merely an accessory feature of an institutional setting controlled and regulated more than ever by social authority."[1] Instrumental pursuits, particularly the expansion of the productive apparatus and the growth of commercial capitalism, were permitted to the extent that they did not threaten to abridge the social obligations sustained in the prevailing cultural traditions. In Habermas' words, the system of work received its legitimation "from above."

S. N. Eisenstadt suggests that the basic condition and, simultaneously, the basic dilemma for the stability of a transitional society such as eighteenth-century England is that power holders require and receive both traditional legitimation and various types of free-floating resources and support—resources and support, that is, which are flexible, not "embedded in traditional, ascriptive groups or committed for more or less fixed goals."[2] In these circumstances, the exercise of power is accorded legitimacy so long as the development and provision of free-floating resources are circumscribed within the limits established by traditional structures of authority. In Eisenstadt's words, the task is

> to regulate and channel the more active groups and free-floating resources, and to link them constantly to the more traditional forces in common political frameworks and organizations. The . . . effective exercise of political power was largely dependent on the ability to maintain such regulation.[3]

Often, however, a dialectic emerges as these two sources of support enter into contradiction. On the one hand, there is a tendency to continue the legitimation of power by abiding by the traditional system of authority; on the other, there is a tendency to generalize and expand power by increasing the amount and kind of free-floating resources. This second tendency entails a denial of the traditional authority structures and a separation, a freeing, of the economy from social obligations. The establishment of a self-expanding industrial base and a self-regulating market presupposes the elimination of social constraints; yet the elimination of these constraints would seriously erode the traditional bases of support and legitimacy. An appreciation of this dilemma is essential to a full understanding of the operation of English society in the last half of the eighteenth century.

A primary concern of this chapter is to demonstrate the two-dimensional qualities (partially reflected in the tension between traditional and free-floating legitimations) characteristic of England in the eighteenth century, particularly between 1750 and 1790. After examining the subsystem of instrumental action, the subsystem of symbolic interaction, and, in turn, the mediation of the two as it is influenced by the norm of reciprocity, the goals and structure of popular social protest are studied and explained with reference to the work and interaction dialectic. The social constraints on economic and productive activity are emphasized throughout this analysis.

SUBSYSTEM OF INSTRUMENTAL ACTION

Mercantile capitalism, which arose shortly after the breakdown of feudalism in the fifteenth and early sixteenth centuries, provided the organizing principles for the economy of eighteenth-century England.[4] Though the mercantile system began to wane after mid-century, it continued to exert a significant impact on all aspects of social life. Under feudalism, questions concerning the possession and rights accruing to the ownership of land, transfer of land, and organization of labor were subject, not to market regulations of buying and selling, but to legal and administrative rules. While mercantilism had managed by the eighteenth century to extricate trade and commerce from the restrictions and peculiarities of local markets, in Polanyi's words, it "never attacked the safeguards that protected these two basic elements of production—labor and land—from becoming objects of commerce."[5] Thus, the economic system generated by mercantile capitalism was still embedded in basic social relations. As a consequence, little systematic mobilization of foodstuffs and produce for market exchange had occurred; nor, as we shall see below, had anything approaching a viable labor market developed. Moreover, prior to mid-century the creation and maintenance of many capitalistic organizations depended to a great extent on governmental support. In many respects, then, mercantile society paralleled the feudal order. Where the productive forces and economic activities under feudalism were regulated by the custom and tradition apparent in town charters, tenancies, and guilds, those under mercantilism were guided by statutes and ordinances delivered and enforced by a political authority which received its legitimacy from communal traditions.

Generally, mercantile capitalism has been examined with reference to its international aspects—the creation of national wealth and a favorable balance of payments through foreign trade. Although largely overlooked, the domestic policies established by the mercantile system are of crucial importance. In England these domestic policies were framed in a well-ordered system of laws and regulations under which, as Charles Wilson notes, "the preservation of social order took precedence over economic progress."[6] Throughout most of the eighteenth century, public protection for certain industries, and governmental regulation of wages and prices, although rapidly declining from the 1790s on, were common. Indeed, as we shall see, any contradictions between the goals and requirements of the national government and those of economic expansion were invariably settled in favor of the former.

Mercantilist doctrine gave recognition to a kind of corporate responsibility which required the government to be sensitive and responsive to problems of general welfare. Throughout the mercantilist period, there was an abundance of legislation designed, as William Appleton Williams notes "to create and sustain some balance and order in the process of economic development and in its attendant social consequences."[7] Relief laws, for instance, "were predicated upon the idea that poverty, instead of being a personal sin, was a function of the economic system, and that the general welfare was the responsibility of the government."[8] Under mercantilism, in short, economic and productive activity were governed by standards which subordinated utilitarian to moral concerns, and as a result, domestic economic policies were formulated to be consonant with the prevailing social order. In effect, these domestic policies served to confine the formation of capital to either commercial endeavors involving finance or to investment in landed estates. Even into the 1770s, credit and investment opportunities for industrial capital remained few; and, often, what new industrial capital was created proved to be unproductive in the context of the strict regulations of the mercantile system. Indeed, the very rapid industrial expansion, growth of production and trade which was initiated in the late 1750s was a product, not of industrial, but of commercial capital—or, more particularly, finance capital: wages, not machinery, constituted the bulk of production costs.[9] As Deane and Cole have found, while industrial capital contributed little to the overall growth of the national product, land continued to be England's most important capital asset in this period.[10]

Until the close of the eighteenth century, land—followed by finance, trade, and industry—continued to be the major source of wealth. At least until the 1780s, much of the increase in industrial output resulted from the expansion of the domestic system of manufacture which was worked primarily by agricultural laborers. Although real wages rose during this period, the rise in demand for industrial products resulted from an expansion of agricultural investment, not from an increase in per capita consumption.[11]

In their study of British economic growth, Deane and Cole observed that the first significant acceleration took place between 1745 and 1760 in conjunction with a sharp increase in agricultural investment. Accompanying this increase, and the attendant improvement of agricultural techniques, were the first systematic attempts at transforming land into capital. The mechanism of transformation was enclosure; and from 1750 on, there was an enormous increase in the number of enclosure bills presented to and enacted by Parliament.[12] The widespread enclosing of open fields and engrossing of farms not only facilitated improved agricultural methods but also enabled the landed interests to more easily convert their holdings into instruments of capital formation. Eventually, of course, the concentration of land resulting from the enclosure movement contributed to the emergence of industrialization. But for a long time, the capital creation which was made possible by the enclosures benefited the landed interests more than it did the industrial capitalists.

With land as the fundamental capital asset of eighteenth-century England, industrial expansion was both rare and discontinuous. The economic expansion generated by agricultural means, although significant, occurred largely within traditional institutional boundaries. The economy, as E. P. Thompson rightly suggests, was infused with moral imperatives.[13] One of the key social foundations in which economic expansion was embedded was kinship. Landed estates were apportioned to families rather than individuals; recruitment to most trades and crafts was made on the basis of kin-ascribed criteria; and, more importantly, in the context of the domestic system of manufacture, the nuclear family served as the basic unit of production. With specific reference to the cotton-weaving industry, Neil Smelser describes the domestic system.

> The father wove and apprenticed his sons into weaving. The mother was responsible for preparatory processes; in general she spun, taught the daughters how to spin, and allocated the picking, cleaning, drying, carding, etc. among the children.[14]

This kind of household production, which was essential to the agriculturally oriented society, was controlled more by custom than by market considerations. Of more concern to employers than how the work was completed "was that the finished goods should be delivered at the end of the week or fortnight prescribed by custom."[15] Under this system, little differentiation developed between agricultural and industrial sectors, as manufacturing work was usually distributed evenly among families.

Although weakened with the emergence of the factory system in the 1760s, the organization of manufacture along the lines of the domestic system continued in a more or less viable way throughout much of England well into the nineteenth century. Unpredictability marked the domestic system of manufacture. In the first place, the largest amount of capital utilized in production was offered in the form of raw materials, and thus could be removed quickly from the productive process. Typically, work orders were given out and returned at unspecified and irregular intervals. This combined with the absence of a functioning credit system, and with the presence of a monetary system continually hampered by a shortage of coin, to inject a relatively high degree of instability into the manufacturing process. Given this instability, the domestic system "retained the casual, leisurely flavors of country life and carried it over into this transitional phase of industrial life."[16]

Not surprisingly, unemployment in mercantile England was commonplace, not only in the countryside and towns, but in the cities as well. Work was contingent both on the fluctuations of commerce and on the vagaries of nature. In the often lengthy periods of unemployment, workers attempted to scrape a living off their small plots of land (although this alternative was increasingly eliminated with the onset of the enclosure movement), relied upon relatives or neighbors for assistance, or received relief benefits from parish agencies. Given the frequency of unemployment, laborers received protection from the Poor Law and the Statute of Artificers, both originally implemented in the mid-sixteenth century. As Polanyi observed, together they constituted the foundation of the 'code of labor' which prevailed in England for most of the eighteenth century.

The Statute of Artificers influenced labor organization in at least three ways: it required the enforcement of labor, both in rural and urban districts, thereby giving legality to the workhouse system; it provided loose guidelines for the public assessment of wages; and, most significantly, it set a minimum standard of seven years apprenticeship binding on all skilled trades and crafts.[17] Complementing the Statute of Artificers was the Poor Law, which essentially decreed:

> that the able-bodied poor should be put to work so as to earn their keep, which the parish was to supply; the burden of relief was put squarely on the parish, which was empowered to raise the necessary sums by local taxes or rates. These were to be levied upon all householders and tenants, rich and non-rich alike, according to the rental of the land or houses they occupied.[18]

With the parish serving as the basic unit for the distribution of poor relief, widespread migration was discouraged, and establishment of a regional market for labor was impeded.

Economic and industrial expansion was limited by the social obligations expressed in the institutional framework. Prior to 1760 such expansion occurred, not as a result of the introduction of new industrial techniques (although some were available), but was generated by a differentiation of existing units of production. When, after 1770, a rapidly growing population intensified demand, and thereby necessitated a greater reliance on improved industrial techniques, the direction and amount of change taken by the productive apparatus and economy were still subject to regulation. The large-scale introduction of mechanical equipment into the manufacturing process, which took place between 1770 and 1780, did, however, serve to initiate the gradual transformation of commercial capital to industrial capital.[19] As Paul Mantoux observes, "through the introduction of machinery and the consequent concentration of the means of production, the hold of commercial capital was riveted on industry, and the manufacturer in the modern sense of the word took the place of the merchant-manufacturer."[20] Around the 1780s the commercial strength of the country began to be related to its industrial strength. Despite this gradual but highly significant transformation, industrial expansion continued into the 1790s on a very uneven course, with some industries, like the metal industry, almost completely mechanized, and with others, such as the weaving industry, still organized about the domestic system.

These variations among industries were paralleled by wide geographical variations. As a consequence, no national markets and, for the most part, no regional markets could develop. Specialized markets were established about local industries, but most regional exchange was transacted at seasonal fairs. T. H. Ashton describes the established procedures associated with these ad hoc markets with reference to the recruitment of labor:

> The determination of wages was a matter for bargaining between masters and men. . . . Custom played a large part and the tradition of apprenticeship had an influence on both supply and demand. The market for labor was far from perfect. In agricultural and mining areas the workers attended the annual fairs to offer themselves for hire; and Spitalfields market served as an employment exchange for the poor women silk weavers of London. Employers sometimes gave notice of vacancies in local newspapers, and in cases of urgency made use of the town crier. The office of overseer of the poor, the inn, and the house of call of the tramping artisan, all served

as centers of information. Most often, however, it was by word of mouth from one man to another that news of opportunities of employment was spread.[21]

Prior to the 1760s this imperfect method of procuring labor posed no severe problems. While several large factories employing a substantial number of workers existed, the predominant forms of manufacture were carried out either by means of household production or by a capitalist with a small number of workers under his supervision.

With the rise of large-scale manufacture between 1760 and 1780 the deficiencies of the traditional market system began to be felt. During this period, several attempts were made to perfect regional and even national markets. The improvement of transportation and communication, largely through the creation of a massive series of navigable waterways, was begun. Accompanying this development, was the growing advocation of the authorization of free trade, and the emergence of serious efforts aimed at eliminating governmental intrusion in economic and industrial activities.[22] This early defense of a self-regulating market-propounded by the new school of classical economists—was accompanied by sporadic attempts on the part of the rising industrial capitalists to separate the economy from social constraints.[23] Through the last half of the century, however, all these efforts were met by the protest and opposition of the laborers. And, as Ashton noted, "whenever the peace of the metropolis was threatened by disputes about wages [Parliament] tended to fall back on the traditional system of legitimation."[24]

Not until the 1780s did the strength of institutional controls begin to be seriously compromised. It was also during the last twenty years of the eighteenth century that industrial expansion was concentrated: the mechanization of the textile industry, the application of steam power, and the vast improvements in the technology of coal and iron, all contributed to a tremendous increase in output.[25] In Eisenstadt's terms, the support which could be provided by free-floating resources was becoming more significant than the support supplied by cultural traditions. It is essential to recognize, however, that England was still without a fully integrated market system. The standards of manufacture, the conditions of labor, and the determination of prices and wages were still under institutional control; and they would remain so, at least partially, until the nineteenth century.

Of particular importance to the organization of economic and industrial activity during this period was the role of the laborer. While regarded as a major source of national wealth under the mercantile system, the laboring population of eighteenth-century England did not receive benefits commensurate with its generally supposed contributions. What accounted for this was a prevailing belief in what Edgar Furniss has labeled the "utility of poverty."[26] Essentially, this meant that the national interest required that most of the population be confined to poverty conditions. Only the pain of low wages and 'hard times' could stimulate the laborer to assume diligent and disciplined work habits. As a contemporary, Arthur Young, remarked, "Every one but an idiot knows that the lower classes must be kept poor or they will never be industrious."[27] The doctrine of the 'utility of poverty,' although formally subscribed to, was modified in practice. As will be examined in greater detail below, the laboring classes had considerable impact on the standards employed in regulating wages and work conditions.

Accompanying the rapid economic growth beginning in the 1750s and 1760s was the weakening of the 'utility of poverty' argument. A more sympathetic attitude toward the laboring population, one which retained the view of labor as the foundation of national wealth, emerged. According to this position—which, by the third quarter of the century, had been widely advanced—an improved standard of living was a necessary incentive to adequate work effort. The proponents of this view were quite cognizant of the immediate implication of their argument; namely, that the wants and needs of the laboring classes be given priority over those of the rich. Thus, it was urged that the newly won benefits of economic and industrial expansion be somewhat redistributed. One observer of this period has found that this concern with the increasing disparity of the allocation of wealth and resources "inspired various egalitarian proposals, and [moreover], appeals for a more equal distribution of wealth or a wider diffusion of property became frequent enough to constitute a characteristic feature of contemporary literature."[28] This new position soon undermined the older mercantile view of the necessity of maintaining the bulk of the working population in conditions of economic distress. In contradistinction to their mercantilist counterparts, the classical economists expressed a less rigid view of the working class: their position exhibited "less carping, less preaching of the early-to-bed, early-to-rise variety, and there was more tolerance of distinctively human behavior."[29] Although this position was gaining adherents, its most significant implications—those relative to redistribution—were never implemented. Nevertheless, this position did contribute to a number of important changes.

Typical of these changes was the modification of Poor Law policy and practice brought about with the enactment of the Gilbert Act in 1782. Previously, Poor Law relief was allocated primarily to the old and infirm. While temporary relief was available for the unemployed, it was discouraged, mainly because it was inconsistent with the notion that 'hard times a better worker makes.' Pressure from workers, as well as other groups in society, to improve Poor Law policies along more equitable lines came with the recognition of the growth of resources and capital which society had at its disposal. The passage of the Gilbert Act represented the culmination of this pressure. In moving away from the inadequacies of prior policy, the Gilbert Act stipulated that

> relief was not merely to be granted in the customary form of temporary subsidies at times of sickness, bad trade, or high prices, a practice which had never ceased in many parishes, and which was already on the increase; it was also to be provided as a guarantee of maintenance during an indefinite period.[30]

In short, the Gilbert Act obligated the government to maintain an adequate standard of living for the workers either by providing them employment or with relief in aid of wages.

The Gilbert Act was one part of the well-ordered system of protective laws and regulatory principles upon which mercantile capitalism rested. In effect, these principles introduced moral overtones to economic and industrial relations, creating a sense of responsibility which infused most social activities. As Furniss remarked, these principles of regulation usually operated as a just distributive force, as "the principles appealed to were of social justice and national expediency, not those of economic theory."[31] As they pertained to the worker, these regulatory standards contributed to the determination of what standard of living, what conditions of work, how much wages, in short, of what kind of protection ought to be given in justice to the laboring man. In these circumstances, "the notion of *economic objectivity*—of an economy operating according to laws of its own, independent of man's conscious will," received little development and even less support.[32] The economic closely intermingled with the political; and to the extent that the political continued to rely upon traditonal legitimations, social obligations took precedence over market considerations.

Although Parliament began to formally abandon some of the social constraints on the market in the 1760s, informal controls persisted, as local authorities continued to respond to workers' threats by initiating a reestablishment of traditional arrangements. By the 1780s, even these informal sources of control began to be diminished. In 1785, the General Chamber of Manufacturers was formed for the purpose of organizing a broad-based alliance in opposition to the regulatory principles and practices supported by the government. Although it would be incorrect to associate the aims of the Chamber of Manufacturers with laissez-faire doctrines, it is true that the organization sought to extirpate those policies which impeded unlimited commercial expansion. In discussing the interests of these manufacturers, Mantoux observed that they "were naturally opposed to regulation of any kind, whether of persons or things, of technical processes or labor conditions. They were determined to be the sole masters of production, unfettered by any limitation or control."[33] Not entirely successful, the Chamber of Manufacturers did manage to achieve a general relaxation of the regulatory policies, both formal and informal; and, more importantly, its influence was sufficient to impede the enactment of further controls. What prohibited a more extended renunciation of the regulatory system was, as previously, the refusal of the laborers to allow a complete breakdown of protective safeguards.[34]

But the manufacturing interests, by this time involved with the prospects of industrial capital as well as commercial capital, did not require a complete breakdown of traditional regulations to accomplish their aims. The factory system was first systematically introduced in those areas of England less encumbered by institutional controls, and the first industries to undergo extensive mechanization were those which, by virtue of their recent origin, were not yet ensconced in traditional and legal restraints. Especially important in this regard was the cotton industry. During this period, cotton manufacture grew rapidly. Not subject to time-honored customs, and now beyond the hold of governmental controls, the cotton industry incorporated a succession of new mechanical techniques which very shortly increased its complexity and made it the model of the large-scale factory system. As Mantoux remarked, the cotton industry "grew up all the quicker because [it] had not to break down too many habits and traditions. . . . The fact is, that with regard to this new industry the government had no definite policy at all."[35]

The technical advances made in the cotton industry spread to all other major industries during the next twenty years; and, in a somewhat discontinuous manner, industrial capitalism began to take root. If industrial capitalism was to grow, however, the remaining regulatory principles had to be abolished. Even here, the precedent was set by the cotton industry. When, in the 1780s, the government decided to apply an excise tax on cotton materials, the manufacturers combined to successfully pressure the House of Commons to reverse the decision. Upon their return to Lancashire, the manufacturers were met by a hugh procession of supporters bearing banners reading: "Let Commerce flourish forever! Freedom restored! May Industry never be cramped!"[36] This issue concerning the freedom of eonomic and industrial activity from social controls would be raised again and with much greater intensity in the years to come. For now, however, economic expansion and significant transformations of the productive apparatus continued to be abridged by the moral codes embodied in institutional controls.

SUBSYSTEM OF SYMBOLIC INTERACTION

All societies are based on domination and oppression. Since force alone is most inadequate for maintaining stable and enduring organizational

forms, domination is invariably accompanied by the development of ideologies which serve to justify the exercise of force. In preindustrial capitalist
England, the predominant ideology embodied "a higher category, over
and above the social value system and its institutions, from which their
legitimacy [could] be rationally derived or attacked."[37] Inclusive of both a
conforming and a critical reason, this ideology possessed a substantive content in terms of which legitimacy was granted to or withheld from the existing order.

The higher, trans-systemic category to which the ideology of eighteenth-
century England (and, in turn, the institutional controls over economic and
productive activity) was linked was the doctrine of natural law. While a concept of natural law existed as early as Aristotle, the modern development of
natural law doctrine was initially formulated in the seventeenth century.[38]
In this latter form the predicates of natural law received continued and
extensive expression throughout the eighteenth century. Based on the assumption that values are immanent in reality—that is, in the nature of
things—the doctrine of natural law allows normative prescriptions for
social action to be deduced from nature. These normative prescriptions
carry a moral imperative which obligates all men to act or refrain from acting
in particular ways. Thus, from natural law can be deduced a set of natural
rights and duties which nature has accorded man. On the basis of these
natural rights, furthermore, it is possible to establish what is, by nature, just.

Two related implications are suggested by this exposition of the natural
law doctrine. First, since all rights are natural rights, the positive or conventional laws of civil society are not to be created *de nove*; rather, they are
to be formulated in accordance with those values immanent in nature.
Natural rights are not contingent upon positive laws: on the contrary, these
laws merely reflect, are declaratory of, natural rights. Accordingly, the
principal aim of society, as William Blackstone insisted in 1765,

> is to protect individuals in the enjoyment of those absolute
> rights which were vested in them by the immutable laws of
> nature . . . [since] this law of nature being coeval with mankind
> and dictated by God Himself, is, of course, superior in obliga-
> tion to any other. . . . No human laws are of any validity if
> contrary to this.[39]

Since the laws of civil society are subsidiary to natural law they can be examined and evaluated with reference to a higher category. Thus, the second
implication in the natural law doctrine—and this is clear in Blackstone's
remark—is that positive or conventional laws cannot be imposed; rather,
they must be consented to. This bears directly upon the problem of legitimacy.
To the extent that positive laws diverge from natural law, they should not be
adhered to; to the extent that government, intentionally or inadvertently,

abridges natural rights, it should not be supported. Government, in this context, arises as a moral necessity out of the natural rights of man; it is a government of laws, but of laws which are reflective of the fundamental nature of mankind.

The conforming tendencies contained in natural law ideology were expressed as rationales for legitimating the prevailing arrangements. In general terms, this involves, as Weisskopf observes,

> not simply a submission to and acceptance of the existing order . . . [but] a rationalization of this order . . . [since a] higher interest is used to justify the existing order by arriving at the conclusion that its cognitive, normative and institutional aspects are rooted in the natural order of things.[40]

While the natural law ideology was thus able to confirm the established order, it was also capable of challenging its legitimacy. In its critical form it "develops a cognitive, normative and institutional system which is different from [that of existing society] and uses it to attack the existing order."[41] Thus, in its conforming orientation, the natural law ideology stresses the duties which derive from natural law; and in its critical form the rights accorded man by natural law are emphasized. Below, the conditions under which conforming reason gives way to critical reason will be specified.

In eighteenth-century England, the confirmatory aspects of natural law ideology were rooted in the premise that nature made all men alike but not equal. E. P. Hurlbut summarized this position:

> Uniformity of *kind* but inequality of *powers*, seems to have been the rule of Nature when she formed the character and appointed the destiny of the various members of the human family. . . . [And] so far as human legislation has gone, it has left [the individual] as it found him—strong if he were strong before, and weak, if he were weak. It has guaranteed the *freedom* of his nature, not the *powers* of it.[42]

Thus, while nature has conferred the same rights upon all men, some are better equipped to exercise these rights than others. With regard to these others—the young, the immature, the inexperienced, the socially or psychologically defective—it is the responsibility of government to provide them with protection.

The protection and restraint issued by the government was done so under the name of the common good. As a law of nature, the "common good" or the "greatest possible happiness" was also employed to establish the justice of the positive law of property. Richard Cumberland, in *A Treatise of the Laws of Nature,* stated the case typically:

> We have seen how the nature of things imprints on us . . . a knowledge of good and evil, even of that which is common to many, as is that by which we know the causes of generation and corruption. I now proceed to consider, that the matter and motion, in which the powers of a human body, as of all other parts of the visible world, do consist, have a finite quantity, and certain limits, beyond which they cannot extend themselves. Whence flow these most evident axioms concerning all natural bodies: That the same bodies cannot at the same time be moved toward several places . . . so as to be subservient to the opposite wills of the several men; but that they are so limited, that they can be determined by the will of one only, unless several conspire to one and the same effect or use.

Based on this argument, Cumberland later wrote:

> It follows, that men, who are obligated to promote the common good, are likewise necessarily obligated to consent, that the use of things and labor or persons, so far as they are necessary to particular men to enable them to promote the public good, should be so granted them, that they may not lawfully be taken from them, whilst the aforesaid necessity continues; that is, that those things should, at least during such time, become their property, and be called their own. . . . It is, therefore, evident, that the nature of things discovers, that it is necessary to the happiness, life, and health of every particular person, upon which all other advantages depend, that the uses of things should be limited, at least for a time, to particular persons exclusive of others.[43]

This long passage contains the key elements of the conforming reason embodied in natural law ideology. Implied in nature is an absolute and inviolable right to property. Restricted by natural law, the positive law of civil society and, accordingly, the power of government—if they are not to lose the consent of the people—must not abridge this right.

Natural law ideology rationalized the existing social order by portraying it as part of the natural order of things. As long as it remained declaratory of the natural law, the established society warranted popular consent. But—and this point cannot be overemphasized—this rationalization of the status quo had to be logically consistent with the broader implication of natural law doctrine; that is, it could not deny that all men shared the same basic natural rights, despite the assertion that some people were better enabled to practice these rights. The solution to this problem was that government along with these 'superior' people assumed the responsibility of protecting the natural rights of the less able. Since this action would be consonant with natural law, it should be consented to by all involved. Stated in this way, the conforming reason of natural law ideology took the form, in John Stuart Mill's words, of a "theory of dependence."

There were two central elements to the theory of dependence. The first was that the existing status order, with a few exceptions, was unalterable. The second element concerned the poor or, more generally, the laboring population. As members of the lower orders, the poor and the laborers (often the two categories were indistinguishable) were viewed and treated as children. Responsibility for the protection of their natural rights had to be partially assumed by the higher orders. Thus, civil legislation, in concert with the dictates of natural law, was established to facilitate the protection of the natural rights of those who comprised the bottom status levels. Accompanying the protection of these rights were specific duties. What developed, then, was a reciprocal relationship between the higher and the lower orders. A set of mutual obligations emerged which, given the nature of natural law and the corresponding positive laws of civil society, was binding on all parties. The best description of the particulars of the theory of dependence was offered by Mill in his *Principles of Political Economy.* Summarizing the outlines of this eighteenth-century rationalization of the existing order, Mill wrote:

> The lot of the poor, in all things which affect them collectively, should be regulated *for* them, not *by* them. . . . It is the duty of the higher classes to think for them, and to take responsibility of their lot, as the commander and officers of an army take that of the soldiers composing it. This function the higher classes should prepare themselves to perform conscientiously, and their whole demeanor should impress the poor with a reliance on it, in order that, while yielding passive and active obedience to the rules prescribed to them, they may resign themselves in all other respects to a trustful *insouciance*, and repose under the shadow of their protectors. . . . The rich should be in *loco parentis* to the poor, guiding and restraining them like children. Of spontaneous action on their part there should be no need. They should be called on for nothing but to do their day's work, and to be moral and religious. . . . Their superiors . . . should do all that is necessary to ensure their being, in return for labor and attachment, properly fed, clothed, housed, spiritually edified and innocently amused.[44]

Entailed by the theory of dependence was a series of reciprocal obligations between the rich and the poor, the rulers and the ruled. Where the former were required to make available specific provisions, the latter were obligated to reciprocate by diligently performing their laboring tasks.

This matrix of reciprocal relationships was firmly embedded in the status order. While natural law conferred rights and duties upon all, the specific execution of these rights and duties was a function of status. The sense of obligation, which pervaded the eighteenth-century ideology, proceeded from the relation of status to the higher category of natural law. The authority of the existing order rested upon the natural law justification of the obligations associated with each particular status. As long as these obligations remained normatively binding, the legitimacy of the prevailing arrangements was virtually assured. In this traditional authority relation, the higher orders and the lower orders, as Bendix noted, thought "of each other as an inferior or superior extension of themselves."[45] When, as was the case throughout most of the eighteenth-century, the higher-status orders were generally responsive to the needs and demands of the laboring poor, the application of authority was often viewed as a nonpartisan action, one consistent with natural rights. It is clear, then, that natural law ideology—and, more specifically, the derivative theory of dependence—provided a rationalization of the existing order which assigned, to those who benefited from the perpetuation of this order, both privileges and duties. When these duties or responsibilities were not adequately met, the legitimacy of the social order and, more particularly, of those obligations associated with the lower status orders, was severely challenged. Guiding these challenges was the evaluation of the current situation made possible by the categories of natural law and natural rights. We find in these circumstances a shift from conformity to critical reason.

The critical expression of natural law ideology appeared sporadically from the 1720s on, in the various campaigns for constitutional reform. Common to these efforts to reform positive law was a constant appeal to natural rights, the rights of the freeborn Englishman protected by the original Saxon constitution in accordance with natural law. Thus, the modified constitution of government was examined in light of the 'higher,' unwritten, nonrational constitution which nature had conferred upon man.[46]

Directly connected to the issue of constitutional reform was the eighteenth-century tradition of *Commonwealthman*. Demanding civil and religious liberty, the Commonwealthmen kept alive in their writings and programs the traditions and struggles which earlier culminated in the seventeenth-century Glorious Revolution. The Commonwealthmen—or, as they are also known, the Independent Whigs—were comprised largely of Dissenters, the nonconformists to the Anglican church. While several major contributors to the Commonwealthman tradition defy any religious categorization, it is of great significance that the typical figures and the key ideas of this tradition were centrally influenced by Dissent. The importance of the Commonwealth-man tradition in sustaining the critical aspects of natural law ideology through-out the eighteenth century cannot be overstated. In this regard it is useful to note that the proportion of Dissenters in the total population rose from 4 percent in 1715 to 20 percent by the 1790s, the period which marked the beginning of the first serious challenge to the authority relations of English society.

In her important study, *The Eighteenth-Century Commonwealthman,* Caroline Robbins outlined the two fundamental principles of the tradition. The first "insisted that an Englishman was entitled to be ruled by laws to which he himself had consented, wherever he was, and the [second] ex-tended this right to all of mankind."[47] Influenced by the Lockean theory of natural rights, the Commonwealthman tradition maintained that the de-cisions, policies, and practices of the state were subject to scrutiny by all. Decision-making agencies were thus held accountable for their activities. The revolutionary implications of the Dissenters' interpretation of the Lockean position arose from the secularization which the interpretation brought to bear on political discourse. According to this interpretation, it is the individual conscience, not the positive laws of state, which is declaratory of natural rights. It was at this very point, as Staughton Lynd remarked, that "they broke with the Lockean thesis that man is the passive product of circum-stance, and affirmed what they liked to call 'the dignity of human nature.' "[48]

The emphasis on individual conscience underlay much of the critical thrust of Commonwealthman thought. Natural law, because it was above the king and magistrates and was accessible to all people through their consciences, was necessarily the ultimate standard of authority. All public measures and governmental activities were to be examined in light of this higher law before they were granted legitimacy. Thus, authority did not proceed from the rela-tion of the status order to natural law; it issued forth from the relation between conscience and natural law. What this interpretation of natural law ideology suggests is of the highest importance, for it redefines the exist-ing order as something which has to be acted upon. The established status order was no longer perceived as unalterable: consequently, the legitimacy of this order was open to question. Writing in 1751, Cato presented the typical Commonwealthman argument on this point, noting that the Inde-pendent Whig

> scornes all implicit faith in the State, as well as the Church. The Authority of Names is nothing to him; he judges all men by their Actions and Behavior, and hates a Knave of his own

Party, as much as he despises a Fool of another. He consents not that any Man or Body of Men, shall do what they please. He claims a right of examining all public Measures and, if they deserve it, of censuring them. As he never saw much Power possessed without some Abuse, he takes upon him to watch those who have it; and to acquit or expose them according as they apply it to the good of their country, or their crooked Purposes.[49]

Based on this conception of natural inherent rights, the Commonwealth-man tradition urges popular resistance to any decision made within the context of civil legislation that was capable of abridging these rights. Laws formulated independently of the knowledge and consent of those governed by the laws were to be resisted and, if necessary, overthrown. While this did not involve a denial of the necessity of political domination, it did constitute a challenge to the nature of domination. Regarding this latter point, the Dissenting tradition transferred the burden of proof from the individual seeking to exercise his rights, to the state engaging in limiting this exercise. Thus, political domination could be consented to; insurrection was justifiable. Stated in this critical form, the natural law ideology eliminates the practical implications deriving from the notion of social contract. As Elie Halevy has pointed out,

When men have adopted a position of legitimate insurrection, what is the point of saying that they are rising because the contract which should have guaranteed their rights has been violated, instead of saying, more simply, that they are rising because their rights have been violated? These 'absolute rights' are held . . . to constitute the compact itself. . . . [Thus] the expression of the contract becomes a figurative way of representing the idea of moral obligation.[50]

The virtual dissolution of the social contract thesis and, corresponding to this, the shifting of the location of obligations from the status order to man's inalienable rights, were the consequence, in Lynd's words, of the "restoration of conscience to the center of man's experience."[51] The immediate implication of this shift was a redefinition of the gnosiological character of natural law. All men, the common men as well as those of the higher orders, through their consciences, possessed the ability to know and understand the rights established by natural law; these rights as truths become self-evident. In 1774, John Cartwright wrote:

We are told that these men have a right to more, those to less, and some to none at all. But a title to the liberty of mankind is not established on such rotten foundations: 'tis not among mouldy parchments, nor in the cobwebs of a casuist's brain we are to look for it; it is the immediate, the universal gift of God.[52]

Increasingly during the last quarter of the eighteenth century, the Commonwealthmen focused the critical interpretation of natural law ideology on the injustices associated with the concentration of national wealth and with the centralization of political power. They found that society as presently organized did not warrant legitimation, and that the civil legislation formulated by the government did not merit consent. Before the end of the century, this critique of English society was to gain much public support, particularly from the newly emerging political clubs and corresponding societies.[53] And it is appropriate that a Commonwealthman, Richard Price, summarized the aims of the popular insurrectionary movement which began to spread through England in the 1790s. "Restore to mankind their rights," he warned the government, "and consent to correction of abuses, before they and you are destroyed together."[54]

In summary, the justification of political, economic, and social domination offered by the natural law ideology contained both a conforming and a critical reason. The ideology could be and was used to confirm and to critically evaluate the established structures and institutions. Expressed as conforming reason, the natural law ideology initiated what Marx called a system of false consciousness. Since, however, false consciousness was derived from an ideology which simultaneously contained an anticipation of more just social arrangements, the dissolution of false consciousness required not the elimination of the ideological framework itself, but an emancipatory process—one mediated by reflective activity capable of demonstrating how and why the anticipations embodied in the prevailing consciousness were negated by existing structural tendencies. The Commonwealthman tradition gave sustained expression to the critical implications inherent in the eighteenth-century ideological consciousness. As we shall see below, these critical implications also received articulation in the oral culture, the institutions, communities, and in traditions of the laboring classes. Eventually, these two sources of critical reason were to converge; and, as a result, the legitimacy of English society increasingly underwent attack. To understand why this was so, it is necessary to examine the nature and operation of the norm of reciprocity during this period.

THE NORM OF RECIPROCITY

Prior to the onset of industrial capitalism, English society, with class divisions not yet fully crystallized, was hierarchically arranged with the landed aristocracy situated at the top. Power in this society was strongly associated with property relations. William Marshall wrote at the time, "Landed property is the basis on which every other species of material property rests; on it alone mankind can be said—to live, to move, and have its being."[55] Until the latter part of the eighteenth century, the political— rather than the proprietary—relation to land was emphasized. Authority relations revolved around the status order; accordingly, the landed aristocracy, in the absence of a viable centralized administrative agency, had the major influence on the decision-making process.

In an essay on the eighteenth-century 'political man,' J. H. Plumb examined this situation and suggested that there prevailed at the time two distinct yet related political worlds: a political establishment comprised of the landed elite and a political nation populated by those with no or little property holdings. The first world was

> a tight political establishment, linked to small groups of powerful political managers in the provinces, who controlled parliament, the executive and all that was effective in the nation, and outside this, [a second world] an amorphous mass of political sentiment that found expression in occasional hysteria and impotent polemic, but whose effective voice in the nation was negligible.[56]

Plumb's distinction between a political establishment, which had effective control over the decision-making apparatus of society, and a political nation, which generally acceded to these decisions (and only infrequently displayed its discontent in some aimless and unorganized way), is only partially accurate. For while such a political establishment did have a significant say in the framing of national policies, all decisions were made within a matrix of institutional traditions—which protected the rights of the governed and the obligations due them by the decision makers. Should any decision repudiate these rights and obligations, the legitimacy of the existing order would be revoked. To clarify this important point it is useful to again consider Eisenstadt's analytical remarks.

As noted at the beginning of this chapter, Eisenstadt found that the autonomy of a society's decision-making apparatus from traditional prescriptions is contingent upon the extensive development of free-floating resources (such as money and various types of exchangeable commodities) and upon a free-floating population not precommitted to particularistic values. With their development restricted until the close of the eighteenth-century, free-floating resources and support remained subsidiary to those based upon traditional legitimation in the form of natural law ideology. As we have seen, embodied in these traditional prescriptions were certain obligations which the decision-makers were required to fulfill if their power was to be granted legitimacy. Thus, throughout the eighteenth century, reason was

still committed to a substantive content; rationality was not content-free—
that is, it was not free-floating. The critical implications located in committed reason served to establish the boundaries within which power could
be applied.

Contrary to Plumb's portrayal, then, the political establishment could
not arbitrarily make decisions. All major decisions had to be made in such
a way that traditional legitimation would be maintained. When decisions,
policies, and practices were pursued with a disregard for these boundaries,
they were met by widespread opposition. Thus, unlike the laissez-faire
decision-making policies which would predominate in the nineteenth century,
choices in the eighteenth century were

> made between alternative goals and a decision reached as to
> what the nation ought to make of herself from the potentialities
> of her resources. Once this decision [was] made, the process
> of evaluating individuals and social classes on the basis of
> their fitness to contribute to the attainment of the national
> purpose, of evolving concepts of the duties of the various
> classes and creating sanctions to enforce these duties, of ma-
> nipulating the industrial organization, of apportioning rewards
> for services—the entire framework of public policy . . . —
> [followed] logically.[57]

Throughout this period the normative standards of natural law ideology
guided the decision-making activities of the government. The government
—the decision makers and power holders—was held accountable to these
standards and, more specifically, to the people whose natural rights were
conferred by these standards.

In part, what permitted the propertied class to exercise political power as
authority was its ability to develop and maintain an effective patronage
system. In a society where there were no central administrative agencies
capable of making policies and appointments, and where there was at best a
blurred distinction between personal and official influence, patronage permeated the social hierarchy from top to bottom. Extending throughout
society, the patronage system made recruitment on all levels—from Court
appointments to relief listings—a matter of politics. As Harold Perkin notes,

> If government patronage controlled the most lucrative, private
> patronage controlled the most numerous appointments: most
> church-livings, salaried country, borough, and parish offices,
> merchants' and lawyers' clerks, estate agents, chaplains, secre-
> taries, tutors and governesses, and the whole pyramid of
> domestic service, sometimes extending to the very labourers
> on the estate or home farm.[58]

Within the rigidities of a property-based status order, it was an effective patronage system that facilitated the maintenance of traditional legitimation. Under these circumstances, the exercise of political power relative to the decision-making process was confined to the limits imposed by rank, tradition, and kinship. Until late in the century, authority accrued to the power of local administration, not to that of the national government. The prevailing feeling was that "obedience and tranquility were most effective when they depended not on the means of compulsion or on the existence of administrative apparatus but on the natural social sanctions of a local community."[59]

An analysis of the dynamics underlying the relation between power and authority must take place through an examination of the operation of the norm of reciprocity. The status order in eighteenth-century England depended for its legitimacy on the adequate fulfillment of the obligations established by the norm of reciprocity. Indeed, the stability of the status order was directly associated with how effectively the decision makers met these obligations. When the rulers failed to adequately respond to these obligations, social protest on the part of the ruled resulted. Given a stratification system organized on the basis of status, conflict groups were primarily status groups. Through the relation of these status groups political authority and domination were expressed. And, since embodied in these status relations were obligations, rights, and duties, political domination was somewhat circumscribed. This is not to deny the existence of an oppressor-oppressed relation, but only to emphasize the accountability of the former to the latter. As previously noted, the norm of reciprocity entails, not equivalence of response, but adequacy of response as culturally defined. The important point is that in the eighteenth-century status order, negative experience could be and was placed into a relational matrix; that is, negative experience was attributed to the nature of the status relations. The cause of negative experience was interpreted as a violation of the reciprocal obligations built into the status order. When such violations occurred, whether they were the consequence of design or natural events, the confrontation of status groups quickly transformed into the confrontation of political groups wherein the legitimacy of the status order was challenged.[60] And, because of the immediacy of authority in all hierarchical relationships, social conflict, when it did occur, assumed very specific forms.

Reciprocity between the rulers and the ruled took the form, as Mill noted, of a theory of dependence. The rulers were obligated to make available specific provisions to the ruled. And, while they rationalized these obligations in terms of an alleged responsibility for the care of the inferior and immature, the performance of these duties were required if their authority was to be left unchallenged and their power unabridged. Thus through the norm of reciprocity, the oppressed did set restrictive limits to, and demands upon, their oppressors. The patronage system can be viewed as an expression of the reciprocal obligations established between the rulers and the ruled. In return for their loyalty and support the dominated expected protection; and in time of need, the guarantee of at least a subsistence livelihood. Both of these obligations were normally met through the patronage system. Thus, as even the poor laws illustrate, the landed aristocracy had duties as well as rights, duties which had to be adequately fulfilled if social opposition was to be avoided. Throughout the century, whenever manifestations of unfulfilled obligations arose (such as an inadequate supply of food or an exorbitant rise in prices), they were invariably met by riots and protest which sought to physically reestablish patterns of adequate and just response.[61]

Subordination in this context involved negotiation. The strategies of negotiation which emerged from the interaction between the 'polite,' patrician culture of the gentry and the plebian culture of laborers were characterized, as Thompson notes, by a certain theatrical style.[62] The popular culture of the laborers and the poor was essentially a 'playful culture' which exhibited horizontal solidarities, a distinct consciousness, and a refusal to assume a deferential stance. The gentry—partly, no doubt, as a consequence of the presence of an inadequate standing army—not only tolerated the popular culture but often responded to the demands it generated. This "permissive attitude to the robust, unchristian popular culture, a certain caution and even delicacy in the handling of popular disturbance, even a certain flattery extended to the poor as to their liberties and rights," suggests to Thompson

> some reciprocity in the relations between rich and poor; an inhibition upon the use of force against indiscipline and disturbance; a caution [on the part of the rich] against taking measures which would alienate the poor too far, and [on the part of the poor] a sense that there were tangible advantages to be gained by soliciting the favor of the rich.[63]

In terms of this reciprocity—this negotiated subordination—the aims and aspirations expressed in popular culture had considerable impact on the activities of the rulers. For, although the popular culture was not yet a revolutionary culture, it was a critical culture, one which spawned riots when obligations were unfulfilled and traditional rights abridged. Fully aware of this, the authorities were usually careful to follow the rules of the game established through negotiation.

Prior to the widespread enclosing of open fields and engrossing of farm lands, which began in the second half of the century, the specific obligations derived from the norm of reciprocity were associated with the allocation of land. During this time, most people possessed plots which were arranged in such a way that they had to be worked in accordance with common rules and regulations. Within each community, moreover, there existed areas of common land which were used for grazing and farming purposes by all members of the community. The usage of these common lands was perceived as a definite right by those in the lower status orders.[64] When the enclosure movement began to impede this form of reciprocity, riots occurred throughout the country. In 1757, in the face of this opposition, Parliament enacted legislation which "directed the commissioners for enclosures to pay into the hands of the Poor Law authorites certain compensations 'to be applied towards the relief of the poor in the parish or township where . . . wastes, woods, and pastures had been enclosed.' "[65] As Hobsbawm notes, until the 1790s the government responded favorably to these riotous activities either by compelling the reestablishment of adequacy of response or by replacing the old obligations with new obligations.[66]

Until the last decade of the eighteenth century, the obligations and duties established by the norm of reciprocity were generally and adequately met. The legitimacy of the status order was maintained: natural law ideology was, with a few exceptions, used to affirm the prevailing social arrangements. In order for this confirmatory expression of natural law ideology to be preserved, it was necessary for the powerholders in society to maintain some controls over the productive apparatus and the economy in general. Once productive and economic changes were allowed to proceed in such a way that status obligations could no longer be fulfilled, the legitimacy of the status order was called into question as riots developed quickly, almost spontaneously. Because the government quickly responded to these threats, by acceding at least partially to the demands of the rioters, normalcy was usually reestablished. Once grievances were redressed and an adequacy of response was restored, opposition disappeared.

SOCIAL PROTEST

Popular uprisings were a common feature of eighteenth-century social life. The most systematic treatment of these preindustrial protest activities is found in the recent works of E. J. Hobsbawm, George Rudé, and E. P. Thompson. According to these historians, the participants in popular uprisings retained a strong attachment to traditional values and practices, which served to both create a meaningful sense of order and animate a "constant and continuous presentation of demands for the 'restoration' of 'lost rights,' such as the 'just wage' and 'just price.' "[67] Just as the demands and objectives of the participants were inherited from the remembered past, so too was the structure of their agitation. As Thompson observes, these popular uprisings exhibited a pattern of behavior which had originated several centuries earlier, and "which repeats itself, seemingly spontaneously, in different parts of the country and after a passage of many quiet years."[68]

Although protest emerged spontaneously, often in the form of direct action riots and frequently characterized by a playful or festive posture, it was not undisciplined.[69] Targets were precisely and discriminately selected, and property, not people, was assaulted and destroyed. More often than not, the agitation occurred in the older, more cohesive, more traditional communities. Rudé, in a summary of the dynamics of these uprisings, notes that the participants were

> fired as much by memories of customary rights or a nostalgia for past utopias as by present grievances or hopes of material improvement; and they dispense[d] a rough-and-ready kind of 'natural justice' by breaking windows, wrecking machinery, storming markets, burning their enemies in effigy, firing hayricks, and 'pulling down' their houses, farms, fences, mills, or pubs, but rarely by taking lives. The riots, then, [were] the characteristic and ever-recurring form of popular protest, which, on occasion, turn[ed] into rebellion or revolution.[70]

Thus, direct action protest was legitimated by reference to traditional standards. The protesters, Thompson notes, "were informed by the belief that they were defending traditional rights or customs; and, in general, that they were supported by the wider consensus of the community."[71] Moreover, it was in accordance with these traditional rights that the legitimacy of the prevailing status order was measured. Defined with reference to the doctrine of natural law, these measures were infused with a sense of social responsibility. As we have seen, if the 'higher orders' refused or were unable to meet their obligations—or, in other words, if the 'ancient rights' of the 'lower orders' were abrogated—the existing status order was discredited.

The popular uprisings of the eighteenth century, then, arose primarily in response to unfulfilled obligations. Underlying these agitations by the laborers and the poor was the assumption, supported by past experience, "that the authorities would be sensitive to [their] movements, and probably also that they would make some sort of immediate concession."[72] This assumption— or, perhaps more accurately, this heritage—was grounded firmly in the existing moral economy. Although the moral economy was subject to increasing attack by advocates of laissez-faire from the 1760s on, its principle of market supervision (markets should be controlled so that "the poor should have the opportunity to buy grain, flour, or meal first, in small parcels, with duly-supervised weights and measures") and its principle of consumer protection (in terms of which millers and bakers "were considered as servants of the community, working not for a profit but for a fair allowance") remained in operation.[73] In the context of this moral economy, popular agitation usually focused around price and wage concerns. Whenever prices and wages were allowed to fluctuate with market considerations—that is, whenever traditional institutional controls over economic and productive activity were relaxed or abolished—riot and crowd activity would invariably ensue. During these occasions rioters would intimidate vendors and employers in an effort to reestablish traditionally sanctioned price and wage scales. Often they would prevent the transportation of needed foodstuffs out of their locality; and, just as frequently, they would take control of the marketplace to ensure the continued availability of certain goods at what they considered adequate prices.[74]

That these direct action uprisings never developed into enduring protest movements was chiefly due to the responsiveness of the 'higher orders.' As long as the rich and powerful met their obligations by providing an adequate standard of living, by making food readily available at suitable prices and by regulating wage rates, the likelihood of protest was remote. In short, the threat of riot and challenge to authority disposed the rulers to maintain institutional regulations on prices, wages, the distribution of foodstuffs, and the productive process itself.[75] The popular uprisings were effective, as Thompson remarks, "in getting corn to market; in restraining rising prices; . . . in intimidating certain kinds of profiteering . . . [and in signaling] the rich to put the machinery of parish relief and of charity—subsidized corn and bread for the poor—into good repair."[76] In sum, superimposed upon and restraining the market economy, the moral economy protected traditional obligations from infringement by economic and industrial growth. Any denial of the social responsibility affirmed by this moral economy initiated protest activity which, if left unabated, would have certainly weakened the stability of the status order. Riotous activities in eighteenth-century England can be classified according to their primary goals as political, economic, or industrial. Cross-cutting this dimension is a second one, which is concerned with whether such activities resulted from spontaneous, popular direct action or from "the deliberate use of the crowd as an instrument of pressure, by persons 'above' or apart from the crowd."[77] Where the first category characterizes the revolutionary crowd with insurrectionary aims and practices, the second represents the "Church and King" mob, a mass of laborers orchestrated by aristocratic interests to react against the progressive forces in society. While this distinction is a useful one, in that it emphasizes the dissimilarities of the different types of protest action, it overlooks an important point. In practice, both the revolutionary crowd and the "Church and King" mob involved a conflict between the rich and the poor, the powerful and the powerless, the oppressor and the oppressed. Moreover, both arose and achieved an intensity of outburst under conditions of unfulfilled obligations. Thus, despite the reactionary slogans associated with the "Church and King" mob, this form of social protest activity, like the revolutionary crowd, contained—however undefined—a critical orientation.

This point receives solid documentation below, in an examination of representative industrial, political, and economic protest activities.

The industrial disorders which occurred in London in 1768-1769 are typical of those protest activities which were initiated from 'below.' As economic conditions worsened and traditional controls were abandoned, vigorous agitation quickly replaced the calm which had previously characterized the metropolis. While most of the industrial poor participated in the various protest activities, the most significant disturbances were generated by the coalheavers, the seamen, and the silkweavers.

Although lacking deliberate coordination, the protest activities of the coalheavers, seamen, and silkweavers were nearly identical in form and content. All three sets of disturbances were reactions against the abrogation of traditional rights, and each constituted a demand for the reestablishment of the protections of the moral economy. Thus, the coalheavers demanded a tightening of the Act of 1758—which, as presently formulated, permitted employers to avoid institutional regulations at their convenience; the seamen insisted that the authorities prevent their employers from reneging on customary obligations; and, similarly, the silkweavers rioted for official regulation of their industry.[78] In each instance, there existed a combination of new and old tactics and goals; and the result was a progressive radicalism that emerged out of a traditional context. Direct action riots, as well as petitioning, occurred alongside more organized and highly disciplined activities. While 'spontaneous' groups engaged in the destruction of looms and other equipment, and in the threatening of employers, there were attempts to form enduring organizations along trade union lines.[79] Conservative goals oriented toward paternalist protections were raised along with the more progressive goal of enhancing the laborers' role in the decision-making process. Better organized than their predecessors, the industrial rioters of 1768-1769 exerted sustained pressure upon their employers and the authorities; and the disturbances they produced subsided only after their demands received an adequate response.[80]

Coinciding with these industrial riots was a series of political disorders revolving around the "Wilkes and Liberty" movement. Despite continuous interaction between the industrial and political riots, there was never an attempt to merge the two into a unified movement. The Wilkite riots—both in their guiding ideology and in their structure—closely resembled the industrial agitations, although the former, essentially a political activity, was a middle-class movement and the latter, with its industrial concerns, was a movement of the laboring class.[81] For our purposes, the Wilkite riots are important because they clearly reflect the underlying cooperation which existed between the lower and middle classes in preindustrial social protest activities.

Beginning in the late 1760s and providing repercussions lasting into the middle of the next decade, the "Wilkes and Liberty" movement is a good example of riot and crowd activity emerging in response to the decision makers' break with traditional obligations and liberties. This whole period was marked by rapidly rising food prices (especially bread prices in the countryside), an increased application of taxes on basic provisions, and an intensification of the enclosure movement. As a consequence, opposition to the existing order grew from the mid-1750s on. This discontent was manifested in the rural hunger riots and urban industrial riots and, eventually, in the significant support received by the "Wilkes and Liberty" movement. The crowd which supported Wilkes was typical in every sense of the traditional eighteenth-century crowd; its actions were not fully organized; nor had it attained a sufficient degree of self-consciousness to be able to specify common aims and goals. However, the importance of the "Wilkes and Liberty" movement is that it occurred at such a time to provide a channel through which the political awareness of the oppressed could begin to be articulated.

The immediate stimulus of the "Wilkes and Liberty" movement was the House of Commons' refusal, both in 1768 and in 1769, to permit John Wilkes to sit for Middlesex, a position to which he was elected four times. Wilkes was declared ineligible by the House because, at the time of his election, he was imprisoned for seditious libel. This charge had been brought against Wilkes for his activities as editor of *The North Briton,* a journal which frequently published satirical attacks against the government and king.

Wilkes' defense of his journalistic activities, as well as his argument for being allowed to take his seat in the House of Commons, rested upon the traditional notions of rights, liberty, and protection. In his appearance in court Wilkes addressed the judges by insisting:

> The liberty of all peers and gentlemen, and, what touches me more sensibly, that of all the middling and inferior set of people, who stand most in need of protection, is in my case to this day to be finally decided upon a question of such importance as to determine at once whether English Liberty shall be a reality or a shadow.[82]

By thus associating his situation with the broader curtailment of normative obligations which was taking place at the time, Wilkes successfully sought the support of the discontented lower class. Indeed, after Wilkes had been elected to the House of Commons despite strong opposition from the government and the king, many laborers participated in a victory celebration which was simultaneously an expression of their grievances. The *Annual Register* described the scene.

> The rabble was very tumultuous; . . . The mob paraded the whole town from east to west, obliging every body to illuminate and breaking the windows of such as did not do it im-

mediately. The windows of the Mansionhouse, in particular,
were demolished all to pieces, together with a large chandelier
and some pier glasses, to the amount of many hundred pounds.
They demolished all the windows of Ltd Bute, Lord Egmont,
Sir Sampson Gideon, Sir William Mayne, and many other
gentlemen and tradesmen in most of the public streets of both
cities; London and Westminster.[83]

Despite increased repression such riots continued for the next several years,
until the government both reversed its decision on the Wilkes matter and
restored regulatory controls which assured an adequate standard of living.

While the strongest support for "Wilkes and Liberty" remained located
within the areas surrounding London and Westminster, the movement
quickly gained in numbers throughout England. As earlier noted, prior to
the "Wilkes and Liberty" movement popular insurrectionary activities prevailed in many localities. However, these outbursts occurred in a discrete
and uncoordinated way. The "Wilkes and Liberty" movement, by articulating the critical achievements of natural law ideology, brought to these
isolated economic and industrial disputes a coherent set of political guidelines. One contemporary observer, noting this relation between industrial
disputes and the political movement associated with Wilkes, commented:

> Artisans of almost every denomination . . . combined for an
> advance of wages, and their discontents, and disobedience to
> the laws led them to join often, in numbers, those mobs which
> the consequence of the elections for Middlesex frequently
> produced.[84]

The interaction between the industrial riots and the "Wilkes and Liberty"
movement is highlighted by Rudé's detailed and careful study. Among
Rudé's findings, first was that Wilkes received his greatest electoral support
in those districts of Middlesex experiencing a growth in population: "The
mainstay of Wilkite support lay not so much in the urban area as a whole . . .
as in the populous commercial parishes lying to the east and north of the
City."[85] Second, those who participated in the riotous activity associated
with "Wilkes and Liberty" "tended to be wage earners rather than self-
employed craftsmen, peddlars or small proprietors, but they were rarely
criminals, vagrants or the poorest of poor, and insofar as any parts of the
metropolis may be said to have been more riotous than others, they were the
City, the Strand, Southwark, Shoreditch and Spitalfields rather than . . .
the shadier alleys of Holborn."[86] Third, after examining the criminal records
listing those rioters who were arrested, Rudé suggests that the most active
and vociferous supporters of the movement came from the lower status

orders: of those implicated in "Wilkes and Liberty" riots and demonstrations, "[t]he greatest majority were, in fact, labourers, servants, journeymen, small craftsmen, or petty traders."[87] Fourth, as is clear from the above, "Wilkes and Liberty" attracted support from wide sections of both the 'middling' and laboring populations.[88]

The evidence Rudé presents is clear enough. The "Wilkes and Liberty" movement supplied an organizing base and a set of articulated aims which attracted extraordinary support from large numbers of the newly emerging entrepreneurial and working classes. However, while the support from both groups was equally strong, the nature of support differed significantly. Where the 'middling' group displayed its commitment by launching a series of successful petition drives in Wilkes' behalf, the laborers engaged in disturbances in which they attempted to physically bring about a natural justice. A second important difference between the two groups concerns the interpretations which each brought to the Wilkite demand for liberty and the restoration of rights. The entrepreneurial supporters of the movement interpreted the cry for liberty as a cry for freedom from governmental regulations of the economy. Conversely, the laborers—as they demonstrated quite clearly in their industrial riots—regarded liberty and justice as possible only in the context of institutional controls. What is crucial to recognize at this point is the operation of critical reason. The critical expression of natural law ideology afforded evaluative categories which the oppressed groups— the middling and lower classes—used to discredit the legitimacy of the existing order. These critical categories anticipated *alternative* tendencies: on the one hand, laissez-faire principles of organization; on the other, communal principles of organization. The anticipatory content was ambivalent. A choice had to be made as to which tendency was to be realized.

The struggle to achieve the power to make this choice would occupy much of the next century. Until this struggle, it was not uncommon to find what in the next few years would become the bourgeoisie and the proletariat coordinating their actions in opposition to the aristocracy, the government, and the king. Although in the 1770s the decision makers of England were still a good twenty or thirty years away from explicitly abrogating the normative prescriptions upon which their traditional legitimation rested, the "Wilkes and Liberty" movement afforded a prototype of what was to come. The significance of the movement is aptly summed up by Rudé.

> For all its immaturity and lack of definition, the cry of 'Wilkes and Liberty' was a political slogan and stirred the political passions of not only freeholders and freemen but of the unenfranchised craftsmen and journeymen, who were its most vocal and enthusiastic promoters. This was something new in the nation's political life and raises the popular movement

associated with Wilkes above the level of the mere food riot
or [other] such blind outbursts.[89]

The "Wilkes and Liberty" movement, like the industrial disorders of the
same period, drew its strength from the revolutionary crowd. A second major
form of social protest was the preindustrial mob, which is commonly contrasted to the revolutionary crowd and regarded as a collection of riffraff
guided by reactionary aims and controlled by external interests. However, a
careful examination indicates that the mob, far from being passive and manipulated, was active and assertive in its selection of targets; and, like the
revolutionary crowd, it directed its hostilities against the higher orders during
periods of unfulfilled obligations. Despite the reactionary slogans under which
it marched, the mob physically expressed "a certain desire among the poor to
settle accounts, if only briefly, with the rich."[90] Responding—often inco-
herently and certainly without the articulation which characterized the Wilkes'
supporters—to the abridgement of customary and natural rights, mob participants contributed to the growing assault on established authority relations. To
demonstrate the critical content of mob activity three representative cases, each
allegedly manipulated by aristocratic and governmental interests, will be
briefly examined and analyzed: the provincial hunger riots of the 1760s; the
Gordon riots of the 1780s; and the Priestley Riots of 1791.

The hunger riots which pervaded southern England in the summer and
fall of 1766 are regarded as "the most extensive rural disorders" of the
eighteenth century.[91] Intense and tightly disciplined, drawn exclusively
from the poor and laboring classes, the rioters managed to secure temporary
control over large areas of the countryside. Typically, these rural riots were
instigated by unfulfilled obligations—in this case, the failure to provide an
adequate supply of food at suitable prices. Although the shortage of food
appears to have been the consequence of natural processes, the people of
the lower orders interpreted the problem as one of artificial scarcity, a
deliberate denial of the social responsibility embodied in traditional constraints and mandated by natural law. In their attempts to force a reduction
in prices and prevent the transportation of needed provisions out of the
locality, the hunger riots sought to reimpose the principles of the moral
economy.

The primary target of the hunger rioters was the middleman—the miller,
the baker, the grain dealer—who was clearly benefiting in the shift from a
purely local to a more regional marketing system. Unlike the disturbances
of 1757, the riots of 1766 avoided confrontation with the landowners and
the gentry magistrates. This fact, combined with the wide encouragement
the rioters received from the government, has caused the participants in
these hunger riots to be viewed as a 'loyal mob.' In this light, the direct

action assaults, the intimidation, and the destruction of property brought against the middlemen by the rioters have been portrayed as activities controlled from above: the lower class, in short, performed the 'dirty work' of the landowners.

This portrayal is highly simplistic: for while it recognizes the manipulation of the lower orders by their 'betters,' it fails to attend to the manipulation of the landowners and the gentry magistrates by the rioters. Although the government was quick to encourage the attacks against the middlemen, these attacks were initiated by the laborers and the poor. Moreover, there is some evidence to suggest that the support from above was motivated, not by an intolerance of the middleman, but by a desire to avert the assaults on the 'higher orders' that were so frequent in the 1756-1757 disturbances.[92] In this sense, the response from above was partially manipulated from below. By confirming the activities of the rioters, the landowners and gentry magistrates not only diverted potential attacks but also presented the appearance of abiding by traditional obligations. Thus the encouragement which the rioters received from the authorities came in the form of support, not control; and this support—this reaffirmation of traditional rights—was essential if the authorities wished to avoid attack.

Like the hunger riots, the Gordon Riots of the 1780s are often presented as a classic example of mob activity. These disturbances were ostensibly organized by the Protestant Association in its drive to convince Parliament to repudiate pending legislation which called for partial toleration of the Catholic religion.[93] Under the banner of "No Popery" the mob's hostility was mobilized by the middling elements of the Protestant Association and was unleashed against the property and people in the predominantly Catholic districts of London. In this way—it has been suggested—the commercial and Protestant interests employed the laboring population in their struggle against the government.

Although the ensuing riots proceeded under religious slogans, their orientation was clearly social and political, reflecting—in Rudé's words—the "belief that Englishmen were 'free' and not 'slaves,' and did not starve or wear 'wooden shoes'—such as foreigners in general and Papists in particular."[94] That political grievances, more than religious bias, underlay the Gordon Riots is made clear in the selectivity with which the assaults were launched. The Catholic districts attacked were those which housed the residences of the wealthy and influential; the poorer districts, where the Catholic workers and indigent resided, were rarely the scene of riotous assaults.[95] Thus, after "the priest and the schoolmaster had been dealt with, it was the gentleman, the manufacturer, the merchant or the publican, rather than the craftsman or wage earner, who was the main object of the rioters' attention."[96] Given the careful discrimination used by rioters in determining their targets, it is misleading to characterize their actions as aimless and incoherent. Indeed, it appears that in many cases the rioters employed "No Popery" slogans to justify their assaults against the rich.

Although the disturbances usually commenced in or around Catholic districts, they often spread to other areas of the city. On numerous occasions, city business houses and the residences of certain justices were stoned and burned; jails, including the Newgate and Fleet prisons, were attacked, and prisoners freed; and there was at least one attempt to besiege the Bank of England.[97] It is noteworthy that these riots, as they occurred both within and outside the Catholic districts, resulted in few casualties, and were marked by only minimal looting. On the whole, it appears that sociopolitical more than religious grievances were given expression in these disturbances. An article on the Gordon Riots written in 1780 for *The New Annual Register* recognized this:

> It is certain, that it would be unjust to impute to the Protestant Association . . . the whole of the mischief that ensued. . . . Some of the common people probably engaged with more readiness in the riots, from the unpopularity of the administration, at least among persons of that class: and, perhaps, so much violence and disorder could not have happened under any administration, which had been universally respected by the common people.[98]

Horace Walpole concurred. "The Pope needs not be alarmed," he wrote. "The rioters thought much more of plundering those of their own communion than his Holiness's flock."[99] Anti-Catholic rhetoric tended to conceal the rioters' repudiation of existing authority relations. To be sure, the rioters were anti-Catholic; but they were also vehemently opposed to the abridgement of rights and the denial of social responsibility.

The Priestley Riots occurred in Birmingham in 1791, and the vast majority of their participants were drawn from the industrial artisans and laborers of the area. Like the Gordon Riots, the Priestley Riots are considered representative of the passive mob, manipulated by governmental and aristocratic forces to blindly abolish emerging liberal organizations and political societies, In this particular case, the rioters directed their opposition against Joseph Priestley and the people associated with his activities. Priestley, a Unitarian minister and active Dissenter, was a major figure in the campaign to repeal the Test and Corporation Acts which imposed restrictions on the public life of Dissenters. By July of 1791, Priestley and the New Meeting reform society, of which he was a member, had been openly accused of constituting a threat to "Church and King." Coming from local authorities and the pulpits of Anglican churches, these accusations provided a license for the mob activity which ensued.

Concentrating on Dissenting establishments and the property of key Birmingham dissenters, the rioters looted, sacked, and pulled down businesses and residences. While little physical harm was done to the persons of individual dissenters, their safety was clearly threatened. Less political than the Gordon Riots, the Priestley Riots nevertheless demonstrated a displeasure of the existing order on the part of the laboring population. This is suggested by R. B. Rose, who notes that there were several underlying reasons for the mob's assault on selected targets.

> Both Russell and Taylor were justices of the peace, and Taylor had been High Sheriff of the County. Humphreys was accused of allowing his clerks to read seditions and republican literature at the warehouse. William Hutton, a historian and stationer suffered exceptionally badly. . . . As a commissioner of the Birmingham Court of Requests, a court for small debts, he had earned much unpopularity. "He had," his daughter remarks, "compelled ten thousand blackguards to pay their just debts and at this time of general license they were let loose upon him."[100]

Thus there is some indication that a latent class struggle was being expressed along with the animosity toward dissenting and republican ideas. When viewed in terms of the broader social developments, which by the 1790s had entailed an increasing abrogation of traditional rights, these riotous activities were not simply reactionary: for they reflected a solid disenchantment with established social arrangements.

While the provincial hunger riots, the Gordon Riots, and the Priestley Riots resulted in much aimless and unwarranted destruction, the social and political motivations, as well as the religious, ethnic, and economic ones which underlay them, must not be ignored. These riots were much more than the blind reactions of the hungry and the hateful; they represented, with varying degrees of political awareness, a defense of traditional customs and naturally ordained rights. Thus it was not the Irish, the Catholics, and the Dissenters who were assaulted; rather, it was the wealthy and influential Irish, Catholics, and Dissenters. In these instances, the rioters were not blind, passive, and manipulated. Their targets, carefully selected, were people who had benefited at their expense. While it is clearly true that many of the rioters were indeed prejudiced against ethnic and religious minorities, it is equally true that they seized these opportunities in order to repudiate the established order.

The immediate impact of the eighteenth-century riots—and this holds more for the revolutionary crowd than the mob—entailed, not drastic societal change, but a reestablishment of or compensation for traditional normative obligations. The long-term impact, however, was significant. In effect, these riots enhanced the awareness of different and contending interests. Initially, this resulted in a clearer separation of the critical and conforming elements of natural law ideology; and, on a more concrete level, it resulted in the emergence of middle-class political societies such as the Yorkshire Association, and a variety of working-class organizations, including trade unions, and political clubs such as the London Corresponding Society. In short, these riots and social protest activities enabled the political nation to be better equipped in dealing with the political establishment. The radicalism which was to blossom in the first few decades of the nineteenth century—in the form of both philosophic radicalism and militant working-class consciousness—could trace its roots to the eighteenth-century riots and mobs.

Summary

Eighteenth-century English society was characterized by the basic features of what has been earlier described as two-dimensional society. The allocation of wealth and resources, the distribution of products, and the decisions and policies which were made and implemented were all expressive of underlying social obligations and relationships. Incorporated in the status order, these normative obligations were directly associated with the legitmacy of society. Whether the existing order was approved or discredited depended largely on the extent to which the various status orders adequately fulfilled their obligations. Thus, political domination was significantly shaped by these normative prescriptions. The activities of the decision makers were circumscribed by these overarching cultural patterns.

Not only did these normative obligations shape the relationships between the powerful and the powerless, the rich and the poor, but they also served as the basis for guiding economic and productive activity. As we have seen, under mercantile capitalism major questions concerning the direction and pace of economic growth and productive development were dealt with in accordance with cultural traditions. Thus, while economic and productive activity operated under criteria of instrumental or purposive rational action, these kinds of activity received their legitimacy from the normative prescriptions linked to the status order. As a consequence, rationalization proceeded both formally and substantively. Throughout the century, but especially from 1760 on, English society extended its technical mastery over the external forces of nature. However, despite the growing attacks on the moral economy, this increase in the technical control over nature was not allowed to extend to society. The historical opportunities for progressive emancipation were enhanced.

With this substantive content, the natural law ideology which developed in eighteenth-century England embodied both a conforming and a critical reason, and thus was capable of legitimating both the prevailing arrangements and the oppostion to these arrangements. Often these two categories would become entangled, resulting in such instances as the Gordon Riots and Priestley Riots, wherein affirmative slogans would combine with oppositional practices. The important point, however, is that the affirmation and the criticism of society derived from categories which were not reducible to the society itself. Reason continued to be committed to fundamental human values: it was not yet free-floating—that is, content-empty or value-free.

In its critical form, natural law ideology anticipated a more progressively emancipated form of social organization. This anticipatory content served three general and related purposes. First, it contained the evaluative principles which were used to critically scrutinize the present order. Second, it offered alternatives to the existing arrangements by identifying the tendencies (laissez-faire principles *and* communal principles) contained in and suppressed by these arrangements. And, thirdly, the anticipatory content provided transcendental criteria for social action.

This emancipatory consciousness had a practical side which is evidenced by the always physical and often violent activities carried out by the eighteenth-century rioters in their attempts to restore a 'natural justice.' Since these activities offered a serious challenge to the legitimacy of the established order, the decision makers were quick to come to terms with the grievances of the common people. Beyond this, they sought to avoid potential outbursts of popular discontent by protecting the regulatory controls established by cultural tradition. Accordingly, changes in economic and productive organization were effected within an institutional framework which embodied the particular rights as well as duties accorded to the lower status orders. Expressed through the norm of reciprocity, these rights afforded some degree of protection to the oppressed. Indeed, when these rights were abridged, conforming reason gave way to critical reason.

Throughout most of the century, the protest activities of the common people were more or less successful, as the government maintained a system of regulation which subordinated instrumental concerns to the preservation of the social order. By the 1790s, however, the government's ability to retain these institutional controls, and to give continued assurance of adequacy of response from all status orders, was severely hampered. Although industrialization had been taking place since the 1760s, the decisive turning point occurred in the 1780s. The period from 1780 to 1800 marks the first steady and sustained period of economic growth in England's history. During this twenty-year period, the population in industrial and commerical counties increased by approximately 33 percent as compared to a 26 percent increase over the previous thirty years, while predominantly agricultural counties experienced a decline in their growth from 20 percent to 11 percent over the corresponding periods.[101] Moreover, it has been estimated that from 1760 to 1803 the contribution of agriculture to the total national income fell from 27.7 percent to 22.3 percent, while the contribution made by manufacture, trade, and distribution interests rose form 32.2 percent to 45.9 percent.[102] Accompanying these developments were the growth in numbers and power of the capitalist class and the extension of free-floating resources. Where the first factors promoted oppositon to the government's maintenance of institutional controls, the second offered the decision makers an alternative mode of support to traditional legitimation. In short, the decision makers could now afford to dissociate themselves from cultural traditions. A revolutionary working class consciousness began to emerge out of this background at the turn of the century.

NOTES

1. Karl Polanyi, *The Great Transformation* (Boston, 1944), p. 67.

2. S. N. Eisenstadt, *The Political Systems of Empires* (New York, 1969), p. xiv.

3. Ibid., p. 301.

4. For a concise examination of the development of mercantilist doctrine, 1500-1750, see William Grampp, "The Liberal Elements in English Mercantilism," *Quarterly Journal of Economics* 66 (November, 1952): 465-501.

5. Polanyi, *The Great Transformation,* p. 70.

6. Charles Wilson, *England's Apprenticeship, 1603-1763* (London, 1965), p. 375.

7. William A. Williams, *The Contours of American History* (New York, 1961), p. 44.

8. Ibid.

9. Wilson, *England's Apprenticeship,* pp. 359, 292.

10. Phyllis Deane and W. A. Cole, *British Economic Growth, 1688-1959, Trends and Structures* (Cambridge, 1962), pp. 94, 157.

11. Ibid., pp. 90-93. On the continued importance of agriculture and commerce as major sources of capital after 1750 see Dorothy Marshall, *Industrial England, 1776-1851* (New York, 1973), p. 172. Also R. M. Hartwell, *The Industrial Revolution and Economic Growth* (London, 1971), p. 269.

12. See Deane and Cole, *British Economic Growth,* p. 94.

13. See E. P. Thompson, "The Moral Economy of the English Crowd in the Eighteenth Century," *Past and Present* 50 (February 1971): 83-87.

14. Neil Smelser, *Social Change in the Industrial Revolution* (Chicago, 1959), pp. 74-75.

15. T. S. Ashton, *An Economic History of England: The Eighteenth Century* (London, 1955), p. 76.

16. Wilson, *England's Apprenticeship,* p. 345.

17. Polanyi, *The Great Transformation,* p. 86. Also see T. K. Derry, "The Repeal of the Apprenticeship Clauses and the Statute of Artificers," *Economic History Review* 3 (January, 1933): 67-87.

18. Polanyi, *The Great Transformation,* p. 87. Clearly reflected here is the Settlement Law of 1662 which tied the poor relief system to the parish of origin. The stipu-

lations of the original law, the law's effect on eighteenth-century poor relief policy, and its modification in 1795 are examined, respectively, in: A. E. Bland, et al., eds., *English Economic History, Select Documents* (London, 1914), pp. 645-649; G. D. H. Cole and Raymond Postgate, *The British Common People* (New York, 1961), pp. 126-127; and in Phyllis Deane, *The First Industrial Revolution* (Cambridge, 1965), pp. 144-145.

19. See Hartwell, *The Industrial Revolution and Economic Growth,* pp. 117-118.

20. Paul Mantoux, *The Industrial Revolution in the Eighteenth Century* (London, 1961), p. 250.

21. Ashton, *An Economic History of England*, p. 219.

22. See, for instance, the position of David Hume as presented in Wilson, *England's Apprenticeship,* p. 353.

23. See William Grampp, "On the Politics of the Classical Economists," *Quarterly Journal of Economics* 62 (November 1948): 714-747.

24. Ashton, *An Economic History of England,* p. 218.

25. See Asa Briggs, *The Making of Modern England, 1783-1867* (New York, 1959), p. 18.

26. See Edgar Furniss, *The Position of the Labourer in a System of Nationalism* (New York, 1957), pp. 117-125.

27. Arthur Young as quoted in Furniss, *The Position of the Labourer*, p. 120.

28. A. W. Coats, "Changing Attitudes to Labour in the Mid-Eighteenth Century," *Economic History Review* 11, No. 1 (1958): 49.

29. Grampp, "The Liberal Elements in English Mercantilism," p. 482.

30. A. W. Coats, "Economic Thought and Poor Law Policy in the Eighteenth Century," *Economic History Review* 13, No. 1 (1960): 50.

31. Furniss, *The Position of the Labourer,* p. 157.

32. Maurice Dobb, *Studies in the Development of Capitalism* (New York, 1947), p. 200.

33. Mantoux, *The Industrial Revolution,* p. 393.

34. Ibid., pp. 451-460. (See also the discussion under the "social protest" section in this chapter).

35. Ibid., p. 258.

36. Ibid., p. 259.

37. Walter Weisskopf, *Alienation and Economics* (New York, 1971), p. 34.

38. For the shifts in the category of natural law from the Aristotelian to the modern usage, see Leo Strauss, *Natural Right and History* (Chicago, 1953).

39. William Blackstone as quoted in Julius Stone, *Human Law and Human Justice* (Stanford, 1965), p. 88.

40. Weisskopf, *Alienation and Economics,* p. 34.

41. Ibid.

42. E. P. Hurlburt, *Essays on Human Rights and Their Political Guaranties* (New York, 1853), pp. 28, 35.

43. Richard Cumberland, as quoted in Hans Kelsen, *What is Justice?* (Berkeley, 1957), pp. 154-155.

44. J. S. Mill, "Principles of Political Economy," in *Class and Conflict in Nineteenth Century England.* Edited by P. Hollis, (London, 1973), p. 364.

45. Reinhard Bendix, *Nation-Building and Citizenship* (New York, 1969), p. 49.

46. The nature of the 'ancient constitution' (and its impact on the development of historiography in the seventeenth and early eighteenth centuries) is examined in J. G. A. Pocock, *The Ancient Constitution and the Feudal Law* (Cambridge, 1957).

47. Caroline Robbins, *The Eighteenth Century Commonwealthman* (Cambridge, 1959), p. 9.

48. Staughton Lynd, *Intellectual Origins of American Radicalism* (New York, 1968), p. 20.

49. Cato as quoted in Robbins, *The Eighteenth Century Commonwealthman* p. 120. ("Cato" was a pseudonym for John Frenchard and Thomas Gordon.)

50. Elie Halevy, *The Growth of Philosophic Radicalism* (New York, 1928), p. 138.

51. Lynd, *Intellectual Origins,* p. 30.

52. (John Cartwright as quoted) Ibid., p. 37.

53. The impact of the Commonwealthman tradition on American radicalism is examined in Lynd, *Intellectual Origins* and in Bernard Bailyn, *The Ideological Origins of the American Revolution* (Cambridge, 1967).

54. Richard Price as quoted in Robbins, *The Eighteenth Century Commonwealthman,* p. 377.

55. William Marshall, as quoted in Harold Perkin, *The Origins of Modern English Society, 1780-1880* (Toronto, 1969), pp. 41-42.

56. J. H. Plumb, "Political Man," in *Man versus Society in 18th-Century Britain,* ed. J. Clifford (New York, 1968), p. 12.

57. Furniss, *The Position of the Labourer,* p. 202.

58. Perkin, *The Origins of Modern English Society,* pp. 44-45.

59. Briggs, *The Making of Modern England,* p. 100.

60. See Walter Shelton, *English Hunger and Industrial Disorders* (Toronto, 1973), Chapter 2.

61. G. D. H. Cole and A. W. Filson, *British Working Class Movements, 1789-1875* (New York, 1967), pp. 20-21.

62. See E. P. Thompson, "Patrician Society, Plebian Culture," *Journal of Social History* 7 (Summer, 1974): 382-405.

63. Ibid., p. 395. While Thompson recognizes the strong influence of reciprocity on eighteenth-century status relations, he suggests that "paternalism was as much theater and gesture as effective responsibility," (p. 397). In his discussion of the moral economy, however, he observes that reciprocity entailed certain responsibilities which, when neglected or ineffectively carried out, gave rise to riot or mob activity.

64. See Mantoux, *The Industrial Revolution,* pp. 146-155, and Furniss, *The Position of the Labourer,* pp. 211-219.

65. Mantoux, *The Industrial Revolution,* p. 171.

66. See E. J. Hobsbawm, "Machine-Breakers," *Past and Present* 1 (February, 1952): 66.

67. George Rudé, *Paris and London in the Eighteenth Century* (New York, 1970), pp. 22-23.

68. Thompson, "The Moral Economy of the English Crowd," p. 108.

69. See Thompson, "Patrician Society, Plebian Culture," pp. 399-402. As we shall see in Chapter 3, this playful feature of popular protest existed well into the nineteenth century.

70. George Rudé, *The Crowd in History* (New York, 1964), p. 6.

71. Thompson, "The Moral Economy of the English Crowd," p. 78.

72. E. J. Hobsbawm, *Primitive Rebels* (New York, 1959), p. 111.

73. Thompson, "The Moral Economy of the English Crowd," p. 83.

74. Ibid., pp. 98-106. For other specific examples, see R. B. Rose, "Eighteenth Century Price Riots and Public Policy in England," *International Review of Social History* 6 (1961): 286-287.

75. Indicative of this pressure is the fact that in large towns and cities a large amount of bread was kept on hand; and in the countryside, especially after the 1782 passage of the Gilbert Act, the authorities were obligated to maintain an adequate standard of living for the workers either by providing them employment or relief in aid of wages. The relative calm in the north and southeast of England and in London during the early 1760s largely resulted from the magistrates' energetic maintenance of institutional controls. See Shelton, *English Hunger and Industrial Disorders,* pp. 37, 155.

76. Thompson, "The Moral Economy of the English Crowd," p. 123.

77. Thompson, *The Making of the English Working Class*, pp. 62-63.

78. See Shelton, *English Hunger and Industrial Disorders,* pp. 169, 186-188, 193-199. Also, J. L. and Barbara Hammond, *The Skilled Labourer* (London, 1936), pp. 205-216.

79. See Shelton, *English Hunger and Industrial Disorders,* pp. 172-175 (coalheavers), 191 (seamen), 194-195 (silkweavers).

80. Ibid., pp. 182-183, 199. Regarding the coalheavers, a more effective act replaced the Act of 1758. The silkweavers were more successful as the Spitalfield Act of 1773—which remained operative until 1824—restored traditional protections to the industry. See also Hammonds, *The Skilled Labourer,* p. 216.

81. Shelton, *English Hunger and Industrial Disorders,* p. 148, notes that one significant difference is that "the courts gave heavier sentences to lower-class hunger and industrial rioters than to middle-class political rioters."

82. John Wilkes as quoted in George Rudé, *Wilkes and Liberty* (New York, 1962), pp. 26-27.

83. (*Annual Register* as quoted) Ibid., p. 43.

84. (Duke of Grafton as quoted) Ibid., pp. 90-91.

85. Ibid., p. 81. Also see pp. 82-85.

86. Ibid., p. 15.

87. Ibid., p. 183.

88. Ibid., p. 184.

89. Ibid., p. 197.

90. Rudé, *Paris and London*, p. 329.

91. Shelton, *English Hunger and Industrial Disorders,* p. 21.

92. Ibid., pp. 109-113.

93. For a description of the Catholic relief measure enacted by Parliament in 1778 see George Rudé, "The Gordon Riots," *History Today* 5 (July, 1955): 429-430.

94. George Rudé, "The London 'Mob' of the Eighteenth Century," *The Historical Journal* 2, No. 1 (1959): 13-14.

95. See Christopher Hibbert, *King Mob* (New York, 1958), p. 145. Also, George Rudé, "The Gordon Riots: A Study of the Rioters and Their Victims," *Transactions of the Royal Historical Society,* 5th series, No. 6, (1955): 93-114.

96. Rudé, "The London 'Mob' in the Eighteenth Century," p. 12. Also see S.

Maccoby, *English Radicalism, 1762-1785* (London, 1955), pp. 305-325.

97. See Rudé, "The Gordon Riots," *History Today,* pp. 434-437 and Hibbert, *King Mob,* pp. 106-116.

98. *New Annual Registrar* as quoted in Maccoby, *English Radicalism,* pp. 305-306.

99. Horace Walpole as quoted in Hibbert, *King Mob,* p. 168.

100. R. B. Rose, "The Priestley Riots of 1791," *Past and Present* 18 (1960): 76.

101. See Deane and Cole, *British Economic Growth,* pp. 40-49, 66, 105.

102. See Peter Mathias, "Social Structure in the Eighteenth Century: A Comparison by Joseph Maisse," *Economic History Review* 10 (1957): 30-45.

CHAPTER 3

The Crisis of Power and Authority, 1790-1832

During the last twenty years of the eighteenth century the mechanization of the productive process began to occur at an increasingly rapid pace. By the turn of the century the factory system, although not yet the dominant mode of production, had become commonplace, and England was in the midst of its period of sustained economic growth. This situation posed a serious dilemma for the dominant powers. On the one hand, further economic and productive expansion required the separation of the economy from social obligations—in short, a denial of social responsibility—which would precipitate widespread social protest. On the other hand, any refusal to allow continued growth would further weaken an already depleted treasury and intensify the opposition of the emerging entrepreneurial class. Taking the route of industrial and economic expansion, the rulers after 1795 greeted popular uprisings with repression, not concession; and over the first half of the nineteenth century they proceeded to dismantle most of the traditional protections against the vagaries of the market.

The preindustrial tactics with which the workers and poor initially responded to this denial of social responsibility were easily enough contained. At the same time, however, traditional values and customs were strengthened. The workers created protective communities, with institutions and organizations designed to maintain social obligations. Within these communities, and in terms of the traditional standards they sustained, the workers distinguished themselves form other segments of society. No longer regarding themselves as constitutive of a lower status order dependent upon and naturally extended from the higher orders, they developed a distinct class identity and consciousness.[1] Traditional collectivist values drawn from the remembered past and emphasizing social responsibility were at the core of the working class communities of the early nineteenth century. "It is this collective self-consciousness, with its corresponding theory, institutions, discipline, and community values," writes Thompson, "which distinguishes the nineteenth-century *working class* from the eighteenth-century mob."[2]

Although distinguished from the mob, the working class is historically continuous with it. One important reason why the mob never matured into a class was the fact that its demands—couched in terms of rights as defined by the established norm of reciprocity—were generally acceded to. Now, with industrial expansion taking precedence over traditional legitimation, these demands could no longer be easily met. Consequently, the traditional values of protection, provision, and dependence had to be fulfilled by members of the working class themselves, through their own institutions and organizations. Once the creation of these institutions was accomplished the workers began to reassert their rights, not in terms of the 'rights of the lower orders,' but in Thomas Paine's term of the 'rights of man.'[3] Indeed, during these years many of the vehement conflicts were fought not over economic issues but over issues concerned with equality and justice.

The primary purpose of this chapter is to examine how and explain why the English working class emerged from the contradiction between the system of instrumental action and the system of symbolic interaction. Special attention will be devoted to the relationship between changes in political domination and corresponding shifts in working class social protest. Here, following Raymond Williams and Nigel Young, I will focus on the communalist and collectivist strains embodied in working class institutions.[4] This is essential, for "although the working class has an oral and written tradition of some importance, its culture has been creatively articulated in a fundamentally institutional fashion rather than in an ideological (or literary) one."[5]

INSTRUMENTAL ACTION: CHANGES IN ECONOMIC AND PRODUCTIVE ACTIVITY

As noted in the previous chapter, the convergence of industrialism and capitalism occurred largely within the interstices of society, in those areas and occupations where traditional constraints had yet to develop. Despite the existing restrictions on the kind and extent of industrial techniques which could be incorporated into the productive process, the factory system— by virtue of its spectacular success in stimulating an enduring pattern of economic growth—quickly became the model of most new productive endeavors. By the close of the eighteenth century, as Deane and Cole find, the economy was expanding at the rate of 1.8 percent per annum (or 19.1 percent per decade). "After 1785," they observe, "both total output and population were growing much faster than before, but the former now began to draw decisively ahead of the latter. For the first time, per capita output started to increase by nearly nine percent per decade."[6] Although the acceptance and incorporation of industrial productive techniques rapidly increased during this period, the agricultural sector remained predominant until well into the nineteenth century.

In a recent paper, E. A. Wrigley suggests three related criteria of industrialization: expansion of total output; an increase in real incomes per head; and a constant transformation of material technology.[7] According to these criteria, and despite the continued predominance of the agricultural sector, English society was undergoing industrialization by the turn of the century. Over the first quarter of the nineteenth century, the compound rate of growth in the real product averaged 2.9 percent per annum.[8] Employing Hoffman's indexes of production, Gayer (et al.) found an extremely large advance in the expansion of total production (from 4.4 to 5.2 percent) during the years 1793-1801.[9] Corresponding to this growth in total national product was a tremendous increase in money wages between 1790 and 1850. While there was only a negligible improvement in real incomes during the Napoleonic war years, a more significant advance in real incomes occurred in the ensuing years.[10] An increase in the proportion of net national products investment accompanied these changes. Observing the rise in the stock of reproducible capital from the mid-eighteenth century onward, Deane and Cole write "that an average annual rate of capital formation of under 10m. per annum in the early 1780s had been raised to over 20m. per annum by the early years of the nineteenth century."[11]

It is clear that by 1800 industrialism had become a potent force in English society. Confronted with the process of industrialization and the sustained economic growth it engendered, capitalist principles of exchange and organization required modifications aimed at the abandonment of the moral economy. During the late eighteenth century many towns and old industries (such as the weaving industry) formally complained to Parliament about the infringement of traditional protections generated by the widescale introduction of the factory system. Initially, Parliament tended to appease these grievances; but, by the turn of the century, statutes were enacted which were expressly designed to facilitate free trade and the incorporation of industrial techniques. Either implicitly—by refusing to sanction violations of common law regulations, or explicitly—through the passage of legislation, Parliament acted to expedite the mobilization of land, food, and, most importantly, labor through market arrangements.

As industrialization advanced, the capitalist principles of exchange were expanded to include labor. Under mercantile capitalism, markets existed primarily for the exchange of products, and market relations exerted only a minimal influence on labor. Now labor, like land and food, was to be treated as a commodity to be exchanged in the market. By including labor under the category of commodity, these revised principles suggested the need for drastic social reorganization, beginning with the elimination of impediments to the extension of market relations. C. B. Macpherson describes the essential features of the new market society entailed by these principles.

> Without any authoritative allocation of work or rewards, the market, responding to countless individual decisions, puts, a price on everything, and it is with reference to prices that the individual decisions are made. The market is the mechanism through which prices are made by, and are a determining factor in making, individual decisions about the disposal of energies and the choice of utilities.[12]

According to these principles, prices and wages should be determined exclusively by market considerations unhampered by noneconomic factors.[13] Thus, it became necessary to explicitly distinguish the economy from society, the private from the public realm. Decisions and choices to be effected in the former were not to be influenced by concerns emanating from the latter. However, activities carried out in the market, by virtue of the market's self-adjusting capacities, could only enhance the public good. In short, any effort to subordinate the self-regulating features of the market economy to the institutional regulations of society would have detrimental effects. The implication of these assumptions, as Macpherson notes, was that "human society can only be a series of relations between sole proprietors, i.e., a series of market relations. . . . No traditional concepts of justice, natural law, or divine purpose were needed."[14] The practical effects of this argument proved to be immense in the course of the next several years. Before examining these ramifications, it is necessary to detail the significant transformations in the nature of exchange and production engendered by the burgeoning industrial capitalism.

Beginning in the early 1800s the introduction of power driven machinery effected considerable change upon the methods of production. Throughout the first quarter of the century, however, small-scale industries and established forms of manufacturing persisted alongside the factory system.[15] Emphasizing this point, Hobsbawm writes:

> The Industrial Revolution did not merely replace cottage or slum workshops by the factory, but multiplied both domestic industry and factories; the former either on direct dependence of the latter (as in cotton weaving), or in the rapidly expanding branches of production as yet quite untouched by the factory (as in the garment industry), or in the industries whose scale remained small even when they adopted new power.[16]

As a result of this situation traditional regulations of working conditions and wages coexisted for a time with market determinations. Unskilled labor remained under customary controls while the rising numbers of skilled laborers operated with respect to market calculations.[17]

By 1810 contractual practices had begun to supersede apprenticeship arrangements. In 1813 a statute was enacted repealing wage-fixing customs. And in 1829 one observer could comment that

> The condition of the labourer had been sufficiently determined . . . to discourage the frequent interposition of a magistrate in respect of wages. That the labourer might bargain for what he could get, and that the market would always be supplied in proportion to the demand: that the question was best left to individual contract rather than maximums or minimums to be fixed by authority—were maxims beginning to gain ground. The enabling of magistrates to interfere between man and man in these matters was seen to be as foolish as it was tyrannical.[18]

This preeminence of contract over custom was largely a consequence of the growing concentration of both capital and industrial holdings which occurred during this period.

The advance toward concentration received its overriding impetus from the new technical innovations being employed in the factory system. The use of spinning jennies in the 1780s, the introduction of steam power at the turn of the century, and the incorporation of the power loom around 1825 all had the effect of creating rival systems of production which could operate more efficiently and at a lower cost than the domestic industries. Faced with this competition, small manufacturers reluctantly adopted the new machinery and techniques.[19] Lacking the resources of the larger enterprises, these attempts were doomed to failure. Thus, the initial expansion of the domestic industry brought about by industrialization was reversed as centralization proceeded.

Accompanying the utilization of mechanical innovations was a more specialized division of labor and an increase in the rate of production. Trade, credit, and capital expanded: indeed, as the factory system became the predominant unit of production, the joint stock company emerged as the major financial form;[20] and occupational differentiation intensified as an almost automatic response to the exigencies of the market and the necessities of the situation. The rather serious ramifications which this unregulated expansion entailed for the problem of work discipline and, more generally, for the nature of domination are examined in detail below. The impact of the new industrial methods on economic growth warrants prior analysis.

During the first thirty years of the nineteenth century, manufacturing gained predominance over agriculture in terms of the number of both jobs and investment opportunities provided.[21] In particular, the textile, mining, iron and steel, and transport industries experienced a very rapid expansion, thereby encouraging new investment and effecting a significant growth in the available stock of reproducible national capital. Between 1800 and 1832, Deane and Cole estimate, the national income increased by about 50 percent while national reproducible capital increased by about 70 percent.[22] After 1815 the rate of investment quickly increased, and the rate of capital accumulation became stronger than for any previous period.

Whatever expansion occurred in agricultural and domestic industry output was primarily a function of the extension or improvement of customary methods. Operating under traditional regulations, industries in these sectors rarely installed mechanical devises and procedures. Those that did, proved incapable of withstanding the competition offered by the larger establishments. Investment, accordingly, was confined largely to those areas of the economy where, unhampered by institutional controls, technological improvements could be easily made. In the cotton industry, for instance, "between 1783 and 1802 . . . capital grew by about 8 million and there was another wave of investment in cotton mills in the early 1820s."[23] Similar increases in investment occurred in the coal, iron, and wool industries.

The major channels of investment, especially between 1790 and 1800, were geared to the establishment of a viable infrastructure. The continued practice of enclosure, the construction of roads, bridges, turnpikes, and harbors, and the improvement of inland navigation absorbed much of the invested capital.[24] Encouraged by the increased output and the incomes which these developments produced, the government not only extended banking privileges—thus facilitating the availability of cheap, short-term capital—but also, in 1793, permitted an advance of exchequer bills to be made to private interests for the purpose of investment. Parliament's actions allowed wide access to easy money, and signaled the growing subordination of traditional customs to industrial and economic expansion.

The first ten years of the nineteenth century witnessed an economic boom.[25] The general rate of investment increased as a great deal of capital was channeled into the construction of new factories. This rapid rise in investment was expedited by a number of developments. With governmental checks relaxed, the Bank of England was able to more easily finance private trade.[26] This generated wide speculation in commodities which, in turn, served to encourage the establishment of joint-stock companies. These developments were strengthened by other governmental activities, such as the passage of the Combination Acts which prevented workers from organizing for purposes of wage increases. These factors interacted to bring about an expanding market economy.

Over the next several years, economic expansion was impeded somewhat as the number of investment outlets declined, as a consequence of the war with France. While the economy stagnated during this period, a number of major changes occurred which were to constitute the basis upon which the self-regulating market was to be established. In 1812 the government repealed the Order of Council which had previously served to regulate the extent and content of trade. Beginning in the same year, a detailed reorganization of the London Stock Exchange was initiated. With a codified set of rules and regulations and a growing number of member companies, the Stock Exchange became a determinate influence on economic activities. By 1826 several pieces of legislation encouraging the further development of joint-stock companies were passed in response to a wide demand by members of the aristocracy—and especially by members of the middle class—for shares.[27] In the years immediately following the Napoleonic wars, the arguments in favor of free trade gained in intensity and support.

The years between 1820 and 1832 were ones of economic prosperity. With expanded resources at its disposal, manufacturing extended its use of mechanical processes. Productive output, incomes, and the scale of private investment all increased. Joint-stock companies grew at an enormous rate, and the government persisted in the direction of facilitating free trade by passing tarriff reforms and by modifying the banking system in accordance with investment requirements. The market economy had finally attained a steadiness of movement.[28]

The economic and productive transformations which took place between 1790 and 1832 had profound consequences for English society. First, as Dorothy Marshall notes, "men who were neither landowners nor gentlemen could nevertheless create wealth through possession of factories and foundries."[29] Thus we find industrial capital and, alongside it, finance capital beginning to exceed commercial capital in importance. Corresponding to this shift in capital was a shift in political power. Strategically employing their resources, the entrepreneurial interests applied effective pressures to the decision-making process; and eventually, in 1832 and after much dispute, the franchise was extended to the middle class. Emerging from these developments was a set of policies and practices which distinguished the economy from society in such a way that decisions made in the former would be free from noneconomic compulsions. Among the more significant consequences was, of course, the breakdown of the traditional framework. While this had broad ramifications, the most immediate, at least as far as the new entrepreneurs were concerned, were in regard to the problem of work discipline.

Worker discipline constituted a concern of manufacturers even before the widespread advent of power-driven machinery. The central workshop concept, as Sidney Pollard demonstrates, evolved independently of mechanization and largely for the purpose of enabling manufacturers to establish a minimal degree of control over the workers and the work process.[30] These preindustrial central workshops exhibited a kind of natural division of labor; and new skills emerged more as a result of successive subdivisions of work process and less in response to the installation of new technology. This situation underwent transformation in the 1780s and 1790s with the adoption of technological innovations.

With the introduction of these innovations, the central workshops were converted to the factory. Now, as new skills became increasingly determined by machine technology, the division of labor became highly specialized. The most common method of diffusing the skills required to operate the new machinery was the recruitment of laborers from firms which had previously utilized industrial techniques.[31] As these developments intensified, the problem of worker discipline became of more serious moment. Manufacturers were no longer merely concerned with controlling the availability of a semipermanent labor force. The factory system required workers capable of performing regular, methodical, and routine tasks. Accordingly, the methods of discipline were directed toward the adaptation of workers to the dynamics of factory production.

As the factory system gained in importance, the need for a full-time labor force became paramount. The operation of machinery required the regular attendance and routinization of the workers. Pollard puts the matter well:

> What was needed was regularity and steady intensity in place of irregular spurts of work; accuracy and standardization in place of individual design; and care of equipment and material in place of pride in one's tools.[32]

While the new work skills themselves were relatively easy to acquire, the proper rational attitudes which presuppose the adoption of such skills were absent. The use of a cash stimulus to bring about such a rational orientation was impeded by traditional customs and by the prescriptive norms imposed by established trades. Until the first decades of the nineteenth century, workers continued to regulate their activity in accordance with traditional holidays, fairs, and days of religious celebration. Irregular attendance was, therefore, commonplace.

> "St. Monday" and feast days, common traditions in domestic industry, were persistent problems. The weavers were used to "play frequently all day on Monday and the greater part of Tuesday, and work very late on Thursday night, and frequently all night on Friday." Spinners, even as late as 1800, would be missing from the factories on Mondays and Tuesdays, and "when they did return, they would sometimes work desperately

> night and day, to clear off their tavern score, and get more
> money to spend in dissipation.''[33]

Throughout most of the period in question, work discipline constituted a crucial problem for the success of the factory system. Not only was it troublesome to create a stable work force, but the prior matter of labor recruitment was also difficult. As we shall observe later, the government contributed to the resolution of the second problem by instituting changes in the relief system which, by compelling migration, effected the beginnings of a permanent labor market. The first problem, involving the implementation of new work rules, was dealt with primarily in the context of the factory system itself. In Pollard's words, the capitalist became simultaneously a disciplinarian.

The capitalist as disciplinarian had at his disposal three basic methods of imposing work discipline and standardization: deterrents, wage incentives, and the formulation of a new work ethos.[34] The use of deterrents—dismissal, fines, punishment—occurred frequently at the beginning of this period, but they quickly proved ineffective and gave way to wage incentives. While payment by results existed among many industries in the eighteenth century, the unit of payment was the productive group. As applied during the first quarter of the nineteenth century, however, forms of wage incentives applied to individual rather than group productivity. Accompanying the widespread implementation of wage incentives was a series of concerted efforts by the capitalists to make workers more respectable—that is, more amenable to the methodical requirements of the factory system. Insisting that workers and their children regularly attend church services and school, the capitalists mounted a campaign aimed at equating leisure with idleness and idleness with sin; time was to be constantly occupied whether by work or by self-improvement. Although these campaigns had little immediate impact on the workers themselves, they were highly successful in mobilizing middle class opinion, redefining attitudes toward the poor (the poor were poor because they were idle) and, ultimately, in effecting significant policy changes.

The intense involvement in matters of worker discipline had roots, not only in a concern for technological superiority, but also in the changing nature of domination. While there is some dispute as to whether or not the increasing specialization and growing centralization represented by the factory system enhanced technical efficiency, there is no doubt that these developments seriously weakened the workers' control of product and process.[35] The division of labor engendered by the convergence of industrialism and capitalism, as Stephen Marglin observes, resulted "in the change of the workmen's choice form one of how much to work and produce, based on his relative preferences for leisure and goods, to one of whether or not to work at all, which of course is hardly much of a choice."[36] As specialization intensified, the workers were increasingly deprived of control over product; and as the factory system grew in prominence, their control over process was similarly eliminated. The practice of worker discipline, then, was geared to reducing the workers' power over the production process. Discipline and supervision, accordingly, were class issues.[37] When they are viewed exclusively in terms of technological superiority we lose sight of an essential point—namely, that through these mechanisms the capitalists were asserting domination over the workers.

At the core of the pervasive efforts to establish worker discipline was the attempt to change the workers' conception and experience of time. If the transition to a mature industrial society was to be successful, time had to be compartmentalized, artificially regulated, and synchronized to the mechanics of technology. This reordering of time was an indispensable condition for the restructuring of work habits and the cultivation of rational attitudes. Indeed, work discipline, as it involved the transformation of the conception and experience of time, assumed a momentous importance in the making of the English working class.

Preindustrial time was based almost exclusively on experience, and measured, when it was, in accordance with the compulsive rhythms of nature. Throughout most of the eighteenth century, work, both in village and domestic industries, was task-oriented; as such, it was shaped by the predominant conception of time as cyclical and experientially based. In an insightful analysis of "Time, Work-Discipline, and Industrial Capitalism," Thompson emphasizes the major features of task-oriented time.

> First, there is a sense in which it is more humanly comprehensible than timed labour. The peasant or labourer appears to attend upon what is an observed necessity. Second, a community in which task-orientation is common appears to show least demarcation between "work" and "life." Social intercourse and labour are intermingled—the working day lengthens or contracts according to the task—and there is no great sense of conflict between labour and "passing the time of day." Third, to men accustomed to labour timed by the clock, this attitude to labour appears to be wasteful and lacking in urgency.[38]

The villager, the farmer, the outworker in the domestic industry, did not confront the problem of 'free-time' or 'leisure' which was to become so important in the nineteenth century. Work, play, and ritual continuously flowed into one another as nature and tradition dictated. The task and not the timepiece regulated productive activity.

As long as the manufacturing industry remained organized about the domestic system or the small-scale, central workshop, task-oriented work could prevail. However, the installation of new machinery and the concomitant increase in specialization demanded the synchronization of man to the productive process. Time was measured quantitatively as human activity was geared to the machine. As Thompson notes, "a general diffusion of clocks and watches [occurred] . . . at the exact moment when the industrial revolution demanded a greater synchronization of labour."[39] Accompanying these developments was a separation of time into 'work time' and 'personal time,' the former being devoted to worthwhile pursuits, the latter occupied by leisure and idleness. Time, like labor, had to be converted into a commodity: time was not to be passed, but to be spent.[40]

Throughout this period attempts at abolishing the elements of play associated with preindustrial traditions proliferated. The comprehension and value orientation provided by the 'rules of experience' were regarded as impediments to the routinization required by technological work. As one observer remarks,

> With the coming of industrialism little was heard of the old incentive to labour which had existed in [preindustrial] society—joy, competition, craftsmanship, social responsibility. Work was now frankly regarded as an imposition which only a strong constitution could bear; idleness was the natural state.[41]

Thus the rules of experience were to be replaced by the laws of science. Ultimately, the transformation in the conception of time which these developments entailed would have the effect of lifting choice out of the domain of human experience and placing it in the domain of science.[42] The elements of tradition and remembrance would be superseded by those of scientific prediction as the guiding criteria in the making of choices.

By the fourth decade of the century, the program of worker discipline initiated by the capitalists had combined with the suppression of workers' organizations, culture, and leisure activities to successfully impose the required work habits. This involved not merely a process of technological conditioning—that is, a reconceptualization of the workers' time-sense; but it included, as well, a reordering of the workers' time-measurement; and, as will be analyzed in the next chapter, this development enhanced the process of labor exploitation.[43] These changes, however, were not accomplished easily. As we shall see, they met with widespread and often violent resistance by the workers.

We have observed that the convergence of industrialism and capitalism entailed the breakdown of traditional institutional controls over economic and productive activity, and the suppression of customary work habits.

The essential requirements for further development of industrial capitalism—
the availability of easy money and the establishment of a viable labor market—conflicted with the preexisting trade regulations and protective controls. In the face of this, one contemporary wrote,

> In the beginning of the nineteenth century it would be a grati-
> fying circumstance to have old prejudices removed, and to see
> a committee of the House of Commons occupied in clearing
> the Statute Book of all Acts concerning . . . important manu-
> facture. . . . Thus it would at once be freed from the fetters
> which have so long bound it, and henceforward its operations
> would go on . . . unconstrained.[44]

The principles of laissez faire enunciated in this passage gained adherents
among the growing numbers of manufacturers and entrepreneurs. Manufacturer's associations, which arose in the 1780s and 1790s for the purpose
of industrial lobbying, became a significant political force by the turn of the
century.[45] Responding to the growing pressure applied by the emerging
middle class and to the increasingly influential doctrine of classical political
economy, and encouraged by the expanding base of resources and support
promised by continued economic growth, Parliament acted (or, in some
cases, refused to act) in such a way as to facilitate the implementation of
laissez-faire policies.

In summary, during the period 1790-1832 the system of instrumental
action came into conflict with the established ideological consciousness.
Where previously the decision makers would seek to restore a balance between
the two, they now attempted to abrogate traditional constraints in order to
further industrial and economic expansion. We begin to find at this point:
the increasing separation of the economy from society; the replacement of
substantive controls with purposive-rational rules and regulations; and the
redefinition of the standard of living from the quality of life to the quantity
of life.[46] The dismantlement of economic controls began to proceed systematically from 1815 on. Trading restrictions were removed; taxes on consumer goods were reduced; the Justice of the Peace's authority to fix wage
rates was repealed; and, through an extensive revision of monetary and
banking policies, the restrictions imposed on transactions in money and
shares were virtually eliminated. The repeal of the apprenticeship clauses of
the Statute of Apprentices in 1814 preceded these policy changes. The system
protected by this Elizabethan Law required craftsmen to serve a seven-year
apprenticeship in order to practice a trade. While many of the trades protected
by the clause petitioned for its maintenance, the capitalists persuaded Parliament to repeal it on the grounds that, in the words of one master, "if men
were compelled to be bound for seven years, and those who have been so

bound were to combine together, that let their demand be ever so exorbitant we must comply with that demand, or have our goods perish."[47] With this repeal, craftsmen were left without protection and compelled to enter the market as another commodity.

SYMBOLIC INTERACTION: THE STRUGGLE OVER IDEOLOGICAL ALTERNATIVES

As the adequate fulfillment of traditional obligations was increasingly precluded, the conforming reason of natural law ideology lost much of its affirmative thrust. Reality, subsequently, was redefined as something to be acted upon. There were two different interpretations within this redefinition, each rooted in one of the contending alternatives anticipated by the critical reason of natural law ideology. Where one interpretation was couched in the language of laissez faire and urged man, as ego, to reshape society by reshaping himself, the second was articulated in communalistic terms and urged man, as a member of society and a participant in history, to improve himself by transforming society.

Eventually these interpretations came into conflict with one another. At the heart of this conflict was the struggle over which of the objectively possible alternatives contained in society was to be implemented. In short, this clash between the middle class and the working class was a struggle involving historical choice. However, it is important to note that at the beginning of and occurring sporadically throughout this period, the working class and middle class jointly participated in opposition against the landed and aristocratic interests. The critical thrust of the two contending inter- pretations provided, on occasion, a common ground of action. Thus, to take one example, both the middle class and the working class opposed the government's taxation of the press. But their grounds for this opposition differed. Middle class commentators argued that such taxation prohibited free exchange by involving the government, not merely in the marketplace of ideas, but in the marketplace of economic exchange. Workers, on the other hand, maintained that taxation, by raising the cost of papers and periodicals—thereby severely restricting the number of workers who could afford to purchase them—weakened the viability of a distinct working class press and, in so doing, closed off channels of communication and solidarity. Despite different justifications, the similar conclusion reached by both sides allowed some coordination of effort to ensue.[48]

Both the middle class doctrines of laissez faire and the working class doctrines of communalism were critical of the existing order, offering a comprehensive attack on its legitimacy. Where the former attempted to mobilize the people against the aristocracy, the latter sought to mobilize the workers against the other classes in society. However, with the complete discrediting of the theory of dependence, the common ground on which the middle class and working class could converge collapsed. In the confrontation that followed, the middle class was able to form an alliance with the aristocracy. On the basis of this alliance, middle class interests were often translated into governmental policy. In the following pages, the outline and the impact of the middle class ideology are examined with the aim of demonstrating how its critical components were transformed into a conforming orientation.

Reinhard Bendix notes that during the early years of industrial capitalism the rising entrepreneurial class attended, not to the formulation of an ideology, but to matters of expediency: "What stands out in [the] reaction of the early entrepreneurs . . . is their utter unconcern with ideas of any kind, and their complete preoccupation with the affairs of the moment."[49] A similar unconcern existed on the part of the government. As both Mantoux and the Webbs have observed, Parliament's attitude toward the reduction of regulatory and protective controls was initially ambivalent. Although many of Parliament's actions at this time had the effect of facilitating industrial and economic expansion at the expense of traditional controls, these actions were "not as yet influenced by any conscious theory of freedom of contract."[50]

The first systematic attempts at formulating a coherent set of laissez-faire principles occurred around 1810. About this time political clubs, scholarly circles, and periodicals advocating free trade and freedom of contract greatly increased in number. In this context, Parliament became more receptive to laissez-faire arguments, and repealed a number of clauses which had permitted workers to petition grievances on the grounds that all interference in economic matters was inimical to economic growth. In 1808 a Select Committee of Parliament rejected a request for a minimum wage bill, by arguing

> that no interference of the Legislature with the Freedom of Trade, or with the perfect Liberty of every individual to dispose of his time and his labour in the way and on the terms which he may judge most conducive to his own interests, can take place, without violating general Principles of the first Importance to the property and happiness of the community.[51]

Before the second decade of the century had concluded, a general movement for the implementation of laissez-faire policies had developed. Prior to the practical application of these policies, however, it was first necessary to disassociate political authority from its traditional bonds.

This break with traditionalism essentially entailed the elimination of the theory of dependence. However, as Bendix rightly observes, this denial of social responsibility and obligation presented two fundamental problems: "How could the 'higher classes' deny their responsibility for the poor and at the same time justify their power and authority over them? How could the poor be taught self-dependence without developing in them a dangerous independence?''[52] Proposed solutions to these problems came from three major sources: Thomas Malthus' writings on population, the political philosophy of the Utilitarians, and classical political economy. While there were several significant points of disagreement among the three, each overlapped with the others to produce the logically consistent justification for the abrogation of social responsibility which underlay the middle class critique of the established order.

In his 1798 *Essay on Population,* Thomas Malthus attempted to scientifically repudiate the notions of progress formulated by Condorcet and William Godwin. By demonstrating with a pseudo-mathematical formula that population tends to increase at a faster rate than subsistence, Malthus suggested that the 'higher orders,' by taking responsibility for the poor, only compounded an already serious problem. Such responsibility constituted an interference with an irreversible law of nature and was detrimental to society, since it discouraged the exercise of foresight and prudence which alone could bring about an approximate balance between population and subsistence. In short, Malthusian theory contended that, first, poverty and indigence are inescapable features of social life and, second, the responsibility for poverty and misery rests with the poor and miserable. Malthus, accordingly, was vehemently opposed to the continuation of traditional forms of assistance to the poor, the unemployed, and the underemployed. In particular, he scorned minimum-wage provisions and the poor relief system as antithetical to the prosperity of English society.

The eighteenth-century poor relief system variously incorporated certain wage-fixing policies which regulated the workers' income in accordance with some conception of an adequate standard of living. In many cases, for instance, relief was administered on a scale of assistance established in relation to bread prices and the number of children which a family had. The right to subsistence, then, was consecrated by tradition and custom.[53] Malthus was especially opposed to this, and insisted that the right to subsistence be replaced by the right to work.

Around the turn of the century, the increasing supply of agricultural labor met with a decline in demand. This situation became quite acute in the depression years following the war. During this period the poor rates expanded at a rapid pace. Given that the allocation of poor relief benefits was administered by local parishes, migration from agricultural areas to industrial towns was severely impeded; for once a worker left his parish there was no guarantee that he could receive assistance elsewhere. Most detrimentally affected by this system were the landowners—who were compelled to bear much of the financial burden, and the manufacturers. In the early stages of industrialization, the manufacturers benefited from the poor relief system which allowed them to pay less than subsistence wages. Now, since they required a surplus pool of labor and an extensive labor market, they found the restrictive aspects of the poor laws to be inimical to the factory system. Initially, both the landlords and the manufacturers reacted to this situation in an ad hoc manner. The former began pulling down cottages in an effort to compel migration from the local parishes; and the latter voluntarily increased their taxes so the town could afford to maintain relief assistance.[54] These makeshift, often ineffective solutions began to give way between 1815 and 1820, a period that witnessed a huge increase in the expense of the poor relief system. Over this same period we find a profound redefinition of attitudes toward the poor; and throughout the next ten years, until the passage of the Poor Law Amendment Act of 1834, middle class opinion received explicit and systematic shape in the form of laissez-faire doctrines. As the power of the middle class grew, these opinions began to be felt in Parliament. In 1824 the *Report on Labourers' Wages* attributed most of the problems encountered by workers (and, indeed, many of the difficulties faced by the agricultural and industrial sectors of society) to the poor relief system.

> Men who receive but a small pittance know that they have only to marry, and that pittance will be augmented in the proportion to the number of their children. . . . An intelligent witness, who is much in the habit of employing labourers, states that when complaining of their allowance they frequently say to him: "We will marry, and you must maintain us."... But there was one thing better than to marry and have a family, and that was to marry a mother of bastards. . . . As one young woman of twenty-four with four bastard children put it: "If she had one more, she would be very comfortable."[55]

The imprint of Malthus on this passage is unmistakable. Indeed, throughout this period it was largely Malthus' criticisms of the poor relief system which were relied upon. These criticisms were essentially three-pronged. First, he contended that the old Poor Law was an institution which encouraged population growth by allotting assistance payments for children. Secondly, related to this, the poor relief system fostered imprudent marriages, thus all but eliminating one of the major checks against population growth. Finally, and most importantly, Malthus maintained that the subsistence guaranteed by the poor laws promoted the most dangerous ideas—that men had an absolute right to subsistence. What should be perceived as an act of benevolence and received with gratitude, was regarded as obligatory.

The inculcation of moral restraint among the poor was required; and this could be accomplished only with the removal of subsistence provisions.

Only by transferring responsibility from society to individuals could these related problems be eradicated. Malthus summarized his position, as follows:

> Nothing perhaps would tend so strongly to excite a spirit of industry among the poor as a thorough knowledge that their happiness must always depend principally upon themselves; and that if they obey their passions instead of their reason, or not be industrial or frugal while they are single to save a sum for the common contingencies of the married state, they must expect to suffer the natural evils which Providence has prepared for those who disobey the repeated admonitions.[56]

"The repeated admonitions," of course, were Malthus' own. They were repeated initially by the middle class and later by the government in an effort to justify new policies. As James Huzel has discovered, the vast majority of government studies and reports between 1824 and 1834 were completely consistent with the Malthusian position.[57] Malthus' influence on governmental policy and action culminated in 1834 with the enactment of the New Poor Law (the Poor Law Amendment Act). The New Poor Law abolished the general category of poor and replaced it with the more specific classifications of 'honest poor' and 'labouring poor.' Distinguished from the first category which referred to those physically incapable of working, the second category concerned those who were unemployed. The new relief system was designed principally to deter the unemployed from applying for poor relief. The key stipulations of the law were: "(1) No relief except within a workhouse to the able-bodied; (2) Such relief to be less 'eligible' than the most unpleasant means of earning a living outside; (3) Separation of man and wife to prevent child-bearing."[58] The New Poor Law and similar legislation not only allowed for the expansion of the national labor market—a crucial contribution to the development of an industrial reserve army in the urban areas, but also typified the growing attempts at displacing social obligations with individual responsibility. Thus Engels was only slightly exaggerating when he stated: "It is . . . Malthus' theory of population—and the new poor law to which it gave rise—which represent the most flagrant warlike aggression of the middle classes against the workers."[59]

Malthusian theory, with its emphasis on individual responsibility and exact scientific analysis, had a central influence on the formulation of Philosophic Radicalism. However, where Malthus merely presented a scientifically phrased renunciation of social responsibility, Philosophic Radicalism—which rested largely on the Utilitarianism of Jeremy Bentham and the classical political economy of James Mill and James MacCulloch—supplied a morality and a political philosophy supportive of laissez faire. Stating the problem positively as a defense of individual rights, Philosophic Radicalism offered an optimistic picture of the future in contrast to Malthus' stark pessimism.

Insisting that all social phenomena are reducible to laws, the Philosophic Radicals maintained that the resolution of society's ills required a program guided by rational scientific analysis. Underlying this argument was a morality infused with the notion of egoism. Bentham's self-preference principle, or principle of universal egoism, was the master assumption upon which this morality was founded. This principle implies the following:

> Since the sum total of happiness is made up of the individual units, is it consequently not enough, in order that all may be happy, for each one to be egotistical? . . . The proof . . . that all men are egotistical is that the human race subsists: for on the prudence of the individual depends the persistence of the race.[60]

Society, in this view, is a harmony of egoistic interests.

According to this morality, man is not merely an 'infinite appropriator'; he is also an 'unlimited desirer of utilities.' The 'right' of unlimited appropriation, which received justification in terms of the rationality and morality of infinite desire, acted, as Macpherson perceptively notes, as an incentive to continuous exertion.[61] From this standpoint the maximization of individual utilities emerged as the preeminent criterion of the good society. In contrast to Malthus, Bentham and his fellow Philosophic Radicals related scarcity to infinite desire or satisfactions, not to material resources. And, on these grounds, "the rational purpose of man becomes an endless attempt to overcome scarcity. The attempt is endless by definition, but only by engaging endlessly in it can infinitely desirous man realize his essential nature."[62]

In the context of economic optimism, Philosophic Radicalism retained Malthus' scientifically phrased repudiation of social responsibility, and—especially in the 1820s and early 1830s—provided an effective platform for the mobilization of middle class opinion. Although some fundamental disagreements prevailed within Philosophic Radicalism, they were not severe enough to prevent the formulation of a general system of laissez-faire thought.[63] The two most important aspects of this thought were the emphasis on utility over obligation and the distinction between the public and the private.

With its analysis of English society guided by a morality of prudence and a conception of man motivated by utilitarian concerns, Philosophic Radicalism opposed the natural law notion of obligation with the notion of utility. In its essential outlines, the argument contended that the establishment of rights and obligations presupposed the restriction of liberty. On a more elementary level, the imposition of obligations entailed the elimination of a pleasurable state, if not the application of pain. "*Therefore all obligation is an evil.* If an obligation is to be justified, it cannot contain in itself the principle of its own justification . . . it can only be justified on the ground that it is a necessary evil, endowed with a relative utility";[64] that is, an obligation is to be permitted only if the evil it engenders can be compensated for by the utility—the services—it provides. Rights and obligations, then, are established by social legislation and are, therefore, revocable. What is immutable is the principle of general interest, which has utility as its object. Thus, "it is through the general interest that the rights of [man] are discovered, and not the general interest through the rights of man."[65] Determined by the general interest, obligations and rights are infused with moral overtones only by virtue of their utility.

Utility was the overriding criterion for evaluating all institutions, policies, and activities in society. Hence, in the political economy associated with Utilitarianism, liberty, equality, and justice are examined with reference to their usefulness. Not surprisingly, the egalitarian thrust of classical political economy is reduced to an argument for the expansion of the middle class. Inequality, it was claimed, was a natural and necessary condiction. However,

> the plan of distribution applied to the matter of wealth which is most favorable to the universality of subsistence, and thence, in other words, to the maximization of happiness, is that in which, while the fortune of the richest . . . is greatest, the degrees between the fortune of the least rich and that of the most rich are most numerous—in other words, the graduation most regular and insensible.[66]

In other words, the liberty of the middle class served the general interest by encouraging the development of an intelligent and productive group of people free from both the vices of the imprudent laborer and the excesses of the unproductive rich. The middle class, in short, was the most useful class and, ipso facto, warranted the rights of liberty and equality.

Although rights and obligations are in no way natural, they can be established through morality and legislation if justified on the grounds of social utility. This involves an artificial identification of interests spontaneously generated by nature.[67] Malthus' law of population is an example of natural utility, as are the laws regulating the natural distribution of wealth. With regard to the latter it was suggested that, given the laws of economic exchange, the distribution of wealth—when unhampered by noneconomic (artificial) compulsions—will result naturally in the creation of a viable middle class. Thus, not only did the middle class meet the standards of social utility, but it satisfied those of natural utility as well.

While the artificial laws of social utility were the responsibility of the Utilitarians, the natural laws of economic exchange constituted the domain of Political Economy.[68] Expressed by this division of concern is the notion that economic activity significantly differs from social activity in that it is not amenable to human legislation.[69] In economic pursuits, human activity is governed by nonhuman laws; when these laws are tampered with, distress unavoidably results. Thus, the separation of society and economy, the distinction between the public and the private, must be institutionalized. Prior to examining the extensive influence these arguments had, first, on the middle-class campaign to obtain the franchise, and later on the elimination of social constraints on the market, it is essential to more carefully assess the rationale for distinguishing the social and the economic.

As society (the product of artifices) increasingly was contrasted with economy (the work of natural processes), the distinction between social and natural utility became elaborated as a distinction between the public and the private realms. The public-private dichotomy eventually received a more specific rendering in the form of the distinction between the state and society. Included within the domain of the state are moral, juridical, and legislative matters. The government was realized, therefore, as the artificial identification of interests, and, as a consequence, was involved in the formulation of human laws in accordance with the criterion of social utility. In this context, as Hannah Arendt notes, society becomes identified with the economy, and as such comprises the arena wherein individual egos, governed by natural laws, enter into a natural identification of interests.[70] The position of the Philosophic Radicals on this score is summarized by Halevy:

> Founded on these bases, it is incessantly appealing to two distinct principles . . . the one in virtue of which the science of the legislator must intervene to identify interests which are naturally divergent; the other in virtue of which the social order is realized spontaneously, by the harmony of egoisms.[71]

Thus there are two separate spheres, each having its own logic and rationality. For progress to proceed, the relationship between these two spheres must be carefully conceived.

As a necessary evil, the state or the public realm could not interfere with the economic activity that took place in society. Since the state, as an artifice, could be justified only by its utility, it was morally responsible to carry out those projects—such as the creation of an infrastructure—which the private realm could not or would not do.[72] Any direct intercedence into the private realm by the state would constitute the subjugation of natural processes to artificial ones. If, however, the state refrained from such interference, the public good would be enhanced. Thus, public space must be subordinated to private space. The implications of this position are of some import. As O'Neill has recently argued, one-dimensionality is rooted in this concept of society "as a field in which the private pursuit of economic interests produces public benefits without political intervention.''[73] The previous view that public benefits were created by the public control of private pursuits was undermined and replaced with the argument that the best choices were those determined naturally, by market considerations. Pre-established goals, couched in tradition and expressive of social responsibility, had to give way to a decision-making process animated by technological rationality.

The program of Philosophic Radicalism ultimately resulted in the positivization of natural law. The eighteenth-century distinction between the state of nature and the state of society was superseded by the distinction between the state and society.[74] In this formulation, rights and obligations could only be derived from the state. However, these rights and obligations, since they were artificially conceived in the public realm, were established at the expense of personal liberty. Accordingly, it was only in the private sphere that individual liberty—personal choice guided by the egotistical goal of maximizing individual needs—was possible. Stated in this way, the distinction between state and society entails a reconceptualization of positive law. With natural law ideology, positive law was morally sanctioned by virtue of its isomorphism with natural law; with Philosophic Radicalism, positive law is sanctioned by force. Thus, positive law or public legislation must be formulated on the basis of the interests of all people in society.[75] Rooted in this argument was the demand for the extension of the franchise to the middle class. Not only would a limited franchise extend the rights to vote and of representation to the (soon to be) majority, but it would also be socially useful—since the members of the middle class, as indicated by their vast property holdings, were the most intelligent, diligent, and prudent actors in the private sphere. Moreover, a limited extension of the franchise on the basis of property would serve as an incentive to the poor to be more virtuous in their private lives. Thus it was suggested that the inequality of property would eventually promote political equality.[76]

By the mid-1820s Philosophic Radicalism had been almost unanimously accepted by the merchants and manufacturers of the middle class. And, as many observers have noted, during this same period the impact of Philosophic Radicalism on governmental activity—from the Repeal of the Statute of Apprentices in 1814 to the Reform Act of 1832 and the New Poor Law of 1834—was visibly decisive. The arguments opposing state regulation, or more appropriately, social responsibility, were infused with the ''scientific'' findings of Malthus, Bentham, and Ricardo. Typical of these arguments was the one launched against the passage of the Factory Acts which would regulate child labor. The opposition to the Factory Acts rested on the following grounds: (1) Children encountered miserable working conditions only in the small factories which, through free competition, eventually will be eradicated. (2) Government interference would constitute an obstacle to free competition, thus impeding the destruction of small factories and, on a more general level, causing economic distress. (3) Such interference would abridge the private and therefore natural responsibility which parents have for their children. (4) Regulation of hours, therefore, would interfere with the liberty of parents and, (5) more generally, with the liberty of free labor.[77]

The principles of political economy implicit in this argument were presented for popular consumption as well. Systematic attempts at popularizing the laws of political economy resulted in the proliferation of middle-class-sponsored periodicals written especially for the working-class audience. The intent of these periodicals was to present the tenets of classical political economy as constitutive of an established and undeniable science. R. K. Webb, in his study of the working class reader, outlines the major features of this popularized version: The economy was portrayed mechanistically as a mechanism operating independently of human and social forces, and the ultimate benefits of mechanized production were glorified. In addition, the canon of freedom was emphasized in contrast to the restrictive effects of trade unionism; and the positive association between moral restraint and personal and social improvement was given wide circulation. Finally, and perhaps most significantly, was "the proposition that the interests of the working classes and of the middle classes were the same—the forwarding by all possible means of the interests of and increase of capital."[78]

Webb's evidence indicates that many workers had regular access to this popularized version of political economy. Many more workers, however, were introduced to Philosophic Radicalism, not by pamphlets, but by the drastic changes on their lives and expectations effected by the policies and programs it advanced. In their response to these ideas and the programs they promoted, the workers formulated an alternative ideology, one critical of both aristocratic power and middle class utilitarianism.

Critical reason: Communal principles and working class institutions

Throughout most of the eighteenth century, industrial and economic disputes were usually short-lived, and they rarely extended into explicit political struggles. As we have seen, whenever changes were implemented which had the effect of weakening institutional controls—that is, whenever obligations were left unmet—laborers, often in the form of direct action protests, appealed to the government which usually reinstated the controls or compensated with new controls or benefits. And, as the Webbs remarked, as "long as each section of workers believed in the intention of the governing class to protect their trade from the results of unrestricted competition" no enduring opposition and no distinct consciousness could form.[79]

Radical thought during this period, as evidenced by the Commonwealthmen and such activities as the "Wilkes and Liberty" movement, was oriented toward reform and animated largely by the deciphering of the critical implications contained in the relation between the constitution and natural law ideology. Until the mid-1790s critical reason—as expressed by both the manufacturers and the laborers—was consistently couched in the language of constitutional reformism. By the turn of the century, significant differences in the conceptualization and, especially, in the practice of critical reason began to emerge. While both the middle class and the working class expressed their demands in a democratic rhetoric, the organizational techniques each developed to implement these demands diverged. Where the former developed lobbying and pressure groups, the latter formed combinations.

One initial factor in the clarification of the two contending interpretations derived from critical reason was the continued reliance on natural law in opposition to the arguments based on utility. An important contribution to the maintenance of natural law ideology was Thomas Paine's *Rights of Man,* published in two parts in 1791 and 1792. As is evident in the title of his work, Paine insisted that man as an individual possessed a number of natural and therefore inalienable rights: "the intellectual rights, or rights of the mind, and the various rights possessed by every individual of acting with a view to his personal well-being and happiness, in so far as the exercise of these rights does not threaten the natural rights of other men."[80] Alongside natural rights are civil rights, such as the acquisition of property, which are derived not from nature but from a social contract. Obviously, then, Paine accepted the distinction between state and society, but he did so without reducing rights and obligations to artifices. Thus, while in agreement with the Utilitarians and political economists that there should be an institutionalized separation of government and economy, Paine diverged from them by insisting that every man, by virtue of his existence, warranted political equality.

It was in his refusal to accept the utilitarian standards of Philosophic Radicalism that Paine's importance largely resided. Democracy or, more particularly, political equality should be accorded not on the basis of social utility but because it is a natural right of all people. The basic problem with this position is that economic equality is neglected. In his *Political Justice* (1793), William Godwin implied this criticism of Paine in his argument that equality of opportunity was a more fundamental matter than political equality. What is highly significant about Godwin's demand for an egalitarian society is that it was rooted not in the notion of natural rights but in the notion of utility.

Like Philosophic Radicalism, Godwin placed utility at the core of his morality. In both systems natural utility was expressed as the natural identification of interests. For the Philosophic Radicals this meant that all people in society (as distinct from the state) possessed identical aspirations. The rich and poor alike had an interest in improving their material conditions; hence the acquisition and possession of private property had both natural and social utility. Working from the same principle, Godwin maintained that the existence of economic inequalities impeded the expression of the natural identification of interests.[81] Not only are the rich of no social utility but, more importantly, private property is effectively antithetical to the general interest. Godwin wrote, "Those who, by fraud or force, have usurped the power of buying and selling the labour of the great mass of the community, are sufficiently disposed to *take care that they should never do more than subsist.*"[82] Thus the persistence of private property perpetuates economic inequality and, in so doing, suppresses the natural identification of interests. If society is to progress in a just—that is, socially useful— manner, the redistribution of wealth is required. And, once egalitarianism is brought about on this level, the state becomes obsolete, for economic equality will assure political equality.

Paine and Godwin, in their different ways, clarified the communal principles of critical reason in contrast to the laissez-faire alternative. Although many of their ideas eventually became familiar to the working population, it is too much to claim for them a determinate influence on the development of the workers' ideological consciousness. The distinctive working class consciousness which began to emerge at the turn of the century had its origin in the institutions created by the workers themselves.

The 1790s witnessed numerous attempts on the part of workers throughout England to organize themselves into associations for the purpose of mutual protection. During these early years workers' associations sought to gain Parliamentary relief through two primary means, the petitioning of Parliament and the mobilization of public support. When, instead of assistance, these efforts were met with governmental repression of workers' combinations, the workers were compelled to create new organizational forms. It was in the development of these new forms that the ideology of the working class took root.

Although the workers often couched their grievances in economic terms, they were actually concerned with the broader issue of the breakdown of traditional protections. As one observer notes, "to lose control over one's own (and one's family's) labour was to surrender one's independence, security, liberty, one's birthright."[83] The weakening of institutional controls was generally viewed as an arbitrary act which warranted a critical stance toward the established order. The workers' opposition, then, certainly was linked with traditionalism. But this association with traditionalism was not an irrational attempt to deny the 'foreboding strangeness' of the future. Rather, it resulted from a deliberate act of resistance toward the encroachments upon the justice and security afforded by traditional obligations. In this way, the association with traditionalism often produced a critical and radical perspective and eventually served as the foundation of the working class consciousness.

The link with tradition allowed the worker to retain a set of standards with which he could criticize the new industrial society. As Thompson writes, "the factory-hand . . . was . . . the inheritor . . . of *remembered* village rights, of notions of equality before the law, of craft traditions."[84] Through remembrance the worker was able to encounter the present and anticipate the future with reference to historical time: he could locate himself both in history and society. In this light, we should not view the discontent of the workers merely as a response to economic inequality. Rather, along with J. L. Hammond, we should recognize that

> The real passion of the working class revolt of this time was partly inspired by the envy of wealth, but ultimately in the main by a hostility to a view of life which outraged the poor man's self-respect and gave to his higher wants no place at all in his values.[85]

Thus the workers' opposition was directed against cultural as well as economic impoverishment; and, in its former mode, it entailed a revolt of imagination.

In the confrontation between the traditions nurtured in the protective communities of the workers and the requirements of the industrial capitalism, the past was imaginatively reconstructed; the social life of the eighteenth century was glorified as a 'Golden Age.' From this remembered past the workers drew the criteria with which they judged the present situation as illegitimate. This use of the remembered past to criticize the present order has been commonly and mistakenly viewed as a misguided attempt to deny the real changes which had occurred by demanding a return to a fictional past. Typical of this view is the following:

> The view that the period before the Industrial Revolution was a sort of golden age is a myth. Many of the evils of the early factory age were no worse than those of an earlier period. Domestic spinners and weavers in the eighteenth century had been 'exploited' by the clothiers as ruthlessly as the factory operatives were 'exploited' by the manufacturers. . . . Men, women, and children worked long hours for low wages under the domestic system as under the factory system. . . . It was [only] because the factories brought the workers under one roof that it became possible to detect bad conditions which had formerly been hidden in isolated cottages and workshops.[86]

While there is no doubt that exploitation and oppression pervaded eighteenth-century England, there is good reason to question the suggestion that the myth of the Golden Age was indicative of certain retrogressive tendencies in working class protest activity. Upon close examination, this myth can be accurately read as an expression of the workers' resistance to the denial of social responsibility and their recognition that a better society was possible. As such, the myth of the Golden Age was an essential part of the workers' ideological consciousness.

During the first quarter of the nineteenth century, as Asa Briggs observes, the concept of class had begun to replace the earlier notions of the 'chain of connection' and 'bond of attachment' as the descriptive category of hierarchical and domination relationships.[87] In direct contrast to the previous categories, the concept of class reflected the elimination of social obligations and responsibility from hierarchical relationships. In class society worth is extrinsic; it has to be achieved. With this shift it became possible for the workers to more easily distinguish their interests from those of other classes.

What facilitated the worker's identification of common interests was the retention of traditional values and institutional forms. Not only did these enable workers to give meaning to their shared experiences, but they also served to clearly differentiate the working class ideology from that of the middle class. In the face of the incessant destruction of cultural traditions (exactly what the middle class urged), the working class was compelled to reconstruct these traditions, to remould them in accordance with the new challenges offered by class society.

Given the more explicit and intensive kinds of repressive mechanisms which were implemented from the turn of the century on, the reconstruction of traditions was carried out in conjunction with the reconstruction of working class communities. In a sense, form and content were united. Deprived of open expression, the workers were driven underground where they were to form an unsurpassed solidarity. It was there that the secret tradition, so crucial to the unification of form and content, was born and nurtured. The major manifestation of the secret tradition is to be found in the early trade unions. As H. A. Turner notes, the early unions exhibited a structural simplicity founded upon communal ties and relationships. Accordingly, the formal disbanding of a union by the government resulted only in a temporary setback; for the workers were still able to maintain close association with one another and, on this basis, develop informal mechanisms capable of achieving the same goals as the open trade union.[88] As repression increased, secrecy grew into a moral code of conduct and assumed a crucial role in working class consciousness. Thompson describes the typical operation of this code of conduct.

> At work no leader or deputation need approach the employer
> with the men's demands; a hint would be dropped, an over-

> looker would be prompted, or an unsigned note be left for
> the master to see. If the demands were not met there was no
> need . . . for a formal strike; men would simply drop away or
> singly give notice.[89]

Pervading working class communities and institutions, in the friendly societies and in the trade unions, were the ceremony and ritual characteristics
of eighteenth-century traditions, now hidden but still effective. Working-
class communities became reorganized to meet the obligations recently denied
by the middle class and the government. Working-class institutions were
created to foster self-discipline and self-protection: if traditional protections
were to be reinstituted, the workers themselves would have to do it. Thus
the working-class ideology, emphasizing self-respect, was built on these
communities and institutions.

Under these conditions of secrecy emerged what David Lockwood has
called a 'proletarian consciousness.' According to Lockwood, proletarian
consciousness results from the concentration of workers in an occupational
community in which a strong sense of shared occupational and communal
experiences reinforce the group's solidarity. The distinctive cultural networks which developed in these occupational communities not only strengthened internal cohesion but also served to create an image of society in terms
of a dichotomous or two-class power model. Lockwood writes, "Thinking
in terms of two classes standing in a relationship of opposition is a natural
consequence of being a member of a closely integrated industrial community
with well-defined boundaries and a distinctive style of life."[90] It comes as
no surprise, then, that the middle class devoted much energy to the weakening of working class communities and traditions. For, out of these communities grew a political consciousness which transformed the revolt of
imagination into social revolt.

The workers' reconstruction of their communities was affected by a
significant change in the experience of domination. Prior to examining how
and why these reconstructed communities and traditions emerged into social
conflict, it is worthwhile to briefly analyze the nature of this change.

Domination and legitimacy in crisis

Prior to the advance of industrial capitalism, domination was rooted in
the structure of the status order. Expressive of status relationships, the
legitimacy of domination rested upon the responsiveness of the higher orders
to the lower orders. In this way the authority of the established order was
constantly open to challenge. When responsiveness was not forthcoming,
authority was seriously questioned. During the first third of the nineteenth
century this situation began to change. The emerging middle class rapidly

gained in strength, both numerically and economically, and began to demand a greater share of political power. Eventually, the center of power began to split in two, one half remaining within the governmental apparatus, the other located in the economy. Political power, until 1832, remained formally in the hands of the aristocracy. Although entrepreneurs and individual capitalists had significant influence on the decisions made in this realm, the aristocrats were still the ultimate decision makers.[91] Economic power, in contrast, resided in society and rested upon the natural identification of interests. Here the decision maker was the market.

Paralleling this shift in the focus of power was a shift in the nature of legitimacy. With its stability seriously weakened by the conflicting attacks launched by the middle class and the working class, the government had to decide which kind of support—the strong cultural orientations offered by the workers or the increasing free-floating resources provided by the entrepreneurs—would be most beneficial. By siding with the latter, the government abandoned in effect its ties with traditional authority: now its legitimacy would rely more closely on the continued expansion of free-floating resources. Political decisions, accordingly, would have to be made in a way constant with the dictates of economic growth. In short, the government had to be responsive to the economy, and the state had to assure that economic activity would proceed unhampered. The state, then, was responsible for suppressing any attempts at maintaining traditional protections.

With this realignment of power, working class demands and agitations were redefined as illegitimate and illegal. From 1795 on, a large number of repressive measures were implemented. New legislation not only restricted the scope and composition of public meetings, but also made it a treasonable offense to publicly criticize the government.[92] As a result, the number of trials and prosecutions brought against workers increased dramatically. Moreover, it was not uncommon to find repressive legislation accompanied by physical violence. Workers' rallies frequently attracted the army or local militia which, on such occasions as the Peterloo Massacre of 1819, physically and arbitrarily attacked the participants. Repression became the tool with which the workers would be transformed into free-floating resources. Lord Melbourne, in his 1832 letter to district magistrates, expressed this view:

> In these circumstances, I am commanded by his Majesty to express his confident expectation, that all who hold the commission of the peace will act with the promptitude, decision, and firmness which are so imperatively required, and that they will exert themselves for the prevention and suppression of all meetings which shall be called together for an illegal purpose . . .; for the detection and punishment of all unlawful combination and conspiracy . . . and for the encourage-

ment and protection of his Majesty's peaceable and well-disposed subjects.[93]

Workers demanding an adequacy of response were now viewed as seditious; working-class organizations and the mobilization of workers within their own communities were regarded as conspiratorial.

Typical of the repressive legislation enacted during this period were the Combination Acts of 1799 and 1800. The Combination Acts formally stipulated a practice which had existed in common law for a number of years with the intent to facilitate prosecution. Essentially, the Combination Acts prohibited the formation of any combinations, regardless of their purpose. It is instructive to note, however, that despite the existence of many employers' combinations, not one employer was prosecuted under the Acts. Enforcement was applied exclusively to workers' organizations. Basically, the Acts

> made liable (for the first offense) to three months in gaol, or two months' hard labour, any working man who combined with another to gain an increase in wages or a decrease in hours, or solicited anyone else to leave work, or objected to working with an other work-man. . . . Appeal was forbidden unless "two sufficient sureties in the penalty of twenty pounds" were provided . . . [but] the sustaining of a defense was made difficult by a provision that anyone who contributed to the expense of a person convicted under the Act would be fined £10 and the receiver of the subscription another £5 . . . [moreover] defendants were forced to give evidence against one another.[94]

The Combination Acts were used in various ways. Only irregularly invoked against artisan groups, they were systematically enforced against combinations developing among highly specialized and technical occupations. Most commonly, the Acts were enforced to weaken a particular union at a critical moment in its development, or to destroy a working-class association once it became successful and effective.[95]

The Combination Acts represented only one aspect of a more general policy of enhancing a repressive state apparatus which was employed constantly to break up working-class organizations, trade unions, and traditional protective customs. This policy generated an increasing reliance on force and violence. Shortly after the Peterloo Massacre of 1819, the notorious Six Acts were passed, extending and formalizing the repressive legislation approved from the turn of the century on. The Six Acts enabled the state: (1) to prohibit military exercises, training, and, by implication, demonstrations by private bodies; (2) to authorize the search of private houses, without warrants, on the suspicion of there being illegal arms therein; (3) to quickly expedite proceedings against suspected offenders; (4) to restrict the right and limit the size and composition of public meetings; (5) to punish 'libelous' statements made against the government and constitution, and thereby limit the right of free speech; and (6) to increase the stamp duty on working-class periodicals, putting them beyond the expense of their intended audience.[96]

As a consequence of these developments, many working class activities became legally regarded as criminal in nature. Not surprisingly, then, the first systematic efforts at creating a viable police force emerged at the end of this period. The London police force was established in 1829 with the Metropolitan Police Act; and within ten years this 'new police' model had spread throughout the country.[97] The new police were assigned to patrol the communities of the 'dangerous classes,' and their primary task was to prevent and control crime and disorder. By the late 1820s many working class traditions and customs were classified as criminal and disorderly.[98] Thus, the modern police force arose in the midst of intensified class tensions, and was empowered to control the threat of riot and revolution. In this way, the landed aristocrats and industrial capitalists could deny the existence of class conflict. As Allan Silver writes, they "turned toward a bureaucratic police system that insulated them from popular violence, drew attack and animosity upon itself, and seemed to separate the assertion of 'constitutional' authority from that of social and economic dominance."[99] The new police, in short, reflected well the shifting nature of domination in these transition years. And this change in domination was based on the more fundamental change from a status to a class society. Social and political domination became associated directly with economic requirements, and was no longer circumscribed by a normative framework entailing obligations and responsibilities; domination began to be legitimated to the extent that it permitted economic growth.

The working-class consciousness was shaped in large part by this new experience of domination. During this period of trade union illegality and repressive legislation, the workers were forced to go underground, where they acquired a sense of solidarity and invaluable experience in surreptitiously creating new tactics and methods of a protective and occupational nature. The context of secrecy which evolved gave a consequent opacity to working-class activities and culture, an opacity which impeded governmental attempts to destroy traditional institutional frameworks.

From 1795 to 1832 domination and legitimacy, power and authority, were in a state of crisis. In their communities and institutions, in their very culture, the workers maintained the traditional standards of the past. With these standards they critically evaluated the new arrangements of industrial capitalism, not merely in cost-of-living terms, but in terms of dehumanization, inequality, and injustice. They would not legitimate domination which took place independent of substantive rationality. The workers demanded responsiveness; and when they received none, they reacted initially as their predecessors had. Ineffectual in these new times, mob and riot activity eventually gave way to more organized forms of social protest.

SOCIAL PROTEST

Prior to the turn of the century, social protest was usually directed toward the restoration of certain rights and obligations. Conflict very rarely threatened the structure of the status order, and class consciousness can hardly be said to have existed. Even throughout the last decade of the eighteenth century, when protest activities were better organized and more highly defined, class consciousness remained of subsidiary importance. As we have seen, opposition was often directed against the aristocracy and involved some coordination between the entrepreneurs and the workers. The critical reason of natural law ideology had yet to be sufficiently differentiated into its laissez-faire and communal alternatives; thus it continued to provide a common meeting ground for the two opponents of the aristocracy.

With the weakening of aristocratic power, the alternative possibilities contained within the existing order and expressed in critical reason were clarified. Although the middle class and working class continued to form alliances in opposition to the aristocracy, the struggle gradually focused on which of the alternatives was to be actualized. As governmental stability came to rely more and more upon sustained growth, laissez-faire principles were employed increasingly to justify the social repression engendered by class society. However, these principles and the new system of domination and inequality which they intended to justify were critically evaluated and repudiated in terms of the communal alternative adhered to by the workers. This evaluation and repudiation initiated a process of destruction and reconstruction. Initially, the workers encountered the new arrangements with preindustrial tactics, strategies, and aims. Direct action, however, was contained easily enough. In response, the workers refashioned traditional values so as to formulate a critique of political economy, exploitation, and the 'unproductive classes' of society, and they reorganized protest activities to meet the new form of domination. As a consequence, the social repression of the emerging industrial capitalist society was perceived as illegitimate and experienced as intolerable. The social protest which ensued was more than an attempt to negate the recently established order: it also aimed to realize a better society.

This reconstruction of traditional values and institutions will be examined now. The focus is on the interaction of economic and productive activity with the changing ideological consciousness. During the first twenty years of the nineteenth century, the economy was in a cyclical depression, with both wages and prices following a more or less uneven movement. At the same time, new productive techniques associated with technology and the factory system appeared. The widespread experience of increasing insecurity and greater regimentation, which these developments produced, served as the background for the creation of the working class consciousness. Linked to preindustrial moral codes, this consciousness was capable of assessing the new experience in other than economic terms. And, as we shall see, this capacity to assess economic exploitation and oppression in terms other than those supplied by the economy itself gave working class opposition its critical edge.

The emergence from preindustrial forms

During the closing years of the eighteenth century, as we have seen, the authority of the landed aristocracy underwent serious challenge from both the laboring population and the rising industrial bourgeoisie. Not only were these two groups united by a common enemy; they also adhered to the general principles contained in critical reason. With the contending alternatives embodied in critical reason not yet clearly defined, the working class and the middle class had a common ground upon which they could meet. However, during the first third of the nineteenth century, when the conflicting interpretations of natural law ideology began to emerge, it was still common for working class protest activities to receive active support and guidance from various middle class sources. Writing in the *Communist Manifesto,* Marx and Engels recognize this continued alliance as a necessary one:

> At this stage . . . the proletarians do not fight their enemies, but the enemies of their enemies, the remnants of the absolute monarchy, the landowners, the non-industrial bourgeois, the petty bourgeois. . . . In all these battles, the bourgeois sees itself compelled to appeal to the proletariat, to ask for its help, and thus, to drag it into the political arena.[100]

In mobilizing the working class as a political force, Marx and Engels continue, the bourgeoisie at the same time "furnishes the proletariat with weapons for fighting the bourgeoisie."[101] What is suggested here, of course, is that the proletariat must be forced to assume forms of conflict appropriate to industrial capitalist society; it must be "dragged into the political arena" by the middle class. Against this view will be proposed another which suggests that the emergence of working class protest from preindustrial forms is prompted by the workers themselves.

In the last decade of the eighteenth century, the number of trade clubs formed by workers and political societies created by entrepreneurs increased significantly. Usually concerned with issues and problems associated with particular localities, these associations nevertheless provided some organizational stability to oppositional activitiy. Communication was established between the various clubs and societies with two important consequences. First, problems were no longer viewed as being confined to local conditions: this made the opposition more national in character. Secondly, the link between working class and middle class agitation was strengthened. About this development, Gwyn Williams notes:

> The most remarkable feature of this period is not really the growth of organised societies, but the unprecedented *diffusion* of political ideas, often related directly, in their turn, to strictly *local* experience. Without this awareness of wide and deep *penetration,* of some unseen but permanent minority which at any crisis might suddenly become a majority, the whole clanking apparatus of [governmental] intimidation . . . [is] meaningless.[102]

Constitutionalism resided at the core of these diffused political ideas. Protest activities, whether on the part of the working class or the middle class, were directed toward the restoration of ancient liberties and rights accorded to the 'free-born' Englishman. Occurring shortly after the French Revolution, the spread of these ideas and the increasing coordination which they reflected were viewed by the government with apprehension and alarm.

Perhaps the most significant working class association created at this time was the London Corresponding Society. Modeled after middle-class political societies and composed largely of skilled workmen (weavers, carpenters, shoemakers, watchmakers), the L.C.S. was primarily concerned with the dissemination of political ideas.[103] Centered in London, the L.C.S. served as a center of communication and information for workers' associations in many of the towns affected by industrial changes—such as Manchester, Sheffield, and Leeds. Although influenced by and sympathetic to the French Revolution, the L.C.S. followed the doctrines of Paine and retained a faith in the constitution. Its activities, accordingly, were always carried out in the open, its goals and methods always subject to public scrutiny.

The demands put forth by the L.C.S. were couched in terms of natural rights and justified with reference to the constitution. Its programs aimed for, in George Veitch's words, "a harmony of the doctrines of natural rights and social contract in order to prove man's right to a share in the government of his country."[104] Universal suffrage and annual parliaments became key goals of the L.C.S., and petitioning of Parliament became the advocated means. In a public address issued in 1792 the Society made its programs clear: "Reform, not anarchy," was the goal; "Reason, firmness, and unamity," not violence, was the method.[105]

In its goals and methods, its ideology and organization, the L.C.S. closely resembled the oppositional associations developed by the middle class. At the same time, however, the L.C.S.—as is true of popular societies and trade clubs in general—exhibited a general orientation similar to that which characterized direct action mob and riot activity. Although more enduring than preindustrial conflict groups, these associations continued to be guided by the customary belief in the responsiveness of government to traditional obligations. In this context, protest activities generally were viewed by the participants less as weapons of social change and more as ways of conveying discontent to Parliament. In short, while these societies and clubs adopted many of the features of middle class political associations, they retained their attachment to the traditions of the preindustrial crowd, and their protest activities tended to remain merely symbolic expressions of grievances.[106]

With the onset of repressive measures, this situation changed. Political societies (especially those of the workers) and trade clubs reacted by reshaping the aims and structures of their associations, making them suitable for the clandestine operations that were required. Governmental repression of the L.C.S. commenced in 1793. Following an initial period of refusing to even consider the submitted petitions, Parliament commissioned a series of sedition trials which effectively weakened the formal channels of communication both within the L.C.S. and between it and other corresponding societies. Despite this repression, the L.C.S. experienced a significant increase in membership, from 5,000 members in 1792 to 10,000 in 1795.[107] Accompanying this growth was the reappearance of direct action protest and the virtual disappearance of petitioning attempts. In 1795, "[w]ave after wave of food riots, price-fixing actions, seizures of grain, broke over region after region. . . . Millers and corn factors were attacked. In several places the militia mutinied."[108]

Governmental response took the form of an intensification of repressive controls. In 1795 the Two Acts were passed, making incitement of contempt of the government a treasonable offense and restricting the scope of public assembly. The prosecutions carried out under the Two Acts brought about the gradual disintegration of the L.C.S. Taken with the Combination Acts, the Two Acts made public political activity virtually impossible for the workers. It was at this point that workers' associations went underground.

Operating clandestinely, workers associations remained historically continuous with the preindustrial ideals of the mob and the riot. However, these traditions began to be redefined in accordance with the new experience. Natural rights now had to be protected by the workers themselves. Protest, therefore, had to become more than a symbolic expression of grievances. Organizational reconstruction accompanied this ideological reconceptualization, and working class communities and associations assumed a more combative posture. Protest activities became more highly organized; and demands to Parliament were replaced with calculated attacks on the wealthy farmer, the factory owner, and the institutions of industrial capitalism. By the 1820s, Patricia Hollis notes, the workers saw as their enemy "capitalist economics rather than aristocratic privilege, property rather than taxes, a profiteering middle-class rather than a parasitic upper class."[109]

The common ground—the undifferentiated critical reason of natural law ideology—upon which the laborers and entrepreneurs converged had shriveled by the first decade of the nineteenth century. Over the next twenty years, as the distinctive and contending interests of the two classes emerged, the relationship was transformed from one of cooperation to one of conflict. Crucial to this transformation was the nature of the governmental repression which occurred in the 1790s and early 1800s. As is evident in the Two Acts and Combination Acts, governmental repression was directed primarily against workers' associations. As a consequence, the repressive measures enacted during this period intensified political domination while relaxing controls on economic exchange. In effect, this meant that the government partially was acceding to the demands of the middle class to extirpate the economy from traditional regulations. The peculiar nature of this domination—which was pursuant to the government's program of realigning the basis of support and legitimacy—provided many benefits to the entrepreneurial interests. Conversely, the workers now had to contend with both an intensified political domination and a spreading economic domination. The middle class, now stockholders in the apparatus of domination, was an enemy.

Despite the growing opposition between the working class and the middle class, it was not uncommon throughout the first third of nineteenth century for the two classes to be allied in opposition to the government. During this period middle-class strategists made concerted efforts to mobilize workers' associations behind their causes, thereby securing greater leverage in their bargaining with the government and aristocratic interests. As Briggs has found, middle class attacks on 'aristocratic tyranny,' 'hereditary opulence,' and 'social injustice' invariably were accompanied by "an appeal to the working classes ('joint victims' of the monopolists) and by an attempt to win over tenant farmers."[110] While the alliance was a tactical one for the middle class, it was none the less so for the workers.

Workers' associations entered into alliance with their middle class counterparts only when they could potentially benefit. Thus, alliances were formed on two general grounds, either in opposition to the taxation policies of the government or in opposition to political domination. Representative of the first instance was the alliance formed against the Corn Law of 1815— which prohibited the importation of foreign corn as long as the domestic price of native corn remained below 80 shillings a quarter. The middle class, buttressed by the advocacy of free trade put forth by the classical political economists, called for the repeal of the law on the grounds that it favored income made from rent over profits generated by capital. The workers lined up against the Corn Laws, but not because the law discriminated against capital: rather, they opposed the law because it continually threatened the maintenance of even a subsistence standard of living, by raising the price of wheat.[111] Although the Corn Laws were not repealed until 1846, many other measures which impeded free trade, as documented earlier, were rapidly eliminated. As a result, the economic policy of the government no longer served as a basis for a working-class - middle-class alliance.

The second ground for alliance—namely, opposition to political domination—was more significant. The middle-class leaders employed the doctrines of political economy and Philosophic Radicalism to back their demand for the extension of voting privileges and the right of representation. The workers, on the other hand, advocated universal suffrage, not as an end in itself but as a means of transforming society.[112] When these superficially similar demands were phrased in terms of general suffrage, an alliance was formed: the result was the passage of the Reform Act of 1832 and the extension of the franchise to the middle class.[113]

An extremely tense atmosphere surrounded the passage of the Reform Act. From 1829 to 1831 militant workers' associations proliferated in response to both economic crises and the nonresponsiveness of the government. Threatened by an increase in working-class political activity, the Whigs, who dominated Parliament at the time, recognized the necessity of incorporating the middle class into the parliamentary system. They reasoned that "any plan must be objectionable which, by keeping the Franchise very high and exclusive, fails to give satisfaction to the middle and respectable ranks of society, and drives them to a union, founded on dissatisfaction, with the lower classes."[114] Designed to avoid this possibility, a Reform Bill was introduced in Parliament in 1831. Essentially, the Bill had two provisions: First, it proposed to abolish the numerous small, so-called rotten boroughs and to reassign representation to the growing industrial towns such as Manchester and Leeds; and, second, it intended to extend the franchise to the middle class in these boroughs and to the tenant farmers in the countryside.[115] The Bill received widespread support, not only from the middle class but also from many working class groups which had assurances that, once in Parliament, the middle-class representatives would use their power to implement manhood suffrage. What actually happened, of course, was that after the passage of the Reform Act the middle class distanced itself from its working-class supporters, and it more closely attended to the formation of alliances with the *ancien régime*.

The passage of the Reform Act represented the incorporation of the industrial bourgeoisie into the circle of political power, and thus contributed to the strengthening of the barriers which the working class had to over-come at a time when revolt seemed most feasible. As Thompson maintains, "the fact that the revolution did not occur was due . . . in part to the skill of the middle-class Radicals in offering exactly that compromise which might, not weaken, but strengthen both the state and property-rights against the working class threat."[116] With this development, the old view of politics as a struggle of the working and middle classes against the aristocracy was virtually eradicated.

Contrary to Marx and Engels, then, working-class social protest did not receive its weapons from the middle class. While it is certainly possible to demonstrate a number of cases of alliance between the two classes, it is equally possible to demonstrate, especially after 1815, that these alliances were entered into by both sides for tactical reasons. That the pressures pro-duced by these alliances usually resulted in changes beneficial to the middle class does not allow us to infer that the workers were used, or that their participation was manipulated. Rather, the middle class benefited because of the shift in domination and legitimacy from traditional orientations to free-floating resources, which began at the turn of the century.

How, then, did working-class agitation advance from preindustrial forms? The process was self-generating, originating in the traditions and practices, and sustained by the organizations and institutions—the trade unions, religious groups, and benefit societies—established in the protective com-munities of workers. Through these organizations and institutions, the remembered rights and liberties inherited by the industrial worker were imaginatively reconstructed; and, in response to the changing conditions of domination, this communal celebration of the past sparked the emergence of new forms of social protest.

The revolt of imagination: Remembrances and ritual

Corresponding to the changing form of domination and to the realignment of power was a change in the aims, methods, targets, and organizational skills of working-class protest activity. After an initial phase of widespread rioting, which differed from earlier riots in deliberation and trans-local organization, working-class protest acquired a more concerted orientation. In the period from the mid-1820s to the early 1830s—generally considered the most explosive epoch of working-class agitation, a significant upsurge in industrial actions in the new manufacturing districts converged with an intensification of agrarian riots.[117] While there were some important struc-tural differences between the industrial and agrarian actions, the two were linked directly by an underlying consciousness. The importance of this ideological consciousness, especially with regard to historical continuity, was alluded to previously. What requires emphasis here is how this ideological consciousness injected the element of imagination into the working class protest of the period. In analyzing the role of imagination in protest and revolt, it will be necessary on occasion to reconsider the problem of time.

The relationships between the techniques of factory production, work discipline, and the linear conception of time have been examined already. This examination indicated how the linear conception of time had the effect of 'deconstituting' the historical-generational background of domination, and thereby impeding the dominated from giving meaning to immediate experiences.[118] A number of factors prevented this from occurring before the early 1830s. First was the uneven pattern of development which temporarily resulted in the concurrent expansion of the factory system and domestic industry. Old productive techniques, social relationships, and cultural standards persisted alongside the new, giving continued expression to traditional ways. Secondly, the pattern of migration from rural to urban areas was a several-step process, usually involving two generations. This pattern of migration from countryside to town and from town to city was gradual enough so as not to weaken traditional relations.[119] The third and most important link with the past is found in the ideological consciousness of the workers.

Reference has been made to the common appearance of the myth of the viewed as an indication of the regressive tendencies of the workers, recognition of the past—by emphasizing a common history—provided a fundamental basis for the development of a working-class political community. Although the workers demanded the restoration of the past, the content of these demands constituted a call for the progressive reorganization of society. Derived not from the real historical past but from a fantasized past, the better society symbolized in the myth of the Golden Age never existed. Rather, it represented a future society which could and should be actualized. In this context fantasy possessed a critical thrust which partially fueled the workers' delegitimation of society. The possibility of critique which is contained in fantasy has been described by Marcuse:

> The truth value of imagination relates not only to the past but also to the future: the forms of freedom and happiness which it invokes claim to deliver the historical *reality*. In its refusal to accept as final the limitations imposed upon freedom and happiness by the reality principle, in its refusal to forget what *can be*, lies the critical function of phantasy.[120]

As fantasy the 'myth of the Golden Age' was a symbol which gave shared historical meaning to the new experience of domination. As an exercise in imagination it supplied indications of hope for a better society; and in the presence of hope we find the possibility of revolt.

This mythical portrayal of the past as the 'good life' did not conceal the injustices of the past. In a kind of inversion, the injustices of the past were incorporated into conceptions of the present. For the 'good life' to be realized these injustices had to be eradicated. Thus the workers demanded a society—like preindustrial society—based on social responsibility and protective of human rights, and a society—unlike the present one—without economic inequality and an unaccountable political structure. In short they sought to negate, not the products of industrialization, but the laissez-faire principles which underlay the organization of these products.

Informed by the remembered past, the ideological consciousness of the workers was incongruent with the attempts at restructuring temporal experience associated with work discipline. The concerted efforts to bind human time to mechanical time were, in effect, efforts to strip man of his past and thereby make him resigned to the present. By enhancing the ability to forget, submissiveness and renunciation could be sustained. Thus, the concern with the past displayed in working class agitation should be read, not as retrogression, but as resistance to the submission of human qualities to mechanization. Again, we turn to Marcuse for the subtle implications of the relation between remembrance and resistance.

> To forget is also to forgive what should not be forgiven if justice and freedom are to prevail. Such forgiveness reproduces the conditions which reproduce injustice and enslavement; to forget past suffering is to forgive the forces that caused it—without defeating those forces. The wounds that heal in time are also the sounds that contain the poison. Against this surrender to time, the restoration of remembrance to its rights, as a vehicle of liberation, is one of the noblest tasks of thought.[121]

Remembrance, the act of remembering—of making active in the present that which has occurred in the past—allows the dominated to place themselves in history and society, to refuse to repeat that which has previously failed, to actively confront the sociohistorical causes of the prevailing domination, and in so doing, to transcend the one-dimensionality of linear time.[122]

Arising out of the protective communities, protest activity in this period became more organized and coordinated. No longer regarded as a symbolic expression of grievances—a signal to the dominant powers to meet their obligations by reestablishing traditional protections, social protest was now seen as a legitimate means for gaining more or less permanent control over the village, the town, and the work place. Following this redefinition of purpose was a shift from the mob to the movement. In the Luddite riots lasting from 1811 to 1820, and ten years later in both the Swing movement launched by the agricultural laborers and the trade union movement in the industrial areas, the spontaneity characteristic of the earlier popular up-risings was subordinated to more organized practices.

Each of these movements was guided by standards drawn from the re-membered past. The stories of Ned Ludd and Captain Swing, and the Owenite portrayal of villages of cooperation, were all based on the myth of the Golden Age.[123] The theme of each was similar. The framework-knitter, the farmer, the small artisan, or the factory worker was being denied his right to an adequate standard of living; his traditional values and skills were being subordinated to the machine and the market; and, despite the pride he took in his work, he was being systematically turned into a pauper. The 'un-productive classes' of society—the parson, the landlord, the manufacturer and entrepreneur, the government and monarchy—are indicted for their part in undermining the basis of eighteenth-century society. In the past these people "listened to the complaints of [the] tenantry and remedied their grievances"; but now they insisted that "[e]very man can do what he pleases with his own."[124] To meet such nonresponsiveness the workers must take matters into their own hands by wrecking machines, burning hayricks, initiating strikes, or organizing a moral economy outside of the market economy. Through such means industrial society will be infused with social responsibility, and a better society, one built upon collective control and cooperation, will result. Thus, although guided by the myth of the Golden Age, these movements were not retrogressive; for upon the revival of 'ancient rights,' progressive aims, new precedents, and conceptions of the future were made. The uses of the remembered past by the Luddites, Thompson observes, "contained within them a shadowy image, not so much of a pa-ternalist, but of a democratic community, in which industrial growth should be regulated according to ethical priorities and the pursuit of profit be sub-ordinated to human needs."[125] In Luddism, as in the Swing and industrial movements, the criteria which defined future objectives and guided social action were embodied in the remembered past.

The impact of the past mirrored in the ideological consciousness was present as well in the formation of working-class communities and conflict groups. The ritualism and play, the refusal to separate work and leisure, so characteristic of laboring communities in the eighteenth century, remained in existence throughout the first third of the nineteenth century. The methods and techniques employed by the workers were borrowed in part from Non-conformist religious sects. Given the ceremony, ritual, and transcendental categories inherent in religious doctrine and practice, it is not surprising that workers' associations so often affiliated with religious sects.

Not only did the use of religious class meetings and religious imagery allow the workers to circumvent the Two Acts and Combination Acts, but it also improved the technique of working-class agitation. Through class meetings organizational skills were acquired, and networks of communication and channels of recruitment were established, as were mechanisms for the collection and distribution of financial resources from and to the community. Organized as religious sects, workers' associations permeated all aspects of working-class life. Thev offered, albeit in spiritual terms, a forum for the expression of the collective suffering and aspirations of the community. They afforded some degree of economic protection in times of distress, and they provided a basis for insurrectionary activity.[126]

The form and content of working-class social protest were shaped by these organizational experiences, and were guided by an ideological consciousness which engendered a sense of historical continuity. The industrial and agrarian riots we will examine below featured many of the collective practices and rituals found in preindustrial actions; and the participants in these riots often adhered to the symbols of the past. In their analysis of protest during this period, Hobsbawm and Rudé write:

> There was always a certain ceremonial attending such operations. The leader might wear a white hat or ride on a white horse; flags were carried, and horns were blown . . . to arouse the villagers and warn them of the rioters' approach. In the earlier (and later) days, when the militants were more inclined to fear detection, raiding parties might blacken their faces and do their work at night; but as the movement developed, riots took place in open day, and were public performances and at times assumed a festive air.[127]

With ceremony and ritual combined with imagination and remembrance, the form and content of working-class protest converged. In the response to the new experience of domination, symbol and structure interacted with and transformed one another. In this way, the revolt of imagination coincided with the revolt against social domination and led to the most explosive period of class conflict in England's history.

The methods, techniques, goals, and organization of working-class agitation were distinctively associated with the experience and history of working-class life. The emergence of social protest from preindustrial forms occurred not by middle-class manipulation but by working-class assertion. An analysis of particular protest activities generated by the workers in response to industrial capitalism will bear this out.

Case Studies

The emergence of working-class social protest from preindustrial forms took place most rapidly in those areas and among those occupations directly under the impact of industrialization. In most rural and many mining areas the methods and aims of social protest were virtually indistinguishable from those of eighteenth-century agitation practices. As Dorothy Marshall remarks, many of the rural rioters "still cherished the belief that if only the King and his ministers realized their distress they could take steps to end it."[128] With the extension of the productive, distributive, and exchange techniques of industrial capitalism, protest activities in these areas were soon reshaped to better deal with the new domination. Important in this regard was the intensification of repression against the workers, as typified by the Peterloo Massacre and the Six Acts. While there were significant, most often occupationally based, differences among working-class protest activities during this period, and no national organization to speak of, the timing of various protest activities and the demands made by the various protesting groups coincided often enough to give the appearance of a working-class movement.

Within this movement, forms of social protest activity varied, at times significantly, as a result of the uneven development of industrial capitalism. Despite such variation, it is possible to discern three major types of protest organization—one, characteristic of workers whose occupations were intermediate between the domestic system and the factory system; another, found among agrarian and rural occupations; and the last, exhibited by the new industrial workers. The first form emerged in the Luddite riots; the second in the Swing riots of 1829 and 1830; and the third in the industrial agitation and trade union disturbances. In the early 1820s there was some overlap between Luddism and industrial protest, and in the late 1820s and early 1830s industrial agitation was closely linked with the political reform movement and loosely connected with agricultural uprisings of the Swing movement. These three forms of working-class protest are representative, not exhaustive, of the shapes assumed by the workers' revolt.[129] Nevertheless, they do suggest the great extent to which the working-class challenge permeated the agrarian, the industrializing, and the industrialized sectors of English society.

Luddism   Luddism is typically viewed as an exercise in futility carried out by a band of naïve and shortsighted people convinced that they could stop progress by smashing a few machines. This view, like so many others concerned with the English working class, is a distorted one. The Luddite movement, which began in 1811 and lasted until 1820, often engaged in machine breaking; but this activity occurred only rarely, in an indiscriminate and arbitrary way. Moreover, the hostility expressed in these activities was directed, not against machines, but against the dehumanizing social relations induced by an advancing mechanization of production. Ultimately, Luddism represented an attempt by the workers to acquire decisive control over the productive and distributive mechanisms of society.

Machine breaking was not an end in itself; it was a tactic, and not a new one. Wrecking, Hobsbawm reminds us,

> was a traditional and established part of industrial conflict in the period of the domestic and manufacturing system, and the early stages of the factory and mine. It was not directed only against machines, but also against raw material, finished goods, or even the private property of employers, depending on what sort of damage these were most sensitive to.[130]

Under the existing conditions—the illegality of combinations and certain public assemblies, the increasing strength of the army, and the inability of many workers to subsist for even a short while without work—machine breaking was the only effective mode of work stoppage that was available.

Luddite riots, however, involved much more than machine breaking. Provision shops and grain dealers were attacked, often in retaliation for either high prices or the inaccessibility of goods. Many raids were carried out in an effort to acquire firearms and other weapons. In Nottingham, where no new machinery had been introduced, Luddism gained a strong foothold; and the ensuing riots entailed, not the destruction of machines, but attacks upon employers who refused to yield to workers' demands for a regulated wage scale.[131] In the midlands, the center of Luddism, there was little, if any, opposition to labor-saving machinery. "The midland Luddites," as Darvall noted, "were using attacks upon machinery, whether old or new, as a means of coercing their employers into granting them concessions with regard to wages and other matters."[132]

During the first decade of the nineteenth century, a series of bad harvests and rising wheat prices placed an enormous burden on the workers' struggle for survival. Over the same period, the countryside was rapidly becoming the chief location of new industrial enterprises which benefited from the absence of strict regulations and the availability of a cheap labor force. Initially organized as small establishments, the new factories differed little from the domestic system, and existed side-by-side with agricultural industries. With the expansion of industrialization, however, the two came into conflict and the worker was caught in the middle. On the one hand, agricultural employers refused to adequately increase wage rates; on the other, the factory system subordinated craftsmanship to tedious tasks. Luddism arose in this context as a response to both the denial of social responsibility and the employers' attempts at (1) producing cheap 'cut-up' goods and (2) vitiating the skills associated with traditional crafts and trades. As a writer in the *Nottingham Review* (1811) observed,

> The immediate results of this new system of manufacture are that the market is stocked with these worthless goods and that

those who continue to make hose "in a tradesmanlike manner," must either make them cheaper or starve.[135]

In a strong sense the Luddite riots were an expression of pride in craftsmanship and work. Control of the productive apparatus and the market
would prevent the further production of inferior quality goods, would
mitigate the constantly fluctuating price of food, allow regulation of wages,
and protect more humane social relationships.

Although Luddite riots were usually organized about specific and limited
goals, the Luddite movement as a whole sought to maintain the moral economy. "What was at issue," writes Thompson, "was the 'freedom' of the
capitalist to destroy the customs of the trade, whether by new machinery,
the factory-system, or by unrestricted competition, beating-down wages,
undercutting his rivals, and undermining standards of craftsmanship."[134]
In this light, the Luddite riots become more than industrial disturbances:
they become acts of political sedition.

Luddism had its roots in—and indeed reflected the strong sense of solidarity that prevailed in—working-class communities. Although only a
handful of workers participated in any particular riot, the community at
large supplied continuous and widespread support to the whole range of
Luddite activities.[135] This support permitted the Luddies to maintain the
secrecy of their operations, thereby impeding governmental attempts at
suppression. That such considerable support was forthcoming is still another
indication that Luddism was not merely confined to machine wrecking.
Luddism's more general concern with questions about the nature of production and distribution, the loss of trade induced by the introduction of
new frames and the arbitrary nature of decision making, was what attracted
extensive sympathy and support.

If Luddism was a shapeless movement, it was so out of necessity. And, in
this case, lack of shape should not be equated with lack of unity. What
differentiates the Luddite riots from the isolated and symbolical riots of the
preindustrial era is the concerted manner in which they occurred. As Thomis
notes

> There were civil wars, religious riots, food riots and industrial
> riots in the previous two centuries, but there never had been
> such wide-scale industrial riots occurring simultaneously with
> food riots in an industrial revolution context.[136]

More organized and systematic, the Luddite riots constituted a major advance over previous forms of working-class agitation.

Deliberation clearly characterized the Luddite movement. In many areas,
Luddites circulated documents and letters in an effort to create viable chan-

nels of communication and thus to better mobilize support. Friendly Societies and similar agencies were often established to provide benefits to community members in times of distress. In this way Luddism became firmly entrenched in the local communities. The support the Luddites received in return proved indispensable when, after 1812, the government began both to infiltrate Luddite organizations and to introduce the military into Luddite areas on a massive scale. Within the protection afforded by the local communities, the Luddites were able to construct secret yet complex organizations which remained impervious to repressive measures for several years. A vivid description of these highly organized, clandestine operations appears in an 1812 edition of the *Leeds Mercury*:

> The first object of these rioters seemed to be the breaking of machinery; but they had in many instances resorted to measures infinitely more alarming, namely, demanding of arms; and even carried them off. . . . Sometimes the rioters were under the control of leaders; and were distinguished not by names but by numbers; were known to each other by signs and countersigns, and carried on all with the utmost caution. They also took an oath that "they would not reveal anything . . . under the penalty of being put out of existence." They adopted and submitted to a military discipline; they had regular muster-rolls. . . . They also had their Committees and Sub-Committees, and countersigns, by which they made their written communication. . . . It further appeared that two-pence a week was appointed to be paid by each member to their respective Delegates.[137]

The opacity of working-class culture and community enabled Luddism to persist in an effective and threatening way.

Given this relation between Luddism and the working-class community, it is virtually impossible, as Darvall suggests, to distinguish between Luddism and the other popular movements of the time.[138] For instance, a very similar movement emerged in 1816 among the agricultural laborers of East Anglia. These riots also were initiated by the employers' denial of traditional responsibilities and the authorities' refusal to meet age-old obligations. In a letter prepared by the laborers and addressed "To the Gentlemen of Ashill" these considerations were expressed clearly:

> You do as you like, you rob the poor of their common rights, plough the grass up that God sends to grow, that a poor man may feed a Cow, Pig, Horse, nor Ass; lay muck and stones on the road to prevent the grass growing. . . . There is 5 or 6 of you have gotten the whole of the land in this parish in you

own hands and you would wish to be rich and starve all the
other part of the poor of the parish.[139]

Tactics similar to the Luddites were employed. Less solidly organized than
the Luddites but better organized than the eighteenth-century rioters, the
East Anglian rioters engaged in such activities as machine wrecking, arson
(outbuildings and office buildings were the prime targets), breaking into
shops, and distributing of goods. In June, 1816, a group of laborers secured
temporary control over the town of Littleport.[140] Not only were the methods
and techniques of attack employed by the East Anglian rioters so similar to
the Luddites, but on a number of occasions the Luddites worked in concert
with various laborers' associations. In some cases, Luddite riots received
financial backing from occupational and trades groups, and in all cases
the rioters were afforded protection and sustenance whenever such was
required.[141]

To reduce Luddism to an exercise in machine breaking is to seriously
misread the historical data. Machine breaking was a tactic made necessary
by the prevailing conditions and sanctioned by traditional customs. Often
the rioters merely disassembled rather than destroyed the machines. In the
main centers of Luddism (the framework-knitting districts of Nottingham,
Leicester, and Derby, the cropping district of the West Riding, and the
cotton weaving district of South Lancashire) wrecking manifested a general
concern with political objectives.[142] While the intensity and scope of Luddism
varied from one area to the next, the varieties of Luddism did coalesce into
a single movement, displaying similar insurrectionary motives and a similar
pattern of development. Luddism, in short, was an insurrectionary movement with progressive and radical aims, and with a firm organizational base.

The Luddite movement had a considerable impact on English society. In
its reaction to Luddism, the government perfected the new repressive policies
and, in the process, established important contacts with middle-class interests.
However, while the policies of governmental domination were being improved, so too were the techniques and tactics of working-class agitation.
From the experience of Luddism, workers acquired organizational skills
and the recognition that the problems they confronted transcended local
boundaries.

With the passage of two bills in 1811 and 1812, the government commenced efforts to eliminate the threat posed by Luddism. The first bill, an
extension of the Watch and Ward act, enhanced the powers of local magistrates to deal with rioters. The second converted frame breaking from a
minor to a capital felony.[143] Soon after the enactment of this legislation,
apprehended rioters were either executed or transported out of the country.
From 1812 to 1818 the implementation of repressive measures steadily advanced, and many Luddites were prosecuted under the Combination Acts as

well. In 1819 the Six Acts were passed, and within a year Habeas Corpus was suspended and the giving and taking of secret oaths were declared a criminal offense.

Accompanying this spate of repressive legislation was the government's introduction of troops to the disturbed areas. An army of 12,000—six times greater than any military contingent used in previous domestic disturbances— was employed to suppress Luddism.[144] The strengthening of military and civil force was paralleled by the creation of a permanent spy network. Faced by a public unwilling to provide information about the Luddites, the government began a systematic program of infiltration. Unprecedented in its scope, the infiltration and military occupation of Luddite areas was eventually effective in reducing the severity of protest activities.

Through its repressive legislation and use of troops the government played a crucial role in the suppression of Luddism. Given the local bases of Luddism, however, the chief figure in the implementation of repression was the local magistrate. Serving as a kind of liaison between the government and the manufacturing interests, the local magistrate was instrumental in negotiating a common front for the two previously opposed forces. As an intermediary, he helped to solidify the growing middle-class legitimacy of the government, by directing governmental resources to the protection of private enterprises. One consequence of this new relationship was that many factory units were able to increase in size, despite Luddism. Through the competition of the 'free market' economy, now protected from the intrusion of noneconomic compulsions by the government, smaller enterprises—if not already besieged by Luddite attacks—either went out of business or were incorporated into the new, more centralized enterprises. These larger establishments presented a less vulnerable target to the Luddite rioters.

Although Luddism failed to achieve its more insurrectionary objectives, its contributions to working-class protest was significant. Occurring when it did, Luddism brought to the forefront the hitherto hidden interests shared by the middle class and the aristocracy. In so doing, Luddism helped infuse many working-class communities with a distinct identity and a spirit of independence. Moreover, Luddism served as a demonstration that well-organized and carefully planned activities would both seriously reduce the power of the beneficiaries of existing society and receive support and legitimacy from working-class communities. The lessons learned by the Luddites would be practiced again.

The Swing movement   The major impact of the enclosure movement was felt at the close of the eighteenth century, when the agricultural industry became mechanized and land became an important commodity. Accompanying this revolution in agriculture was a disregard for traditional rights. In the absence of these common rights and the resources they supplied, the small farmer, the squatter, and the cottager also became commodities. As the Hammonds write, "in an unenclosed village . . . the normal labourer did not depend on his wages alone . . . he received wages as a labourer, but in part he maintained himself as a producer. . . . Now, with all his auxiliary resources . . . taken from him . . . he was . . . a wage earner and nothing more."[145] The enclosures brought about the agrarian proletariat.

Dispossessed of rights and resources, stripped of wage and price protections, and prevented by settlement laws from migrating in search of jobs, the rural laborers entered a period of stark pauperism. The government's response to this situation, and to the laborers' demands for a reinstatement of controls and allotments, was the Speenhamland system of poor relief established in 1795. As we have seen, Speenhamland replaced the previous regulations on adequate wage rates with a guarantee for a minimum family income based on subsistence requirements. Although Speenhamland policy violated the major thrust of the classical economic doctrine, it was not a complete anathema to the middle-class position, since the poor relief supplements it provided did allow employers to pay less than subsistence wages.

The scope of transformation associated with enclosures was immense. The concentration of land holdings and the mechanization of agriculture created the rural proletariat. The large reserve army of labor located in the countryside contributed to the growth of small-scale industries and attracted new and larger enterprises. Cash payment and contract became the prominent relations as the bond of responsibility between employer and laborer disappeared. The impact of these changes by 1830 are illustrated by Hobsbawm and Rudé:

> Instead of the village community (as symbolized by open field and common) there was no enclosure. Instead of mutual aid and social obligation, there was now the Poor Law, administered exclusively by the rulers of the countryside. Instead of family, patronage or custom, there was now the straightforward nexus of wages, which bound the landless to the landed.[146]

With the exception of two disturbances in 1795 and 1816, laborers' discontent over these changes took the form of small, largely ineffective riots directed against unemployment and rising prices. It was not until the late 1820s that the agrarian proletariat offered a serious challenge to the power and authority of the established order.

Rebuilding after the war years, the English economy remained on a line of steady improvement throughout most of the 1820s. Although the benefits of economic prosperity did not normally filter down to the workers, the position of the agrarian laborer did experience some minor advances. In

1828, however, the economy entered a downswing. Not only did rural unemployment and prices increase, but there was simultaneously a surge of opposition by the rate payers against the rising cost of the poor relief system. The worsening of economic conditions certainly contributed to the tension which gave rise to the agrarian movement.

Along with economic distress, the agrarian laborers were once again subjected to an attack on their culture and the defenses it contained. Following the government's denial of social responsibility, the agrarian proletariat, like its counterparts in the towns and urban centers, formed protective communities and institutions wherein tradition and belief in natural law were nurtured. With the government's infringement of these protective communities, and with the disregard of community decisions by employers, we find another source of social tension.[147] The agricultural uprisings which broke across the English countryside between 1828 and 1830 sought to establish both an improved economic position for the rural laborers and a defense of traditional customs. In the attempt to achieve these objectives, the Swing movement weakened the stability of English society.

The Swing riots began as a symbolic expression of discontent over the infringement of laborers' rights. The movement quickly acquired a more practical thrust, however, as its objective became more clearly defined. From a call for the restoration of traditional social relations, the Swing movement shifted to a demand for the redistribution of societal resources. This demand received partial legitimation from fantasy. Originally passed by word of mouth, and in 1830 published in autobiographical form as *The Life and History of Swing, The Kent Rick-Burner,* the Swing myth, discussed earlier, was known throughout rural, working-class communities. As a mixture of metaphor and fact, fantasy and actuality, the 'autobiography' of Swing contained a portrayal of the past as a Golden Age and gave clear expression to the disaffection common throughout the countryside.

Like the Luddite riots, the Swing riots were rooted in and supported by locally based communities. Governmental attempts at acquiring information about and bringing prosecutions against riotous activity were impeded by an uncooperative community. Considerable support was given to the agricultural laborers, not only by village craftsmen—mechanics, smiths, carpenters—but also by many of the remaining small farmers. Still bound by traditional obligations and a sense of social responsibility, and certainly aware of the vulnerability of their position, these groups rallied in support of the agrarian proletariat against the government and industrial capitalist interests.[148]

The Swing movement began in the cereal farming regions, spread westward to Dorset, then northward to Bucks, until it covered much of the English countryside. While Swing riots were evident from 1828, the movement achieved its greatest momentum in 1830, when agricultural protest attained insurrectionary proportions for several months. During this period, some communities and villages participated more vigorously than others in the Swing movement. Since all the agricultural districts experienced similar levels of economic distress and insecurity, this variation in participation must be attributed to other, noneconomic factors. The first such factor concerns the size of the village. Larger villages which served as trade and communication centers were often the scene of the most militant Swing activity. Independence is a second factor. Villages which contained a high proportion of nonfarm laborers (again usually the large villages) were most closely associated with Swing. Nonfarm laborers—such as craftsmen whose traditions and rights were maintained in craft associations, and laborers employed in small-scale industry whose traditions were sustained in community institutions—possessed, if not actual independence, a sence of independence. Contributing to this sense of independence were the Nonconformist religions usually predominant in these communities. Also important was population stability. In those villages where established parish roots had been maintained, where the protective communities had time to grow and take shape, Swing activity was very much in evidence. Finally, those communities with a previous history of labor disturbances were most prominent as participants in the Swing riots.[149]

The Swing riots, then, were far more than 'rebellions of the belly.' The rioters—the overwhelming proportion of whom were between the ages of 18 and 35, many married with families, and most reported to have possessed 'good character and high moral qualities'—were defending their rights, their skills, their traditions and their communities against the infringements of the rich.[150] They were validating themselves and their institutions, and, in so doing, undermining the legitimacy of the established arrangements.

The Swing movement exhibited a fair degree of coordination. Swing contingents in the various districts were linked by a crude yet operative network of communication. More important, however, was the connection afforded by a shared ideological consciousness and a common experience of economic distress. The immediate aims of securing adequate wage and price controls and abolishing agricultural unemployment, as well as the long-range objectives concerned with the partial redistribution of wealth and the establishment of a society built upon social responsibility, were shared by all the communities active in Swing. This ideological coordination did not, however, impinge upon the methods employed by local Swing groups. Depending upon both the structural conditions of the community and the particular issue at hand, wage riots (involving taking control of the market), arson riots (aimed at rick burning), or the destruction of threshing machines would be carried out. The methods employed varied with the occasion and the available opportunities.

In its multiformity of method, the Swing movement represented a slight advance over Luddism. However, the Swing riots did exhibit a more precise selection of targets. The parson, the squire or landlord, and the farmer were the major targets of Swing. The standard used by the rioters to select their targets was clear enough: those people who refused to abide by the decisions agreed to by the community were summarily attacked.[151] While some degree of secrecy was involved in the decision-making process, its utilization was nowhere as extensive as it was with Luddism. This process of target selection differed from that which characterized the eighteenth-century riots. In the preindustrial disturbances, selection was usually confined to a general category of targets not selected by the rioters themselves. Thus, in the anti-Popery riots, the rioters restricted their attacks to rich and influential Catholics; but the initial selection of Catholics as targets was determined externally. In the Swing riots the situation was different: target categories were selected by the rioters themselves in accordance with standards rooted in the laboring community. And these standards—according to which, property was a legitimate object of attack, and life was not—were, as Hobsbawm and Rudé note, "the diametrical opposite of their betters' for whom property was more precious to the law than life."[152]

Just as the aims and targets of Swing were shaped by the community, so too were its organizational features. The organization of Swing activities was based upon village voluntary associations which were originally formed for protective purposes. The collective practices which grew out of these associations contained elements of customary village ritual.[153] Protest activities, which often arose spontaneously in the village marketplace, acquired strength as participants went from house to house and farm to farm mobilizing support.

The government's reaction to the Swing movement, as to Luddism, involved the combined extension of physical and legislative repression. As previously, the major responsibility for repressing the rioters resided with the local magistrates. With the spread of riotous activity, however, government troops were quickly dispatched to the countryside. As a consequence, by 1830 there were over 1,900 rioters in jail awaiting trial for their activities.[154]

Despite this, the riots continued unabated. The seriousness of the situation prompted the government to assume greater responsibility in the suppression of the Swing movement. Commencing in December, 1830, the government authorized a number of special commissions charged with formulating and implementing strict legal restraints which would facilitate the prosecution of rioters. The primary objective of these commissions was to deter further participation by severely punishing the imprisoned rioters.

The first special commission, held in Winchester, set the precedent for those which followed. What is interesting about the report submitted by the commission is its mixture of paternalism and laissez faire. The commissioners justified the severity of their suggested punishments by first arguing that the riots had the effect of dissolving "that bond of mutual kindness which

ought to unite the various classes of society for the common benefit of all."[155]
At the same time, the rioters were interfering with individual—that is,
property-rights. The report notes:

> it is the undoubted right of every subject of the kingdom to
> employ his capital and to conduct his business, whether engaged
> in agriculture, commerce, or manufactures, in such manner
> as he may think most conducive to his own interest, unless
> where the wisdom of Parliament has controlled him by legis-
> lative restrictions.[156]

Advanced in this dual justification is the distinction between the public and
the private—the former characterized by mutual kindness, the latter by
individualized interests. In order for the benefits of the public realm to be
established, the rights inherent in the private realm first had to be secured.

With this aim in mind the commission began its work. The most crucial
aspect of this endeavor entailed the redefinition of a capital felony. The
commission suggested that the following acts be categorized as capital felonies:

> 1st. Such as arise out of the statues passed for the prevention
> and suppression of riotous and tumultuous assemblies.
> 2nd. The crime of arson.
> 3rd. Robbery from the person.
> 4th. Robbery or stealing in dwelling-houses to which may be
> added other felonies *not* capital; viz.
> 1st. The sending of threatening letters.
> 2nd. The destruction of or damaging with intent to destroy
> or render useless threshing-machines, or any machine or en-
> gine prepared for or employed in any manufacture.[157]

The results of these proceedings, once accepted by the government, had
an immediate impact. Arbitrary arrests became frequent, and those arrested
usually were given severe sentences.[158] It was at this time that the local police
force was transformed into a permanent agency of control. More important,
however, were the implications of the extension of criminal law. Now, the
demand for wage and price controls (that is, for adequacy of response) was
defined as robbery, and those issuing such demands were subject to capital
punishment. In effect, traditionally sanctioned customs and practices were
declared illegal, and in some cases their exercise was punishable by death.
Thus, the government's reaction entailed not only the suppression of Swing
riots but certain aspects of working-class culture as well.

The achievements of the Swing movement must be seen as limited ones.
Swing activities undoubtedly contributed to a number of parliamentary
reforms concerned primarily with poor relief policy and practice. Minimal

wage concessions were won and maintained for several years after the termination of Swing. In many districts the use of threshing machines declined, effecting a partial reduction of rural unemployment.[159] The major achievements of Swing—the delegitimation of governmental and monarchical authority, and the challenge to state and middle-class power—were short-lived. The government, largely through repressive measures and partially through occasional concessions, had the Swing movement effectively contained by 1831.

In *The Village Labourer,* the Hammonds refer to the agrarian riots as "The Last Labourers' Revolt." This description receives some support from the findings of Hobsbawm and Rudé. They observe that, after the suppression of Swing, the discontent of the agrarian proletariat was expressed in unplanned, isolated acts of terrorism. Revenge became the primary objective. With the termination of Swing, which was accompanied by the suppression of worker traditions and institutions, there is "a new note of embittered despair, a dark atmosphere of hatred and vengeance, which is on the whole absent in 1830."[160] It was a despair born from the lack of hope and in the absence of alternatives; in short, it was a despair rooted in the emerging one-dimensionality.

Industrial protest With the passage of the Combination Acts at the turn of the century, workers' associations were trapped in a matrix of severe restrictions, and trade unions were declared illegal. Disguised as Friendly Societies and community clubs, these associations and clubs prevailed. Rooted in the informal institutions of the working-class community, they exhibited a remarkable organizational continuity. As Turner observes, despite formal sanctions, the "essential work-place units survived informally . . . and could maintain their links with each other; the re-erection of an open organization was an easy matter."[161] In this way the mobilization capabilities of the communities were preserved.

From 1800 to 1819 the emerging industrial districts such as Lancashire, Leeds, and Sheffield witnessed numerous industrial disturbances. Beginning in 1804 and lasting until 1813, the Lancashire cotton weavers participated in a series of strikes. In 1814, framework knitters, often in conjunction with Luddism, actively opposed the mill owner and the magistrate through turnouts and riots. In 1819 the colliers at Lancashire, St. Helens, Nottingham, Leeds, and Tyneside vigorously protested the absence of economic regulations and the arbitrary, nonresponsive character of the decision-making process.[162]

These disturbances shared at least two features in common. They were locally based and, because of this, easily repressed. Although there were several attempts during this period to organize regional and even national associations of workers, none succeeded.[163] Unlike the village communities, the industrial communities located in the large manufacturing areas were occupationally homogeneous. While this homogeneity was important to the creation of internal solidarity, it often impeded coordination between communities and different occupational groups. Thus, as Turner finds, older occupations such as handweaving gave rise to defensive associations which tended to protest in periods of economic distress. The newer occupations, less concerned with the protection of traditional craft standards, formed aggressive associations inclined to become active in periods of economic boom.[164] Unable to overcome these differences, industrial disturbances remained confined to isolated localities and, as a result, were quickly suppressed.

The period between 1820 and 1830 was, in the words of G. D. H. Cole, "the seeding-time of working-class ideas and organizations."[165] During these years the number and intensity of industrial protest activities declined, but this decline was accompanied by three important developments: the emergence of a working class press; the repeal of the Combination Acts; and a renewed alliance between the working and middle classes. A viable working-class press began to take shape following the Napoleonic Wars. The major obstacle faced by the working-class press was governmental repression. With the Six Acts, the government imposed heavy stamp duties upon newspapers, with the intent of raising their cost beyond the means of the workers. Violating this law, the working-class press continued unstamped publication; and, despite several setbacks, at least a dozen papers and periodicals had widespread circulation in working-class communities by 1830.[166]

By the late 1820s, the unstamped press emerged as the primary medium of communication among the various working-class groups and communities. Carrying announcements and reports of local meetings and activities, it encouraged and facilitated cross-regional and cross-industry contact. Through the working-class press, the factory worker, the artisan, and the builder were able to define a set of common interests. Beyond this, the unstamped press acted as a link between the industrial associations and the rural participants in the Swing Movement.[167] Serving as a nucleus for the still disparate industrial communities, the unstamped press focused on both immediate and long-range problems. Not only did it engage in fund raising to aid particular communities in times of distress; it also sought to provide ideological coherence. Examined in a larger context, local grievances were shown to have societal causes and, consequently, remedies which could be made possible by concerted and organized action on a national scale.[168] In this way, the working-class press helped to unify the industrial laborers, despite existing variations in the conditions of their work.

What enhanced the ability of the unstamped press to serve as a medium of communication for the geographically and occupationally disparate workers' associations was the repeal of the Combination Acts in 1824. Soon after, most of the existing organizations shed their clandestine modus operandi, and numerous new organizations, largely trade unions, were created. Although the repeal was amended in 1825 to limit the activities of the rapidly expanding associations, the 1825 act did little to impede the increasingly militant practices of these groups.

The repeal of the Combination Acts received steady and significant support from middle-class circles. Adherents to the new economics insisted that the repeal would have the effect of reducing, not intensifying, trade union activity. Their argument was founded on

> the idea that wages were ruled by the inexorable laws of Political Economy, and that Trade Union action was powerless to affect them save within a narrowly restricted field. . . . [Hence, the] freedom to combine would soon teach the workers the futility of kicking against the pricks, and induce them rather to collaborate with the employers in increasing the 'wages fund'—which depended on the employers' profits—than to wage a useless war against Capitalism.[169]

Although guided by different aims, the working and middle classes did form a coalition in support of repeal. This alliance was operative several years later when the question of political reform arose. As we have seen, workers' associations, assuming that universal suffrage constituted a partial yet progressive step toward societal reorganization, were active in the agitation for the Reform Bill. Although this support eventually was betrayed, the partcipation of workers' associations was not without beneficial results. By closely observing the organizational activities of such middle-class societies as the Birmingham Political Union and the National Political Union, the workers gained a recognition of the importance of a coordinated national organization.

These three developments occurring in the 1820s had a forceful impact upon industrial protest activity. On the organizational level, workers' associations became more open and better able to establish contact with one another. Ideologically, a more coherent and unified set of objectives began to emerge. Combining the communalism of Robert Owen with Ricardo's labor theory of value, the industrial workers further distinguished themselves from the 'unproductive classes' of society, and demanded a full appropriation of the products of their labor—or, in other words, an end to exploitation and capitalism.[170] By 1829 a number of large unions had been formed; and during the next several years attempts were made to organize them into a general union capable of realizing these demands.

It is possible, then, to talk of a working-class movement by 1829. The great industrial and political agitation which arose at this time resulted in the formation of the National Association for the Protection of Labour, in 1830. Centered in Manchester, N.A.P.L. was initially an affiliation of twenty trade unions, but within a year grew to represent 150 unions comprising 100,000 members. Although the majority of members were textile workers, the potters, millwrights, blacksmiths, mechanics, and miners were also represented. The association's paper, the *Voice of the People,* attained a weekly circulation of 30,000 by 1831.[171]

Unable to financially sponsor a general turnout of its members, N.A.P.L. took the route of encouraging successive individual turnouts by the member trades. Initially achieving moderate success, this practice eventually failed when the employers agreed to a general lockout. After several months of intransigence, N.A.P.L. funds decreased to the point where continued assistance to the striking workers was impossible, and the workers were compelled to return to their jobs. Still convinced of the need for a general union, the N.A.P.L. set out to expand its base.

The primary impediment to the establishment of a general industrial union was the Yorkshire Clothiers' Union. The workers' movement in Yorkshire, unlike the one in Lancashire, retained its secrecy after the repeal of the Combination Acts. Two closely related reasons explain why the woolen and worsted workers of this region continued operating as a 'secret order.' The Yorkshire workers had a long history of protest activity, a history which extended throughout the first quarter of the nineteenth century. Given the illegality of these activities during this period, the workers were compelled to develop clandestine organizations complete with secret oaths. As these organizations spread throughout the district, their accomplishments grew. Two consequences derived from this success. The workers decided after 1824 to maintain the clandestine form of organization; and the government and the employers intensified their attacks on the Yorkshire unions.[172] In response to the increased repression, the Yorkshire workers' associations became even more secretive and subsequently more opposed to the open organization proposed by N.A.P.L.

The gap between the Yorkshire and Lancashire movements was bridged in 1834 with the formation, largely under the direction of Robert Owen, of the Grand National Consolidated Trades Union. The aims of the G.N.C.T.U. were clearly insurrectionary. "Its immediate object," Cole notes

> was nothing less than the entire supersession of Capitalism and competition by a Co-operative system of workers' control. It aimed, not only at controlling industry, but at superseding Parliament and the local governing bodies and at becoming the actual government of the country.[173]

In this way the G.N.C.T.U. synthesized the goals and tactics of cooperation and trade unionism.

By 1832 the N.A.P.L. had been severely weakened, and its place of prominence in the Lancashire movement became occupied by the Operative Builders' Union. Known for its aggressive orientation, the O.B.U. had at this time a membership of 40,000, and its influence extended from Lancashire to Birmingham. The O.B.U. served as the basis of the G.N.C.T.U. which claimed a membership of 500,000 in 1834.[174] Contributing to this membership was the Yorkshire Trades' Union movement which, sympathetic to the Owenite cooperative movement, affiliated with the general union.

Owenism received wide currency among the industrial workers, and it contributed significantly to the insurrectionary phase of trade unionism. At its beginning around 1820, the Owenite movement engendered a radicalism strongly tinged with paternalism. Owen's scheme for a society organized about villages of cooperation would be implemented, he felt, by the governing class: the new society would be forged by reason, not by class struggle; it would be made not upon the ruins of the old but outside the boundaries of the old. Thus, while Owenism challenged and criticized industrial capitalist society, it constituted no serious threat to that society.

Initially, Owenism gained its strongest support among artisans; and in 1824 the London artisans formed the London Cooperative Society. Several years later, this base of support widened to include workers from all occupations. What attracted such widespread support was the Owenite doctrine which consisted of a curious blend of millenarianism and an ideology of work discipline. It was, in a sense, a recognition that the tools of industrialism—the factory system—could, if properly used, allow the workers to bring about a secular millenium. Underlying this recognition was a celebration of the cooperative village, a celebration which borrowed from the myth of the Golden Age and its glorification of eighteenth-century village life. This concern with the past was directed toward the present. As Thompson observes:

> So far from being backward-looking in its outlook, Owenism was the first of the great social doctrines to grip the imagination of the masses in this period. . . . What was at issue was not the machine so much as the profit-motive; not the size of the industrial enterprise but the control of the social capital behind it.[175]

It was this emphasis on collective control and cooperation, this stress on infusing social responsibility into industrial society, which gave Owenism its appeal to the artisan, the skilled laborer, and the industrial poor. Restorative of traditional obligations, yet respectful of recent industrial achievements, Owenism produced a critique of the prevailing arrangements which, because it appealed to both sentiment and reason, won the support of the underemployed and the relatively secure craftsmen, the unskilled and the highly skilled laborers.

Prior to 1832, the Owenite movement avoided political and even industrial disputes, preferring to work outside the prevailing social arrangements. The aim of cooperative societies, rapidly multiplying in the late 1820s, was not the organization of trade combinations but the creation of self-sufficient communities capable of bringing to fruition the conditions necessary for the equality of their members. Writing in 1831, Alexander Campbell offered a useful account of the operation of these communities.

> These societies are generally composed of the working classes; and their capital, held in small shares, payable in installments, is to be applied to the following objects: The purchasing at wholesale prices of such articles of daily consumption as the members require, and retailing out to them and others at the usual retail prices, adding all profits to stock for the further object of giving employment for members who may be either out of work or otherwise inefficiently employed, and thereby still increasing their capital to obtain their ultimate object—the possession of land, the erection of comfortable dwellings and asylums for the aged and infirm, and seminaries of learning for all.[176]

The Owenite movement remained distinct from other workers' movements until 1832 when, in the aftermath of the Reform Act, workers' agitation intensified. In the midst of this renewed activity, Robert Owen became convinced of the need for concerted organization, and launched his plan for a "grand general union." At the core of this plan was cooperative production. Owen approached the trade unions with a proposal for establishing a National Equitable Labour Exchange which would provide jobs and goods to workers as an alternative to strike pay, and would thereby enhance the position of the unions during turnout periods. Ultimately, these enterprises of cooperative production and exchange would serve as the basis for workers' control in industry.[177] On the basis of cooperation the G.N.C.T.U. was created.

That the G.N.C.T.U. accomplished only limited objectives in its two years of existence is partially attributable to the existing economic downturn. More important, perhaps, are two other factors. First, the leaders of the organization, confident that its strength would continue to increase, followed a gradual line of attack which combined industrial disturbances with the development of a societal-wide cooperative program. They assumed, incorrectly it turned out, that the G.N.C.T.U. would prevail for more than two years. The second impediment is found in the increasingly repressive measures applied by the government against the union since its inception. Parallel to the government's attacks were those of the middle class.

With the emergence of militant trade union activity in 1829, employers combined within the various trades to initiate a series of lockouts which had the effect, usually after several months, of weakening the incipient unionism. The lockout continued to be used against the G.N.C.T.U., but now more systematically in the context of a general anti-union policy. One purpose of the lockout was to force returning workers to sign statements renouncing any further union activity. Employers in Leicester, Lancashire, Leeds, and Derby adhered to this policy. The resolutions passed at a meeting of employers at Derby in December, 1833 typify the general objectives of the policy.

> That, as great numbers of the workmen in Derby have joined the Trades Union, with a view to control their employers, and for purposes which the latter believe to be destructive to their interests and utterly subversive of that free agency which the Unionists claim for themselves, these employers are compelled by necessity to unite in their own defense, and do now resolve, unanimously. That each of them will immediately cease to employ every man who is a member of the Trades' Union, and will not receive or take back into his service any man who continues to be a member of that Union, or of any other Union having similar objects.[178]

The employers' position in this struggle was enhanced by the government which encouraged the adoption of measures designed to suppress union activity. Beyond this, the government informed the employers that they could rely on it to "take the most prompt and efficient measures to repress disorder."[179] With explicit government support, the anti-union movement rapidly spread throughout the industrial areas of England.

As the lockout began to be used in response to and, in many cases, in anticipation of union activity, the capacity of the G.N.C.T.U. to fund the growing number of unemployed workers was weakened immensely. When more militant practices were followed they were met immediately by harsh governmental repression. In 1834 six Dorchester laborers were arrested and found guilty of administering secret oaths. For this 'crime,' the six—later known as the Tolpuddle Martyrs—were sentenced and transported out of the country.[180] The stringency of this sentence symbolized the government's new policy toward convicted workers. This, combined with the employers' ability to maintain enduring lockouts, undermined the G.N.C.T.U. When many of the crafts—such as the masons—broke with the union, it was reduced to a largely ineffectual organization.

One crucial factor which impaired the general union's response was rooted in its organizational structure. Both for tactical and financial reasons, the national agency of the G.N.C.T.U. retained ultimate control over union activities. Strikes and more militant practices required the authorization of the national office. As a consequence, the spontaneity characteristic of earlier forms of protest activity was extremely difficult. The immediate result was factionalism. Operating independently, the remaining unions were faced with three options: protest and suppression; the formation of cooperative societies; or, accommodation to the prevailing arrangements. Most opted for the third; a few for the second; and none for the first.

In the process of accommodation, the traditions and institutions of the working-class community deteriorated: concern became focused on the present, not the past and future. When trade unions were rebuilt in the late 1830s they were conceived along narrow lines. Exclusively oriented to particular trades, and expressing moderate aims, the new unions resolutely prepared themselves to become parts of industrial capitalist society. The Cooperation Movement experienced a similar transformation. "The new Co-operation was no longer a gospel of revolt, much less of revolution. [It] developed as . . . a field for the investment of working-class savings as well as an expression of the Victorian ideals of self-help."[181] Thus, in the absence of communal traditions and institutions, the workers' movement devolved into organizational conservatism. But this is the topic of the next chapter.

SUMMARY

Throughout the first third of the nineteenth century, the English working class was on the threshold of revolution. In the late 1820s and early 1830s workers in agricultural, industrializing and industrial areas engaged in numerous forms of protest activity, all aimed at undermining the then solidifying foundations of industrial capitalism. Given the uneven development of industrial capitalism, there were significant differences in the organization, the grievances and the demands of the workers' social protests. In spite of these differences, a working-class movement developed. The movement was often shapeless, lacking both established boundaries and effective channels of communication. Yet the movement also exhibited a certain opaque unity, a unity which derived not so much from organizational links as from a shared ideological consciousness which provided a sense of historical continuity.[182] A class consciousness or, in Lockwood's terms, a proletarian consciousness was shared by the Luddites, the Swing rioters, and the unionists. From the symbolism of 'Ned Ludd,' 'Captain Swing,' and the Owenite 'village of cooperation' emerged a similar image of the good society, one which directly repudiated industrial capitalism. The factory worker, the artisan, and the dispossessed farmer shared a common objective: the establishment of a society built upon social responsibility. On the basis of this objective, which looked through the past to the future, the diverse protest activities of this period came together to constitute a working-class revolt.

The maintenance of tradition in working-class communities and institutions allowed a sense of integrated experience. When, with the onset of industrial capitalism, social responsibility was denied, the proletariat, both in the countryside and in the manufacturing centers, developed alternative arrangements and parallel institutions to secure its traditional protections. The regulation of wages and prices, the protection of workers in times of unemployment, now denied by the government, became the task of the workers themselves. In their communal institutions, the workers preserved the norm of reciprocity which had regulated relationships in the eighteenth century.

By 1810 the contradiction between industrial capitalism and the communal traditions of the working-class community greatly intensified. The continuing elimination of customary controls converged with systematic efforts to destroy these communal institutions. The intent was not only to achieve a free labor market but one comprised of disciplined, reliable, and motivated laborers. The source of this contradiction resided in the government's shift from traditional orientations to free-floating resources as the key element of legitimation. Partially determined by the rising governmental expenditures incurred in the wars against France, this shift initiated a significant social realignment. The middle class was becoming a junior partner in the decision-making process: a new apparatus of domination, one which would span State and Society by 1850, was launched.

Confronted with this new, more extensive form of domination, the workers retained their traditions and, with them, the standards of legitimacy incongruous with the prevailing arrangements. The denial of social responsibility was negated by practical reference to ritual and custom. The past was imaginatively reconstructed as a Golden Age and used to critically evaluate the present. In the workers' struggle against the present, this portrayal of the past was transformed into a portrayal of the future as the beneficial features of the present were added to it. In this way the negation was negated. The critical standards rooted in tradition became future-oriented, transcendent of the present.

What is important to recognize about this process of transcendence is that it involves both ontological necessity and moral imperatives. The tendencies contained (ontologically rooted) in English society at this time could not be actualized merely as a matter of historical necessity. They could only be actualized by those for whom they were meaningful. The ideological consciousness of the workers, precisely because it was linked to communal traditions, made the communal tendencies located in society meaningful to the beleaguered workers. They fought to actualize these tendencies; that is, they struggled for a better society because that society *ought* to be. Although the transcendent criteria that guided social protest reflected real structural possibilities, they acquired a motivating force only after they were made meaningful in terms of working-class culture. The dialectic which occurred was not confined to the substructure: its dynamic was not determined by ontological necessity alone. Rather, it was a dialectic between structure and culture, wherein ontological necessity became subjectively meaningful.

That there was no working-class revolution in England during this period goes unquestioned. The argument presented here is that the working class was on the verge of revolution. The reasons why a revolution never materialized are clear enough. The organizations comprising the working-class movement were new and somewhat immature; they lacked sufficient funds and other resources. Communication among them was established but generally inadequate; societal-wide coordination was difficult. When confronted by a cohesive, well-stocked, and fully armed enemy—the government and the middle class—the workers' movement, not surprisingly, was easily contained. What is surprising, however, is the virtual absence of later working-class attempts to make industrial capitalist society more responsive and responsible. Why was it that hope gave way to despair, and struggle guided by objectives was replaced by revenge? And, in turn, why was it that attempts at undermining industrial capitalism were converted into attempts at becoming an integral part of that system? What happened to the transcendent criteria that previously shaped social conflict? In preparing to answer these questions in the next chapter, we would do well to consider the observation of the Hammonds:

> in an age of such rapid invention and development it was easy to slip into the belief that the one task of the human race was to wrest her secrets from nature, and to forget how much of the history of mankind is the history of the effort to find a tolerable basis for a common life.[183]

NOTES

1. See Asa Briggs, "The Language of 'Class' in Early Nineteenth Century England," *Essays in Labour History* (London, 1960), pp. 43-73.

2. E. P. Thompson, *The Making of the English Working Class* (New York, 1963), p. 424.

3. R. K. Webb, *The British Working Class Reader* (New York, 1955), pp. 38-41 documents the wide working-class audience received by Paine's writings.

4. See Nigel Young, "Prometheans or Troglodytes? The English Working Class and the Dialectics of Incorporation," *Berkeley Journal of Sociology* 12 (1967). Also, Raymond Williams, *The Long Revolution* (New York, 1961), pp. 325-328.

5. Young, "Prometheans or Troglodytes?", p. 14.

6. Phyllis Deane and W. A. Cole, *British Economic Growth, 1688-1959* (Cambridge, 1962), p. 80.

7. E. A. Wrigley, "The Process of Modernization and the Industrial Revolution in England," *The Journal of Interdisciplinary History* 3 (1972): 226-227.

8. Deane and Cole, *British Economic Growth,* p. 170.

9. A. D. Gayer, et al., *The Growth and Fluctuation of the British Economy* (New York, 1953), p. 43.

10. See Deane and Cole, *British Economic Growth,* pp. 22-27.

11. Ibid., p. 262.

12. C. B. Macpherson, *The Political Theory of Possessive Individualism,* (New York, 1962), p. 55. While a model of the "possessive market society" was systematically developed by the early eighteenth century, it was not until the end of the century that its specific features began to be implemented on a wide scale.

13. See E. J. Hobsbawm, "Customs, Wages, and Work-Load in Nineteenth-Century Industry," in *Essays in Labour History,* p. 113.

14. Macpherson, *The Political Theory of Possessive Individualism,* pp. 264-265.

15. See Arthur Redford, *Labour Migration in England, 1800-1850* (Manchester, 1964), pp. 41, 186. Also see Zygmunt Bauman, *Between Class and Elite* (Manchester, 1972), pp. 7-8.

16. E. J. Hobsbawm, "The Standard of Living During the Industrial Revolution: 1964), pp. 41, 186. Also see Zygmunt Bauman, *Between Class and Elite* (Man-

17. See Hobsbawm, "Custom, Wages, and Work-Load," pp. 115-120.

18. As quoted in Daphne Simon, "Master and Servant," in *Essays in Labour History* (London, 1960), pp. 197-198.

19. See Mantoux, *The Industrial Revolution in the Eighteenth Century,* pp. 264-265.

20. See R. M. Hartwell, *The Industrial Revolution and Economic Growth* (London, 1971), pp. 127-128.

21. Deane and Cole, *British Economic Growth,* pp. 144-145. Also see Phyllis Deane, "Capital Formation in Britain Before the Railway Age," *Economic Development and Cultural Change* 10, 3 (1961).

22. Deane and Cole, *British Economic Growth,* p. 304.

23. Ibid., p. 366.

24. Ibid., pp. 358-364.

25. For specific investment figures see Gayer, et al., *The Growth and Fluctuation of the British Economy,* pp. 66-69.

26. Ibid., p. 77.

27. Ibid., pp. 406-440. On the adaptation of the legal system to the economy see Hartwell, *The Industrial Revolution and Economic Growth,* pp. 244-250.

28. Ibid., pp. 174-211.

29. Dorothy Marshall, *Industrial England, 1776-1851* (New York, 1973), p. 92.

30. See Sidney Pollard, *The Genesis of Modern Management* (Baltimore, 1965), pp. 22-23.

31. Ibid., p. 207.

32. Ibid., p. 213.

33. Ibid., pp. 213-214. Also E. P. Thompson, "Time, Work-Discipline, and Industrial Capitalism," *Past and Present* 38 (December 1967): 76.

34. See Sidney Pollard, "Factory Discipline in the Industrial Revolution," *Economic History Review* 16, 2 (1963): 260-269.

35. See Stephen Marglin, "What Do Bosses Do? The Origins and Functions of Hierarchy in Capitalist Development" (Research Paper, Harvard University, May, 1971), pp. 3-11.

36. Ibid., p. 4.

37. Ibid., p. 44.

38. Thompson, "Time, Work-Discipline, and Industrial Capitalism," p. 60.

39. Ibid., p. 69.

40. Ibid., p. 61.

41. Keith Thomas, "Work and Leisure in Pre-Industrial Society," *Past and Present* 29 (December, 1964): 62. Also see Sebastian de Grazia, *Of Time, Work, and Leisure* (New York, 1962), p. 265.

42. The problem receives some consideration in Arnold Thackery, "Natural Knowledge in a Cultural Context: The Manchester Model," *American Historical Review* 79 (1974): 672-709.

43. See Thompson, "Time, Work-Discipline, and Industrial Capitalism," p. 80.

44. As quoted in Mantoux, *The Industrial Revolution,* p. 270.

45. J. M. Norris, "Samuel Garbett and the Early Development of Industrial Lobbying in Great Britain," *Economic History Review* 10, No. 3 (1958): 450-460.

46. See Hobsbawm, "The Standard of Living During the Industrial Revolution: A Discussion," *Labouring Men* (London, 1964), pp. 120-125.

47. As quoted in T. K. Derry, "The Repeal of the Apprenticeship Clauses and the Statute of Artificers," *Economic History Review* 3 (1931): 86.

48. See Patricia Hollis, *The Pauper Press* (London, 1970), pp. 14-22 and Joel Wiener, *The War of the Unstamped* (Ithaca, 1969), pp. 20-51, 115-136, 237-239.

49. Reinhard Bendix, *Work and Authority in Industry* (New York, 1956), p. 88.

50. Sidney and Beatrice Webb, *The History of Trade Unionism* (London, 1935), p. 53.

51. "Report of the Select Committee on the Cotton Weavers' Petition, 1808," as quoted in Marshall, *Industrial England,* p. 145.

52. Bendix, *Work and Authority in Industry,* p. 78.

53. See Elie Halevy, *The Growth of Philosophic Radicalism* (New York: 1928), p. 207, and H. L. Beales, "The Historical Context of the Essay on Population," in *Introduction to Malthus* (London, 1953), p. 13.

54. See Redford, *Labour Migration in England,* pp. 81-92.

55. "Report of Labourers' Wages, 1824," as quoted ibid., p. 83.

56. Malthus as quoted in James Huzel, "Malthus, the Poor Law, and Population in Early Nineteenth-Century England," *Economic History Review* 22 (1969): 432. Also see Thomas Malthus, *An Essay on the Principle of Population and Its Effects on Human Happiness* (London, 1890), pp. 458-459.

57. Huzel, "Malthus, the Poor Law, and Population," pp. 433-437.

58. G. D. H. Cole and Raymond Postgate, *The British Common People* (New York, 1961), p. 276. Also see Polanyi, *The Great Transformation,* pp. 255-260.

59. Frederick Engels, *The Condition of the Working Class in England, 1844* (Stanford, 1958), p. 320.

60. Halevy, *The Growth of Philosophic Radicalism,* p. 477.

61. See C. B. Macpherson, "Democratic Theory: Ontology and Technology," in *Political Theory and Social Change* (New York, 1967), pp. 206-209.

62. Ibid., p. 211.

63. The nature of these disagreements is examined in Halevy, *The Growth of Philosophic Radicalism,* pp. 192-212, p. 285.

64. Ibid., p. 37.

65. Ibid., p. 180.

66. (John Bowring as quoted) Ibid., p. 366.

67. Ibid., p. 127.

68. See David Ricardo, *Principles of Political Economy and Taxation* (London, 1891), p. 1.

69. On another level, Ricardo's tripartite division of society, in terms of which it charges the landowners with parasitism, reflects the growing class antagonism of the period. See Harold Perkin, *The Origins of Modern English Society, 1780-1880* (Toronto, 1969), pp. 215-223.

70. Hannah Arendt, *The Human Condition* (Chicago, 1958), pp. 22-78.

71. Halevy, *The Growth of Philosophic Radicalism,* p. 508.

72. On the connection between this aspect of Philosophic Radicalism and Adam Smith's doctrine, see William Grampp, "On Manufacturing and Development," *Economic Development and Cultural Change* 18, 3 (1970): 452.

73. John O'Neill, *Sociology As a Skin Trade* (New York, 1972), p. 22.

74. See Jürgen Habermas, *Theory and Practice* (Boston, 1973).

75. Ibid., p. 85, and Halevy, *The Growth of Philosophic Radicalism,* pp. 431, 494-500.

76. See Christopher Bickford, "The Improving Principle: Changing Attitudes Toward Social Mobility in England, 1700-1860" (dissertation, University of Connecticut, 1971), p. 310.

77. See Kenneth Walker, "The Classical Economists and the Factory Acts," *Journal of Economic History* 1 (1941): 174. A series of factory acts eventually were passed before mid-century. However, it would be incorrect to view these acts as a reaffirmation of social responsibility. As we shall see in the next chapter, these acts are better understood in the context of the increasing tension between the aristocracy and the middle class.

78. Webb, *The British Working Class Reader,* p. 99.

79. Sidney and Beatrice Webb, *The History of Trade Unionism,* p. 47.

80. See Halevy, *The Growth of Philosophic Radicalism,* p. 187. Paine develops his attack on Burke in *The Rights of Man* (New York, 1908), pp. 1-21.

81. Halevy, *The Growth of Philosophic Radicalism,* p. 209.

82. (Godwin as quoted) Ibid., p. 215.

83. Thomas, "Work and Leisure," p. 63.

84. Thompson, *The Making of the English Working Class,* p. 194, emphasis added.

85. J. L. Hammond, "The Industrial Revolution and Discontent," *Economic History Review* 2 (1930): 227-228.

86. W. O. Henderson and W. H. Chaloner, "Editor's Note," in Engels, *The Condition of the Working Class in England,* p. xiii.

87. See Asa Briggs, "The Language of 'Class,' " pp. 43-73.

88. H. A. Turner, *Trade Union Growth, Structure, and Policy* (Toronto, 1962), p. 85.

89. Thompson, *The Making of the English Working Class,* p. 514.

90. David Lockwood, "Sources of Variation in Working Class Images of Society," *Sociological Review* 14 (May, 1966): 251.

91. Aristocratic control of Parliament continued even after the 1832 Reform Act. See G. Bingham Powell, "Incremental Democratization: The British Reform Act of 1832," *Crisis, Choice, and Change* (Boston, 1973), pp. 109-110.

92. See Cole and Filson, *British Working Class Movements,* p. 74.

93. Lord Melbourne as quoted in J. L. and Barbara Hammond, *The Skilled Labourer* (London, 1936), p. 45.

94. Cole and Postgate, *The British Common People,* p. 173.

95. See A. Aspinall, *The Early English Trade Unions* (London, 1949), Ch. 19; and Thompson, *The Making of the English Working Class,* pp. 507-508.

96. See Cole and Filson, *British Working Class Movements,* pp. 167-170.

97. The organizational implications of the Metropolitan Police Act are examined in Charles Reith, *British Police and the Democratic Ideal* (London, 1943), pp. 31-40. For the tremendous upsurge in the concern with crime between 1812 and 1828 see J. J. Tobias, *Nineteenth-Century Crime in England* (New York, 1972), p. 100.

98. See Roger Lane, "Crime and the Industrial Revolution: British and American Views," *Journal of Social History* 7, 3 (1974): 290.

99. Allan Silver, "The Demand for Order in Civil Society," *Criminal Justice in America* (Boston, 1974), p. 160.

100. Karl Marx and Frederick Engels, *The Communist Manifesto* (Peking, 1970), pp. 41, 43.

101. Ibid., p. 43.

102. Gwyn Williams, *Artisans and Sans-Culottes* (New York, 1969), p. 66.

103. See Henry Collins, "The London Corresponding Society," *Democracy and the Labour Movement,* p. 110. For a specific breakdown of the trades represented in the L.C.S. see Cole and Postgate, *The British Common People,* p. 153 and Thompson, *The Making of the English Working Class,* pp. 155-156.

104. George Veitch, *The Genesis of Parliamentary Reform* (London, 1913), p. 206.

105. (L.C.S. address as quoted) Ibid.

106. See Williams, *Artisans and Sans-Culottes,* p. 9.

107. See Collins, "The London Corresponding Society," p. 114.

108. Williams, *Artisans and Sans-Culottes,* p. 99.

109. Hollis, *Class and Conflict in Nineteenth Century England,* p. xxi.

110. Briggs. "The Language of 'Class,' " p. 60.

111. Powell, "Incremental Democratization," pp. 122-123 characterizes this and all middle-class-working-class alliances between 1815 and 1820 as 'defensive coalitions.'

112. See Thompson, *The Making of the English Working Class,* pp. 827-828; Briggs, *The Making of Modern England* (New York, 1949), p. 245; and A. L. Morton and George Tate, *The British Labour Movement, 1770-1920* (London, 1956), p. 78.

113. A good summary of franchise restrictions prior to 1832 is found in G. D. H. Cole, *British Working Class Politics, 1832-1914* (London, 1941), pp. 3-14.

114. H. Cockburn as quoted in Briggs, "The Language of 'Class,' " p. 56.

115. See Morton and Tate, *The British Labour Movement,* p. 62.

116. Thompson, *The Making of the English Working Class,* p. 817. Also see Powell, "Incremental Democratization," pp. 128, 136.

117. See George Rudé, "Protest and Punishment in Nineteenth-Century Britain," *Albion* 5, 1 (1973): 3-5.

118. See Herbert Reid, "American Social Science in the Politics of Time and the Crisis of Technocorporate Society: Toward A Critical Phenomenology," *Politics and Society* 3, 2 (1973): 202-203.

119. See Michael Anderson, *Family Structure in Nineteenth Century Lancashire* (Cambridge, 1972).

120. Herbert Marcuse, *Eros and Civilization* (New York, 1955), p. 135.

121. Ibid., p. 212.

122. See Victor Gioscia, "On Social Time," in *The Future of Time,* pp. 73-141.

123. On the Ned Ludd myth see Malcolm Thomis, *The Luddites* (New York, 1972);

the myth of Captain Swing is presented in "The Life and HIstory of Swing, the Kent Rick-Burner," in K. Carpenter, ed., *The Rising of the Agricultural Labourers* (New York, 1969); the appeal of the Owenite 'Villages of cooperation' is discussed in Thompson, *The Making of the English Working Class,* pp. 864-866.

124. "The Life and History of Swing," pp. 6-8.

125. Thompson, *The Making of the English Working Class,* p. 552.

126. See Robert Wearmouth, *Some Working Class Movements of the Nineteenth Century* (London, 1948), chapter 2; and Hobsbawm, *Primitive Rebels,* chapter 7.

127. E. J. Hobsbawm and George Rudé, *Captain Swing* (New York, 1969), p. 211.

128. Marshall, *Industrial England,* p. 84.

129. In view of the strong increase in criminal commitments during this period, many argue that certain criminal activities be classified as a type of working-class social protest. Crimes such as poaching, arson, destruction of manufacture goods, and breaches of the peace are regarded as politically motivated pursuits. See Rudé, "Protest and Punishment"; J. J. Tobias, *Crime and Industrial Society in the 19th Century* (Oxford, 1967); J. L. and Barbara Hammond, *The Village Labourer* (London, 1936), pp. 162-175; and A. J. Peacock, *Bread or Blood* (London, 1965), pp. 38-54.

130. E. J. Hobsbawm, "The Machine Breakers," *Past and Present* 1 (February, 1952): 58-59.

131. See J. L. and Barbara Hammond, *The Skilled Labourer,* pp. 257-258.

132. Frank Darvall, *Popular Disturbances and Public Order in Regency England* (London, 1934), p. 5.

133. *Nottingham Review,* December 6, 1811, as quoted in J. L. and B. Hammond, *The Skilled Labourer,* p. 227.

134. Thompson, *The Making of the English Working Class,* p. 549.

135. See Hobsbawm, "The Machine Breakers," pp. 63-64; and Thomis, *The Luddites,* pp. 154-155.

136. Thomis, *The Luddites,* p. 145.

137. *Leeds Mercury,* July 11, 1812 as quoted in Wearmouth, *Some Working Class Movements,* pp. 6-7.

138. Darvall, *Popular Disturbances and Public Order,* pp. 177-185.

139. As quoted in Peacock, *Bread or Blood,* p. 65.

140. Ibid., pp. 110-115.

141. See Darvall, *Popular Disturbances and Public Order,* p. 180.

142. Ibid., pp. 23-26.

143. See J. L. and B. Hammond, *The Skilled Labourer,* p. 267.

144. See Darvall, *Popular Disturbances and Public Order,* p. 2.

145. J. L. and B. Hammond, *The Village Labourer,* p. 82.

146. Hobsbawm and Rudé, *Captain Swing,* pp. 36-37.

147. See ibid., p. 98; and George Rudé, "English Rural and Urban Disturbances on the Eve of the First Reform Bill, 1830-1831," *Past and Present* 37 (July, 1967): 89-90.

148. See J. L. and B. Hammond, *The Village Labourer,* pp. 224-259; and Hobsbawm and Rudé, *Captain Swing,* pp. 61-64, 244-246.

149. See Hobsbawm and Rudé, *Captain Swing,* pp. 180-188.

150. Ibid., p. 247.

151. Ibid., p. 223, pp. 312-358.

152. Ibid., p. 288.

153. Ibid., pp. 61-69.

154. Ibid., p. 258.

155. "The Charge of the Honourable Baron Vaughn to the Grand Jury of the County of Southampton," December 20, 1830, reprinted in Carpenter, ed., *The Rising of the Agricultural Labourers,* p. 4.

156. Ibid., p. 5.

157. Ibid., p. 6.

158. See J. L. and B. Hammond, *The Village Labourer,* pp. 248-300.

159. See Hobsbawm and Rudé, *Captain Swing,* pp. 296-298.

160. Ibid., p. 285.

161. Turner, *Trade Union Growth,* p. 85. Also see Frank Munger, "Participation and Militancy in Industrial Revolution England" (paper presented at A.S.A. national convention, Montreal, August, 1974), p. 13.

162. Aspinall, *The Early English Trade Unions,* pp. 313-342.

163. See G. D. H. Cole, *Attempts at General Union* (London, 1953), p. 8 and Turner, *Trade Union Growth,* p. 51.

164. Turner, *Trade Union Growth,* pp. 75-77.

165. G. D. H. Cole, *A Short History of the British Working Class Movement, I* (New York, 1930), p. 79.

166. See Hollis, *The Pauper Press,* pp. 107-155.

167. See Cole and Filson, *British Working Class Movements,* pp. 256-258; and Webb, *The British Working Class Reader,* pp. 104-112.

168. See Hollis, *The Pauper Press,* pp. 259-275.

169. Cole and Postgate, *The British Common People,* p. 233.

170. See, for example, Thomas Hodgskin, *Labour Defended Against the Claims of Capital* (London, 1922, originally, 1825).

171. See Cole, *A Short History,* p. 107; and *Attempts at General Union,* pp. 176-186.

172. See Cole, *Attempts at General Union,* pp. 84-87.

173. Cole, *A Short History,* p. 124.

174. See S. and B. Webb, *The History of Trade Unionism,* p. 135.

175. Thompson, *The Making of the English Working Class,* p. 804.

176. As quoted in Sidney Pollard, "Nineteenth-Century Cooperation: From Community Building to Shopkeeping," *Essays in Labour History,* pp. 84-85.

177. The shift in Owen's personal views on this matter is discussed in W. H. Oliver, "Robert Owen and the English Working-Class Movements," *History Today* 8 (1958): 787-796.

178. As quoted in Cole, *Attempts at General Union,* p. 86.

179. Ibid.

180. Ibid., pp. 127-136.

181. Pollard, "Nineteenth-Century Cooperation," pp. 108-109.

182. See Rudé, "English Rural and Urban Disturbances," pp. 99-100.

183. J. L. and B. Hammond, *The Skilled Labourer,* p. 381.

CHAPTER 4
Legitimation and the Suppression of Imagination

The Reform Act of 1832 formally sanctioned the alliance between the middle class and the landed aristocracy. As the process of industrialization advanced, a number of disputes, all centered around the general issue of free trade versus limited (aristocratic) protections, scarred this alliance. Despite these disputes, the structure of power, as Thompson observes, continued to develop upon a "complex interpenetration of aristocratic privilege and commercial and industrial wealth."[1] Two factors especially worked to prevent a serious break in the alliance. The first was the acceptance by each class of the fundamental rules of the political game. Disagreements were to be settled in Parliament. The second, and at this stage the most important in maintaining viable relations between the two groups, was the shared opposition to workers and their associations.

Workers in both agrarian and industrial areas responded to this realignment, and to the deterioration of traditions which it signaled, with a series of protest activities. However, for the reasons examined in the previous chapter, workers' opposition was safely contained by 1834. While many working-class organizations persisted, their aims and activities over the next several years were minimal and isolated. Over these same years we find the extension of measures intended to suppress the institutions and associations—in short, the culture—of the working class. This period sees a concerted effort by the government and various middle-class groups to stamp out the recreation and ceremony so important to working-class communities. When combined with such legislation as the New Poor Law of 1834 and the phenomenal growth of the transport system which facilitated widespread emigration, these efforts seriously damaged the cultural framework of England's working class.

This suppression of working-class culture marks the beginning of one-dimensionality. During this initial phase, the distinctiveness of working-class culture was not abolished, but its critical thrust was dulled. The institutions and evaluative standards of the culture became flattened out, emptied of imaginative content. Although this culture still sustained the separation between 'us' and 'them,' its capacity to formulate alternatives to the established order was severely blocked. In this context protest became more a matter of revenge and less a striving for a better society.

By mid-century this phase of one-dimensionality, which entailed a pragmatic acceptance of the existing arrangements, gave way to a second phase which involved a normative acceptance. The labor aristocracy, constituting a small but significant segment of the working class, expressed in their 'new model' unions and cooperative societies a basic agreement with the principles of industrial capitalism. Protest thereafter was circumscribed within a general set of unquestioned presuppositions. Here lies the beginning of the incorporation of the working class into the established social order.

At the core of this working-class accommodation to the established order was the self-legitimating capacity of industrial capitalism. With the suppression of communal values and practices, the advancement of industrial capitalism, as the Hammonds remarked, "made people think that their society was to be judged solely by its commercial success. . . . The test of success was the test of profits: if a society could make its social and political conditions favorable to the earning of high profits that society was prosperous."[2] In this way the economic system provided its own standards of legitimation. No longer subject to external criteria of assessment, the economic system established a content-free ideology which replaced the anticipatory ideology and the transcendent criteria of social action which it contained.

Issuing from this self-legitimating process was a new form of domination. Now people viewed their domination as derivative not from other people but from objects—a self-regulating market, the laws of supply and demand, and the science of political economy. From this perception emerged two implications. First, objects, unlike people, could not be morally bound by normative obligations and duties.[3] And, secondly, the dominated could no longer understand their situation in terms of social and personal relationships. Rather, since everybody operated under the same 'objective laws,' their place in society could only be understood by attributing it to personal inadequacies. Both of these developments, hypostatization and the shift from a relational to a attributional image of social inequality, intensified the spread of one-dimensionality.

In the period to be examined in this chapter, the changes which began at the turn of the century are completed. The elimination of the theory of dependence, the suppression of imagination, the elevation of mechanical time, the distinction between the public and the private—that is, the separation of economic activity from noneconomic compulsions—were all established. Clearest of all was the increasing adaptation of the legal system to the system of production. The convergence of industrialization and capitalism made necessary the establishment of national markets for consumer goods and labor, the creation of a stable monetary and credit system, the concentration of capital, the elaboration of flexible investment policies, and the development of a mobile labor force. The changes in the legal system, made throughout this period, facilitated industrial expansion. As Polanyi maintains, these legislative changes established three basic principles:

> that labor should find its price on the market; that money should be supplied by a self-adjusting mechanism; that commodities should be free to flow from country to country irrespective of the consequences—in brief, a labor market, the gold standard, and free trade. A self-inflammatory process was induced as a result of which the formerly harmless market pattern expanded into a sociological enormity.[4]

The organization of a self-regulating market as required by the incessant growth of industrial capitalism presupposed the transformation of land, labor, and capital into commodities. Once this transformation was completed by the adaptation of the institutional framework to the productive forces, structural changes became self-generating.

In sum, where previously the institutional framework was dialectically interdependent with the system of work, it now becomes almost totally determined by the system of labor as comprised by the productive forces and market organization. Cultural values are less expressive of substantive rationality and social obligations, and more expressive of the efficiency and calculability demanded by formal rationality. Just as the institutional framework becomes adaptive to the system of labor, so too does the political system. The relational qualities of power and domination are now more indirect and less visible, as they are mediated by a system of labor capable of generating its own legitimacy. While social protest and opposition is still possible in these circumstances, it is a distorted kind of protest and opposition, without direction or goals. As political domination becomes increasingly disguised, social protest becomes largely a response to economic crises, and protest movements become exclusively oriented to economic concerns. A possible concept of social freedom capable of guiding opposition and giving meaning to negative experience is repressed, as conflict and struggle occur in an unchallenged universe of discourse.

SYSTEM OF INSTRUMENTAL ACTION

Capitalism had existed in some viable form in England since the seventeenth century. Only when capitalism became associated with industrialism, however, was the two-dimensional quality of social life undermined. New techniques such as the steam engine, the water frame, the spinning jenny, and the carding engine made feasible the centralization of production, the mobilization of large numbers of workers under one roof, and more or less permanent technological change. By the mid-1830s, though the English economy remained strongly dependent on agriculture, and though remnants of the domestic system continued to persist, the convergence of industrialism and capitalism had been firmly secured. From this point on, the expansion of factory production and economic growth proceeded with few interruptions. In the 1840s a 'second industrial revolution' began, centering around the perfection of techniques, the improvement of administration in both political and industrial realms, and, most importantly, the development of a national transportation system.

After 1832 there began a period of very rapid and largely domestic economic development, which lasted until the close of the decade. Throughout this period the rate of industrial output advanced considerably as investments in factories, new equipment, and, to some extent, in railroads, increased.[5] Much of the enormous growth which took place is surely attributable to the encouraging atmosphere generated by the Reform Act. On a practical level, manufacturers and industrialists were now in a better position to effect legislative changes on behalf of economic expansion. The New Poor Law of 1834, for example, by abolishing the link between wages and poor relief, expedited the formation of a national labor market. As Redford finds, more than four-fifths of 4,684 Poor Law migrants between 1835 and 1837 went to the textile districts of Lancashire, Cheshire, and the West Riding.[6] By encouraging, if not actually compelling, long-distance migration, the New Poor Law greatly contributed to the onset of economic prosperity.

Under these conditions of prosperity, industries expanded by both diversifying prevailing techniques and introducing new ones. Accompanying this expansion of existing industries was the proliferation of newer, usually small, industries. Not only did this establish a highly competitive situation; it also effected a dramatic change of the labor force. For with a greater reliance on more complex machinery it became possible to employ, at cheaper wages, women and children in the place of adult males. By 1840 the results of these developments appeared in full force. The use of machinery simultaneously engendered a steady advance in productive output and—by permitting a reduction in the employment of adult males—a drop in wage rates. As a result, production had to be stockpiled. In the absence of any limited liability protections, the majority of small enterprises, and several of the larger ones, found it impossible to acquire outside funds, and eventually went out of business. A severe depression, lasting throughout the early 1840s, afflicted the English economy.

In large part, the depression was the result of overproduction, a situation determined by the lack of adequate distribution and consumption arrangements. Accordingly, extensive efforts were directed toward the development of a viable transport industry. While roads and canals were built, and the foundations of a shipping industry were established, the bulk of investment capital was channeled into the railroad industry.[7]

Such heavy expenditures required, of course, the creation of new levels of capital formation which, in turn, had the effect—as Deane and Cole observe—of "directly stimulat[ing] the growth of large-scale heavy industries— themselves highly capital-intensive."[8] Thus the railway industry, and the transport industry in general, by serving as outlets for investment and capital accumulation, by securing new areas of trade, and by establishing improved distributive arrangements, contributed much to the revival of economic prosperity in the mid-1840s.

Infrastructural growth was initiated and maintained by the availability of easy money in the capital market. This was made possible by the Bank Charter Act of 1844. The Bank Act of 1833 had extended flexibility to borrowing and lending practices, thereby stimulating the elaboration of a national credit system. The removal of old usury laws, along with the reduction of interest rates and penalties for debtors, greatly enhanced the availability of short-term funds for investment purposes. The 1844 Act went beyond this by not only extending credit opportunities but also by guaranteeing the credit issue with a metallic reserve, three-fourths of which was constituted by gold.[9] By the end of 1844, capital was readily available for investment purposes.

Quickly following the Bank Charter Act was the repeal of numerous protective acts—the Corn Laws in 1846, the Navigation Acts in 1849, and import duties in 1853. Other important legislation included the Factory Act of 1847, which restricted the hours which women and children could work, and the Companies Act of 1855 which—by vastly extending the principle of limited liability—encouraged a rapid capital flow into the manufacturing industries. While the political machinations surrounding these legislative actions are essential to an understanding of the shifting power relations between the middle class and the aristocracy, it is sufficient now to note that these changes had two immediate consequences: the strengthening of free trade, and the reduction of unemployment. By 1850 the economy had fully recovered, and England entered the 'golden age of capitalism.'

Three important and related developments grew from these successful attempts to strengthen the market economy. The first was connected with the agitation which precipitated the passage of the Factory Acts—limiting the working day for women and children and eventually reducing the average daily work hours for all laborers. Faced with these restrictions on work hours, manufacturers were compelled to innovate and to rely more heavily upon improved industrial techniques. As a result, productivity continued to increase despite the shorter hours. What took place, in Marx's terms, was a shift from absolute to relative surplus value. That is, the base of surplus value—capital expansion—became a self-renewing process free of any externally imposed limits. "For," as Marx writes, "the movement in the course of which it adds surplus-value, [becomes] its own movement, its expansion, therefore, [becomes] automatic expansion."[10] As we shall see, this had significant implications for the norm of reciprocity.

With this shift to relative surplus value, and greater emphasis on the productive apparatus itself, technology became a cumulative and self-generating process. Technological growth and, subsequently, economic expansion assumed a pattern of compulsive sequences where innovation was compelled by an imbalance in one of many interrelated units which comprised a particular technique.[11] With the self-expanding tendencies of capital, this self-generating capacity of technology provided the foundation for a long period of sustained industrial and economic growth.

As the factory system began to permeate society, the prominence of contractual work agreements grew correspondingly. Not only did these contractual arrangements make for a more fluid labor force; but, as Stanley Udy observes, they allowed for certain developmental possibilities as well. The contractual arrangement, Udy writes,

> produces an organization composed of an aggregate of individuals, rather than an already constituted well-knit group [and] . . . thus moves the work organization a step away from social determination, allows for the development of a distinctively organizational culture, and makes possible the enhancement of technical efficiency.[12]

Thus, as the system of work becomes disengaged from social determination, differentiation and the development of free-floating resources occur without impediment. The growth of free-floating resources—including here political support and cultural identifications, as well as manpower and economic resources—assumes a flexible and autonomous character, and influences political authority significantly by allowing the legitimacy of power to come from the system of work itself.[13] As Marx notes in another context, "as soon as capital as such comes into existence, it creates its own prerequisites . . . through its own process of production; . . . [it thus] proceeds from itself, creating the presuppositions of its maintenance and growth."[14] In this way the institutional framework lost its ability to regulate the system of work.

These developments received extensive recognition in 1851, at the Great Exhibition held in Hyde Park. Containing over 100,000 exhibits, the Great Exhibition served to symbolize the achievements of English industry and wealth. The triumphs of technology and the market economy—"progress," it was called—here were made visible and celebrated. Industrial superiority was equated with the good life. "The themes of the Great Exhibition," J. F. C. Harrison remarks, "were intended to be as moral as material. To honour the gospel of work and the Smilesian virtues [of self-help] was a main object of the venture, and there was much reference to 'the working bees of the world's hive.' "[15] The Great Exhibition was a celebration of the successful separation of the economy from society and social obligations. It was a veneration of a self-adjusting market and a self-generating technology. Before the decade was over, the whole of England was viewed as a Great Exhibition, and the celebration of industrial capitalism lay at the core of Victorian ideals.

SYSTEM OF SYMBOLIC INTERACTION

In the Victorian period, working-class culture was objectified, emptied of its creative dynamic, and became less able to supply meaning and alternatives to daily experience. The human element, heretofore conspicuously visible in the creation of culture, was suppressed, and traditional standards of pride and social responsibility were replaced by criteria of efficiency and profitability. Unlike natural law ideology where laws were declaratory of human rights, the laws developed under industrial capitalism—scientific laws, particularly the laws of the market—were viewed as *independent* of man. In this context, Birnbaum notes, there emerged "a gap (indeed, an abyss) between men and the meanings and mechanisms of a world they [were] not quite able to experience as theirs."[16] The constriction of experience accompanied the advance of industrial capitalism and the extension of formal rationality. Stripped of its commitment to substantive concerns, rationality became 'free-floating,' restricted to assessing the most appropriate—that is, the most efficient—means for the acquisition of goals supplied by the system of production itself. Culture came to express the creative power of the instrument, not of man.

Under these conditions, fundamental questions pertaining to the very nature of society and of social relations give way to more limited, less critical questions which can be resolved without superseding the boundaries of the existing social order. As the determination of goals was surrendered to objectified forces, what was once questioned became converted into unchallenged presuppositions. Concern was reduced to concern over means, over instruments. Freedom and equality as well were reduced to instruments, interpreted in terms of economic behavior and not political action.[17] In the private realm all were free to do as they please; and, given the lack of state interference, all allegedly shared equal opportunities. Confined to the instrumental sphere, the power of reflection—the negativity contained in remembrance and the anticipation of the future inherent communal values—was minimized. The sense of human presence, the sense of being able to actively shape the social world, was subjugated to abstract time and space. The present absorbed all else, and one-dimensionality took firm root.

In part, the weakening of working-class institutions and traditions was the direct result of increasing industrialization. In the late 1830s industrial occupations began to gain prominence over agricultural occupations, and a corresponding increase in the rate of urbanization took place.[18] Crucial to this period of industrial growth, as we have seen, was the rapid advance of the transport industry, the railways in particular. The advent of the railways contributed to the development of a transient, highly mobile labor force, and was thus instrumental in undermining many of the enduring features upon which working-class communities were built. Thus industrialization had a significant impact on working-class traditions. However, the 'impersonal' effect of industrialization was preceded—indeed, it was presupposed—and accompanied by a more direct and intentional attack on the underpinnings of the working-class solidarity.

The working-class community, as we have seen, supported a kind of integrated experience which synthesized play and work, non-instrumental and instrumental activity, and the past, the present and the future. In the eighteenth century, work and play in many instances were almost indistinguishable.[19] Hiring fairs, in particular, were always festive and playful occasions. During the first third of the nineteenth century, work and play became more distinct, but were not compartmentalized into discrete categories of activity. Many traditional holidays continued to be celebrated. The practice of St. Monday persisted; singing and the reading of stories to the factory operatives while they worked were common. Before play was formalized and confined to particular times and well-defined places, before it was restricted to children and portrayed as a trivial, if not irresponsible activity, it was essential to the protest activities which issued forth from working-class communities. Spontaneity, innovation, flexibility, and a defiance of conventional proprieties all marked the workers' protest. Ceremony, merrymaking, and play, deriving from, reinforcing, and expanding beyond the shared oral culture of the working-class community, were common attributes of the agrarian and industrial revolts.[20] Indeed, as Robert Malcolmson finds, working-class festivities and popular recreational assemblies tended to incapacitate the existing means of social control, and were often the scene of violent agitation.[21]

It is important to recognize that play was still not separated from the reality of working-class life; and this reality was confronted, not denied, in play. Play gave fantastic expression to political aspirations, and enabled a critical assessment of the existing reality. Fantasy enriched and revitalized life, providing new meanings, transcendent visions, and conceptions of a better future. The playful celebration of an imaginary universe, thus, could quickly be converted into an active repudiation of the established arrangements. Only when play is dissociated from reality, when work time is separated from free time, does it lose its political implications and progressive thrust. Detached from life, play merely provides an innocuous haven from the burdens of the real world, while fantasy devitalizes experience. Prevented from confronting reality, play becomes, if not retrogressive, certainly apolitical, simply offering the appearance of freedom in an unfree world. By constricting play, by severing the linkages between play and real concerns, and thus fragmenting experience, the rebellious disposition sustained in the working-class community would be weakened.

The non-fragmented experience provided by the working-class community was in large measure the source of the workers' distinctive consciousness, and was essential to the shaping of their demands and activities in line with a sense of social responsibility. While serious, widespread efforts aimed at destroying this feature of working class social life had been in existence since the turn of the century, it was not until the 1830s and 1840s that these efforts became concerted and, as it turned out, successful. Under the banner of moral improvement, the government—relying on both force and legislation—and a variety of middle-class-sponsored propaganda associations worked together to extirpate the 'barbaric' exercises inhibitive of the growth of respectability among the workers.

While the professed reason for this move against working-class play and recreational activities was the moral improvement of the working class, the actual reasons have more to do with the aggrandizement of aristocratic and industrial interests. Play was now associated with idleness, and, as such, was an obstacle to a reliable, methodical, obedient, and productive work force. Labor discipline, a prerequisite for sustained industrial and economic growth, could only be furthered, it was argued, with the suppression of play.[22] Accordingly, an ironclad distinction had to be made between work and play, production and idleness, maturity and childishness.

A more efficient labor force would immeasurably strengthen the national economy. The prohibition of popular recreations, along with the reduction of holidays and fairs, would not only contribute to this efficiency and reliability; it would also foreclose the major sources of the imprudent expenditure of workers' time and money. Following such changes—the argument went—time and money would be channeled into the market. Hence, the attacks on working-class recreational assemblies were guided less by moral improvement than by profitability. It is significant in this regard that those fairs "which blended pleasure with business were usually much more resilient than those which were strictly for pleasure; when a fair became economically redundant . . . it was much more liable to attack."[23]

Combined with the intent to extend labor discipline and strengthen the national economy, was a third, perhaps more important, motivation behind these efforts. I am referring, of course, to the aim to contain working-class social protest activity. Fairs, celebrations, and football matches not only emphasized shared traditions; they also brought together a great number of people. It was not uncommon on these occasions for large crowds to get out of control and to visibly express their grievances. Of more significance than these ad hoc outbursts, however, were the more permanent and threatening kinds of opposition engendered and protected by an integrated and meaningful community. By breaking through this integration, by restraining the creative dynamic of working-class culture, a critical step would have been taken toward the neutralization of working-class protest. Thus, in condemning community football matches and in making cockfighting and bull-baiting illegal, governmental and middle-class reformers were condemning and outlawing traditional practices which gave shape to working-class social life. The contention that these actions were genuinely motivated by a concern for moral improvement is at best a weak one. As Brian Harrison remarks, the Royal Society for the Prevention of Cruelty to Animals—typical of the many associations formed at this time to bring respectability to the workers—"attacked the dogfights and cockfights of the poor but ignored the foxhunting and gameshooting of the rich. . . . [Other sports, such as steeplechasing and stag hunting] were sometimes even publically defended by R.S.P.C.A. spokesmen."[24] Working-class recreational activities were barbaric in many respects; but they also were potentially threatening. The condemnation they received derived not only from an interest in moral improvement but also from a concern with eliminating the sources of working-class rebelliousness.

The relatively high degree of success achieved by the moral improvement program is attributable, not to persuasion and conversion, but to the government's ability to make and physically enforce legislative changes. The frequent application of considerable governmental force against popular recreations was justified by the need to protect the public order and the operation of the free market economy. Games and matches of various sorts were often, especially in the 1840s, ended forcibly by the police, and their participants usually arrested and prosecuted. Footballers were commonly charged with destroying property and interferring with business transactions. The *Derby Mercury,* in 1842, condemned matches on the grounds that

> The inhabitants never know anything of the business until they see the crowds of vagabonds upon the grounds, who forcibly take possession of some field suitable for their purpose, and not only bear down all resistance on the part of the owner, but set at defiance the exertions of the magistrates and peace officers, to stop their lawless proceedings.

The article goes on to urge an 'efficacious plan,' later incorporated into governmental policy, which included

> instructing the peace officers and others to take particular notice, not only of the parties, and their seconds and bottle-holders, but also of the principal ringleaders . . . and any other persons on the ground who refuse to assist the peace officers, and afterwards to indict them.[25]

By defining working-class, traditional practices as criminal, the government could easily move to restrain them. Not only did this benefit the factory owner in terms of an improved labor discipline; it also enhanced the position of the landed aristocracy by freeing it from many of the customary obligations which had persisted in the rural areas.

The middle-class contribution to the 'elevation' of the workers consisted of mechanics institutes, philanthropic societies, religious associations, and educational reform. Central to these endeavors was the ethic of self-improvement, given its most forceful expression and promoted most intensely by evangelicalism.[26] A revival and a reinterpretation of certain major aspects of Puritanism, evangelicalism regarded personal salvation largely as a matter of individual responsibility and self-denial. To assure that each individual employed his moral ability to work out salvation, evangelicalism directed its many middle-class adherents to engage in ceaseless proselytizing and to establish societies for moral reform and the improvement of manners.[27] Working-class play activities, because they deterred religious worship and the strict observance of the Sabbath, and, more importantly, inhibited the moral sobriety and self-improvement necessary for salvation, received the scorn and the serious concern of the evangelical campaign for social reform.[28] Play was antithetical to religious proprieties; and it was incumbent among the middle class to infuse a sense of moral earnestness among workers, to allow the workers the opportunity to save themselves.

Although evangelicalism was partially embraced by the few relatively prosperous segments of the working class (the labor aristocracy, about which more is said below), its immediate importance is found elsewhere.[29] Not only did evangelicalism supply moral overtones to the growing assaults on the working-class community; it also extended the scope of these attacks. While the government and the industrial interests were concerned with separating play and work, free time and work time, evangelicalism aimed to assure that free time be expended just as profitably as work time. Self-improvement entailed obedience to God, as well as to the methodical rhythms of factory production. More permeable than Puritanism, the evangelical ethic was more open to the secular influences of the period. Generally optimistic, justifying benevolence in terms of its utility for personal regeneration and social peace, and satisfied that the moral improvement of the individual was the source of progressive social change, evangelicalism concentrated much of its energy on the constriction of working-class play.[30]

With the encouragement and support of the government, the middle class incorporated the ethic of self-improvement into their programs of educational reform. As reflected in an official report, the *Minutes* of 1846, these programs combined a conception of economic expansion as benevolent with a strong denunciation of working-class decadence.[31] It was suggested that the salvation or self-improvement of the workers must be initiated from above; the barbaric, yet potentially explosive, traditions of the workers had to be eradicated. A viable educational system was proposed to assume the duties neglected by working-class parents. In such a system, where the teacher and the school were under direct governmental control, children would learn how not to waste their time, and they would be partially protected from the scandal, sedition, and moral iniquity which abounded in working-class communities. The children, unlike their parents, would learn to express the proper deference to their social superiors.[32] Thus educational reform, as Johnson notes,

> promised an expansion of . . . markets and a pacification of . . . work-forces. Above all, it neatly redistributed guilt away from the [middle class] makers of a social revolution onto those who suffered most from it. . . . It gave to particular interests the appearance of a universal benevolence.[33]

The aim was to weaken working-class traditions and, in turn, "to determine . . . the patterns of thought, sentiment, and behaviour of the working class."[34]

By mid-century much of traditional, working-class culture had been weakened. For many workers, play and recreational activities came to be viewed as trivial pursuits; but for many more workers, participation in such noninstrumental activity left them open to physical attack and prosecution. Unsurprisingly, after the 1850s the appearance of traditional holidays, games, matches, and fairs in working-class communities visibly and rapidly declined; and with it, disappeared the spontaneity which heretofore had sparked working-class resistance and opposition to the established order.

The attack on play and recreation was accompanied by an intensification of earlier efforts to promote and apply the linear, mechanical conception of time. As the suppression of the play element in working-class communities advanced, as the integrated experience generated within these communities was shattered, time became reified, detached from human experience, and encapsulated within the standards of formal rationality. In this way, the reconceptualization of time served as an essential aspect in the maintenance of social control. With the growing acceptance of the linear conception of time, the public and the private distinction became reinforced, labor discipline improved, and progress became defined as quantitative, organic growth. Founded upon mechanical time was the preeminence of science, the emphasis on facts, and the repudiation of values as a crucible of sentimentality. When 'time is money' it loses its transcendent character.

With the mechanization of time came the compartmentalization of work and life, the workday and free time. This distinction closely paralleled that between the private and public realms. In the work place, as in the private sphere, activities and decisions were governed by the market. In the public realm, however, decisions were guided by public opinion. Free time, accordingly, could be profitably spent in refining one's ability to contribute to a considered and effective public opinion. It is precisely this reasoning which leads John Stuart Mill to equate liberty with leisure and suggest that the workers devote their free time to the pursuit of higher activities in an effort to acquire the accoutrements which warrant their being awarded the franchise.[35] By occupying their free time with exercises in self-improvement, it was argued, workers would gain a political liberty commensurate with the equality provided by the market economy.

Behind this argument lay a hidden agenda. For, free time dedicated to the refinement of moral sensibilities was depoliticized time. With the rigid demarcation of work and life, the creative thrust of the noninstrumental was subjugated to existing forms. The social cohesiveness of working-class communities, and the spontaneity of the protest activities they gave rise to, were undermined as performance, and emotions were alienated from one another, packaged discretely in work and life containers. In these circumstances adult play became formalized and methodical; innovative, spontaneous, joyful, and noninstrumental play was confined to childhood. "Aware always of temporal relations and responsibilities," writes Jerome Buckley in summarizing the Victorian attitude towards time, "no adult can contrive or decree the release from time that the child habitually enjoys."[36] Disembedded from human experience, its transcendent elements suppressed, time was now perceived as an objective force within which people were imprisoned.

The constriction of imagination to the instrumental dimension placed social interactions under purposive-rational constraints. As spontaneity was significantly reduced, so too was the capacity to resist the infringements of industrial capitalism. Eventually, a reconciliation—both in pragmatic and normative terms—with industrial capitalist society was effected by the workers. When the established order was accepted, either because there were no demonstrable alternatives to it or because it was perceived as good, questions pertaining to the fundamental nature of society were replaced by questions which presupposed the validity or inevitability of that society. Where, earlier, workers resisted and protested *against* time, now they protested *about* time.[37] The mid-1840s working-class agitation in support of a Ten Hour Bill did not critically examine the nature of prevailing work relationships which had a negative impact on the workers' life. Rather, the necessity of these relationships was taken for granted. Workers demanded not the abolition, but only the modification of exploitative relationships. In effect, the struggle for the ten hour day, as deGrazia points out, "crystallized the workday and in so doing, crystallized free time too."[38] It reflected and reinforced the workers' acceptance of mechanical, compartmentalized time.

The all-out attack on working-class culture not only alienated instrumental from noninstrumental activity; it also damaged the sense of historical continuity which underlay the working-class community. By making the past experiences active members of the present (to "re-member") establishes ment sustained the existing system of domination. For the inability to make past experiences active members of the present (to "re-member") establishes the compulsion to repeat past domination relations.[39] Thus the inability to bring the past into consciousness or into real time prevented the workers from avoiding a repetition of that past.

With this disengagement from a sense of historical continuity, the workers were compelled to relax their hold on a set of categories which gave meaning to their lives and provided standards for legitimating or discrediting the prevailing social arrangements. Meaning and standards of legitimacy were now associated with the formal rationality of the economic and productive system itself. "The problem of systematically rejecting the past," Hobsbawm observes, "arises only when innovation is recognized both as inescapable and as socially desirable: when it represents 'progress.'"[40] Through the suppression of imagination, innovation—usually interpreted as industrial growth and economic expansion—did become viewed as inescapable. And, to the extent that the available evaluative criteria of the social order were generated by that social order, such innovation was treated as representative of a better society: the good society became the society with advancing industrialization and sustained economic growth. In other words, the good society became the existing society.

If the present society was good, the future society would be better. "Yet the future society would be 'better,'" Buckley explains, "only insofar as the present was already good."[41] Thus the future came to be regarded as a fulfillment of the present, not the past. Progress was defined as a process of quantitative, incremental improvements, and was measured with reference to how far society and its members had distanced themselves from the past. The refusal to idealize the past, and the obsession with the present which developed from this notion of progress, are typified in Thomas Macauley's *History of England:*

> Those who compare the age on which their lot has fallen with a golden age which exists only in their imagination may talk of degeneracy and decay: but no man who is correctly informed as to the past will be disposed to take a morose or desponding view of the present.[42]

Imagination, fantasy, and remembrance were denounced and eventually constrained. As a consequence, working class culture became flattened out and harnessed to the existing order.

This significant transformation of working-class culture is highlighted in Martha Vicinus' examination of the shifting nature and role of nineteenth-century working-class poetry.[43] As an integrating factor in the working-class community, the importance of poetry and songs cannot be overestimated. Norms, values, and traditions are more easily presented and better retained in these forms. Prior to the onslaught on working class culture, these poems and songs were integral to the process of remembrance; traditional themes were sustained, and it was common for present grievances to be assessed in light of past ones. In this regard, Vicinus finds that songs were composed delineating the people who betrayed a union or community decision, and it was often a long while before the song and the betrayers were forgotten.[44] Through such songs and poems, traditional standards were maintained in the context of industrial capitalism.

Through the first third of the nineteenth century, working-class poetry was based almost exclusively upon the workers' experience in their community and its relation to the work place. The poet and his poems were integrally rooted in the working-class community, and it was usually the case that the feelings and emotions expressed were open only to the appreciation of the community's members. While this certainly contributed to the opacity of working-class culture, it also provided that culture with a rich and meaningful symbolism.

Expressive of fundamental feelings, the symbolism of working-class poetry was a significant force in the establishment of community cohesion. Not only was it a central element in ritual and celebration; it was also a valuable means of socializing new members into the community. Linked to the traditional heritage, the poetry and songs of the workers expressed the eighteenth-century emphasis on natural rights; they symbolized the workers' grievances and demands with reference to the abrogation of rights and responsibilities. In this way the poems and songs intended to strengthen the bond between the strikers and rioters and the community. Their purpose was explicitly political; namely, to rally and rouse the spirits of the workers. In analyzing "The Cropper's Song," typical of the political songs found among the workers until the 1830s, Vicinus finds this expressed in "a remarkable sense of personal and communal worth. . . . The croppers are set apart from the rest of society because of their past and future deeds of courage; there is no justification or explanation for their frame-breaking since the song was meant for those who were already Luddites."[45]

In short, working class poetry and songs derived from and were expressive of an integrated experience. They helped to bind the community and, in so doing, they contributed to the elaboration of distinct and meaningful working-class consciousness. Coincident with the attacks on working-class culture, the symbolic richness contained in poetry and song began to wither. Poems and songs were emptied of meaningful symbols developed out of the workers' lives and were replaced by an emphasis on the element of chance or fate inexplicably governing the characters' lives.[46]

At this point, working class poetry increasingly began to reflect the objectification of culture. Gone were the references to the workers' ability to provide solutions to the problems they daily encountered. Instead, the emphasis was on submission to time: with the passage of time, problems would generate their own solutions. For the moment, one could only become reconciled to them. In her analysis of Edwin Waugh's "Come, Mary, Link Thi Arm i' Mine," written in 1855, one of the most popular poems of the period, Vicinus stresses this subjugation to be objectified forces. Unlike earlier working-class poetry, in this poem

> Love and sex . . . are no longer linked metaphorically . . . but are expressed through the cataloguing of material goods. These objects, intended to symbolize the narrator's love, become more important than the emotions they represent, so that the net effect of the poem is little more than a list of what a good man can offer his wife. Both individuals derive their character from these objects, rather than from each other or from their respective vocations, as in earlier weaving poems.[47]

After mid-century, working-class poetry in general gave expression, in form as well as content, to the disintegration of the community. Disengaged from the day-to-day activities of the working-class community, poetry, like play, became restricted to particular times and places. Working-class poetry "came to be a means of expressing and explaining one's emotion on exceptional occasions, such as marriage or death, rather than being integral to one's life."[48] Emotions were separated from performance as play had been separated from work.

As working-class poetry became detached from the working-class community, so did the poet. From 1850 to 1880, the ideological thrust and the political and economic interests of the working-class poet gave way to more sentimental concerns. During this period traditional poetry was replaced by "pure" poetry and dialect poetry. With the exception of the tightly knit communities in the coal mining areas where traditional song writing and poetry persisted, "working men with serious poetic aspirations denied their traditional culture for the ideal of "pure poetry," which they believed was part of the mainstream of English poetry."[49] Where "pure" poetry was infused with a spiritual morality, dialect poetry was promoted as a revival of working-class traditions. Dialect poetry, however, revived these traditions in a framework of middle-class values. Like "pure" poetry, dialect poetry accepted the distinction between work and play and "concentrated on the leisure time activities of the working class and the delights of the family instead of the problems of an industrial urban environment."[50] Education, self-help and temperance were presented to the workers as noble goals. The advantages of sacrifice and thrift over strikes and riots for the alleviation of poor conditions were vividly painted. In short, through the dialect poem the middle class could employ the workers' own language and customs to effectively promote the ethic of self-improvement and the denial of social responsibility. Thus, while a distinctive working-class poetry—and, indeed, a distinctive working-class culture—prevailed, it was drained of its critical thrust.

This gradual middle-class subversion of working-class culture resulted in a complete takeover by the end of century. Dialect poetry was mass-produced in London; it became a profit-making commodity. "Consumption and profit became the watchwords of those writing for the middle-class." Working-class culture was leveled down and brought into line with the emerging mass culture, signaling a new, more extensive, phase of one-dimensionality. Through popular songs and poetry the business interests furnished the worker, as Vicinus observes, "with words to express his feelings, and then with feelings themselves to which he was to tailor his own emotional responses."[51]

Vicinus' findings receive important support from Gareth Stedman Jones' recent study of a working-class cultural institution which became dominant in the last half of the nineteenth century, the music hall. Jones observes that from the 1850s on there is a declining interest in politics among the workers and an increasing demand for entertainment—a demand not for play, it must be emphasized, but for light commercialized entertainment.[52] Attuned to the daily realities of working-class life, the music hall, along with the pub, expanded to meet this demand. Essential to the extensive popularity of the music hall was its recognition of distinctive working-class concerns. Indeed, the impermeability of working-class culture was often reflected in music hall productions. Expressed, as well, was the growing conservatism of this culture. As Jones discovers, the music hall, especially after 1870, developed a fatalistic orientation wherein luck and fate were emphasized, class divisions were accepted as natural, and class was regarded as a fact of life, a life sentence which defied political solution.[53] Class distinctions were maintained, but were shed of their threatening and subversive features.

The "massification" of culture, a more advanced phase of one-dimensionality, would occur only much later. The one-dimensionality which emerged in the mid-nineteenth century involved the leveling down of working-class culture, not its elimination. Here one can agree with Thompson's contention that, beginning in the late 1830s and lasting throughout the century, the workers were occupied with the creation of a collective self-consciousness. But we must contest Thompson's further argument that this development constituted a 'great spiritual gain' for the worker. For, while the suppression of imagination did not entail the abolition of distinctions between the rich and the poor, it did allow these distinctions to be used in such a way that deference moved into the vacuum created by the deline of resistance. Thus, working class culture remained "staunchly impervious to middle class attempts to guide it, but [its] prevailing tone was not one of political combativity, but of an enclosed and defensive conservatism."[54] Not despite, but on the basis of, these distinctive values and institutions, the middle class and the government were able to bring about the accommodation of the working class.

SELF-HELP AND THE TRANSMUTATION OF WORKING-CLASS VALUES AND INSTITUTIONS

In a provocative article, "The Intellectual Origins of Mid-Victorian Stability," Trygve Tholfsen argues that the workers

> were the agents of their own defeat, for in affirming the worth of their class and cultivating virtues of their own choosing, they committed themselves to values enmeshed in a culture that embodied the social presuppositions of the propertied classes. Even a vestigial working class radicalism was co-opted by the system.[55]

The crucial issue in this argument concerns the matter of choice. With the suppression of imagination, the ability to formulate transcendental categories reflective of alternatives contained within society was drastically impeded. Accordingly, the alternatives from which the workers could choose were limited to two: they could accept the established order as inescapable, a form of pragmatic acceptance; or they could accept it normatively. For a long period the majority of workers 'chose' the first option. What facilitated a wider acceptance of the second alternative was the Victorian ethic of self-improvement and self-help. Built upon this ethic, the middle-class ideology was capable of transmuting working-class values and institutions, thereby bringing them into the mainstream of industrial capitalist society. This transmutation involved a shifting of working-class values from the communal to the individual level. Emancipation became redefined as social mobility; independence as self-discipline and diligence. Self-worth was measured in accordance with community participation. The self-help institutions, created along communal principles by the workers at the turn of the century, were reorganized into institutions which provided workers with the social and technical education necessary to become members of the middle class, or served as a means of savings and investment.

Thus—and this is of decisive importance—working-class values and institutions were not eliminated but were disfigured. Accordingly, workers could continue to maintain their values and institutions—at least in name, but now with different consequences. For self-help, independence, and emancipation—all conceived with reference to the individual—were the core values of society at large. The egalitarian society anticipated by the earlier conception and practice of working-class values and institutions had, according to this new conception, already arrived. Tholfsen's argument, then, is a weak one. The workers' decision to become a part of the society they once condemned was really not a decision: for at this time the workers had no choice.

The Victorian ethic of self-help constituted a coming of age for the denial of the theory of dependence. The espousal of self-reliance was a direct extension of the utilitarian and political economic arguments which precipitated the passage of the New Poor Law in 1834. Although it was an extension of the fundamental tenets of Philosophic Radicalism, the ethic of self-help modulated its more stringent tones, as we have seen, by incorporating a strong dose of evangelicalism. More significantly, where utilitarianism and classical political economy focused on the economic realm, self-help attended to the cultural realm: it concentrated on man's spiritual rather than material needs. However, the doctrine of self-help brought to cultural matters the same kind of free trade arguments which were being applied to the economy. Just as the individual improved his economic well-being through self-assertion and initiative, so could he enhance his spiritual well-being in the same manner. And, moreover, like economic betterment, moral improvement can only take place in the absence of state intervention. There emerges at this point the 'free marketplace of ideas.' Both physical and moral being, while still separated (alienated) into distinct spheres, come under the governance of market regulations. The emphasis in both spheres is on individualism.

Arguing that the status order and the theory of dependence had been effectively dismantled, the Victorian ethos insisted that the existing society had successfully replaced troublesome differences with harmonious relations. It was a society in which the rich and the poor, the capitalist and the laborer, by their own initiative could avail themselves of the same opportunities. Duty no longer meant the duty of one status to another. Rather, duty now referred to an individual's duty to himself. The society was so structured that each individual had to assume personal and ultimate responsibility for his or her successes and failures. In this light, the prevailing social arrangements warranted legitimacy, since they provided the individual with sufficient opportunity for intellectual and material improvement.

The Victorian sanctification of the present social order rested on these opportunities for advancement and improvement. The virtuous, diligent, and thrifty individual could achieve, in short stead, respectability and material comforts. The actualization of the good life, at least for these individuals, was at hand. As Tholfsen remarks, Victorian ideology "did not seek to reconcile workingmen to a wretched existence, but to remind them of the great prospects for improvement that lay within easy reach."[56] It was this emphasis upon achievement which the workers latched onto. As a result, the moral, intrinsic dimension of worth was replaced by purely extrinsic criteria. The more an individual, through his performance and sacrifice, approximated the middle-class life, the more worthy he was. Thus, social and personal worth, as Houghton suggests, became measured in terms of "profits, larger plants or firms, personal advancement, professional or social. The test of value, including that of thought, [became] utility in the narrow sense."[57]

The doctrine of self-help gave considerable shape and appeal to the middle-class ideology of industrial and economic expansion. Condemning social and political reconstruction, it portrayed individual improvement as the panacea for existing problems. Prevailing inequalities were attributed, not to social conditions, but to individual inadequacies. Indeed, these inequalities were justified by pointing to those workers who, through their diligence, managed to elevate their social and economic positions. In periodicals, books, and newspapers these frugal and industrious (and therefore respectable) workers received extensive praise. By the mid-1850s there had appeared a proliferation of "autobiographies of self-taught artisans and workers who overcame a lack of education, struggled to borrow or buy books, and who became self-respecting, educated men."[58] The glorification of the self-made man was, in effect, a repudiation of social responsibility. To participate in this glorification the workers did not have to completely abandon their values for new ones. Since the turn of the century, as we have seen, a core element in working-class culture was self-help. Recognizing that they could no longer count on assistance from the "higher orders" or the government, workers established their own institutions and communities within which they assisted each other. Thus, the thrifty and diligent worker seeking to elevate himself by his own initiative and without assistance from the middle class or the government could, with relative ease, justify his activities in terms of working-class values. In its distorted form, however, self-help proclaimed that the middle class and the government could not be obligated to provide assistance, since the responsibility for poverty and miserable living conditions rested not on social relationships but on an individual's lack of ambition. Thomas Wright, a workingman writing in 1867, made this point explicitly. The amelioration of the workers' struggle for existence can only be accomplished, he wrote, by "their having an earnest desire for a better state of things and being capable of self-help," and not by outside help.[59] Self-education would secure what social protest could not.

As an increasing number of workers began to adhere to the doctrine of self-help, opposition to English society gradually assumed a more reformist posture, which was reflected in the transformation of working-class institutions and organizations. The reorganized Cooperative Societies begun in the 1840s and the 'new model' unions founded in the 1850s were not geared for attacking social arrangements but, on the contrary, operated to make workers an integral part of these arrangements. Emancipation was to be established by social and personal advancement; and the tasks of education and the inculcation of frugality became primary goals of these associations. Developed at this time were numerous 'institutions of mental improvement' which were frequently attended by workers

> who wanted not science and the discipline of study, but the opportunity to acquire a little of the cultural elegance which they noted in their social superiors. Instead of classes in chemistry and mathematics, the mechanics' institutes by the 1840's were offering popular lectures, soirées and phrenology.[60]

Self-improvement would achieve for the workers in the cultural realm the same kind of equality of opportunity they allegedly possessed already in the economic realm.

Common to these associations was an eagerness to acquire respectability. But the respectability they sought resided not so much among workers as in the middle class. Many of the documents prepared by working-class organizations after 1850 appear to be addressing a primarily middle-class audience. One such document, published in *Odd Fellows Magazine* in 1837, after delineating how friendly societies have contributed to the moral salvation of the workers, asks the question:

> Can there be adduced a better guarantee for the prosperity of the country, a more striking evidence of the progress of work-

> ing men in all political relations, a more remarkable proof of
> the general spread of education and morality?[61]

The message is clear: an individual becomes worthy by developing his character, and working-class organizations gain respectability to the extent that
they encourage such development.

With the erosion of the critical elements of working-class culture and the
elaboration of the self-help ethic, there developed by the 1860s and 1870s a
pervasive ideological and structural privatization. Workers, indeed all
members of society, were linked unilaterally to the social order as individuals.
Working-class organizations and institutions were increasingly adapted to
facilitate and secure this linkage. The traditional work-centered culture was
being replaced by a culture oriented toward the 'depoliticized havens' of
home and family life.[62] Communal needs were being subordinated to privatized needs which were more readily accommodated by market society.

Following from the privatization of needs was a shift in the working-class
image of society from a relational to an attributional perspective. Where the
former allowed the workers to understand their situation in terms of their
relationship to other orders and classes, the attributional images of society
associated one's current social situation with personal capacities. Poverty
was attributed to a lack of determination, and self-improvement was seen as
the only available remedy. Accountability, like responsibility, was emptied
of its social dimension and attached exclusively to the individual.

The extensive attack, at first brutal and later more subtle in character,
carried out against working-class culture in this period succeeded in dulling
the biting edge of working-class values and institutions. As we shall see, the
workers initially reacted by striking back in vengeance. Gradually this urge
for revenge settled into a despairing acceptance of society; and eventually,
through the ethic of self-help, this despair was replaced by a more or less
unquestioned acceptance of industrial capitalism. While conflict certainly
did not disappear from English society, it did assume a more muted, institutionalized form. In the 1860s, arbitration and conciliation measures were
used extensively to settle labor disputes. The goals as well as the structure
of labor associations had changed drastically. Workers now made quantitative demands—more money and more leisure time—and were justifying
these demands in terms of how their satisfaction would contribute to the
stability and prosperity of society. The belief in social advancement through
individual self-improvement expressed a faith in reform and progress, which
gave this period "a reassuring sense of coherence and consistency."[63]

THE SHIFT FROM POLITICAL TO EXCHANGE
FORMS OF DOMINATION

The legitimacy of society rests largely on the effectiveness with which it
meets the articulated needs of its members. With the blockage of the system

of symbolic interaction, the ability to articulate subjectively felt needs became restricted to individualized expressive forms. Qualitative needs which are best satisfied in a cooperative and communally organized society, were no longer readily expressed: and needs which are not articulated cannot be acted upon. In terms of the ethic of self-help, the articulated needs of many workers—education, individual improvement, achievement—were coterminous with the requirements of industrial capitalism for a reliable, achievement-oriented labor force. Hence the articulated needs of these workers were now satisfied by the prevailing arrangements.[64] With the constriction of 'need articulation,' the regulation of workers' activities by the moral code of the community began to give way to market regulations.

The moral regulations characteristic of working-class communities were rooted in trust. Exchange was socially regulated, and the economic institutions of the community—such as the Friendly Societies—were highly personalized. Through such institutions the moral economy of the eighteenth century was kept alive on a smaller scale until well into the nineteenth century. By 1850, however, the separation of economy and society was nearly complete. Market regulations predominated, and rationality was confined to the techniques of the economy, not to its organization.[65] What transpired, in short, was a shift from socially regulated exchange to economic exchange. Under economic exchange,

> Economic institutions, such as the impersonal market and the contract that stipulates the precise terms of the exchange, are designed to separate concern with distinct objects of exchange from other considerations and to specify the exact obligations incurred in a transaction, thus maximizing the possibility of rational calculation.[66]

Economic exchange requires, then, the extensive availability of free-floating resources. On the most fundamental levels, this requirement means the reduction of social relationships built on trust, the multiplication of contractual relations, and the exclusive application of rationality to instrumental questions. In this way, the object of exchange is detached from all other, noneconomic, considerations.

In the context of economic exchange, property relations became less political and much more productive in character. Pursuant to this was a shift from political to exchange forms of domination. The domination associated with exchange relations was more subtle and less accountable than political domination, depending as it did on the reification of human relationships. Not committed to any substantive goals, people were related to others as things, objects, or commodities. Legitimation, accordingly, was disassociated from the power structure and directly linked to the economic and productive system. Thus domination was connected with the extension of formal rationality. When this happens, the social repression established by domination is one which "disappear[s] from the consciousness of the population because the legitimation of domination has assumed a new character: it refers to the constantly increasing productivity and domination of nature."[67] As long as the conquest of nature proceeded on course—that is, as long as industrial and economic growth and the extension of technical control and purposive-rational action continued—the system would be legitimated. What the domination of nature presupposed, however, was the domination of man, his imagination and traditional heritage.

To appreciate the shift from political to exchange forms of domination it is necessary to examine the realignment of power initiated by the alliance between the middle class and the aristocracy. After the passage of the 1832 Reform Act, entrepreneurs and the industrial bourgeoisie rarely sought election to Parliament. Instead, they exerted their significant influence in extra-parliamentary ways, allying with the Whigs to form a Liberal coalition. As a consequence, Parliament continued to be dominated by the gentry and the landed aristocrats. For a number of years, this situation benefited both interests, and a spirit of compromise, aided by the pragmatic inclinations of classical political economy, prevailed. While the landed aristocracy managed both to prosper and to maintain its political leadership, the industrial interests received legislation favorable to their expansion and investment needs. The government at this time was "something less than 'meddling' . . . and something more than [a] careless, indifferent, *prococurante* government."[68]

By the end of the 1830s, with the economy beginning to stagnate, this working alliance gradually gave way to hostile opposition. Led by the middle-class Radicals, the manufacturing interests attributed the decline of the economy to the continued existence of protective controls on land and corn—the primary sources of income for the landed aristocracy. After the Whigs, who were in large part members of the landed aristocracy themselves, refused to work for the repeal of these regulations, the Liberal coalition was split. Recognizing the futility of initiating repeal through the Whigs, the middle class was compelled to take a new route. Joseph Parkes, active in Radical circles, insisted that "[p]ressure from without will alone rouse the Government. They will otherwise do nothing. Standing still and staring about is their principle and political practice."[69]

In an effort to intensify the 'pressure from without' the manufacturing interests sought to mobilize popular, working-class agitation. Reasoning that such agitation would hasten the repeal of the remaining protective legislation, they incorporated into the free-trade argument the suggestion that repeal would result in an increase in wages. When argument alone did not initiate popular agitation, the manufacturing interests threatened to bring such agitation into existence with a general lockout. In 1842, however, when workers, on their own initiative, shut down factories in most of the country's industrial areas, the manufacturers, now fearful of being unable to control the agitation, reversed their plans; and from this point on they kept their activities and opposition within the institutionalized political boundaries.[70]

Partially centered on the issue of free trade, the animosity between the middle class and the aristocracy continued into the 1840s. From the ensuing struggle, both groups emerged with their positions of power relatively intact. While there is a question as to whether the middle class acquired a slight advantage over the aristocracy in the political realm, it is clear that political power became subjugated to economic power. This latter shift is indicated by the Repeal of the Corn Laws in 1846, and by the factory legislation which culminated in the Factory Acts of 1847.

The Repeal of the Corn Laws in 1846 was followed a year later by the passage of the Factory Acts, which allowed for stricter enforcement of the restricted workday rule for women and children. The importance of these two pieces of legislation is that they typify the relatively wide-ranging changes which formed the tension between the middle class and the aristocracy. Where the middle class supported repeal and opposed factory legislation, the converse was so for the aristocracy. It is noteworthy, however, that despite the two contending sources of support, both legislative changes were made with positive reference to the public-private distinction, and both were justified as being beneficial to social and economic prosperity and self-help.

The opposition to the Corn Laws constituted a more general attack on all the agricultural protections which had been retained for the benefit of the landed aristocracy. Although absolute protections on agricultural goods had been replaced in 1828 with a sliding scale of import duties, the manufacturing interests felt that the higher prices resulting from the existence of the scale contributed to the economic stagnation of the late 1830s. The antagonism against the Corn Laws was organized first in 1838 with the formation of the Manchester Association which, within a year, broadened into the Anti-Corn Law League. Initially led by disaffected Radicals, the League, by the early 1840s, was comprised almost exclusively of middle-class manufacturers and liberals. During its early development, the League devoted its energies and its growing financial resources to propagandizing its contention that the repeal of the Corn Laws would facilitate economic growth and social stability while raising the wages of laborers and the income of farmers. In order to mobilize a broad coalition of support, the League presented its arguments for free trade as a definite solution for the problems besetting English society. Richard Cobden, a leading Radical, presented the typical case for free trade:

> First, it would guarantee the prosperity of the manufacturer by affording him outlets for his products. Second, it would

> relieve "the condition of England question" by cheapening the price of food and ensuring more regular employment. Third, it would make English agriculture more efficient by stimulating demand for its products in urban and industrial areas. Fourth, it would introduce through mutually advantageous international trade a new era of international fellowship and peace.[71]

The aversion to the Corn Laws was converted into an argument for free trade and social harmony. The only obstacle to the acquisition of these related goals was the landed aristocracy. From the beginning, the Anti-Corn Law League was successful in gaining widespread support from middle-class manufacturers and businessmen. By the mid-1840s the League's appeal began to spread to a small but growing group of workers, the labor aristocracy—about whom much shall be said below. What facilitated the continuing expansion of the League was its ready access to the large sums of financial assistance made available by middle-class interests. When the initial usage of these financial resources for propaganda purposes proved of little avail, the league launched a systematic drive aimed at urging its now large membership to acquire the necessary property holdings which would qualify them for the vote. The intent, of course, was to pressure Parliament to repeal the Corn Laws through electoral mechanism.[72] As this recruitment and registration drive reached its peak in 1846, the Corn Laws were repealed.

The repeal, however, cannot be exclusively or even largely attributed to the League's activities, as McCord notes:

> By 1846 all the efforts of the League machine had resulted, at tremendous cost in money and effort, in winning only a few seats. . . . To all appearances the direct power of the League was still not very impressive.[73]

G. Kitson Clark concurs with this analysis. Recognizing the importance of the League and the middle-class agitation it mobilized, he suggests that it would "be equally correct to call [the repeal] 'a concession by the aristocracy,' a timely retreat, that is, from a forward position that had proved to be dangerous. . . . [The aristocrats] had their reward. After the battle the power remained in the same kind of hands as those in which it had rested before."[74]

The repeal of the Corn Laws was expedited not by the Whigs—the former allies of the middle class Radicals, but by the more conservative Tories. This action by the Tories, led by Robert Peel, was of extreme strategic importance, for it muted the middle-class challenge as it was approaching the peak of its strength. As a consequence, the landed aristocracy was able to maintain its position of power, although now in a somewhat weakened form, with little economic sacrifice.[75]

In taking this action the landed aristocracy was giving implicit recognition to the public and private distinction. In a sense, the aristocracy relaxed its claims on the private sphere in order to maintain its hold on the public sphere. This became clear in 1847 with the passage of the Factory Acts. The factory legislation, formulated and acted upon by the same people who repealed the Corn Laws, was justified in terms derived from the public and private distinction. The importance of this legislation for the purpose at hand is two-fold: First, it reflects the continuation of aristocratic power, despite repeal; and, second, it indicates how this power was transformed. That is, the aristocracy retained a decisive say in the political decision-making process. But from this point on, political decisions were introduced into the private sphere only if they could be demonstrated to be essential to the free market.

The factory legislation of 1847 had little novelty about it. The legislation contained provisions aimed primarily at enlarging and improving the enforcement of previous enactments. The restriction of work hours for women and children, the requirement that children receive some schooling, and the creation of a factory inspectorate were all established by the Factory Act of 1833. In an 1844 act, the educational provision was amended to specify the formation of a half-time system "whereby factory children were required to attend school during half the day as a condition of being employed in the factory the other half."[76] Only sporadically enforced, and then usually ineffectively, these acts did little to remedy work conditions.

The purpose of the 1847 act was to allow a stricter, more systematic application of the previously enacted provision. Accordingly, the act clearly stipulated that women and children could work only ten of the fifteen hours between 5:30 a.m. and 8:30 p.m. and, further, that children could enter the workplace only by producing a note certifying school attendance. To assure conformity with these regulations the punitive power of the factory inspectorate was extended. In a sense, the 1847 act sought to simplify factory legislation in an effort to facilitate its application.

By bringing the supervision of factory conditions under the domain of public administration, the factory legislation of the 1840s contributed to the growing centralization of the government; but at the same time, it served to restrict the scope of governmental power. In defending the legislation, the government and, more particularly, the landed interests relied on arguments which associated the factory acts with the moral improvement of the working class. According to this position, the factory acts constituted a furtherance of, rather than an impediment to, free trade. In having to so justify its actions, the government was careful not to contravene the public and private distinction. Indicative of the landed aristocracy's continuing power, the factory legislation also reflected a policy of limited interference into the private realm. As Lubenow notes in this regard,

> In no case was government authorized to do more than super-
> vise the conditions of labour in the factories. In no case was
> government authorized to interfere with the management of
> factory operations unless, of course, these operations had been
> involved in illegal practices. . . . The factory acts, like railway
> legislation, retained the distinction between governmental
> supervision and corporate management.[77]

The earlier situation, wherein economic decisions were influenced by governmental policy, was undergoing a reversal. The scope of governmental power
was being reduced, and the area where market mechanisms could operate
more or less freely of active political control was becoming substantially
enlarged.

Despite significant middle-class opposition, the factory legislation of
1847 prevailed. However, the manufacturers—as had the landed aristocracy
in the aftermath of the repeal of the Corn Laws—managed to solidify their
position. In many of the industrial areas of England, the economic conditions between 1845 and 1847 necessitated a reduction in factory operating
hours. The ten-hour restriction provided for in the Factory Act of 1847,
then, did not have an immediate impact on industrial production. When,
within the next several years, the economy rebounded, the manufacturers
met the new restrictions by introducing a relay system of work assignment.
By dividing factory children into shifts, and thereby assuring the continuous
presence of children in the factory throughout the work day, the relay system
effectively thwarted the hope of the adult male laborers that they would be
included, de facto, under the ten-hour restriction. Declared a lawful practice
in 1850, the relay system allowed the manufacturers to maintain a full productive schedule.[78]

As evidenced in the legislation examined above, the outcome of the struggle between middle-class and aristocratic interests had momentous implications. Under prolonged and sometimes severe attack, the landed aristocracy
managed to retain its hold on governmental power, only at the expense of
restricting the scope of this power. Political decisions in 1850 were made the
same way they were in the late 1830s: influenced by industrial manufacturers,
the landed aristocracy had the decisive input in the decision-making process.
The manufacturing interests still were not concerned with becoming active
participants in government. They concentrated on matters related to production, not politics, and they attended to decisions which were effected in
the private realm, the market. Now, however, the public and the private
spheres were further compartmentalized. Governmental activities became
restricted to those which could be justified as contributory to free trade.
Whether it was factory legislation, or matters relating to health and sanita-
tion, or education, the government defended its actions with reference to the

opportunities they provided for individual improvement. As a result, middle-class consciousness, at the core of which was the ethic of self-help, was immeasurably strengthened.[79] In the political realm, as in the economic realm, individual advancement was equated with social advancement. The legitimation of political decisions became coterminous with a self-sustaining productive and economic system.

THE LABOR ARISTOCRACY

By the 1850s, the ethic of self-help had assumed a prominent place in the programs of the middle class and the government. With many of the disputes between the middle class and the landed aristocracy now muted, if not settled, attention was increasingly devoted to the 'social question'; that is, the workers' place in society. Attempts to answer the social question centered on proposals to infuse working-class values and beliefs with self-help doctrines. Initially, these attempts concentrated upon the 'intelligent laborers,' the labor aristocracy; and every effort was made to clearly distinguish these respectable workers from their disreputable counterparts.

The labor aristocracy consisted of a small but growing group of workers who received higher wages (averaging thirty to forty shillings a week by mid-century), and who were employed more regularly and under better conditions than other workers. This level and regularity of earnings, as Hobsbawm points out, was the most important criterion of the labor aristocracy.[80] What permitted these differentials in wages and work conditions were the exclusionary practices associated with particular occupations. In the late 1830s and early 1840s, the distinction between skilled and unskilled occupations was based, not on features inherent in the occupations themselves, but on whether or not occupational entrance was restricted. At this time the labor aristocracy further demarcated itself from the rest of the working class. trial craft occupations which managed to retain traditional apprenticeship requirements.[81]

With the rise of the new metal industries beginning in the 1840s, the locus of the labor aristocracy shifted. By 1855 'new model' unions had been formed in all of these recently developed industries. The explicit intent of these unions was to improve the bargaining position of the individual groups of workers they represented. Accordingly, procedures were designed which, by limiting entry into these occupations, made the necessary skills scarce.[82] By transforming these newer industrial occupations into professions, the labor aristocracy further demarcated itself from the rest of the working class.

The emergence of the labor aristocracy in the 1840s and 1850s is attributable to the industrial and economic changes of the period. Hobsbawm, in his seminal paper on the labor aristocracy, finds three fundamental and related factors underlying its growth and maintenance:

the decline of domestic work and the corresponding rise of
the factory system; the relative decline of textiles and the old
consumer-goods trades and the rise of the heavy and metal-
working industries; the rise of women labor.[83]

These factors resulted in a process of uneven development which gave rise
to two broadly defined categories of labor; properly qualified skilled labor,
and common labor. The demand of the new industries and of the burgeoning factory system for common labor was easily met. In England, there
existed at this time a relatively large reserve army of labor, predominantly
comprised of women and recent Irish immigrants. Usually, both groups
were paid exceptionally low wages. Certainly this was one factor contributing to the high differentials between common and skilled labor. A second,
more important factor, came from the skilled laborers themselves. Recognizing
that labor, like any commodity, would rise in price the more scarce it became,
they established exclusionary unions which, in the highly competitive economy
of the period, undoubtedly enhanced their bargaining strength.

In short, the emergence of the labor aristocracy was directly related to
economic and industrial developments. The wide differentials which distinguished the labor aristocracy from the mass of common laborers were
determined by the particular nature of the labor market and the industrializing features of the productive apparatus. In terms of the ethic of self-help,
however, these differentials came to be portrayed as a function of superior
moral character. Lavishly praised by the middle class and the government,
the labor aristocracy was used to demonstrate to all workers the achievements made possible by initiative and determination.

By conferring respectability upon and by attributing their social standing
to the personal qualities of the labor aristocrats, the middle class greatly
improved the appeal of self-help. Unlike earlier times, when the middle
class attempted to mobilize the workers in an effort to threaten the aristocracy,
now the middle class "sought to bring about the fullest working class participation in the pursuit of socially approved goals."[84] To secure such active
participation, at least initially, from the labor aristocracy, the objectives
approved by the ethic of self-help were strikingly similar to those expressed
in working-class culture. Independence, self-protection, and social advancement were emphasized. Moreover, in accepting the core elements of Victorian
culture, the labor aristocracy was in no way bound to a strict adherence to
the laissez-faire principles of political economy.[85] The doctrine of self-help,
as earlier noted, concentrated upon cultural (artificial) rather than economic
(natural) matters. However, the diffusion of self-help ideals, to the extent
that they legitimated the prevailing institutions, did impose considerable
constraints on industrial activity. Under these circumstances, as Tholfsen
maintains,

> the maintenance of a critical and even radical stance posed no threat whatsoever to the ideological superstructure of Victorian society. In fact, it merely tended to conceal the extent of working class acquiescence in middle class rule. Thus, while trade unions fought hard against ruthless employers . . . they could win short-run gains, but no more. Because their criticism of errant employers was based on the official values of the culture, the militants had been ideologically disarmed.[86]

Flattened out in the 1840s, working-class values began to be circumscribed within the ethic of self-help in the 1850s and 1860s; and the key element in this second process was the labor aristocracy. Although still cognizant of class differences, the skilled laborers of 1860 no longer challenged the existing inequalities. The institutions and organizations they created did not seek to overturn these discrepancies; they could not, since this was possible only on the basis of individual initiative. Rather, the new cooperative societies and unions aimed primarily at providing opportunities for the expression of such initiative.

As self-help was increasingly accepted by the skilled laborers and their organizations, the labor aristocracy became a status group (in the Weberian sense) within the working class. It was in their leisure-time activities and consumption patterns—the first devoted to self-education and improvement, the second to acquiring those possessions indicative of the intelligent and diligent man—that the labor aristocrats most clearly and self-consciously distinguished themselves from the common laborers. Although the labor aristocracy injected working-class values with the predominant middle-class morality, it did not deny or repudiate its basic class identity. "Insofar as the 'aristocrat of labour' did accept certain values held by dominant groups in his society," R. Q. Gray notes, "he interpreted and reformulated them in terms of his own situation, mediated and diffused them through his own institutions."[87] In this way the labor aristocracy accepted middle-class consciousness without abandoning the working-class situation.

The working-class identity retained by the labor aristocracy was framed in an overriding status identity. In terms of this status consciousness, the worth of individual workers was assessed with reference to respectability and self-improvement. Thus, the class consciousness of the labor aristocracy was transmuted into a level consciousness. "Level consciousness," according to Robert Nisbet, "creates awareness of one's difference from others, rather than one's similarities. In this respect the individual is constantly motivated by distinctions he finds or invents between himself . . . and others."[88] The level consciousness developed by the labor aristocracy emphasized consumptive over productive relationships. While this did not entail the dismantling of the communal base of the labor aristocracy, it did result in separating the communities of the labor aristocracy from other working-class communities, and emptying them of their political thrust. Out of these developments emerged the labor aristocrat as the prototype of Lockwood's 'privatized worker.' Guided by a pecuniary model society, according prestige on the basis of material possessions (for these reflected an individual's character), and instrumentalizing work relationships, the labor aristocrat transformed working-class organizations and community associations into means for the achievement of a middle-class style of life.[89]

Accepting the ethic of responsibility entailed the simultaneous acceptance of individual responsibility. Accordingly, the existing institutions would be granted legitimacy insofar as they facilitated initiative and self-improvement. The legitimacy of these institutions, then, constituted an indirect affirmation of industrial capitalism. As a consequence, challenges to society became muted in a context of reformist policies.

By 1860 the labor aristocracy had completely incorporated the Victorian morality of self-help. Through their institutions and associations, the skilled laborers actively collaborated with the middle class: the middle class was imitated in the cultural realm and bargained with in the economic realm. Attributing its success—which was so widely chronicled in the self-help biographies of the period—to diligence and sacrifice, the labor aristocracy refused assistance to other workers and working-class organizations. By the end of the century, the larger part of the working class accepted the program of accommodation established by the labor aristocracy. When that happened, the denial of social responsibility was completed.[90]

THE NORM OF RECIPROCITY

The denial of social responsibility, which accompanied the labor aristocracy's acceptance of the ethic of self-help, was a direct consequence of the prolonged attack on working-class culture. As the content of working-class institutions became oriented to individual acts of exchange, the incorporation of the labor aristocracy and, ultimately, of the working class in general, proceeded with few interruptions. The key to this process of incorporation was the shift from political to exchange forms of domination.

Industrial capitalism substituted a domination based on a self-adjusting market and a self-generating productive apparatus for direct (and more or less accountable) political domination. Daphne Simon observes that it was a special characteristic of this society "that the ruling class [was] not supported by a privileged legal status, . . . the capitalist *as such* [had] no rights which the wage-earner [did] not have, and their relation to each other [was] not determined by their having a different status but by the contract which they both enter[ed] into."[91] Domination lost its legal and political covering, only to assume the form of exchange relations. In accordance with the organizing principles of market society, in terms of which exchange relations were subject to market rather than human control, men were related to one another instrumentally, as things or means. Engels' study, in particular, is replete with observations concerning the treatment of workers as machines, pieces of property, and inanimate objects.

Mediated through exchange relations, domination became rerooted in, and acquired legitimacy from, the expansion of formal rationality. Authority became reified, a function of the system's ability to reproduce itself. Along with the reification of authority, domination in the form of exchange occurred through the extraction of surplus value. This process was directly involved with the obligation derived from the norm of reciprocity.

With industrial capitalism it became possible to express exchange relations in a precise and quantifiable manner. This marks an important shift from the situation where social obligations—because they were qualitative in nature—were largely unspecified and, therefore, contingent upon the establishment of trust. Now it was possible to regulate exchange in accordance with some principle of equality—that is, to specify obligations in terms of the exchange of equivalents. In short, as sociocultural institutions were divorced from the economy, unspecifiable social obligations were replaced by specifiable economic obligations. Reciprocity, translated as contract, could be satisfied on purely economic grounds; the sanctioning power of reciprocity was no longer built into social relationships.[92] The foundation was thus laid for the later reconceptualization of "rights" and "freedom" in a way compatible with the dictates of industrial capitalism.

The intricate dynamics of domination produced through the exchange of equivalents has received its most thorough analysis in Marx's *Capital*. While primarily a theoretical critique and reconstruction of capitalism, it is a theory strongly informed by the specifics of capitalist development in England and, accordingly, has valuable bearing on this particular discussion. With regard to the exchange of equivalents, Marx writes:

> Every condition of the problem is satisfied, while the laws that regulate the exchange of commodities, have been in no way violated. Equivalent has been exchanged for equivalent. For the capitalist as buyer paid for each commodity, for the cotton, the spindle and the labour-power, its full value. He then did what is done by every purchaser of commodities; he consumed their use-value. . . . [In turn a] metamorphosis, [the] conversion of money into capital, takes place both within the sphere of circulation and also outside it; within the circulation because conditioned by the purchase of the labour-power in the market; outside the circulation, because what is done within it is only a stepping-stone to the production of surplus-value, a

process which is entirely confined to the sphere of production. Thus "tout est pour le mieux dans le meilleur des mondes possible."[93]

In this extremely important passage Marx puts his finger on the hidden, internal dynamics of domination in industrial capitalism. First, in agreement with the classical political economists, he notes the existence of an exchange of equivalents: in exchange for a full day's work the capitalist gives the workers wages representing the value of that work. Terminating their analysis at this point, the classical political economists were hard-pressed to offer a suitable explanation of profit. For them the explanation of profit resided in the superiority of capital over other commodities and/or the superiority of capitalists over other men. Going beyond this point, Marx recognizes that the exchange of equivalents is a superficial occurrence. Taking place behind the back of, but through, exchange relations is the creation of surplus value. For Marx the 'secret' underlying the exchange of equivalents is the value of labor time, which, when examined in the context of the productive process as a whole, reveals the source of profits, capital accumulation and power. He maintains that

> as the value of labour is only an irrational expression for the value of labour-power, it follows, of course, that the value of labour must always be less than the value it produces, for the capitalist always makes labour-power work longer than is necessary for the reproduction of its own value.[94]

Put differently, labor is different from other commodities in that it alone can create value. In the exchange of equivalents, although it appears that all labor is paid labor, the worker is actually paid not for his value-creating potential (labor power), but only for his labor. The value created over and above the cost of actual labor is appropriated by the capitalist, and serves to maintain his power over the workers. Thus, in the exchange relations between capitalists and workers there is a quantitative equality (which is enhanced with the shift to relative surplus value), but these exchange relationships occur in and disguise the context of the more qualitative inequalities developed upon the appropriation and accumulation of surplus value.[95]

The notion of surplus value enables us to recognize how the principles of reciprocity were sustained despite extensive exploitation. Harnessed to the market, the norm of reciprocity was emptied of those personalized, non-rational sentiments that were expressed in a readiness to help others. Instead, the norm of reciprocity now defined obligations in terms of an impersonal and rational calculus of the other's ability to repay. In these terms, the exchange of equivalents gave the appearance that reciprocal obligations were being met. This reinforced the contention of the doctrine of self-help—society owes the individual nothing—and redefined self-realization as a competitive activity. Moreover, as domination and exploitation became depersonalized, objects and laws seemed to take the place of people and interests.[96] In this context, social protest occurred primarily as a programmatic and generally uncoordinated response to economic crises. In the absence of these crises, the exchange relations based on the principle of calculable equality met the minimal and, in the last analysis, the exploitative demands of the norm of reciprocity. Hidden behind these exchange relations, power and domination went unchallenged.

Domination in industrial capitalism rested, then, upon the suppression of imagination, the quantification and privatization of social obligations, and the exchange of equivalents. Together these factors imposed a closed universe of discourse. Meaningful referentials, which would transcend the established system of production and exchange, were without channels of articulation. In this situation of one-dimensionality, the instrumentalization of working-class values and practices occurred. There is a paradox, writes Harold Perkin,

> that the period of most violent class conflict coincided with the period when the real incomes were rising faster than ever before in modern times, and that the transition around mid-century to more harmonious class relations coincided with a deceleration in their rate of growth.[97]

But how paradoxical was this? By mid-century the institutional framework which had previously animated class conflict had been largely minimized. And material deprivation is more easily accepted in the absence of socio-cultural institutions which express social relationships and obligatory rights. Class relations were harmonious in a cultural vacuum.

SOCIAL PROTEST

1848 has been called the year of revolution. Societies across the European continent were rampant with discord, as a massive movement for change threatened to completely undermine the existing order. England was one of the few European countries exempt from an insurrectionary threat. In the year of revolution, the remnants of the Chartist leadership did attempt to link the English workers with the activities on the continent; but the visible failure of its efforts served only to further debilitate an already weakened organization.

From the start, Chartism was organized as a national working-class movement aimed at bringing about societal change through the application of political pressure. The People's Charter, which contained among its Six

Points the demand for universal male suffrage, was presented to Parliament in 1839, 1842, and 1848. Yet, despite the several million signatures which accompanied each presentation, Parliament refused serious consideration to the Charter. In the face of this continuous refusal, Chartism was unable to mobilize anything more threatening than petition drives. There were several reasons for this. First, Chartism was less a national organization than it was a loose federation of regional groups. Within and between these regional groups, moreover, divisions existed between 'physical force' and 'moral force' Chartists, and between those who favored an alliance with middle-class Radicals and those opposed to such an arrangement. The inability of Chartism to establish coordination under a coherent set of objectives greatly impeded the scope of its activity. The kind of workers' uprisings which occurred in Newport, Llanidloes, and Birmingham during the early years of Chartism disappeared after 1845, to be supplanted by petitioning for the Charter and the Land Plan, a cooeprative-like scheme of withdrawal.

Another limitation to Chartism was created by the reorganized cooperative societies and trade unions beginning to emerge in the 1840s. Cooperation and unionism did not share the Chartist strategy of change through political pressure. Indeed, political matters were eschewed by both. The Cooperative Movement of this period sought to make the workers—or, more accurately, the skilled workers—an integral part of society; and unions, while still agents of conflict, engaged in protest only in times of economic distress, and were no longer concerned with infringements upon working-class culture and traditions. Such economically oriented conflict was easily accommodated with the creation of arbitration and conciliation measures in the 1850s and 1860s. Institutionalized in this way, the riots of this period, as Rudé notes, when "compared with the riots of the Regency period and the 1830's and 1840's . . . were hardly worth the name."[98]

After the 1830s social protest in England became, with the exception of several Chartist uprisings, less frequent, less intense, and drastically more limited in scope. To understand this state of affairs it is essential to examine the transformation of cooperation and unionism from oppositional to integrational mechanisms and, second, to analyze the constraints which impeded a fuller development of Chartism.

Cooperation and 'New Model' Unionism

With the dismantling of the G.N.C.T.U. in 1834, cooperation and trade unionism suffered a most serious setback. The Cooperative Movement separated from union activity and took on the features of a small sect seeking to bring the 'Rational Religion' of education to the masses.[99] Unionism during this period was found primarily among artisan groups, and was oriented almost exclusively to economic objectives. Lacking a political thrust, neither cooperation nor unionism offered a threat to the existing order.

Before 1834, cooperation and unionism were firmly integrated in the working-class community and its traditions and customs. To the extent that they, like other working-class associations, provided a sense of certainty and security, they did so as a result of their relationship to these traditional values. With the combined repression of working-class associations and suppression of working-class institutions, the basis of these feelings of security was undermined. What arose was a sense of habitual uncertainty. As Engels writes in 1844,

> The worker knows only too well that employment and food today do not mean employment and food tomorrow. He knows that any whim of his employer or any slackness in trade may throw him back into the morass of unemployment from which he has extricated himself for the time being. He knows that if he sinks into unemployment it will be difficult, and indeed often impossible, to survive. He knows how uncertain is the future for the industrial wage-earner.[100]

For a small group of workers, unionism and—in the 1840s—cooperation came to serve as a means for reestablishing security and certainty. Disengaged from the working-class community, however, unions and cooperative societies redefined security and certainty into economic matters.

As we have seen, the suppression of working-class culture facilitated, at least for the labor aristocracy, the transmutation of working-class values into the ethic of self-help. Following this acceptance of self-help was the transformation of working-class associations into provident organizations centrally concerned with thrift, sacrifice, and education. Actively supported by the middle class and encouraged by governmental legislation, the cooperative movement "exchanged its vision of the 'new moral world' for the more tangible advantages of the 'divi' . . . [and] trade unions, . . . no longer 'schools of war,' [became] schools in which workmen learned to be 'respectable and respected.' "[101] Security now required becoming part of the competitive society; and this is reflected in the restricted nature of the rebuilt associations. As Cole observes, the labor aristocracy's

> Trade Unions, its Friendly Societies, even its successful Cooperative Movement, were carried on under conditions which forbade access to the poorer strata among the workers. Trade Union contributions were too high. Friendly Societies demanded an exercise of 'thrift' which was beyond the reach of the less skilled operatives; the Cooperative Society called for cash from men and women who were compelled to buy on credit if they were to live at all.[102]

As self-help associations, the cooperative societies and unions developed in the 1840s and 1850s were, by their exclusionary character, closely fitted to the competitive dynamics of industrial capitalism. Through these associations and institutions, a reliable and achievement-oriented, skilled labor force was forged. And in 1858 the middle-class press praised these self-help organizations for teaching the lower classes "to think more justly of their fellow countrymen, to feel ashamed of their former prejudices, and to acknowledge that it rests with them and not with any Government to ameliorate their social condition."[103]

Cooperation   Unlike the cooperative movement of the 1820s and 1830s, which considered cooperative production and exchange as alternatives to and eventual replacements for the system of production and exchange engendered by industrial capitalism, the reconstituted cooperative movement of the mid-1840s "saw in the stores and workshops . . . the promises and the fulfillment of a better world, in which . . . the continuance of capitalism, with its capital owners and wage earners, was implicitly taken for granted."[104] Basic to this new form of cooperation was an acceptance of the established order and a substitution of secularism for the millenarianism of previous cooperation. There prevailed, in short, an ideological adherence to the ethic of self-help. With no alternatives to industrial capitalism forthcoming, cooperative societies regarded as their primary task that of enhancing the position of their individual members in the existing arrangements. This was to be accomplished by becoming sensitive to market dynamics, especially to the law of supply and demand, and by providing members with a cultural and social education that would make them self-reliant, reliable, and thrifty. The adherence to self-help, and the concomitant repudiation of social responsibility made by 'modern' cooperation, was expressed at the time in the movement's journal, *The Cooperator*:

> We have seen enough of Communism, enough of the Utopian ridiculous mummery of Socialism. . . . We don't want it; we have seen the new moral world, and don't like it. . . . Let Co-operation be what it is . . . [inculcating] no other spirit but gratitude to God, loyalty to our Sovereign, love to our country, and good-will to all mankind . . . in the cause of constitutional competitive co-operation.[105]

Cooperation no longer offered all workers an alternative to, even an escape from, the established order. It was unable to promise the possibility of an independent community. Instead, for a few workers, cooperation now offered the opportunity for investment and profit making.

The proliferation of cooperative societies, beginning in the late 1840s and continuing throughout the next twenty years, followed upon the widely publicized success of the Rochdale Pioneers—a cooperative venture instituted in 1844. The formation of the Rochdale Pioneers was influenced by a group of Owenite Socialists who had become disaffected from the increasing sectarianism of the post-1834 Cooperative Movement. Initially conceived as a politically and religiously neutral association, established to provide benefits to workers in periods of economic distress, the Rochdale cooperative society incorporated modified principles of capitalism exchange into a framework which remained in basic antipathy to industrial capitalism as such. While stipulating, in direct contrast to trading companies, that, first, each member would have one vote regardless of his or her financial contribution to the Pioneers' store and, second, that the amount of capital each member could hold was to be limited, the Rochdale society also insisted that buying and selling take place only on a cash basis, and determined that surplus would be allocated to members in proportion to their purchases.[106] Upon these two principles, the refusal of credit and the "divi" or dividend on purchases, the Rochdale Pioneers venture distinguished itself from earlier cooperative societies. It was also these two principles which set the Pioneers off from much of the working class, and contributed to a rapid expansion of its capital resources.

The immediate and phenomenal success of the Rochdale Pioneers dramatically lessened its antagonism toward the existing order and the capitalist procedures of exchange and distribution.[107] Through the ethic of self-help, the Rochdale cooperators were able to circumvent any tension which might result from the acceptance of middle-class values and the concomitant relinquishing of working-class values. For the reasons outlined previously, they were easily able to incorporate Victorian ideals in an ideological framework which retained the working-class emphasis on independence and community. From the late 1840s on, the Rochdale cooperative society regarded itself as a self-help institution, inculcating habits of thrift, building reliable and respectable individual characters, and providing a means for working-class savings and investments. By thus linking the stability of cooperation so directly to the stability of prevailing (especially economic) institutions, the Rochdale Pioneers had a vested interest in the continuing growth of industrial capitalism.

Following the model established by the Rochdale Pioneers, numerous cooperative societies developed as self-help institutions, all organized to instill in their members the virtues of middle-class morality. To encourage the extension of the already existing societies, and the growth of modern cooperation in general, the government, with middle-class support, established the Industrial and Provident Societies Act of 1852. Prior to this act, cooperative societies had no legal status and were, therefore, without protection against unjust claims made on their capital reserves.[108] Lacking safeguards for accumulated capital, many of the recently developed cooperative societies deliberately limited their membership and the amount of capital which members could invest and/or save. By the Act of 1852, adequate protections were provided; and, moreover, the Cooperative Movement was both praised and conferred with respectability by the dominant groups in society. Subsequent to this act, the Cooperative Movement quickly spread throughout the labor aristocracy. In 1862 the cooperative societies demanded and received the privilege of limited liability, making them the working-class equivalent of the corporate enterprise.

Modern cooperation had a rather significant impact on the reorganization of trade unions which began in the 1850s. These cooperative societies brought about, in Hobsbawm's words, "the conscious adjustment of skilled workers to the 'rules of the game.' "[109] Cooperative societies contributed to the acceptance of and familiarity with the 'rules of the game' in two fundamental ways. First, by emphasizing frugality and initiative, they helped forge a disciplined and reliable labor force, at least with respect to skilled laborers. Secondly, by successfully incorporating capitalist principles of exchange and distribution, the new cooperative societies appeared to illustrate the advantages forthcoming from a recognition and understanding of market dynamics, trade cycles, and the law of supply and demand. Modern unionism was established upon these two aspects of cooperation. Initially restricted to the 'intelligent,' 'prudent,' and 'determined' laborers—in other words, skilled laborers—new unions were designed to limit membership in order to enhance their bargaining position and, in turn, to raise the price of labor in the market. By so extending the law of supply and demand, they, along with the political economists, were regarding labor as a commodity. Thus submitting itself to the regulations of the marketplace, the new unionism, like the new cooperation, further distanced itself from the moral regulations of the working class community.

'New model' Unionism "Trade unionism," Engels writes in his 1844 study of the working class, "is an ideal preparation for social war."[110] While this statement would have been widely accepted fifteen years earlier, in the 1840s it constituted a serious misreading of the situation. After the mid-1830s, trade unionism was an ideal preparation for integratin with the established the central thrust of industrialization; and, beginning in the mid-1840s, the skilled workers in the newly emerging industries developed their restrictive unions. Both the earlier craft unions and the new industrial unions were exclusive and specialized, set apart from the unskilled majority of workers.[111] In this period, then, especially with the growing influence of cooperation, trade unionism was an ideal preparation for integration with the established

order. Throughout the 1840s, for example, trade unions by and large refused participation in and support to the Chartist Movement.

Although 'new model' unionism formally arose in 1852 with the establishment of the Amalgamated Society of Engineers, it had been anticipated in
general outline by union developments in the 1840s. Restricted to skilled
laborers, the new model trade unions expressed limited and moderate objectives. No longer concerned with societal reconstruction, the new unions
resolutely set themselves to "become integral parts of the structure of the
modern industrial state."[112] Denouncing strikes as detrimental to the stability
of this state, the revived unionism sought to enter into mutual accommodation,
a kind of bargaining relationship, with the middle-class employers.

Structurally, new model unionism differed from the unionism of the
1830s in three major ways. First, it was rigidly exclusive, charging high dues
which could only be afforded by a few. Secondly, it was comprised of discrete
and specialized unions strictly opposed to the formation of a general union.
Exclusionary practices were incorporated to effect the market scarcity of
particular skills and, also, to enhance status distinctions within the working
class. Each specialized union regarded its trade as a profession which, like
all learned professions, warranted protections and privileges from society.
A third distinguishing feature of new model unionism was its inclusion of
certain aspects of modern cooperation. Many of the unions which developed
after 1850 were affiliated with friendly or cooperative societies which operated
on the principles of cash payment and dividends on purchases. Using the
economic rewards through union bargaining to invest in cooperative ven-
tures, skilled laborers rather quickly became accustomed to the logic of
capitalist exchange.[113]

The privatized worker, by Lockwood's definition, engages in trade union
activity for instrumental purposes, not to engender or enhance class solidarity. Trade unions, as a result, lose their affective attachment to the working-
class community and are reshaped in a utilitarian mold.[114] The notion of the
privatized worker is applicable to the labor aristocracy, but only in a limited
way. With the labor aristocracy it was not simply a matter of replacing class
solidarity with instrumental rationality. What occurred, rather, was the
instrumentalization of existing class relations. That is, the labor aristocracy
retained a community and a sense of solidarity; and, moreover, new model
unionism was rooted in this community and solidarity. Community identity
was established, however, by contrasting the character and style of life of
the labor aristocrat with those of the common laborer. Unions, accordingly,
could strengthen community cohesion only by enhancing existing status
differences. As one member wrote about the new unions, "They by no means
seek to place the *superior* and the only average workman upon an equal
footing."[115]

In short, the labor aristocrat can be considered a privatized worker to the extent that his community attachments and union activity were valued for personal or familial status and for the eocnomic benefits they secured. However, insofar as these benefits served to highlight the distinctiveness of the labor aristocracy as a group, they provided the labor aristocrat with a clearly demarcated class identity. As noted earlier, it was this situation which facilitated the labor aristocracy's ready acceptance of self-help values and institutions. The individualized exchange activities of the privatized worker could, in these circumstances, be justified in accordance with working-class standards.[116]

Resting upon a class-based collectivity, then, new model unionism was essentially a mechanism for satisfying privatized needs, to differentiate the 'intelligent' worker from the common laborer. Demanding no longer a redistribution of wealth but now merely an increase in wages, the unions of the 1850s became more acceptable to the dominant powers. Beginning in 1855, consequently, the government enacted legislation which conferred formal recognition upon trade unions. Despite the repeal of the Combination Laws, trade unions were still without legal status since, in terms of common law, they constituted an unlawful constraint on free trade. Not only were union activities restricted, but union funds were in constant jeopardy. To encourage the conciliatory orientation of the new model unions, the government passed the Friendly Societies Act of 1855, which extended legal privileges to unions providing benefit services. This was followed with the Molestation of Workmen Act in 1859, which gave legal recognition to peaceful picketing, and established more broadly conceived rights of combination. This process of legitimating trade unionism was completed in 1867 with the repeal of the Law of Master and Servant, which made the violation of contract a criminal act only when the party committing the violation was a worker.[117]

By according legal status to the unions, the government enhanced their stake in the established order, and thereby precipitated the formulation of even more pacific union policies. Developed in the 1860s and perfected in the 1870s were a number of arbitration and conciliation measures which were increasingly relied upon for the settlement of industrial disputes. The boards of arbitration and conciliation, in which the struggle for wages and work conditions became confined, "had written constitutions with provisions to specify their composition, regulate the timing of their meetings and to stipulate their powers. . . . [T]hey constituted a systematic, orderly method for dealing with industrial disputes which formed the framework for a system of collective bargaining."[118] While the composition of these boards was divided equally between employers' and workers' representatives, J. H. Porter has found that over 80 percent of the arbitrators were either employers, politicians, or lawyers. What this suggests to Porter is that "it is unlikely that [persons] would have been invited to arbitrate if they had not shared the conventional view of political economy.''[119] Not surprisingly, then, the resolution of industrial disputes by boards was usually determined with reference to the current state of the market. By binding itself to these negotiating procedures, new model unionism even further disassociated itself from the noneconomic, substantive criteria of action which earlier guided the workers pursuit of a better life.

Strongly contributing to this institutionalization of union activities and objectives was the London Trades Council, which was formed in 1860. The L.T.C. rose out of the movement for a nine-hour day generated by the building trades. Formally, its domain was confined to the London Trades; but within the next several years it became the central instrument of the "Junta," the eventual leadership group of the trade union movement. Beginning in 1860, the various unions throughout England located their salaried officials in London, where they developed strong ties with each other. Working through the L.T.C., representatives of the Engineers, Carpenters, Ironfounders, and Bricklayers, among others, brought a high degree of centralization to the union movement.

The primary goal of the Junta was to secure legal status for trade unions. In pursuit of this aim, the Junta established close associations with sympathetic middle-class groups. In return for this assistance, however, the Junta was obliged to mobilize trade union support behind the political causes of the middle-class sympathizers.[120] At the same time, the Junta was compelled to more explicitly deprecate the practice of striking, in order to adhere more closely to the individualism emphasized in self-help and political economy. The policies formulated by the Junta, accordingly, were hinged to political reform. As the Webbs observe, the Junta

> believed that a levelling down of all political privileges, and the opening out of educational and social opportunities to all classes of the community, would bring in its train a large measure of economic equality.[121]

Thus, the Junta solidified trade unionism's acceptance of the ethic of self-help, individual advancement, and the separation of the public and private spheres.

From this relationship between the Junta and the middle class grew the impetus for arbitration and conciliation. The almost simultaneous development of 'Lib Lab' politics—an alliance between middle-class liberals and labor—also had its roots in this period. By 1867, when cooperation and trade unionism had been sufficiently adapted to requirements of sustained industrial and economic growth, a second Reform Act was passed and the franchise was brought to certain segments of the working class. This indicated not a victory for the working class, but the successful emasculation of working-class associations, institutions, and values. Cooperation and unionism had been effectively transformed from agents of change to agents of incorporation.

Chartism

The Chartist Movement differed from new model unionism and modern cooperation in two essential ways: it was a popular movement seeking to attract the participation and support of all workers; and from the beginning it was oriented toward political activity. In one sense, Chartism can be viewed as an attempt to mobilize the sense of revenge, despair, and disillusionment which prevailed among the workers in the mid-1830s in the cause of social change. Although proposing to effect change by working through the existing institutions, Chartism is the only serious attempt to initiate class struggle during this period.

Chartism has its roots in the virulent agitation which arose in the manufacturing districts in 1836 with the introduction of the New Poor Law. The antagonism the workers had harbored against the middle class and the government since the 1832 Reform Act considerably intensified when, in the midst of rising unemployment and a sluggish economy, their request for assistance was met with assignment to the workhouse. The hunger revolts which pervaded the factory districts between 1836 and 1839 were largely aimless and unorganized, causing much disruption of, but no significant threat to, the established arrangements. In the efforts to channel this activity to a more effective direction, Chartism was born.

The organizational impetus of the Chartist Movement grew out of the relationship between the Birmingham Political Union and the London Working Men's Association. Revived in 1837 after having dissolved three years earlier, the B.P.U. was a political society comprised of members drawn almost exclusively from the middle class. The B.P.U., even more explicitly than the Anti-Corn Law League, was designed to encourage collaboration between the middle and working classes.[122]

Linked to the B.P.U. by several overlapping members, the most prominent of whom was Francis Place, the London Working Men's Association was founded in 1836 by a group of London workers for educational and propaganda purposes. It was in the meetings of the L.W.M.A. that the idea for a 'People's Charter' originated. With the assistance of Place and other B.P.U. members a Charter was prepared which received the support of the two groups. However, where the middle-class leaders of the B.P.U. regarded the Charter as a first step toward the implementation of worker support for the middle-class opposition to the aristocracy, the L.W.M.A. saw the Charter as a means through which workers could acquire predominant control of society. Shortly after, with the Chartist-inspired struggle in the mining and factory areas, the B.P.U. "lost [its] influence and found [itself] more and more alarmed at the character of working class agitation [it] had helped to create."[123] But by this time Chartism had acquired its own dynamic.

Chartist activity systematically began in 1838 with the launching of meetings and rallies throughout the country, especially in the industrial areas where the agitation against the New Poor Law of 1834 was strengthening daily. The immediate objectives of Chartism, which still retained B.P.U. support at this time, were to publicize the demands contained in the Charter, and to establish a Chartist Convention attended by delegate representatives of all segments of the working class. It was hoped that through such a convention a more formalized movement, if not organization, could be created. Convened in February of 1839, the first Chartist Convention had representatives from most of the industrial districts of England.[124] The deliberations of the convention included a consideration of ways to stabilize the movement (for instance, in the collection of dues and the establishment of communication), and a discussion of appropriate measures for submitting to Parliament a petition in favor of the Charter, which contained 1,200,000 signatures.

Shortly following the convention, industrial unrest assumed more coordination and, consequently, intensified. What were formerly isolated hunger riots became a quasi-national movement, loosely strung together by common agreement with the Charter. Riots in Llanidloes, Birmingham, and Yorkshire had wide repercussions; and throughout industrial England, workers began to organize in disciplined and armed groups.[125] When it became obvious that the petition submitted to Parliament in July of 1839 was being deliberately ignored, this kind of activity increased; and, to a corresponding degree, middle-class support withered.

The most important of the later protest activities was the Newport uprising, which occurred in November, 1839, and typified both the growing interconnectedness of the various Chartist groups and the still inept communication network which existed among them. The strategy underlying the Newport action was as follows: Large groups from three adjacent areas were to have converged upon and captured the town of Newport and, from there, begin an attack on Monmouthshire—where Henry Vincent, a Chartist leader, was imprisoned. The ultimate aim of the uprising was to precipitate similar takeovers throughout the country and, thereby, to precipitate the eventual capitulation of Parliament to the demands of the Charter. On the designated night of attack, only one group, comprised of several thousand colliers, arrived at Newport; and it was easily forced into retreat by the soldiers stationed in the area.[126]

The government's reaction to Chartism, in the aftermath of the Newport uprising, was severe. The leaders of the aborted takeover received death sentences, which were later commuted to transportation for life. Chartist leaders throughout the country were harassed, arrested, imprisoned, and deported. The extensiveness of the government's repression resulted in the virtual collapse of Chartism by early 1840.

Before the close of 1840, however, Chartism had been reorganized with the founding of the National Charter Association in Manchester. The N.C.A. continued adherence to the original six points of the Charter, but differed from earlier Chartism by, first, regarding itself as an exclusively working-class movement and, second, by discouraging the kind of riotous activity which had proliferated in 1839. Emphasizing legal channels of protest, the N.C.A. was an attempt to develop a prototypical political party. Using the language of self-help, although not in the diluted sense employed by coopera-tion and unionism, the N.C.A. sponsored the creation of educational and provident societies which could be used later as a base for mobilizing working-class support.[127] While its program never received complete acceptance, the N.C.A. did serve as the organizational basis for the Chartism of the 1840s.

The Chartist Movement was never able to completely unite the various regional and ideological groups which marched under its banner. Impeding unification were several factors, the most important of which were the con-tinued harassment by the government, the inability to elaborate and articulate a meaningful and comprehensive theoretical framework capable of guiding social action, and growing factions within the Chartist leadership. Shortly after its formation, the N.C.A. experienced a split between 'moral force, and 'physical force' factions. When the N.C.A. leadership opted for the 'moral force' policies, the 'physical force' faction remained in the associa-tion, where it continued adamantly to apply pressure for a more militant approach.

Within the 'moral force' faction, a further split developed over the ques-tion of Chartism's relationship to the middle class. In 1841 and 1842 there were attempts by numerous middle-class associations, in particular the Anti-Corn Law League and the Complete Suffrage Union, to establish ties with the Chartist Movement.[128] During this period, it will be recalled, renewed opposition between the middle class and the aristocracy was being shaped. The Union and—to a lesser extent—the League offered to support the Chartist demand for the franchise on the condition that the Chartists disassociate from and denounce militant-sounding appeals to the workers. Although a small group of 'moral force' Chartists urged an alliance with the middle-class Radicals, a larger segment found such an alliance (which would have subordinated the Charter to such middle-class aims as the repeal of the Corn Laws) repugnant. As Brontere O'Brien said of the middle class in the move-ment's paper, the *Northern Star*:

> We have a perfect right to hold them responsible for those evils—seeing they will never remove themselves, nor suffer us to do so—and that no sane person would think of uniting for

> any purpose with known enemies, our proper business as
> Chartists, is to combine together as one man, not *with* the
> middle class, but *against* them, in order to put an end to their
> usurpations.[129]

As this view gained in prominence, the Chartist opposition to middle-class
associations assumed a more stringent tone. In contradistinction to modern
cooperation and unionism, Chartism explicitly portrayed the middle class
in the most hostile of terms; and Chartist disruptions of League and Union
meetings were extremely common in the early 1840s.[130]

The demands set forth by the Chartist Movement were framed within the
six points contained in the originally formulated People's Charter. As presented in the regulations of the N.C.A., the guiding principles were:

> The right of voting for members of Parliament, by every male
> of twenty-one years of age, and of sound mind; Annual Elec-
> tions; Vote by Ballot; no Property Qualification for Members
> of Parliament; Payment of Members; and a division of the
> Kingdom into Electoral Districts; giving to each district a
> proportionate number of representatives according to the
> number of electors.[131]

The central thrust of Chartism appeared to be directed toward the acquisition
of universal male suffrage. However, this was not entirely the case. In the
first place, the Chartists had repudiated the proposed middle-class alliance,
even though the Union and the League offered to support this particular
Chartist demand. And, as many historians have observed, the Chartists
regarded male suffrage merely as a means whereby broader working-class
objectives involving the redistribution of societal resources—power as well
as wealth—could be implemented.[132] Thus, the Chartist pursuit of the vote
was intended, not as a way of integrating the disenfranchised into society,
but as a way of asserting workers' rights while avoiding unnecessary blood-
shed and repression. Like the machine wrecking practiced by the Luddites
in 1815, the moderate and controlled agitation in support of male suffrage
was the most effective tool available to the Chartists in a period when more
militant activity would have immediately engendered severe repressive
measures.

In May, 1842, the House of Commons rejected the second National
Charter by a vote of 287 to 49. In response to this rejection, to increasing
wage cuts, and to unemployment generated by a faltering economy, numerous
strikes and several riots emerged, the most important being the Plug Plot riots.
These activities, however, were rather quickly contained; and the Chartist
Movement once again suffered a serious setback.

Ambiguity best characterizes the state of Chartism from this point on. Although Engels wrote in 1845 that "[i]t cannot be long before Chartism moves towards Socialism," the fact was that the Chartist program was becoming more and more disjointed.[133] The apparent successes of the Anti-Corn Law League, and the growing acceptance of middle-class morality by the labor aristocracy, combined to weaken the Chartist denunciation of class collaboration, and consequently served to partially redirect the movement's course. The nature of this redirection is typified in the development of the Chartist Land Plan. As initially formulated by Feargus O'Connor in 1843, the Land Plan incorporated elements of Owenite Cooperation. In basic outline, it designed a series of small, peasant villages which would be occupied by smallholders who would be required to pay rent for their cottages, but would otherwise retain the full benefits of their labor. In 1845, the N.C.A. formally accepted the Land Plan by establishing the Chartist Co-operative Land Society with the primary objective being

> To purchase land on which to locate such of its members as may be selected for that purpose, in order to demonstrate to the working classes of the kingdom, firstly the value of the land, as a means of making them independent of the grinding capitalist; and, secondly, to show them the necessity of securing the speedy enactment of the 'People's Charter,' which would do for them nationally what this society proposes to do sectionally.[134]

Thus, the Charter was now to be achieved through the practice of self-help; but in terms of the Land Plan, self-help was to practice by transforming the workers into peasants, not bourgeoisie.

From 1845 to 1847 Chartism was preoccupied with the Land Plan. After extensively publicizing it for a year, the N.C.A. implemented the scheme with the formation of O'Connorville, scheduled to be the first of many Chartist villages. O'Connorville was intended for "the landless, helpless multitude now thronging the filthy lanes, courts and allies of our cities and manufacturing towns."[135] However, while the Land Plan initially struck a responsive chord among the factory operatives in the industrial north, its strongest appeal ultimately resided among the artisans in the smaller towns with declining industries. Importantly, then, the reliance on the Land Plan had the unintended effect of weighting Chartism more in favor of craftsmen and less in favor of factory workers.

The popularity accorded to the Land Plan is attributed by Joy MacAskill to the insecurity and specialization which had become entrenched in industrial capitalism.[136] The Land Plan appealed especially to those artisans whose skills were becoming increasingly obsolete. Unable to meet the standards of modern cooperation and unionism, they regarded the Land Plan as a form of cooperative practice wherein their crafts could be maintained in some combination of agriculture and the domestic system. With the financial collapse of O'Connorville in 1847, however, the scheme's popular support promptly withered away.

The failure of the Land Plan once again left the Chartist Movement in a dormant stage. However, the events on the Continent, culminating with the revolution in France in February of 1848, convinced the Chartist leadership that the time was ripe for a third presentation of the Charter. Just prior to the submission of the Charter to the House of Commons, a convention was held in April, where it was resolved that continued rejection of the National Petition by Parliament would be met by the establishment of a provisional government designed to pressure the Queen and her cabinet to enact the Charter as law.[137] To reinforce this threat the Chartists scheduled a massive demonstration on April 10 on Kennington Common in London.

In preparation for the demonstration the government detached 170,000 constables to meet the 500,000 demonstrators which the Chartists anticipated. When less than 25,000 demonstrators appeared on the Common, the governmental forces were able to summarily contain their activities.[138] Rather than marking the introduction of the age of revolution in England, the events of April 10 clearly highlighted the ineffectiveness of the Chartist Movement. Before the month was out, the House of Commons changed its position on the Charter from one of neglect to one of ridicule. And, although a national Assembly was convened in May, it was terminated after two weeks of constant bickering and indecisiveness on the part of its members. For all practical purposes, Chartism had lost its effectiveness and hope. While the movement was nominally perpetuated until 1858, it had but a minimal program and an inconsequential following. Ernest Jones—perhaps the most militantly inclined of the Chartist leaders, who vehemently repudiated middle-class entreaties in the 1840s, was suggesting in the early 1850s that "there can be no doubt as to the wisdom of allying with the middle classes and their leaders if they offer such a measure of reform as we can be justified in accepting."[139] The shift in Jones' position paralleled the shift in Chartism itself.

Among the more important factors contributing to the failure of Chartism was the extensive use of government force employed against the movement from its beginning. As soon as the hunger riots of 1836 became political riots in support of the Charter in 1839, troops were quickly dispatched; and eventually many industrial areas were assigned a standing military force. From 1839 to the late 1840s thousands of Chartists were arrested and either imprisoned or transported. Most of the Chartist leadership, both on national and regional levels, was incarcerated at one time or another during this period; and this was partially responsible for the disorganized character of the movement.

In its response to the Chartist threat, the government, through the con-tinual intervention of the Home Office, established a stable police force, and perfected and vastly strengthened the domestic capacities of the regular army. In its initial quest for order, the government relied on an auxiliary police force comprised of army out-pensioners. Under local jurisdictions, the efficiency and effectiveness of the auxiliary forces varied considerably. To rectify this, the Metropolitan Police Act of 1839 was passed, constructed so as to bring the police force under centralized control. This Act stipulated the permanent patrolling of districts, and was intended to clarify the pre-ventive role of the police force. Although the Act formally applied to London, it was used as the general model for police forces throughout the country.[140]

Similar changes occurred in the use of military force. In the early phases of Chartism, the Yeomanry, a voluntary military force officered by the landed aristocracy and gentry, and served by small landowners, was used in conjunction with an auxiliary force consisting of Enrolled Pensioners against the Chartist uprisings.[141] Although part of the military apparatus, both of these groups operated under civil authority. When this measure proved inadequate to the task of containing Chartism, the regular army was called in. By the mid-1840s the regular army had a contingent of 30,000 troops exclusively designed for domestic use: the greatest concentrations of these troops were found in industrial districts of England, the strongholds of Chartism.[161] With their mobility significantly enhanced due to the develop-ment of the railway system, these troops were quickly and effectively sent from one troubled area to another.[142]

Facing the well-armed and highly organized opposition provided by the government and the middle class, Chartism's only chance for success lay in a united working class. One impediment to such unity was the growth of the labor aristocracy. In order to maintain their highly distinctive status within the working class, skilled laborers avoided Chartism and engaged their energies in modern cooperation and new model unionism. The self-help institutions of the labor aristocracy differed from self-help Chartism, in regarding political power as an ineffective means for bringing about eco-nomic transformations. Closer to the individualism of middle-class morality than to the collectivism contained in working-class values, the self-help orientation of the labor aristocracy was used to justify the exclusionary character of the skilled laborers' associations. Not only did the labor aris-tocracy refuse assistance to the organizations of the common laborers; it also renounced them. As one working-class observer noted,

> Between the artisan and the unskilled labourer a gulf is fixed. While the former resents the spirit in which he believes the followers of genteel occupations look down upon him, he in his turn looks down upon the labourer. The artisan creed with

> regard to the labourers is, that they are an inferior class, and
> that they should be made to know this and kept in their place.[143]

Thus Chartism, out of necessity, had its major base of support among the unskilled and semi-skilled workers who comprised the reserve army of labor. At a time when such labor was readily available and cheap (there being a heavy reliance upon women and Irish immigrant labor), it became relatively easy to circumscribe the thrust of the Chartist Movement.

The Chartist Movement was always burdened with a disjointed organizational structure and a limited and somewhat incoherent program. More than anything else, however, Chartism's failure resided in its inability to articulate a common ideological bond around which a distinctive and meaningful set of working-class beliefs could crystallize. Unlike previous movements, where a playful return to the past produced images of the future shared by workers with diverse traditions and backgrounds, Chartism lacked a transcendent vision. The alternatives it proposed were either not significantly different from the prevailing arrangements or they were regressive in orientation.[144] To the extent that its formulation of an ideological consciousness relied on the past, it did so unhistorically. There was no attempt to confront the past with the present; and, in the absence of this confrontation, the emergence of transcendent criteria of action was impeded. This unreflective use of the past is clearly illustrated in the Land Plan alternative. The Land Plan proposed a return to the preindustrial village: it vilified industrialization and celebrated the life of the agricultural laborer. There was no recognition whatever of the beneficial possibilities contained in industrialization under the control of the communal principles suggested by the preindustrial village. The problem with the Chartists, Franz Neumann has observed, was that they "did not understand that the clock of history cannot be turned back, that industrialization must be accepted as a fact and that political power must be employed as the decisive instrument for the control of industrialization."[145] Lacking this understanding, Chartism surrendered its political goals by the mid-1840s. Rather than confront the present with memories of the past and anticipations of the future, Chartism tried to deny the present and to return to the past. Caught in the emerging one-dimensionality of industrial capitalism, Chartism could not discern historical alternatives; and, as a consequence, choice became limited to the present.

As a national movement Chartism was constrained by—indeed it partially reflected—the emerging one-dimensionality, the instrumentalization of culture, the constriction of the creative dynamic of play, and the dissolution of meaningful attachments to the past. Despite the increasing success of the assaults on working-class culture and communities, and the subsequent penetration of instrumental rationality, the Chartist Movement—at least for several years—did provide significant and sometimes effective opposition to the established authority structures. What acounts for this oppositon—which was not a mere reaction to economic distress—is the existence of social and geographical locations which had managed to retain a playful attachment to the past. Workers from these groups, communities, and areas sustained a rebellious disposition; and they were the most frequent and most intense participants in the Chartist Movement. Chapter 5 examines these refuges of two-dimensionality to ascertain both their contribution to and the limitations they imposed on the Chartist Movement.

NOTES

1. E. P. Thompson, *The Making of the English Working Class* (New York, 1963), p. 763.
2. J. L. and Barbara Hammond, *The Skilled Labourer* (London, 1936), p. 6.
3. See Mary Douglas, *Natural Symbols* (New York, 1973), p. 90.
4. See Karl Polanyi, "On Obsolete Market Mentality," *Primitive, Archaic, and Modern Economies* (New York, 1968), p. 68.
5. See A. D. Gayer, *The Growth and Fluctuation of the British Economy* (New York, 1953), p. 247-253.
6. Arthur Redford, *Labour Migration in England, 1800-1850* (Manchester, 1964), p. 107.
7. On the extraordinary growth of the railroad industry in this period, see Phyllis Deane and W. A. Cole, *British Economic Growth, Trends, and Structures* (Cambridge, 1962), p. 231; and William Lubenow, *The Politics of Government Growth* (Hamden, Conn., 1971), p. 108.
8. Deane and Cole, *British Economic Growth,* p. 240.
9. See Elie Halevy, *The Age of Peel and Cobden* (New York, 1948), pp. 83-84; and S. G. Checkland, *The Rise of Industrial Society in England, 1815-1885* (London, 1964), p. 344.
10. Karl Marx, *Capital,* vol. I (New York, 1967), p. 154, emphasis added. See p. 314 for the distinction between absolute and relative surplus value.
11. See Nathan Rosenberg, "The Direction of Technological Change," *Economic Development and Cultural Change* 18 (1969): 5, for a clear description of the process of compulsive sequences.
12. Stanley Udy, *Work in Traditional and Modern Society* (Englewood Cliffs, 1970), p. 71.
13. See S. N. Eisenstadt, *The Political Systems of Empires* (New York, 1964), pp. 97-98.
14. Karl Marx, *The Grundrisse* (New York, 1971), p. 107.
15. J. F. C. Harrison, *The Early Victorians, 1832-1851* (New York, 1971), p. 144.
16. Norman Birnbaum, *The Crisis of Industrial Society* (New York, 1969), p. 133.
17. See John O'Neill, *Sociology As a Skin Trade* (New York, 1972), p. 33.
18. The implications of this are discussed in Gareth Stedman Jones, "Working-Class Culture and Working-Class Politics in London, 1870-1900: Notes on the Remaking of a Working Class," *Journal of Social History* 7 (1974): 464-466.

19. See Robert Malcolmson, *Popular Recreations in English Society, 1700-1850,* (London, 1973), p. 15 for examples.

20. See E. J. Hobsbawm and George Rudé, *Captain Swing* (New York, 1969), p. 211.

21. Malcolmson, *Popular Recreations,* pp. 79-80.

22. See ibid., pp. 89-94.

23. Ibid., p. 150.

24. Brian Harrison, "Religion and Recreation in Nineteenth-Century England," *Past and Present* 38 (December 1967): 117-118.

25. *Derby Mercury,* August 10, 1842, as quoted in Malcolmson, *Popular Recreations,* p. 146.

26. See Trygve Tholfsen, "The Intellectual Origins of Mid-Victorian Stability," *Political Science Quarterly* 86 (1971): 79-81.

27. See Ford Brown, *Fathers of the Victorians* (Cambridge, 1961), pp. 4-5; and Noel Annan, *Leslie Stephen* (Cambridge, 1952), p. 113.

28. Evangelicalism was immediately concerned with working-class recreations, but it also opposed aristocratic leisure. See Walter Houghton, *The Victorian Frame of Mind* (New Haven, 1957), p. 245.

29. See Thompson, *The Making of the English Working Class,* p. 740 and Tholfsen, "The Intellectual Origins of Mid-Victorian Stability," p. 88.

30. See Tholfsen, "The Intellectual Origins of Mid-Victorian Stability," p. 83.

31. See Richard Johnson, "Educational Policty and Social Control in Early Victorian England," *Past and Present* 49, 4 (1970): 100.

32. See ibid., pp. 100-108. In the context of educational reform, self-improvement was directly extended to the play activities of working-class children. See Lillian Shiman, "The Band of Hope Movement: Respectable Recreation for Working-Class Children," *Victorian Studies* 17, 1 (1973): 49-74.

33. Johnson, "Educational Policy and Social Control," p. 103.

34. Ibid., p. 119.

35. See John Stuart Mill, *Principles of Political Economy* (New York, 1895); and Sebastian de Grazia, *Of Time, Work, and Leisure* (New York, 1962), pp. 285-288, 350-365. In a sense, Mill is democratizing liberal individualist theory by introducing a second concept of human essence. Man is still an infinite appropriator (the private realm); but now he is also an infinite developer of human attributes (in the public realm). See C. B. Macpherson, "Democratic Theory: Ontology and Technology," in *Political Theory and Social Change* (New York, 1967), pp. 211-217.

36. Jerome Buckley, *The Triumph of Time* (Cambridge, 1966), p. 137.

37. See E. P. Thompson, "Time, Work-Discipline and Industrial Capitalism," *Past and Present* 38 (December, 1967): 85-86.

38. de Grazia, *Of Time, Work and Leisure,* p. 200.

39. See Victor Gioscia, "On Social Time," *The Future of Time* (New York, 1972), p. 104.

40. E. J. Hobsbawm, "The Social Functions of the Past," *Past and Present* 55 (May, 1972): 10.

41. Buckley, *The Triumph of Time,* p. 36.

42. Thomas Macauley as quoted ibid., p. 119.

43. Martha Vicinus, "The Lowly Harp: Nineteenth Century Working Class Poetry" (disseration, University of Wisconsin, 1969); and Martha Vicinus, "The Study of Nineteenth-Century British Working-Class Poetry," *The Politics of Literature* (New York, 1972), pp. 322-353.

44. See Vicinus, "The Lowly Harp," p. 72.

45. Ibid., p. 38.

46. See Vicinus, "The Study of Nineteenth-Century British Working-Class Poetry."

47. Ibid., pp. 335-336.

48. Ibid., p. 337.

49. Vicinus, "The Lowly Harp," p. 143.

50. Ibid., p. 213.

51. Ibid., pp. 329-330.

52. Jones, "Working-Class Culture and Working-Class Politics," p. 140. Jones' focus is on the metropolitan, and especially the London, working-class culture. But he notes that the changes experienced here differed only in degree, not in kind, from the changes in working-class culture throughout society. In the North, for instance, the demand for entertainment was met, not by the music hall, but by professional football. On the infusion of respectability and other middle-class virtues in professional football, see W. F. Mandle, "Games People Played: Cricket and Football in England and Victoria in the Late Nineteenth Century," *Historical Studies,* 15, 60 (1973): 511-535.

53. See Jones, "Working-Class Culture and Working Class Politics," pp. 492-497.

54. Ibid., p. 462.

55. Tholfsen, "The Intellectual Origins of Mid-Victorian Stability," p. 62.

56. Ibid., p. 89.

57. Houghton, *The Victorian Frame of Mind,* p. 111.

58. Bickford, "The Improving Principle," pp. 390-391.

59. Thomas Wright, *Some Habits and Customs of the Working Classes* (New York, 1967; original edition, 1867), p. 2.

60. J. F. C. Harrison, *The Early Victorians,* p. 150.

61. *Odd Fellows Magazine,* July, 1857, as quoted in Tholfsen, "The Intellectual Origins of Mid-Victorian Stability," p. 64.

62. See Jones, "Working-Class Culture and Working-Class Politics," pp. 485-487.

63. Trygve Tholfsen, "The Origins of the Birmingham Caucus," *Historical Journal* 2, 2 (1959): 180.

64. The relationship between need-articulation and legitimacy is concisely and insightfully discussed from a sociology of language perspective by Claus Mueller. See his *The Politics of Communication* (New York, 1973), and "Notes on the Repression of Communicative Behavior," *Recent Sociology* (New York, 1970), pp. 101-113.

65. See K. Polanyi, "The Economy as Instituted Process," *Primitive, Archaic and Modern Economics,* pp. 142-148.

66. Peter Blau, *Exchange and Power in Social Life* (New York, 1964), p. 112.

67. Habermas, "Technology and Science as 'Ideology,'" *Toward A Rational Society* (Boston, 1970), p. 83.

68. Lubenow, *The Politics of Government Growth,* p. 181.

69. Joseph Parkes as quoted ibid., p. 18. This split in the Liberal wing between

the Radicals and the Whigs contributed to the development of the Liberal-Labor coalition some twenty years later. See Frances Gillespie, *Labor and Politics in England, 1850-1867* (New York, 1966), pp. 77-80.

70. See Norman McCord, *The Anti-Corn Law League, 1838-1846* (London, 1958), pp. 124-131.

71. As paraphrased by Briggs, *The Making of Modern England,* p. 314.

72. See McCord, *The Anti-Corn Law League,* pp. 137-154.

73. Ibid., p. 188.

74. G. Kitson Clark, "The Repeal of the Corn Laws and the Politics of the Forties," *Economic History Review* 4, 1 (1951): 12. A key consideration, of course, in the repeal of the Corn Laws was the growing economic distress in Ireland brought about by the famine.

75. See Halevy, *The Age of Peel and Cobden,* p. 106. Peel attempted to have the Repeal of the Corn Laws accompanied by provisions that would shift much of the financial burden from the landed interests to the public domain. He proposed, for instance, that paupers be no longer entitled to receive poor relief from the parish of origin; that the cost of prosecuting criminals and supporting the police be transferred from local to state authorities; and that farmers be permitted to receive governmental credit, in the form of short-term loans, for land improvement. Peel's attempt met with little success. However, over the next several years, as government became more centralized, the state did assume many of these financial burdens.

76. Maurice Thomas, *The Early Factory Legislation* (Westport, Conn., 1970), p. 213.

77. Lubenow, *The Politics of Government Growth,* pp. 145-146, emphasis added.

78. On the use of the relay system to circumvent the factory acts, see Thomas, *The Early Factory Legislation,* pp. 305-306.

79. The influence of the middle class and landed aristocracy struggle on the forging of middle-class consciousness is analyzed in Asa Briggs, "Middle-Class Consciousness in English Politics, 1780-1846," *Past and Present* 9 (April, 1956): 71-72. For a discussion of the constriction of the polity which occurred after 1846, see Moisei Ostrogrowski, *Democracy and the Organization of Political Parties,* Vol. I (New York, 1964), p. 50.

80. See E. J. Hobsbawm, "The Labour Aristocracy in Nineteenth-Century Britain," *Labouring Men* (London, 1964), p. 273; and J. F. C. Harrison, *The Early Victorians,* p. 24. Henry Pelling suggests that the differences between the elite and the common laborers were not significant. The data he uses, however, come from the late nineteenth century when common laborers were following the model established by the labor aristocracy. See *Popular Politics and Society in Late Victorian Britain* (New York, 1968), pp. 36-61.

81. See Turner, *Trade Union Growth, Structure, and Policy,* p. 114.

82. See Hobsbawm, "Labour Aristocracy in Nineteenth-Century Britain," *Labouring Men,* p. 290; and Hobsbawm, "Trends in the British Labor Movement Since 1850," *Labouring Men,* p. 318.

83. Hobsbawm, "The Labour Aristocracy in Nineteenth-Century Britain," p. 281.

84. Trygve Tholfsen, "The Transition to Democracy in Victorian England," *International Review of Social History* 6 (1961): 228.

85. The extent of working-class repudiation of political economy at this time is

discussed in R. V. Clements, "British Trade Unions and Popular Political Economy, 1850-1875," *Economic History Review* 14 (1961): 93-104.

86. Tholfsen, "The Intellectual Origins of Mid-Victorian Stability," p. 69.

87. R. Q. Gray, "Styles of Life, the 'Labour Aristocracy' and Class Relations in Later Nineteenth Century Edinburgh," *International Review of Social History* 18, 3 (1973): 452.

88. Robert Nisbet, *The Social Bond* (New York, 1970), p. 208.

89. See David Lockwood, "Sources of Variation in Working Class Images of Society," *Sociological Review* 14 (May, 1966): 256-260.

90. The strong emphasis on respectability and on 'keeping up appearances,' which developed among the workers between 1870 and 1900 is examined in Jones, "Working-Class Culture and Working-Class Politics," pp. 473-475.

91. Daphne Simon, "Master and Servant," *Democracy and the Labour Movement,* p. 160.

92. On the difference between contract and structural reciprocity, see George Park, *The Idea of Social Structure* (Garden City, 1974), pp. 22-23.

93. Marx, *Capital,* pp. 194-196. Marx's theory of surplus value is important not as an economic theory but as a social theory of class relationships. In this regard, Marx's theory of surplus value, as is shown in Chapter 6, expresses the transformation of the norm of reciprocity in industrial capitalism. See Anthony Giddens, *The Class Structure of Advanced Societies* (New York, 1973), p. 95; and Alvin Gouldner, "Reciprocity and Autonomy in Functional Theory," in *For Sociology* (New York, 1973), p. 222.

94. Marx, *Capital,* p. 539.

95. See Jeremy Shapiro, "One-Dimensionality: The Universal Semiotic of Technological Experience," *Critical Interruptions* (New York, 1970), p. 143.

96. On the depersonalization of exploitative relationships see Steven Marcus, *Engels, Manchester, and the Working Class* (New York, 1974), p. 156; and Thompson, *The Making of the English Working Class,* p. 203.

97. Harold Perkin, *The Origins of Modern English Society* (Toronto, 1969), p. 112.

98. George Rudé, "Protest and Punishment in Nineteenth-Century Britain," *Albion* 5 (Spring, 1973): 4.

99. See G. D. H. Cole, *Attempts at General Union* (London, 1953), pp. 154-155.

100. Engels, *The Condition of the Working Class in England,* pp. 32-33.

101. Royden Harrison, "The British Working Class and the General Election of 1868," *International Review of Social History* 5 (1960): 426-427.

102. G. D. H. Cole, *A Short History of the British Working Class Movement,* vol. II (New York, 1930), p. 19.

103. *Manchester Guardian,* Oct. 15, 1858, as quoted in Tholfsen, "The Transition to Democracy in Victorian England," p. 231.

104. Sydney Pollard, "Nineteenth-Century Cooperation: From Community Building to Shopkeeping," *Essays in Labour History,* p. 102.

105. As quoted in Perkin, *The Origins of Modern English Society,* p. 386.

106. See G. D. H. Cole, *A Century of Co-operation* (London, 1944), pp. 64-65.

107. See ibid., p. 81 for figures on the rapid growth of the Rochdale Pioneers from 1844-1850.

108. See Halevy, *The Age of Peel and Cobden,* pp. 227-231.

109. E. J. Hobsbawm, "Customs, Wages, and Work-Load in Nineteenth-Century Industry," *Essays in Labour History,* pp. 120-121.

110. Engels, *The Condition of the Working Class in England,* p. 254.

111. See Henry Pelling, *A History of British Trade Unionism* (London, 1963), p. 34; and A. L. Morton and George Tate, *The British Labour Movement,* p. 95.

112. Sidney and Beatrice Webb, *The History of Trade Unionism* (London, 1935), p. 180.

113. Two types of new model union organization prevailed. The first assumed the form of a centralized amalgamated society and rested upon cooperative activities and the restriction of the supply of labor. The second consisted of a loose federation of amalgamated societies, and was more active in pressuring for legislation pertaining to wages and work conditions. Although unconnected, both types exhibited a specialized exclusiveness and a concern with reaping more of the benefits of industrial capitalism. See Cole, *A Short History of the British Working Class Movement,* vol. II, p. 63.

114. See Lockwood, "Sources of Variation in Working Class Images of Society," p. 258.

115. Wright, *Some Habits and Customs of the Working Classes,* p. 57.

116. See Zygmunt Bauman, *Between Class and Elite* (Manchester, 1972), p. 121-122.

117. See Pelling, *A History of British Trade Unionism,* pp. 47-48; and Cole and Filson, *British Working Class Movements,* pp. 551-561.

118. V. L. Allen, "The Origins of Industrial Conciliation and Arbitration," *International Review of Social History* 9 (1964): 241.

119. J. H. Porter, "Wage Bargaining Under Conciliation Agreements, 1860-1914," *Economic History Review* 33, 3 (1970): 462.

120. See Pelling, *A History of British Trade Unionism,* pp. 54-57.

121. Sidney and Beatrice Webb, *The History of Trade Unionism,* p. 241.

122. Asa Briggs, "The Local Background of Chartism," *Chartist Studies* (London, 1959), pp. 18-21.

123. Cole and Filson, *British Working Class Movements,* p. 349.

124. See Cole, *A Short History of the British Working Class Movement,* vol. I, p. 145.

125. The uprisings in Llanidloes and Birmingham are examined in Dorothy Marshall, *The Early Chartists* (Columbia, South Carolina, 1971), pp. 220-250. For the Yorkshire outbursts see Frank Peel, *The Risings of the Luddites* (London, 1968).

126. See Cole, *A Short History of the British Working Class Movement,* vol. I, p. 152.

127. On the self-help aspect of Chartism see Patricia Hollis, *Class and Conflict in Nineteenth-Century England* (Boston, 1973), pp. 248-267.

128. See Lucy Brown, "The Chartists and the Anti-Corn Law League," *Chartist Studies,* pp. 352-363.

129. Brontere O'Brien, *Northern Star,* April 24, 1841; in Hollis, *Class and Conflict,* p. 270.

130. See Brown, "The Chartists and the Anti-Corn Law League," p. 361.

131. "A Plan for Organizing the Chartists of Great Britain," August 1, 1840, in Cole and Filson, *British Working Class Movements,* pp. 374-375.

132. See, for instance, Asa Briggs, "National Bearings," in *Chartist Studies,* p. 293; and Thompson, *The Making of the English Working Class,* pp. 827-828.

133. Engels, *The Condition of the Working Class in England,* p. 268.

134. "Rules of the Chartist Cooperative Land Society, 1845," in Cole and Filson, *British Working Class Movements,* p. 399.

135. Feargus O'Connor, *Northern Star,* August 21, 1847, as quoted in Joy MacAskill, "The Chartist Land Plan," *Chartist Studies,* p. 322.

136. See MacAskill, "The Chartist Land Plan," pp. 336-338.

137. See the "Proceedings of the National Convention, 1848," in Cole and Filson, *British Working Class Movements,* p. 404.

138. The Chartists estimated the demonstrators at 150,000, while the authorities put the number at 8,000. After examining the available sources Halevy estimates the 25,000 figure. See Halevy, *The Age of Peel and Cobden,* p. 212.

139. Ernest Jones as quoted in Briggs, "National Bearings," p. 297.

140. See F. C. Mather, *Public Order in the Age of the Chartists* (Manchester, 1959), pp. 97-103. Also see J. J. Tobias, *Nineteenth-Century Crime in England,* pp. 99; and Charles Reith, *British Police and the Democratic Ideal* (London, 1943), pp. 228-249.

141. See Mather, *Public Order in the Age of the Chartists,* pp. 142-150.

142. The perfecting of information-gathering techniques accompanied the strengthening of military and civil force. Spies were common to most Chartist organizations; and, beyond this, the government authorized the Post Office to detain and inspect the mail sent and received by selected Chartist leaders. Also important was the contribution of the middle class which supplied the special constables who supplemented the government's forces. See Mather, *Public Order in the Age of the Chartist,* pp. 153, 218, 80-82.

143. Thomas Wright as quoted in Royden Harrison, *Before the Socialists* (London, 1965), p. 28.

144. See Werner Sombart, *Socialism and the Social Movement* (New York, 1968), p. 143.

145. Franz Neumann, *The Democratic and Authoritarian State* (New York, 1957), p. 261.

CHAPTER 5
The Social Basis of Chartism

One requirement for sustained opposition to the established order is the existence of some basis for creating shared communal meanings with referents external to the prevailing arrangements. As we have seen, such a basis was established by the English workers in the period between 1790 and the early 1830s. Responding to the denial of social responsibility by the government and the emerging middle class, the workers formed protective communities which were loosely linked by a common ideological consciousness. Much of the content of this ideological consciousness was oriented to the past. Traditional values, beliefs, and practices afforded a meaningful framework with which the workers assessed the new and dislocating experiences of industrialization. The categories taken from the past were external to the burgeoning industrial capitalist society, and were initially used to critically evaluate that society. In this interaction between the past and the present, what was originally a retrogressive, ideological consciousness was transformed into a progressive one, anticipatory of a future society. In this way the critical categories became transcendental and, as such, provided goals and guidance to protest activity.

The creative, transcending dynamic of the working class had been diminished, placed under instrumental constraints by the mid-1840s as a result of expanding industrialization, governmental legislation and force, and moral reform campaigns. In the midst of this instrumentalization of culture, Chartism drew its strength from a number of open social locations or sociohistorical spaces not yet absorbed by or adapted to the system of instrumental action. Defined as "relatively open social context[s] in which individuals and groups have, simultaneously, freedom to construct legitimacy for their critical perspectives and access . . . to the larger, routinized social world,"[1] these open social locations managed to retain a sense of integration and of social responsibility, attachments to the past, and a generally noninstrumental orientation toward life. During this period, the major open social locations in English society were found in the religious communities of the Methodist sects, the Irish immigrant communities, and the occupational communities of such socially or geographically segregated workers as the coal miners, iron workers, or small artisans. Strongly attached to the past and protective of the noninstrumental, each of these communities supplied the categories which guided participation in social change.

The communities of the Methodists, the Irish, the miners and artisans closely approximated what Huizinga has described as a "culture that is played."[2] Each embodied and—to a large extent—satisfied communal ideals which stressed mutual responsibility. Within these communities there were winners and losers, to be sure; but both were bound by the same rules. Like the "culture that is played," these communities existed at a distance from the sphere of necessity and utility, and subordinated the instrumental concerns emanating from this sphere to considerations of social obligation. The elements of play and past which distinguished these segments of the English working class were rooted and expressed in the following features:

Marginality

Each was isolated from the mainstream of English social life. The Methodist sects, attacked by both the Anglican Church and the conservative Wesleyan Methodists, were compelled to exist on the outskirts of society. The Irish immigrants, confronted by intense prejudice and pervasive discrimination, remained among themselves in crowded urban enclaves. Concentrated in the North East, the iron workers and coal miners were separated geographically from the industrial and cultural centers; and, in a city like London, artisans employed in declining industries were pushed aside by an emerging labor aristocracy. Subsisting on the margins of society, these communities avoided the direct impact of the instrumentalization of working-class culture.

Communal Responsibility

Traditional social obligations, expressed in an emphasis on mutual responsibility, were sustained in the values and institutions of these communities. The retention of these obligations was made possible in part by the continued noninstrumental orientation of each community. The major working-class strongholds of the Methodist sects were located predominantly in single industry districts comprised of small towns and villages. Avoiding the direct impact of industrialization, the communities in these districts preserved tradition and play, while communities in more urban areas were under attack. The Irish laborers, encouraged to emigrate because their preindustrial work habits suited them for the unpleasant and heavy, manual tasks located at the bottom of industrializing society, were less methodical and reliable than English workers, but more playful and less willing to divide life into work time and free time. A similar refusal to separate the noninstrumental and the instrumental, to dissociate traditional, preindustrial customs and practices from work, characterized the London artisans and the miners. Work and play, the past, present, and future, intermingled in community activities; and participation in these activities, like participation in play, was an end in itself. The resulting affirmation of social responsiblity produced an image and experience of the 'good society' which was incongruous with the present.

Democratic Form of Organization

Complementing the emphasis on communaal responsibility was a deeply rooted sense of equality and fairness. The class meeting of the Primitive Methodists, the "butty" groups of the Irish laborers, and the trade societies of the London artisans and the Newcastle miners were structured to allow the widest participation in the making and implementing of decisions. Characterized by a minimal degree of hierarchy centralization and formalization, each afforded its members the opportunity to actively engage in the creation of social order.

Radical Tradition

The sense of historical continuity found in each of these communities was colored with the spirit of rebellion. Methodism, since the 1730s, had been in continual struggle with the state-supported church; and, from their start in the 1790s, the Methodist sects had engaged in conflict with both the Church of England and the Wesleyan Methodists. Irish immigrant communities were well aware of England's prolonged domination of Ireland, and they were permeated by stories and myths of Irish struggles for freedom. Similarly, the mining and artisan communities still bore the imprint of their active participation in the working-class movements of the first third of the century. In the millenarianism and communitarianism of these communities, the radical traditions were not merely celebrated; they were relived, and resulted in images of the future which rested on the playful relation to the past.

By sustaining the vitality of traditional ideals and customs, these open social locations kept the rebellious disposition alive. Traditional yet relevant religious, ethnic, and occupational value orientations provided the background for the articulation of qualitative needs. Only when manifested politically, however, does the expression of qualitative or communal needs lose its abstract character.[3] Chartism as a national movement failed to provide the well-conceived political outlet necessary for unifying its various bases of support. Lacking a connection between politics and the future, the Chartist leaders were either

> forever looking backward to the former prosperous days of the English laborer and seeking to restore conditions which had forever passed away . . . [or] accept[ing] the changes of the industrial revolution and [seeking] a remedy in the intellectual and moral development and regeneration of the workingman.[4]

In this context, the class consciousness lodged in the ideology of the Methodist, Irish, and occupational communities rarely reached the surface. As a consequence, the traditions sustained by each often proved to be as much a divisive as an integrative force. To take one example, the strong religious ties of the Methodist sects was incompatible with the Catholicism practiced in the Irish communities and the secularism found in the London trade societies, and it occasionally made broad-based alliances troublesome. In large measure, the major deficiencies of the Chartist Movement can be traced to the failure to provide the political expression needed to highlight the commonalities housed in these superficially disparate ideologies. In the analysis which follows, an effort is made to identify the similar values, aspirations, and structures which made these communities the bedrock of the Chartist Movement.[5]

NONCONFORMITY

Methodism arose in the 1730s and 1740s as a reaction to the sectarian Protestantism which then prevailed in English society. Although presuming the existence of a basically corrupt human nature, Methodist theology departed from the Calvinist and Lutheran emphases expressed in eighteenth-century Protestantism, by proclaiming that each person has the potential to enter the domain of the elect. Through rebirth or a process of sudden conversion and regeneration, salvation could be achieved by all. As initially preached by John Wesley, nonconformist theology was oriented to industrious workers (as distinct from the middle class and the poor) whom, Wesley felt, were constrained by social circumstances, not by their individual characters. Among these workers, especially in the mining and small manufacturing areas of the country, Methodism quickly acquired much support.[6] Given its then limited audience, Methodism generally was tolerated by the government and the Anglican Church. However, as the mining and manufacturing districts expanded, Methodism, which even then presented a relatively egalitarian theology and organizational structure, experienced a corresponding growth in size. At this juncture, the government and the Church of England began to express greater concern over the threatening possibilities inherent in the association between Methodism and the lower classes.

A major turning point in the Methodist Revival occurred in the 1790s, in the aftermath of the French Revolution and in the midst of growing agitation in England. The separation of critical reason into its communal and laissez-faire alternatives, which was initiated in this period came to be reflected in Methodism. From a variety of quarters, Methodism was subjected to a barrage of accusations ranging from heresy to sedition. In an effort to mitigate these attacks and avoid further governmental suspicion, the Methodist leadership took a hard line against riots and disturbances.[7] To supplement this position, the leadership, still under the influence of Wesley's teachings, implemented a series of organizational changes which centralized and formalized the itinerent ministry. One group of ministers found these actions contrary to the communal and egalitarian aspects of Methodism; and under their guidance a number of secessions occurred. The Kilhamite New Connexion, founded in 1796, was the most important of these early seceding groups.

Although these secessions were based on political and organizational, rather than doctrinal grounds, important differences in the interpretation of doctrine ultimately arose. Both the Wesleyan Methodists and the seceding Methodists stressed the emotional and experiential elements of salvation, and both agreed that most people could attain the ultimate satisfaction of their own efforts, particularly when these efforts embraced the fraternal spirit of the religious societies.[8] Only through good works was salvation to be acquired. For Wesleyan Methodism, 'good works' was synonomous with methodical, reliable work habits; and later, in the 1840s conversion required the inculcation of self-help virtues; the self-made man was the one who would be saved.[9]

The seceding Methodists regarded good works in a more political context. Here, salvation required the use of individual talents for community improvement. Opposed to the individualistic emphasis contained in both Wesleyan Methodism and the emerging middle-class consciousness, the sects offered their members "a congenial home, where the values and goals were different from those of the wider society, and where unbounded hopes of a future millenium could be indulged."[10] These differences in interpretation were directly related to structural differences. For instance, Wesleyanism exhibited a rigid, hierarchical structure of duties which clearly distinguished the minister from the layman. Among the seceding groups and some of the newly formed sects, on the other hand, an organizational flexibility prevailed and encouraged "a man [to] play an active, key role without having to be ordained a minister."[11] To the workers constructing protective communities in the early years of the nineteenth century, the stress on social responsibility reflected in the ideology and structures of Nonconformity was very appealing.

The contending ideological alternatives which developed within Methodism at the turn of the century received continued elaboration over the next fifty years. Various Methodist sects were often active in working-class movements in industrial and agrarian areas. During this period, the Wesleyans intensified their attack on the political activity of the workers, and devoted their yearly conferences to renewing pledges of loyalty and allegiance to the King and government. It is not surprising, then, that in the 1840s the Wesleyans were firmly in support of the free trade movement, while many of the non-Wesleyan sects were actively engaged in Chartist agitation.

The Halevy Thesis

The classic analysis of the role of Methodism in the political activities of the English working class is offered by Elie Halevy.[12] Halevy contends that Methodism, by providing an ordered and disciplined channel through which working-class discontent could be expressed, contributed greatly to the social stability of England in a period when neighboring societies were experiencing continual upheavals. By making available a relatively innocuous means for the expression of grievances, Methodism had the effect of undercutting the appeal of politically oriented movements. The working-class protest that occurred in England was tame compared to the disturbances which broke out on the continent. Summarizing Halevy's major argument, Richter writes, "When members of the lower classes protested against injustices, they did not feel compelled to attack the system as a whole, nor did their revolt extend to every aspect of the spiritual doctrine. Rather they could appeal to values that were founded on a religious claim, and which were shared by at least a few members of every social class."[13] The tempering effects of Methodism were important in the nineteenth century as well. Methodism again helped subdue the threat to social order posed by growing class antagonism, by making methodical work habits and the virtues of self-help acceptable to many workers through the doctrine of justification of faith by good works.

Thus, the thrust of Halevy's argument is two-fold. First, between the 1730s and the first decades of the nineteenth century, Methodism served as a safety valve through which the hungry, the oppressed, and the dislocated could vent their hostilities without significantly threatening the stability of prevailing arrangements.[14] Secondly, after this period, Methodism became an intermediary between the workers and the dominant ideology in society, translating the value orientations of the latter into a religious doctrine of rebirth.

E. P. Thompson finds some evidence which confirms the positive relationship Halevy draws between Methodism and social stability. However, while recognizing those aspects of Methodist theology which influenced political quietude and justified factory work discipline, Thompson is also sensitive to those elements of Methodism which permitted a rejection of and resistance to the dominant powers. Ideologically, Methodism brought the empirical world into tension with the Kingdom of God; and structurally, it provided workers with organizational forms and skills imbued with a democratic spirit.[15] The potential impact of these contributions were suppressed, according to Thompson, by the reactive cultural pattern in which they were encased. Through this reactive cultural pattern, radical political activity was transformed into religious revivalism.

Thompson contends, then, that Methodism successfully performed a "dual role as the religion of both the exploiters and the exploited."[16] On the one hand, it afforded workers comfort and respect in an otherwise hostile world; and, on the other, it translated political aspirations into a search for moral earnestness. The quest for a better society became a quest for another world which could only be achieved by performing good works in the present. Thus the Methodist communities, very much like the communities of the labor aristocrats, managed to level down working-class values, making them amenable to the dominant value orientations.

E. J. Hobsbawm's analysis of the influence of Methodism on working-class protest diverges further from Halevy's than does Thompson's. Distinguishing the varieties of Nonconformist Methodism more precisely than Halevy, Hobsbawm finds that, while Wesleyan Methodism constituted a stabilizing force in several areas of the country, various sects such as the Kilhamites and Bible Christians were closely connected with politically active working-class movements. This was especially clear with the Primitive Methodists, "the most purely 'proletarian' of the major sects," which, in 1811,

> broke away because the Wesleyans were insufficiently democratic in the matter of preaching by laymen and women, and opposed to the mass propagandist campaigns of the great revivalist 'camp meetings'. . . . [A]mong the northern miners, the farm-labourers, [and] the Staffordshire operative . . . Primitive Methodism was so closely identified with trade unions as to become, practically, a labour religion.[17]

Unlike Thompson who maintains that the workers' participation in and commitment to Methodism followed periods of political defeat, Hobsbawm observes "a marked parallelism between the movements of religious, social and political consciousness."[18] Indeed, Hobsbawm advances the argument that Methodism was a useful supplement, not an alternative, to radical politics. Noting the call for action associated with the Nonconformist sects, he suggests that many workers became involved in Methodism for the same reason they enlisted in more overtly political causes.

Where Thompson tends to support the general implications of the Halevy thesis, Hobsbawm finds little evidence to support the contention that Methodism inhibited insurrectionary activities; indeed, there are some indications that certain segments of Methodism contributed to the organization and ideology of working-class social protest. Although Thompson agrees with Hobsbawm that Methodism provided some legitimacy and organizational skills to the oppositional stance taken by the workers, he maintains that such contributions had the effect of diluting the threatening aspects of the workers' protest. Thompson assumes, then, that working-class political activity would have occurred in a more militant fashion had not the influence of Methodism been so great. But how valid is this assumption?

In the early years of the nineteenth century, when the Combination Acts prevented the establishment of effective laborers' associations, working-class participation in Methodism was widespread. During the 1820s and early 1830s, however, when working-class political clubs and unions proliferated, Methodist support in working-class areas visibly declined.[19] It seems, therefore, that many workers engaged in Methodist activities only after other avenues of political expression had been blocked. In this light, Methodism is seen, not as inhibitory of radical politics, but as a way of maintaining radical politics in the face of repressive measures. While it was true that working-class political activity in the context of Methodism was less aggressive than it may otherwise have been, this is probably less attributable to features of Methodism than to the growing repression which initially compelled the increased working-class participation in Methodism.

In the late 1830s and 1840s, a period beyond the scope of Thompson's study, working-class interest in Methodism was renewed. At this time, Methodism offered the workers one of the few opportunities they had for publicly expressing their discontent. Although the institutional framework of Methodism set limits upon the kinds of activity which could be taken to remedy dissatisfactions, it did extend collective meaning to the workers' suffering and a justification for organized resistance. Given the prevailing repressive measures which effectively precluded public channels of political communication, the Nonconformist sects, to the extent that their ideologies and structures corresponded to those of the working-class community, served as a natural ground on which opposition could be mobilized. In this period,

Methodism constituted an open social location, an historical space within which oppositional values and practices were sustained.[20]

Thus, non-Wesleyan Methodism was as much a political agency as it was a religious one. The value orientation maintained in the sects was in many ways similar to the one which had been expressed in the protective communities of the workers. Indeed, between the two, Thompson notes, was a "continuous thread of communtarian ideas and experiments" expressed through millenarian imagery.[21] By retaining these communitarian and millenarian traditions, the Methodist sects allowed their working-class members to maintain a sense of historical continuity. Encompassed within Methodism, these ideals were outside the attempts directed at adapting working-class culture to the structure of industrial capitalism. As a consequence, the Methodist sects were able to play an integral part in the Chartist agitation. As Rudé has recently commented, the Chartist Movement "tapped a great store of age-old millenial hopes and 'communitarian' ideals and tended to sweep up in its train all the popular demands and aspirations of its day."[22] Much of the credit for the retention of these ideals during a period when critical ideas and practices were being systematically suppressed—and consequently some of the credit for the vitality exhibited by Chartism—must be attributed to the Nonconformist sects.

In this light the Halevy thesis has an applicability which is limited to the middle class. Methodism—or more particularly, Wesleyan Methodism—inhibited a bourgeois revolution, but it did not prevent a working-class revolution. Among middle-class groups, Methodism did not serve as a natural rallying point around which resistance could be mobilized. Almost from the beginning of the century, middle-class political societies and lobbying groups had access to public channels of discourse; and, of course, in 1832 the franchise was extended to include most of its members. Under these conditions, where political expression was possible, Methodism had a stabilizing effect.

Around the last quarter of the eighteenth century, when the shift from traditional orientations to free-floating resources began, we find a striking convergence between the views of the Methodist leadership and those of the emerging entrepreneurial class. During this period the Methodist leaders advocated a position of political neutrality, arguing that any other course would seriously endanger religious pursuits. Framed in religious terms of passive obedience and nonresistance, this politically neutral posture urged loyalty to the King. Duty to the King and government resulted from the view that the achievements of Methodism were made possible by privileges accorded by the government—privileges which bore no relation to industrial or human rights.[23] Anticipated here is the distinction between the public and private, according to which individual rights exclusively hold only with regard to economic endeavors. Following Wesley's dictum that "Religion must necessarily produce both Industry and Frugality and, in turn, Riches," the Methodist leadership sided with the growing support for entrepreneurial values without directly opposing the government.[24]

The claim of political neutrality was continued by the Wesleyan Methodists after the turn of the century. During the Luddite riots, however, this position was abandoned and replaced with a vehement renunciation of the working-class movement. At the Wesleyan Conference in 1819, the 'infidel' workers were exhorted to follow their Christian duty "to be subject to the higher powers, to obey magistrates . . . to submit themselves to every ordinance of man for the Lord's sake."[25] This theme remained a central concern of the Methodist Conferences until the 1850s. What is important to note, however, is that the abolition of a neutral stance by the Wesleyans occurred at a time when the middle class was receiving a greater share of social and economic power. Along with utilitarianism, Wesleyanism provided the middle class with a rather comprehensive rationale for opposing the workers; and, in so doing, it facilitated the alliance between the middle class and the aristocracy.

Through Wesleyanism, the critical values and institutions shaped by the middle class during the eighteenth century were recast along more moderate lines. Middle-class opposition, as it became more clearly distinguished from working-class opposition, was channelled into a socially acceptable direction. In terms of the complementary ideas of privilege and utility, notions of natural right were repudiated, and the established system of inequality was justified. In this way, Wesleyan Methodism complemented the secular intellectual developments of utilitarianism and political economy, and with them comprised the core of a middle-class consciousness which sought to initiate change by working within the prevailing institutional arrangements.

The Methodist Sects

The major working class strongholds of Methodism were predominantly located in single-industry districts comprised of small towns and villages. Experiencing the impact of industrialization later, or in a more muted form than other areas of the country, these districts continued to exhibit viable community ties throughout the period when working-class communities in more urban areas were under attack. Eventually, when these communities also came under attack, their connection with Methodism proved valuable. As repression spread to these areas, it was not unusual for community political leaders to become evangelists in the Methodist sects.[26] By assuming a religious posture and employing a religious terminology, community leaders made use of the only effective public channel of communication at their disposal.

What facilitated the workers' commitment to and participation in the Methodist sects was the basic similarity between the sects and the working-class community. Like that of the working-class community, the value orientation of the sects emphasized communal responsibility and self-worth. In both, self-respect was cultivated, and independent and assertive political attitudes were formed. Both nurtured values and norms which were not bound to the established order. Thus many workers identified with the millenarian emphasis of the sects, because it approximated in several ways the critical ideology of the working-class community. As Harrison suggests, millenarianism was regarded as a revolutionary ideology because the

> change envisioned was not an improvement of the present, but an utter rejection and replacement of it by something perfect. Second, this change was thought to be very near. . . . In fact, some of the joys of heaven on earth could already be foretasted in the community or sect. Third, the change was felt to be inevitable . . . hope was boundless, for human (sinful) nature would be transformed.[27]

Not only did this millenarian thrust encourage and legitimate an oppositional stance, but it did so in a context of historical continuity. As preached by the Methodist sects, this millenarianism reaffirmed many of the traditional working-class values which were then under assault.

Parallels between the protective working-class community and the Methodist sects were found in structure as well as in value orientation. It was earlier noted that the secessions from Wesleyanism were based not on doctrinal disagreements but on political and organizational grounds. The popular or proletarian sects opposed the growing centralization of Wesleyanism, and favored instead a more flexible organization within which the widest possible participation could take place. The organizational techniques introduced into the various working-class communities by the Methodist sects—the class meeting, subscription lists, and communication channels—were eventually incorporated into the institutions of these communities. During the 1820s and early 1830s, even as working-class commitment to Methodism declined, these institutions formed the core of working-class social protest activity. Trade unions and political societies borrowed these techniques with little modification. In 1831, the National Union of the Working Classes officially adopted the class meeting system, and speedily introduced this procedure to many organizations in the outlying provincial areas.[28]

Although these organizations had been severely weakened by the late 1830s, the institutional frameworks upon which they were built were retained in basic outline in the Nonconformist sects. Through the democratic institutions of the Methodist sects, self-respect was maintained in the context of collective practice, as people were encouraged to take an active and creative part in formulating decisions affecting their daily existence. Personal responsibility and communal responsibility were joined, making these institutions even more incongruous with the prevailing developments. Despite the avowed political neutrality of many of the sects, the critical and often radical orientation they sustained and the organizational skills they supplied proved indispensable to the working-class protest of the 1840s.

Although the Chartist Movement shared with the Methodist sects a vehement opposition to the established church and the Wesleyan Methodists, its appeal for Methodist support systematically began only after the implementation of a governmental ban of Chartist meetings. In reaction to this and more forceful measures, the Chartists adopted the policy of regarding their activities

> as essentially religious and on that account place themselves on the same level as Methodist, Baptists, and other denominations. If the Government prohibited class meetings, they would have to forbid Methodists and Baptists from gathering in this way.[29]

The Chartist leadership, then, had very pragmatic reasons for associating with the Methodist sects. Not only would such an association facilitate further activities by making it more difficult for the government to restrain Chartism as a political movement; but, also, such a relationship would enlarge Chartist support. In an effort to establish a working relationship, Chartist leaders sent 'missionaries' to working-class areas where Methodism was strong, and, for a period, encouraged disturbances of the Sunday services held at Anglican Churches.

If the leaders of early Chartism cultivated a relationship with the Nonconformist sects for pragmatic reasons, the members of these sects generally found it easy to combine their religious beliefs and practices with the political beliefs and practices proposed by Chartism. In such places as Leicestershire, Loughborough, Yorkshire, and Newcastle, Chartist organization was coterminous with religious organization. In these areas and many others, working-class commitment to Chartism was mediated by the workers' experience in the sects. Religious meetings, typically devoted to espousing the cause of the just society, were smoothly transformed into class meetings replete with sermons repudiating the unproductive classes and Chartist hymns.[30] The political sentiment tapped by Chartism was embedded in the religious sentiment housed in the sects. Not surprisingly, many Methodist sects served as the organizational bases for local Chartist associations; and, later, Methodist ministers, local preachers, and adherents assumed in disproportionate numbers positions of national leadership in the Chartist Movement.[31]

In short, the Methodist sects were essential to the Chartist Movement. First, they provided the organizational techniques used to recruit new members, acquire funds, and disseminate political and educational information.[32] Along with this, they supplied the Movement with experienced leaders. Finally, and most importantly, in certain areas of the country they made available to Chartism a group of workers who possessed an ideological consciousness capable of discrediting established authority relations, who maintained self-respect and a sense of worth, and who had considerable experience with organizational strategy.

Chartist Activity and Methodism

Chartist activity appeared in most areas where working-class commitment to Methodism was strong. However, the Chartist agitation and disturbances found in these areas varied considerably in terms of frequency, intensity, and militancy. What appears to account for much of this variation is the extent to which the political demands of Chartism were constrained by religious concerns—or, conversely, the extent to which the religious interests of Methodism received political expression. In areas like Birmingham, where Chartism was regarded essentially as a religious movement, Chartism developed a moderate posture; and in places like Yorkshire, where Methodism was viewed as a political movement, Chartist programs and agitation exhibited a more combative stance.

Birmingham Chartism evolved in the context of class alliance. Underlaying this alliance were two factors which minimized the appearance of class distinctions. First, Nonconformity had strong support in both working and middle-class circles. As a consequence, both classes shared the radical tradition embodied in Nonconformity, and both had remained in common opposition to the attempts at restricting the practice of Nonconformist religions. Further enhancing class alliance was the subcontracting, small-scale nature of work organization which existed in Birmingham. Birmingham possessed a wide diversity of occupations; and with the small workshop as the key unit of production, economic and industrial development entailed not an expansion of scale but a multiplication of the existing units. Moreover, skilled laborers constituted a relatively high proportion of the labor force; and this, as Briggs observes, gave Birmingham a higher degree of social mobility than that which existed in comparable areas, and contributed to a "considerable local optimism about the prospects of 'rising in society.' "[33]

Against this background, a strong tradition of cooperation between workers and employers was established in such associations as the Birmingham Political Union. In 1838 and 1839, this tradition of united action was weakened as the workers, under the influence of the Chartist Movement, came to regard the middle class as a betrayer of its interests.[34] Despite extensive efforts on the part of the middle class to maintain class alliance, the workers organized along class lines, and, as Chartists, engaged in agitation which produced much alarm within the middle class.

This agitation was, however, short-lived. With the emergence of the Christian Chartist Movement, the agitation was emptied of its threatening aspects, as the political thrust of Chartism was effectively circumscribed within the moral tones of Nonconformity. In 1840 a Chartist Church was established in Birmingham as a 'politico-religious' society which sought to find solutions to economic, industrial, and political problems in Christian doctrine. Like other Chartist Churches, the one in Birmingham was, in the words of J. R. Stephens, a fellowship "of the weighty and strong-minded people, who now begin in good earnest to ask what is the will of God in these things that belong as well to their earthy as to their heavenly weal."[35]

The Christian Chartist Church immediately transformed the nature of Birmingham Chartism. It quickly gained adherents among the local laborers who saw membership in the Church as a way of maintaining their political beliefs without inviting the repression faced by the militant variants of Chartism. The Birmingham workers also found appealing the emphasis that 'politico-religious' Chartism placed on respectability. Many of the skilled laborers continued to regard themselves as respectable artisans; and the Chartist Church, stressing moral righteousness, allowed the workers to justify certain political views associated with Chartism in terms of respectability. However, as Tholfsen remarks about the Christian Chartists in Birmingham, their "ritual of hymns, prayers, sermons, and tea parties bespoke an impulse to respectability that was incompatible with the continued repudiation of middle class political leadership."[36]

Although the Christian Chartists did not curtail their opposition to the middle class (they refused a proposed alliance with the Birmingham branch of the Anti-Corn Law League), much of the indignation and anger associated with the earlier Chartist opposition was eliminated. The Christian Chartists combined their opposition to the middle class with a virulent repudiation of 'physical force' Chartism. In many respects, their position, with its undercurrents of teetotalerism and temperance, more closely approximated the views of the middle-class Radicals than it did the position of militant Chartism.

The chief effect of Christian Chartism was to soften the workers' antagonism toward the middle class, and thereby establish a situation for the possible renewal of class alliance. Under the direction of Joseph Sturge, middle-class Radicals founded the Complete Suffrage Union in 1842 to take advantage of this situation. Operating on the principles of Nonconformist Radicalism, the C.S.U. accepted the Chartist demand for male suffrage as a way to secure the trust and support of Christian Chartists. Although the C.S.U. managed to attract a small number of artisans, it never received the formal support it had hoped for, and it disbanded in 1845. However, by demonstrating the continued interest on the part of the middle class in establishing an alliance, the C.S.U. had the effect of "ending the political estrangement of the artisan elite," and, in so doing, it reinforced the moderate tendencies of Birmingham Chartism.[37]

The religious undercurrents of Birmingham Chartism contrasted sharply with the politically oriented Methodism characteristic of Chartist activity in Yorkshire and Newcastle. The labor force in these areas was comprised of a relatively small proportion of artisans, most of whom were either concentrated in one particular area or employed in declining industries. There were few and limited avenues of social mobility, and large-scale productive units were common to both areas. As a result, significant differences existed between the workers and the employers. In contrast to Birmingham, there was no tradition of class alliance which could minimize these differences. Workers in Yorkshire and Newcastle had been active in the Luddite riots and, later, in the disturbances of the 1820s and 1830s. Facilitating the retention of this radical tradition of class antagonism was the prevalence of Nonconformist sects. Throughout these areas, with few exceptions, the Methodist sects acquired strongholds of support among the workers and correspondingly little support from the middle class. Religious differences were thus superimposed upon the structural and institutional differences of social class. In this light the sects came to be regarded as political agencies and, as such, amenable to a more militant practice of Chartism.

The bulk of Yorkshire's labor force consisted of factory operatives, primarily employed in the textile industries located in the district. From the beginning of the century, the Methodist sects had acquired good representation among the Yorkshire workers; and in the period of economic distress in the 1830s and 1840s, parts of Yorkshire provided Methodism with its firmest centers of support.[38] Marked by a deep-seated class antagonism which was fueled by the middle-class repudiation of non-Wesleyan Methodism, these areas offered the Chartist Movement a most receptive and enthusiastic audience.

Throughout the early 1840s, Yorkshire was one of the leading centers of 'physical force' Chartism. Chartist activity in Yorkshire was frequent, often violent, and directly involved with the preparations for a national insurrectionary movement. Although no national movement developed, the Yorkshire Chartists engaged in a number of regional protest activities which culminated in the Plug Plot riots of 1842. Confronted with the mounting repression engendered by these riots, Yorkshire Chartism became somewhat subdued; but Chartist organization and, with it, virulent class antagonism remained strong until 1848.[39]

Leeds constituted a significant exception to the militant Chartism found in the other towns and villages of Yorkshire. Unlike many of the smaller surrounding areas, Leeds expressed little interest in the Chartist Movement. At a meeting held in 1838, "Bradford, Huddersfield, and Halifax poured out in their thousands to Peep Green, while the Leeds delegation was not more than two hundred.''[40] In the early 1840s a Chartist group was formed by the artisans, small tradesmen, and shopkeepers of Leeds; but the group took a very moderate approach which was clearly and deliberately distinguished from the militant Chartism found in other areas of Yorkshire.

Leeds, with a relatively high proportion of artisans, a strong tradition of class alliance, and a middle class influenced by Nonconformist Radicalism, was very similar to Birmingham. In its moderation, Leeds Chartism approximated many of the aspects of the 'moral force' Chartism practiced in Birmingham. Unlike 'moral force' Chartism, however, the municipal Chartism which developed in Leeds was devoid of class hostility. Leeds Chartism evolved in the framework of class alliance, and operated within the existing political institutions, concentrating its efforts on municipal elections. Thus Leeds Chartism, in contrast to the Chartism of other West Riding towns, served as an integrating force.

Closer to the militant posture assumed by most Yorkshire workers was the Chartism found among the miners in the northeast of England. Methodist. sects, Primitive Methodism in particular, held a prominent place in mining communities; and they had contributed much over the years to the independent stance taken by miners' associations. Not surprisingly, the Chartist Movement discovered a firm and important base of support in this area. In 1839, Chartist classes were formed on the basis of already existing Methodist classes, and the chapel and meeting rooms of the sects were commonly used for the Chartist gatherings.[41] By the early 1840s there was little difference between religious and political activities, and local Primitive Methodist preachers were often leaders of Chartist groups.

Chartist agitations, comprised largely of strikes and riots, occurred regularly until the mid-1840s, and all bore the imprint of Methodism. A government report dealing with the mining disturbances of 1844, after commending the Wesleyan Methodists for attempting to imbue the mining communities with responsible virtues, castigates the Primitive Methodists for their contribution to the outbursts. The authors of the report found that

> A religious feeling was mixed up in a strange and striking manner with this movement. Frequent meetings were held in their chapels . . . , when prayers were publically opened up for the successful result of the strike. They attended the prayer meetings "to get their faith strengthened," i.e., to encourage each other in the confidence that the strike would succeed.[42]

Methodism, as this description emphasizes, was regarded by the miners as a political movement, compatible with the objectives and practices of Chartism.

With considerable variation in intensity, support for the Chartist Movement was likely to develop in those areas where working-class commitment to Methodism was relatively strong. Conversely, among workers where the Methodist influence was weak and no other open social location was available, participation in Chartist activity was inconsequential. Among London workers, for example, Nonconformity was virtually nonexistent; and—as we shall see later—except for those skilled workers with access to trade clubs, Chartism received very little support, even though most of these workers were as economically distressed as their counterparts in other areas of England. Similarly, in Sheffield, where Methodism was unable to penetrate "the estrangement of the common people,"[43] the workers, for a long time resigned to the existing conditions, were incapable of forming an oppositional base from which Chartism could draw support. Throughout the 1840s, Sheffield workers remained passive, except on a few occasions when they actively opposed the Chartist Movement. In the midst of intense Chartist agitation in other areas of the country, 'The Sheffield Mechanics' Anti-Corn Law Association Committee was founded to organize workers behind the repeal movement. Eventually, this group succeeded in replacing apathy toward Chartism with "monster demonstrations and petitions for the repeal of the Corn Laws, the abolition of monopolies and all restrictions on the importation of food, and for Free Trade."[44] The situation in Sheffield illustrates the difficulty of developing an oppositional stance in the absence of critical standards of legitimacy. Lacking the creative opportunities and experience of tradition provided by the Nonconformist sects, the Sheffield workers conformed to the established order.

THE IRISH

In his 1844 study of the English working class, Engels found "it not surprising that a social class already degraded by industrialisation and its immediate consequences should still be further degraded by having to live alongside and compete with the uncivilised Irish."[45] Engels' statement is included here, not for its accuracy (for it is not accurate), but because it succinctly reflects the popular attitudes toward the Irish held throughout English society. Escaping Ireland in search of jobs, the Irish emigrated to England in vast numbers only to encounter pervasive animosity. All but a few of the Irish immigrants lived desperately poor lives, and, segregated from the wider society, they quickly formed settled communities. In these communities the Irish were free to perpetuate their cultural traditions and institutions.

Irish emigration to England had occurred regularly since the fifteenth and sixteenth centuries. From this time to the early nineteenth century, the great proportion of Irish immigrants were seasonal laborers who would return to Ireland upon completion of the harvesting. The same was true of those Irish laborers brought to England as "blacklegs" during periods of widespread strike activity. Around 1790 the nature of Irish migration to England began to change. As a result of the tremendous growth of Ireland's population, the rate of migration increased significantly; and between 1823 and 1840 the Irish laborers established a large number of permanent settlements in England.[46] By 1841 the Irish population in Britain was about 400,000; and in some areas of expanding industry, such as Manchester and Liverpool, the Irish constituted anywhere from 10 to 25 percent of the labor force.[47]

The pattern of migration which emerged during this period was not destructive of kinship and communal relations; indeed, in several respects it was conducive to their continuation. Large numbers of Irish immigrants tended to concentrate in the growing manufacturing districts where employment opportunities were expanding. It was common for new waves of immigrants to follow the already established routes and to enter the same areas where jobs as well as guidance and support were available.[48] For these later immigrants, the established Irish communities in the industrial districts of England made the transition to an urban and foreign culture much easier than it might otherwise have been made.

The isolation and independence which characterized the Irish working-class communities in England resulted partly from the intense prejudices which prevailed throughout English society, and partly from a strong anti-English feeling held by the Irish. The impediments which prevented a smooth assimilation of the Irish communities into English society were, however, essential to the viable sense of independence which permeated Irish working-class culture. In the first place, many of the immigrants had only recently left Ireland, where active opposition to English rule was extensive and violent. The revolutionary activity in Ireland, for instance, the agitation for Catholic emancipation in the late 1820s, and the struggle for home rule in the 1840s, had continuous bearing on the formulation of Irish radicalism in England.[49]

The continuation of revolutionary activity in Ireland also served to reinforce and renew a viable radical tradition which was rooted in the culture of Irish communities. The Irish workers brought to England memories, stories, and myths highlighting the insurrectionary activities of the Whiteboys and the revolutionary uprisings of the United Irishmen.[50] With these remembrances, their own protest was easily legitimated. One employer, testifying before the Commission of the Irish Poor in 1836, observed that "the Irish are more disposed to turn out, to make unreasonable demands, to take offence at a slight cause and to enforce their demands with strikes and bad language."[51]

The sense of historical continuity contained in this radical tradition was enhanced by Catholicism. Preaching resignation, not action, Catholicism was by no means a critical force in the Irish community. Indeed, the Catholic influence was often a pacifying one.[52] Nevertheless, Catholicism did embody traditional values and practices, and thereby served to remind the Irish worker of his links with the past and his membership in a wider social and historical community.[53] At the same time, Catholicism added to the distinctiveness of the Irish community, further widening the gap which separated it from the larger society.

The Irish workers in England regarded their communities as a continuation of, not a break with, the past. In these communities, Irish life was portrayed in idealized terms, and these images were a source of pride, respect, and self-assertiveness. The culture and institutions of the alien communities, like those presented in the imagined portrayals of Ireland's past, were based on principles of social responsibility. Mutual assistance and loyalty to communal norms comprised the stable foundation upon which these communities were built. As Jackson notes, "in the courts and closes of the Irish rookeries it was usual for those who were slightly more prosperous and in work . . . to club together to provide a loan to enable a streetseller to buy stock . . . [or] to meet the crises of sickness and death."[51] These protective communities, created in the 1830s and 1840s, were very similar to the ones established by the English workers a generation earlier. In both, the cultural and institutional emphases on mutual reponsibility were partially necessitated by a growing denial of social obligations.

The protective features of the Irish communities were related to the fact that the Irish constituted a reserve army of labor which was used as a supplementary work force. In the 1830s and 1840s, there still existed a number of lower grade jobs which could best be performed by traditional labor. The Irish, most of whom were unskilled, proved suitable for these tasks. As Thompson writes, "it was the very success of the pressures effecting changes in the character-structure of the English working man which called forth the need for a [work force] unmoulded by the industrial work discipline."[55] Less methodical, sober, and deliberate than the English workers, the Irish laborers retained preindustrial work habits, and were the obvious choice for the unpleasant and heavy manual tasks located at the bottom of industrializing society. Unskilled and low-graded, the Irish lacked access to existing unions and benefit societies; and, given their position in the occupational hierarchy, they encountered great difficulties in forming their own unions. Accordingly, protective functions could only be performed in the community itself.

The independent posture exhibited by the Irish communities reflected not only a viable radical tradition but also the influence of work conditions. Irish labor was concentrated in the weaving industries, the building trades— particularly canal and railway construction, and the coal mining industry.[56]

Most of these occupations entailed a kind of social and geographical isolation within which the work unit possessed a degree of autonomy not found in the more mechanized industries. In canal building, for instance, the chief unit of production was the butty gang, "a self-governing democracy which would tolerate neither foreman nor overseer."[57] The egalitarian structures and anti-authoritarian attitudes found in such work groups were duplicated in the wider community.

The Irish community in English society was clearly an open social location. The factor of recent immigration and the continuing need for a pre-industrial work force inhibited the 'industrialization of culture' from intruding on the Irish sector of the working class, and allowed the creation of communities with flexible structures and links with the past. Traditional beliefs and practices, ranging from the keeping of pigs, goats, and chickens in dwelling places, to the maintenance of communal sentiment, were readily apparent in the Irish communities. While the raising of animals in the crowded housing developments often lead to unsanitary conditions conducive to the spread of disease, the retention of communal values allowed the Irish worker to discredit the established order, and they provided legitimation to his resistance to the dehumanizing trends of industrial capitalism. As Thompson comments,

> The Irish influence is most felt in a rebellious disposition in the communities and places of work; in a disposition to challenge authority, to resort to the threat of 'physical force,' and to refuse to be intimidated by the inhibitions of constitutionalism.[58]

Residing outside of the expanding system of formal rationality, the Irish community offered its members a place where they could actively transmit the traditions of the past, and where they were free to participate in the creation of their culture. Imagination, fantasy, and remembrance were integral elements in the formation of this culture which contained a critical assessment of English society.

The distinctiveness of Irish culture—the traditional customs and institutions it harbored, the presence of Catholicism, and the unregimented work habits—made the Irish visible targets in a society looking for scapegoats. Anti-Irish prejudice penetrated all segments of English society. Among the workers, the Irish were regarded as strike breakers or cheap laborers who posed a constant threat to job and income security. The dominant powers, whether Whig or Tory, viewed the Irish population as imbecilic, incapable of self-government, and lacking in business skills and intellectual abilities.[59] It seems that only in this shared animosity toward the Irish communities were the workers and their employers on common ground.

Initially, anti-Irish prejudice was exhibited in innocuous and somewhat humorous stereotypes. 'Paddy' was uncertain as to how he should act, and he was reluctant to relinquish his barbaric and outmoded customs. Although his antics were despicable, they were also amusing. 'Paddy' was a figure of hatred, but he also possessed an ineptness and naïvité which made him comical at the same time.

In the 1840s, as working-class agitations intensified, the stereotypes associated with anti-Irish prejudice lost their humorous images. Now, the Irish communities were regarded as a serious menace to the moral standards and institutions underlying English social life. In these circumstances, the Irish were attacked for being dirty, emotionally unstable, dishonest, and untrustworthy. They were unpredictable, unreliable, childish, and primitive.[60] It is clear that the prejudice prevailing during this period was directed against the traditions and flexible structures of the working-class Irish communities. The communal and democratic spirit which pervaded these communities was an obstacle to the establishment of a methodical and reliable work force, but it was conducive to a rebellious disposition. And, it was this rebellious disposition which was characterized as uncivilized, savage, and wild, and later unfavorably contrasted with the self-control, discipline, and respectability preached by Samuel Smiles.[61] Thus the English, especially those of the middle class, were assaulting those aspects of the Irish community which made the Irish workers less resigned to the present and less amenable to the regimentation required by an economy undergoing self-sustained growth. They attacked those features of the Irish community which encouraged play ('childishness'), imagination and fantasy ('emotional instability'), and independence ('unpredictability'). In short, those features of community life which contributed to the rebelliousness of the Irish workers were assailed. Until they were undermined, the Irish remained actively opposed to the established order, and their participation in the Chartist Movement was significant.

Chartism and the Irish

The eclectic character of the National Charter Association permitted the Irish workers to join their English counterparts in movement activity. Given the regional and local bases of Chartist organization, it was possible for the Irish to march under the same banner as the anti-Irish, English workers without sacrificing their independence or cultural distinctiveness. The participation of the Irish workers in Chartist agitation came as no surprise, since they had been active in previous disturbances such as industrial strikes and the agrarian uprisings of the Swing movement.[62]

The Irish played a crucial role in the Chartist Movement throughout its history. Many of the most important leadership roles were occupied by Irish radicals, the most notable being Feargus O'Connor and Brontere O'Brien.

Moreover, as Rachel O'Higgins finds in her examination of criminal trial reports, a considerable number of Irish workers were consistently active in the most extreme Chartist assaults.[63]The Irish community contributed to the leadership, and to the rank and file, a higher proportion of its population than other working-class communities; and, it is important to observe, the Irish influence was most clearly expressed in the 'physical force' segment of Chartism. On a practical level, the Irish were instrumental in the organization of Chartist demonstrations in the early 1840s, and with respect to programmatic issues, they

> did much to mould English Chartist policies and outlooks in the 1840's. [For instance], the participation of the Irish contingent strengthened the 'physical force' element and helped commit the movement to a policy of revolutionary change which was far beyond its resources at that time.[64]

Strong Chartist support developed in all Irish communities regardless of the varying political, economic, and occupational structures that prevailed. In places as divergent as Manchester, London and Liverpool, the influence of the Irish communities on Chartist activity was forcefully evident. In Manchester, where there existed a long tradition of class hostility and conflict, the Irish population, estimated at 34,000, played a prominent role in the Chartist agitation. The largest proportion of Irish immigrants in Manchester, as in Lancashire in general, was employed in the handweaving industry; and, like other weavers in the area, they experienced increasing social segregation throughout the 1830s and 1840s.[65] As a result, the Irish workers in Manchester remained culturally distinct from the English workers, particularly from the factory operatives. This distinctiveness was reflected in Manchester Chartism, which was divided between 'physical force' and 'moral force' advocates for a number of years. The handloom weavers, among whom the Irish were well represented, firmly supported the militant stand while the factory operatives sided with the 'moral force' position.[66] Initially, 'physical force' Chartism prevailed, and, during the early years of the Chartist Movement Manchester was widely regarded as the center of working-class insurrection. After 1842, however, the factory operatives were able to gain control of the local organization, bringing it into line with a more moderate approach. A similar situation existed in London, where the Irish community also contributed significantly to radical politics.[67] Like other unskilled segments of the London working class, the Irish lacked access to unions and trade societies. However, in striking contrast to these workers whose participation in Chartism was inconsequential, the Irish workers were in the forefront of the Chartist disturbances in London.

Not only was the Irish participation in Chartism the most consistent and intense throughout England, it was also the most persistent. While Chartist support among other segments of the working class became increasingly tempered after 1845, the Irish Chartists retained their hard line, and were responsible for most of the Chartist-related disturbances which occurred in the later period of the movement.[68] By 1848 the Irish communities constituted the strongest constituencies of the Chartist Movement. Indicative of this are the attempts by the Chartist leaders to secure a formal alliance with associations like the Irish Confederalists, and the addition of a seventh demand to the People's Charter—namely, the repeal of the Union and the implementation of home rule for Ireland.[69] While these actions did weaken what remaining support Chartism had among the English workers, they also intensified Irish participation; it was almost exclusively upon the basis of this strengthened Irish support that the Chartist Movement was able to survive beyond the failure at Kennington Common in April, 1848.[70]

OCCUPATIONAL COMMUNITIES

Examining the returns to a questionnaire submitted to regional organizations by the Chartist leadership, D. J. Rowe finds that the most enthusiastic responses came from "colliery districts with a strong radical tradition, areas of declining handicraft industry, and, in Bradford (Yorkshire) and Leicester, manufacturing towns with a strong radical tradition."[71] In each of these areas, the success of the Chartist Movement depended upon the existence of community-based organizations which facilitated the political mobilization of workers on local and regional levels.[72] In large measure, these communities were occupationally based, and, like the Irish communities, were able to protect internal social relationships from instrumentalization. The miners, for the most part, were geographically isolated from the larger industrializing society, while the handloom weavers and many of the artisans engaged in the older crafts were socially segregated.

Like the Methodist sects and the Irish communities, these occupational communities constituted open social locations in an increasingly closed society. In these communities, cultural standards incongruous with those of industrial capitalism prevailed, providing legitimacy to oppositional activity. In those areas where the occupational community furnished its members with their only outlet of political expression—for example, among the miners in the North East and Wales and the framework knitters in Leicester—the Chartist Movement was very active. In places like Birmingham and Leeds, however, where occupational communities existed alongside a relatively open political structure, Chartist support was weaker or more moderate in tone. Among those workers who lacked ties to a viable occupational community, regardless of the extent of their economic deprivation, allegiance to and participation in Chartism was slight.

In the mining areas of the North East and Wales, and in the manufacturing district of Leicester, class distinctions between the workers and employers were rigidly drawn. No pretense of social harmony emerged in these areas, and the combative posture the workers exhibited was directly related to a long and strongly held radical tradition. The mining industry had undergone relatively little technological change, and the miners' communities remained largely as they had been in the early decades of the nineteenth century—cohesive, independent, and self-contained.[73] A strong sense of solidarity and class identity permeated these communities. In Leicester, class solidarity had its basis in the crowded lodging accommodations and adjacent factories. As one contemporary noted,

> Associated together in large Factories, communication of ideas and knowledge, the appetite for which perhaps has been sharpened by their sufferings, has led to a wonderful expansion of mind, and at their meetings for the purposes of political discussion, speeches are made by working mechanics which would do honour to any assembly.[74]

In both cases, the occupational communities, with their cultural distinctiveness, pride, and—more practically—meeting places, served as the workers' only avenue of political expression. From the beginning they provided enthusiastic support to the Chartist Movement.

Despite the rapid decline of their unions in the 1830s, the miners in the northeast of England—Durham, Northumberland, and on Tyneside—retained a viable sense of self-respect through their communities. These coal miners and iron workers proved to be among the strongest of Chartism's early supporters. The original Chartist petition was signed by the overwhelming majority of the population in these colliery districts.[75]

The northeast was one of the better-organized regions of the early Chartist Movement, and for a time was the center of 'physical force' Chartism. Coordination among the various mining communities was maintained partially on the basis of contacts established during the earlier union period and partially as a result of the many Chartist 'missionaries' who were placed in the area. As the Chartist Movement in the Northeast assumed a more militant stand by publicly advocating the use of arms in future disturbances, the government instituted a ban on Chartist meetings and freely began to employ an expanded military force against all violations of the ban.[76]

The miners responded to this repression by attempting, in conjunction with the national Chartist leaders, to found a broad-based union. In 1840 the Miners' Association was formed, and very quickly acquired both a large membership throughout the mining districts of Britain and a solid financial base.[77] The Miners' Association remained strongly, although informally, connected with Chartism for several years. Indeed, during this period, many of its personnel and programs, and most of its activities, were inseparable from those of Chartism. With the intensification of the government's reaction against the Chartist Movement in 1843, however, a tactical decision was made to dissociate the Miners' Association from Chartism. Despite a formal declaration of separation, the Association continued along a line of action consistent with Chartist objectives; and the strikes and riots which spread throughout the northeast in 1844 were clearly related to the Chartist Movement.[78]

The relative success of the Chartist Movement in the northeast cannot be attributed to worsening economic conditions. Compared to the lot of the workers in most other areas of the country, the existence of the northeast miners was a prosperous one.[79] Wages were much better, and, in general, were improving. Unemployment posed no serious problem in the northeast; and even duirng the depression of the early 1840s wages and the rate of employment suffered little decline. Throughout the period, the area's industry underwent significant expansion. As a consequence of the shipbuilding and railway boom, heavy capital investment poured into the area, resulting in a dramatic increase in the number of collieries, ironworks, and related metal-producing trades, and a further raising of wages.[80]

A similar economic prosperity prevailed among the colliers and iron workers of Wales. The absence of severe economic distress did not mitigate the radicalism nurtured in the mining communities. As in the northeast, the occupational communities in Wales actively collaborated with one another. In Wales, more than in the northeast, the coordination of communities, which entailed linking rural and industrial workers, was facilitated by Nonconformity.[81]

The Chartist Movement was well received in these communities. Some of the most violent uprisings associated with the early movement, including the unsuccessful Newport uprising, occurred in and around the Monmouthshire industrial valley. As elsewhere, militant Chartist activity in Wales weakened in 1842 and 1843. Although the Miners' Association never gained a foothold in this area, the occupational communities of the Welsh miners remained in hostile opposition to the middle class, and the industrial actions they engaged in continued to bear the imprint of the Chartist Movement.

The situation in Leicestershire differed in several important respects from the one in the mining areas of the northeast and Wales. Leicestershire was the center of the hosiery trade; and, as a result, a large contingent of framework knitters were concentrated in the district, located primarily in the southwest in such towns as Leicester. Until 1845, framework knitting was based on the domestic system of manufacture, with work being performed either

in the home or in a small workshop.[82] In these circumstances, class antagonism, when it arose, was very muted, despite the fact that viable communities
existed in these areas.

In the 1830s the economic position of the stockingers had begun to deteriorate. The government responded by introducing into the area the workhouse provisions of the New Poor Law. This met with widespread social
protest which culminated in growing hostility between the workers and the
middle class. Despite increasing unemployment and class antagonism, the
Chartist Movement initially attracted only sporadic support. However, as
the economic condition of the stockingers steadily worsened in the early
1840s, this changed; and from mid-1841 to the fall of 1842 Chartism rapidly
gained adherents in the area, especially in Leicester.[83] Over these years
Chartist activity in Leicestershire was frequent and often violent, and primarily directed against the regional Anti-Corn Law League—whose members met the depression by raising the rent of the frames. Although the strident
militancy exhibited by the Leicester Chartism became moderated after 1843,
it is significant that Chartism in the area remained viable right through 1848.[84]

An important factor in the persistence of Leicestershire Chartism was the
framework-knitting community. Although these communities lacked a long
radical tradition, they had acquired a sufficiently high degree of autonomy
as a result of the stockingers' struggles with the middle class in the years
between 1837 and 1840. During these years, the knitters forged a distinct
class identity, gained organizational skills, and produced their own leaders.
Not only did the local Chartist leadership draw almost exclusively from the
population of the framework-knitting communities, but, throughout Leicestershire, Chartist support and activity were housed in those areas largely
populated by framework knitters.[85]

The occupational communities created by the miners and the stockingers
provided some measure of social and ideological cohesion in a period of
great dislocations. As a consequence, the workers continued to actively
transmit and recreate a culture which differed from the utilitarian and positivistic values held by the middle class; here, play and fantasy were not restricted to the domain of childhood. These communities engendered a rebellious and challenging attitude among their members, and provided them
with organizational skills, oppositional values which legitimated social protest, and local leadership. As a result, Chartism had wide appeal to these
communities whether they existed in the areas of relative economic prosperity or areas of severe economic distress.

Given the predominance of a single industry in the northeast, Wales, and
Leicester, the occupational communities were simultaneously class communities. They exhibited a marked independence from the local middle
class, and they maintained autonomous institutions. In other places, such as
Leeds and Birmingham, this independence and autonomy were absent.

Occupational communities were not at the same time class communities, as various forms of class alliance existed. Lacking the independence of the mining and framework-knitting communities, the artisan communities of Leeds and Birmingham gave support only to the most moderate segments of the Chartist Movement. In Leeds, as we have seen, the Chartist Movement was effectively circumscribed within the institutions of the middle-class Radicals, the result being a municipal Chartism hooked to the established electoral system. A similar situation prevailed in Birmingham.

Birmingham, it will be recalled, was a town devoid of large-scale, mechanized industries. From the eighteenth century on, the town was heavily dependent on light metal industries, and in the 1830s and 1840s the small workshop continued to be the predominant manufacturing unit in the area.[86] Class relations in Birmingham were relatively harmonious. There was no entrenched capitalist class or industrial bourgeoisie, and the masters who owned the workshops remained on cordial terms with the artisans who operated them. The boundaries between the two were loosely drawn, and social mobility, although uncommon, was certainly possible. The "social structure of Birmingham," as Briggs notes, "made for middle class co-operation with the working classes."[87]

The nature and extent of this cooperation limited the margin of autonomy possessed by the occupational communities in Birmingham. Although the artisan communities retained traditional craft customs, they did not generate a value orientation at odds with that of the masters. The local trade unions were another factor restricting the independence of the artisan communities. Given the long tradition of class alliance in Birmingham, the unions never developed into a threatening movement, and for that reason they did not meet with the brutal repression so common in other areas of the country. Established on the basis of narrowly defined occupational grounds, these communities impeded class organization. Decision making was lifted out of the domain of the community and placed into the hands of the unions, thus creating vertical subdivisions within the community. This structural effect, combined with the unions' acceptance of the existing institutions, set limits upon the 'openness' of the artisan communities.[88]

The Chartist Movement was not immediately accepted in Birmingham. We have already seen that the artisans supported Chartism only after the movement's leadership, with considerable effort, convinced them that they had been betrayed by the middle class. Birmingham Chartism, then, was based on this sense of betrayal and not on the recognition of irreconcilable class interest. Thus, although the artisan communities acquired some degree of class cohesion through their participation in Chartism, the possibility for a reestablishment of class alliance was always present. The artisan communities did assume a more independent posture, but it was an independence circumscribed within the middle-class values of respectability. The Birmingham

Chartists, even throughout the 1839-1842 period of intense agitation, adhered to a 'moral force' position. After 1842, this already moderate stance was further diluted in the form of the Christian Chartist Movement. Accordingly, Birmingham Chartism, although it had a sizeable membership and was active for many years, never deviated from the moderate position which permitted simultaneous opposition to the middle class and the 'physical force' Chartists. Although tempered, the Chartism found in the Birmingham communities was much stronger than that found among workers separated from viable communities. In many of the larger towns and cities such as London, where such communities were absent, the workers expressed a hopeless resignation to the surrounding conditions, and their participation in Chartism was apathetic at its peak.

London, which had a rather large population by the 1830s, was the home of a wide diversity of trades. Only a few mechanized industries were located in the city; and, consequently, factories and huge workshops were present only in small numbers. This situation contributed to the general stability of the city's economy, for it was rare for all the trades to be simultaneously affected by economic downturns.[89] The structure of work prevailing in London was clearly reflected in the structure of the local working class. A large proportion of the workers were employed in the trades. Within this group, however, there existed an informal yet explicit hierarchy. At the bottom of this hierarchy were the lower paid artisans of the older trades—shoemakers, tailors, carpenters, and stonemasons. Residing above them were the artisans employed in trades associated with the production of luxury items—coachmakers, bookbinders, watchmakers, goldsmiths, silversmiths, and jewellers—and the newer artisans, the compositors and engineers, who formed the basis of the emerging labor aristocracy.[90] Outside of this trade hierarchy existed the unskilled and casual labor, the domestic outworkers concentrated in the east end of London, and a relatively large reserve army of labor comprised of unemployed artisans and newcomers to the city—such as the Irish.

Unlike the first two groups of workers who, in the context of the clearly patterned occupational structure, achieved a large degree of internal cohesion, the unskilled and casual laborers—with the exception of the Irish—were disunited. Interpersonal ties among these workers had been severed, and their community was reduced, in Bauman's words, to "an arithmetical total of isolated individuals whose biological needs [were] stripped of social coverings. This in turn . . . made impossible . . . expression of common social interests and therefore an expression of mutual concern."[91] This process occurred most dramatically among the Spitalfields silkweavers. The traditional values and practices of the silkweaving community in London had been completely broken down by the late 1830s.[92] This breakdown was reflected in both the cultural and structural features of the community. On the cultural level, there developed an inhibitory set of values and institutions which were devoid of hope and oriented toward daily survival.[93] Structurally, there were no opportunities for the creation and maintenance of enduring communal relations. There were no private meeting places, no chapels or pubs, where the weavers could congregate as members of a community.[94] In short, the community was a mere aggregate of individuals. The silkweavers had no open social location in which they could create standards for discrediting the established society. As a consequence, these workers did not understand their position in society. Unable to transcend the present, they fatalistically submitted to it.

This dissolution of community bonds did not occur among the lower-ranked artisans of London. In the trade communities these workers maintained, there was a long tradition of working-class political activity dating back to the 1790s. This common tradition was essential to the coordination which developed among the various trades, and was at the core of the oppositional stance they assumed. I. J. Prothero offers a detailed description of the artisan community in London.

> The artisans had their own radical culture and their own organizations—benefit societies, trade societies, mutual improvement societies and political societies. Being based on common trades, these all had several common features. They fulfilled a social function, providing companionship, recreation and solidarity. They often had an intensely local character. In their direct democracy dislike of control by gentlemen they manifested a desire for self-government and independence. Their functions overlapped and they shared to a large extent a common membership.[95]

Thus, the artisan community enabled its members to sustain traditional values, and—through its democratic structures—to actively participate in the decision-making process. Each trade society had its own house of call, where members would frequently meet to discuss pertinent issues and devise programs and strategies. While such decisions were made within the individual trades, they usually reflected the cooperation and custom of united action which underlay the artisan community.[96]

The internal cohesion expressed in the trade societies of the artisans practicing the older crafts was also found in the trade societies of the newer artisans. Among the trade societies of the latter, however, there was no spirit of cooperation. Anticipating the formation of new model unions, these trade societies regarded themselves as commerical and professional endeavors, and they promoted a conciliatory relation with employers. The members of these societies were more specialized and received higher wages than the older artisans, and their organizations were built upon narrow occupational distinctions. The occupational interests which were emphasized over class interests, as Bauman observes, "divided the new artisan stratum from the remaining sections of the working class; they even divided particular sections of the artisan stratum from one another."[97] In this way, working-class values became transmuted into status values which were easily accommodated within the existing order. Thus the newer artisans possessed a standpoint from which they could assess their position in society. But, derived from the prevailing middle-class consciousness, this standpoint generated, not opposition to, but attempts at consolidation with the established society.

The support received by Chartism in London varied significantly among the workers in these three different types of community. During the early years of Chartism, London, experiencing general economic stability and not confronted with the application of the New Poor Law, was a center of quiet and calm. It was only in 1842 that London Chartism began to achieve some significance.[98] Of the three communities examined, the artisan community of the lower-skilled trades offered the firmest support to Chartism, and the silkweavers' community provided the weakest. From the trade communities of the new artisans, Chartism received, not support, but severe denunciations.

Forming the backbone of London Chartism were the workers associated with those occupations ranked at the bottom of the trades hierarchy.[99] Indeed, the Chartist Movement in the city was superimposed upon the organizational structures of the trade societies which comprised the artisan community. Houses of call were used as Chartist meeting places; information was quickly disseminated through the channels of communication already established between the trades; and there was considerable overlap between the memberships of London Chartism and these trade societies.[100] The autonomy, independence, and democratic practices of the artisan community were reflected in the structure and ideology of London Chartism, which maintained internal flexibility and a vehemently hostile view of the middle class.

Contrary to the low-ranked artisans, the Spitalfields silkweavers reacted to the Chartist Movement with extreme apathy. The few Chartist organizations which were founded in the weavers' community all rapidly collapsed when only meager support was forthcoming. After investigating a variety of sources ranging from Chartist membership lists to intra-organizational correspondence, Rowe concludes that there is no evidence whatsoever that the weavers played even an inconsequential role in London Chartism.[101] What is surprising is that, despite several attempts by the Chartist leaders to establish a base among the weavers, not even minimal support was generated. The inactivity of the London weavers cannot be attributed to size, since there were approximately 11,000 weavers concentrated in the east end alone. Nor can it be attributed to economic well-being. From the 1830s on, the silkweavers had experienced severe economic distress. In the 1840s, rising unemployment and declining wages brought them a standard of living much lower than that of the London artisans, and comparable with that of the northern weavers (who, like the London artisans, were active participants in Chartist agitation).[102] What does explain the political quiescence of the London weavers is the one-dimensional situation constraining them. Lacking a viable community which would have provided an open space for sustaining traditions and creating oppositional standards, the London weavers had no way to discredit the prevailing arrangements. While they may not have accepted the justification of domination in terms of self-help and utilitarianism, they were unable to challenge the existing system and, as a consequence, could not legitimate social protest activity.

Conclusion

Chartism was not a movement which rose and fell in accordance with the economic fluctuations of the marketplace. Although economic deprivation was certainly at the base of the Chartist agitation, by itself it was not the driving force of the movement. Economic distress generated much discontent; but for this discontent to be translated into political opposition, it first had to be made meaningful. With the weakening of working-class culture and community, traditional sources of meaning had been undermined. As a result, many workers were unable to make sense of their misery. Lacking access to alternative standards of legitimacy, and unable to accept the prevailing standards, they resigned themselves to the existing order. For other workers, however, categories external to and critical of the current order were made available in Methodist sects, Irish communities, and trade societies. In these open social locations, workers maintained links with the past, and actively participated in the decision making process and the creation of new institutions. These workers comprised the mainstay of the Chartist Movement.

Although these open social locations served as the major arenas of support for the Chartist Movement, they also set restrictions on the effectiveness of the movement.[103] Chartism is conventionally regarded as the first national working-class movement in England. While there is some measure of truth to this view, the fact remains that Chartism was essentially a conglomeration of regional movements and organizations. The difference between these regional (and ethnic and occupational) organizations were significant enough to impede effective organization on the national level. This and other distinctions prevented the establishment of the solid cohesion and agreement necessary for a viable national organization. Thus, while the workers of these communities shared a common experience and a similar oppositional stance, their interpretations of this experience varied. The critical categories employed by each group of workers were derived from different radical traditions; and, although they discredited the established authority relations, they were not conducive to the development of a broadly acceptable set of objectives. Despite this divisive tendency, the Chartist Movement almost surely would have been inconsequential, were it not for the presence of these open social locations which sustained many features of the protective working-class community and which enabled criticism of and resistance to the established system of domination.

NOTES

1. Charles Lemert and Richard Rossel, "Cultural Revolution and the Definition of Reality" (paper presented at the Annual Meeting of the American Sociological Association; August, 1973), p. 16.

2. See Johan Huizinga, *Homo Ludens* (Boston, 1950), Ch. 1.

3. Claus Mueller, *The Politics of Communication* (New York, 1973), p. 9.

4. Harold Faulkner, *Chartism and the Churches* (New York, 1916), p. 74.

5. Although infrequently and poorly expressed, important commonalities underlay and reflected the working-class background of these various traditions. The inarticulate expression of these common goals and orientations tended to make the traditions more divisive than integrative. As to the potentially integrating thrust of such traditions, see George Rudé, "English Rural and Urban Disturbances on the Eve of the First Reform Bill, 1830-1831," *Past and Present* 37 (July, 1967): 99; Herbert Gutman, "Work, Culture, and Society in Industrializing America, 1815-1919," *American Historical Review* 78, 3 (1973): 531-588; and especially, Herbert Gans, *The Urban Villagers* (New York, 1962), pp. 229-262.

6. See Melvin Richter, *The Politics of Conscience* (Cambridge, 1964), p. 20; and Bernard Semmel, *The Methodist Revolution* (New York, 1973), pp. 7-9.

7. See E. R. Taylor, *Methodism and Politics, 1791-1851* (Cambridge, 1935), p. 16; and W. R. Ward, *Religion and Society in England, 1790-1850* (New York, 1973), p. 34.

8. See Semmel, *The Methodist Revolution,* pp. 17-18.

9. See J. F. C. Harrison, *The Early Victorians* (New York, 1971), p. 129 and Gertrude Himmelfarb, *Victorian Minds* (New York, 1968), pp. 279-280.

10. Harrison, *The Early Victorians,* p. 132.

11. Henry Pelling, *Popular Politics and Society in Late Victorian Britain* (New York, 1968), p. 21.

12. Elie Halevy, *A History of the English People in the Nineteenth Century,* vol. I (London, 1949).

13. Richter, *Politics of Conscience,* pp. 305-306.

14. For this period see *The Birth of Methodism* (Chicago, 1971), Bernard Semmel's introduction is extremely valuable.

15. See E. P. Thompson, *The Making of the English Working Class* (New York, 1963), pp. 31, 43-44.

16. Ibid., p. 375.

17. E. J. Hobsbawm, "Methodism and the Threat of Revolution in Britain," *History Today* (February, 1957): 118.

18. E. J. Hobsbawm, *Primitive Rebels* (New York, 1959), p. 130.

19. See Ward, *Religion and Society,* p. 66, and Robert Wearmouth, *Methodism and the Working-Class Movements of England, 1800-1850* (London, 1937), pp. 105-106.

20. A similar situation existed for blacks in the American South where, in the absence of other avenues of political expression, the Churches served as natural rallying points for the struggle against oppression and inequality. See Frank Parkin, *Class Inequality and Political Order* (New York, 1971), p. 75.

21. Thompson, *The Making of the English Working Class,* pp. 47-49.

22. George Rudé, "Review of *The Early Victorians,*" *American Journal of Sociology* 78 (March, 1973): 1325-1326.

23. See Wearmouth, *Methodism and the Working-Class Movements,* pp. 60-68.

24. John Wesley as quoted in Semmel, *The Methodist Revolution,* p. 74.

25. As quoted in Wearmouth, *Methodism and the Working-Class Movements,* p. 179.

26. Pelling, *Popular Politics,* p. 20.

27. Harrison, *The Early Victorians,* p. 166.

28. Robert Wearmouth, *Some Working-Class Movements in the Nineteenth Century* (London, 1948), pp. 66-73.

29. Ibid., p. 136.

30. Ibid., p. 183.

31. See ibid., p. 175 and Ward, *Religion and Society,* pp. 91-92.

32. On the significance of the Chartist Camp Meeting see Wearmouth, *Methodism and the Working Class Movements,* p. 142.

33. Asa Briggs, *Victorian Cities* (New York, 1965), pp. 186-187.

34. See Trygve Tholfsen, "The Chartist Crisis in Birmingham," *International Review of Social History* 3, 3 (1958): 467-468.

35. As quoted in Faulkner, *Chartism and the Churches,* pp. 44.

36. Tholfsen, "The Chartist Crisis in Birmingham," p. 479. Also see Brian Harrison, "Teetotal Chartism," *History* 58 (June 1973): 193-217.

38. See Hobsbawm, "Methodism and the Threat of Revolution," p. 120.

39. See G. D. H. Cole, *A Short History of the British Working Class Movement,* vol. I (New York, 1930), p. 151; and Wearmouth, *Some Working-Class Movements,* p. 188.

40. J. F. C. Harrison, "Chartism in Leeds," *Chartist Studies* (New York, 1959), p. 76.

41. See Wearmouth, *Some Working-Class Movements,* p. 130.

42. As quoted in Wearmouth, *Methodism and the Working-Class Movements,* p. 232.

43. During this period, however, Wesleyan Methodism was a major force in Sheffield. See E. R. Wickham, *Church and People in an Industrial City* (London, 1957), p. 84.

44. Ibid., p. 102.

45. Frederick Engels, *The Condition of the Working Class in England, 1844* (Stanford, 1958), p. 107.

46. See Arthur Redford, *Labour Migration in England, 1800-1850* (Manchester,

1964), pp. 132-164; and John Jackson, *The Irish in Britain* (London, 1963), pp. 3-4.

47. See Harrison, *The Early Victorians,* p. 46 and Jackson, *The Irish in Britain,* p. 7. The population figures given in the 1841 census for the Irish in Britain do not account for the second-generation Irish born in England. These people, who at least equaled those included in the census, faced the same prejudices and restrictions as the immigrant Irish. See Steven Marcus, *Engels, Manchester, and the Working Class* (New York, 1974), p. 197.

48. See Jackson, *The Irish in Britain,* p. 73.

49. See J. H. Treble, "The Irish Agitation," *Popular Movements* (New York, 1970), pp. 152-164.

50. These eighteenth-century uprisings are discussed in James Connolly, *Labour in Irish History* (New York, 1919), and P. B. Ellis, *A History of the Irish Working Class* (London, 1972), pp. 54-81.

51. As quoted in Jackson, *The Irish in Britain,* p. 117.

52. On the pacifying role of the Catholic Church see John Werly, "The Irish in Manchester, 1832-1849," *Irish Historical Studies* 18, 71 (1973): 350-351; and J. H. Treble, "O'Connor, O'Connell, and the Attitude of the Irish Immigrants Towards Chartism in the North of England, 1838-1848," *The Victorians and Social Protest* (Hamden, Conn., 1973), pp. 48-49.

53. See Pelling, *Popular Politics,* p. 32, and K. S. Inglis, *Churches and the Working Class in Victorian England* (London, 1963), pp. 120-123.

54. Jackson, *The Irish in Britain,* p. 114 and Werly, "The Irish in Manchester," pp. 355-357.

55. Thompson, *The Making of the English Working Class,* p. 432.

56. See Jackson, *The Irish in Britain,* pp. 78-87.

57. Ibid., p. 80.

58. Thompson, *The Making of the English Working Class,* pp. 442-443.

59. See L. P. Curtis, *Anglo-Saxons and Celts* (Bridgeport, Conn., 1968), p. 13. For a graphic presentation of the anti-Irish prejudice which pervaded the periodicals of this period see L. P. Curtis, *Apes and Angels* (Washington, 1971).

60. See Curtis, *Anglo-Saxons and Celts,* pp. 51-53.

61. Ibid., p. 84.

62. See Redford, *Labour Migration in England,* p. 162.

63. See Rachel O'Higgins, "The Irish Influence in the Chartist Movement, *Past and Present* 22 (November, 1961): 89.

64. Ibid., p. 92.

65. See Duncan Bythell, "The Handloom Weavers in the English Cotton Industry during the Industrial Revolution: Some Problems," *Economic History Review,* 17, No. 2 (1964): 345; and Briggs, *Victorian Cities,* p. 91. There is some dispute as to the exact proportion of weavers who were Irish. See Duncan Bythell, *The Handloom Weavers* (Cambridge, 1969), pp. 10, 63-65.

66. See Donald Read, "Chartism in Manchester," *Chartist Studies,* pp. 45-48. Also reflected here is the vehement dispute between Daniel O'Connell who urged support of the Anti-Corn Law League, and Feargus O'Connor, the Chartist leader. O'Connell's influence served to impede greater Irish participation in the Chartist Movement. See Treble, "O'Connor, O'Connell," pp. 34-36.

67. I. J. Prothero, "Chartism in London," *Past and Present* 44 (August 1969): 90.

68. The Irish played key roles in the London Rebecca Riots and the Liverpool uprisings which occurred in 1848. See F. C. Mather, *Public Order in the Age of the Chartists,* p. 15 and p. 115.

69. See Elie Halevy, *The Age of Peel and Cobden,* p. 253, and Treble, "The Irish Agitation," p. 164.

70. See Prothero, "Chartism in London," p. 91.

71. See D. J. Rowe, "The Chartist Convention and the Regions," *Economic History Review* 22 (1969): 60.

72. Ibid., p. 64 and Dorothy Thompson, *The Early Chartists,* p. 19.

73. See Marshall, *Industrial England,* pp. 107-108 and Harrison, *The Early Victorians,* p. 42.

74. As quoted in Rowe, "The Chartist Convention," p. 73.

75. See Raymond Challinor and Brian Ripley, *The Miners' Association—A Trade Union in the Age of the Chartists* (London, 1968), p. 11; and William Maehl, "Chartist Disturbances in Northeastern England, 1839," *International Review of Social History* 8(1963): 393.

76. See Maehl, "Chartist Disturbances," pp. 400-407.

77. See Challinor and Ripley, *The Miners' Association,* pp. 8, 60-73.

78. This is the major argument presented by Challinor and Ripley. On this score they differ from other historians, Hobsbawm and Maehl among them, who regard the Miners' Association as an alternative to the Chartist Movement.

79. One exception to the general prosperity that characterized the areas in the northeast was South Shields. Although the workers in South Shields encountered worse economic conditions than their counterparts in Northumberland, Durham, and Newcastle, it is noteworthy that their participation in Chartism was slight. This was partially a result of the extreme fragmentation which prevailed among the South Shields workers. See John Foster, "Nineteenth-Century Towns—A Class Dimension," *The Study of Urban History* (New York, 1968), pp. 292-293.

80. See D. J. Rowe, "Chartism and the Spitalfields Silk-weavers," *Economic History Review,* 20, 3 (1967): 20-21. Also see Maehl, "Chartist Disturbances," p. 391.

81. See David Williams, "Chartism in Wales," in *Chartist Studies,* pp. 220-221.

82. See J. F. C. Harrison, "Chartism in Leicester," *Chartist Studies,* p. 123.

83. Ibid., p. 109.

84. Ibid., pp. 117-118.

85. Ibid., pp. 121-122.

86. See Asa Briggs, "Social Structure and Politics in Birmingham and Lyons," *British Journal of Sociology* 1 (March, 1950): 69-70; and T. W. Freeman, *The Conurbations of Great Britain* (Manchester, 1959), pp. 71-78.

87. Briggs, "Social Structure and Politics," p. 71.

88. See Tholfsen, "The Origins of the Birmingham Caucus," p. 178.

89. See D. J. Rowe, "The Failure of London Chartism," *The Historical Journal,* 11, 3 (1968): 483; and Prothero, "Chartism in London," p. 82.

90. See Prothero, "Chartism in London," p. 84.

91. Zygmunt Bauman, *Between Class and Elite* (Manchester, 1972), p. 10.

92. For many workers who had recently migrated to the East End, it would be wrong to speak of a breakdown of community ties. And, it seems that the majority

of the working class population in the East End was transient in nature; for instance, the population of Bethnal Green had increased from 22,000 in 1801 to 90,000 in 1851. However, the silkweaving industry had been well established in East London for a number of years. When the industry rapidly began to deteriorate in the 1830s, the silkweavers, in substantial numbers, remained in the East End, often relying on casual work in periods of unemployment. In the case of the silkweavers, then, it is accurate to talk about the dissolution of enduring community ties. See Gareth-Stedman Jones, *Outcast London* (New York, 1971), p. 101.

93. See D. J. Rowe, "Chartism and the Spitalfields Silk-Weavers," *Economic History Review* 20 (December, 1967): 490.

94. Ibid., p. 492.

95. Prothero, "Chartism in London," p. 86.

96. See I. J. Prothero, "London Chartism and the Trades," *Economic History Review* 24, 2 (1971): 203-207.

97. Bauman, *Between Class and Elite,* p. 80.

98. See Prothero, "Chartism in London," p. 81; and Rowe, "The Failure of London Chartism," pp. 473-483.

99. See Prothero, "Chartism in London," pp. 103-104.

100. See ibid., p. 100; and Prothero, "London Chartism and the Trades," p. 212.

101. See Rowe, "Chartism and the Spitalfields Silk-Weavers," pp. 484-488.

102. Ibid., pp. 489-490.

103. The focus of this chapter has been on the conditions for mass action; consequently, other, more structural factors, especially those pertaining to the stability of the elite, have been neglected. This neglect should not be read as a failure to recognize that enduring revolutionary or rebellious activity requires the convergence of the two sets of conditions. See Charles Tilly, "The Modernization of Political Conflict in France," *Perspectives on Modernization* (Toronto, 1972), pp. 93-95; and Barrington Moore, *Reflections on the Causes of Human Misery* (Boston, 1973), pp. 178-193.

CHAPTER 6

Competing Explanations of the Incorporation of the English Working Class

By the end of 1860 the working class threat to industrial capitalism in England had been substantially weakened. The institutions and associations of the labor aristocracy were firmly entrenched within the middle-class hegemony, and the common workers were beginning to surrender their despair for hope, as modern cooperation and new model unionism prospered and the franchise was extended to the 'respectable' workers in 1867. The virulent opposition toward the bourgeoisie and the government, and the deep-rooted repudiation of the society generated by industrial capitalism, which characterized working-class communities throughout most of the first half of the nineteenth century, had given way to an acceptance of the established order. Writing about this period, one former Chartist observed,

> In our old Chartist time, it is true, Lancashire working men were in rags by the thousands; and many of them often lacked food. But their intelligence was demonstrated wherever you went. You would see them in groups discussing the great doctrine of political justice. . . . *Now* you will see no such groups in Lancashire. But you will hear well-dressed working men talking, as they walk with their hands in their pockets, of 'Co-ops' and their shares in them, or in building societies. And you will see others, like idiots leading small greyhound dogs.[1]

While there is general agreement that well before the third quarter of the nineteenth century the English working class had been circumscribed by the values, institutions, and structures of industrial capitalist society, considerable variation is found in the various attempts at explaining this incorporation.

The explanation proposed here rests on the demonstration of one-dimensionality, the subordination of symbolic interaction to instrumental constraints. We have seen that, beginning in the late 1830s and continuing through the 1850s, the government and the middle class actively allied to undermine the values and practices, the traditions, of working-class culture. In conjunction with advancing industrialization and capitalist relations of exchange, this effort effected a suppression of imagination, and thereby facilitated further industrial and economic growth. With the suppression of imagination (or, more generally, the suppression of noninstrumental activity through which critical categories are created), working-class social protest became aimless and disorganized. No transcendent criteria capable of guiding social action were forthcoming, and the ideological consciousness of the working-class community lacked viable and meaningful alternatives to the existing arrangements. It became, therefore, extremely difficult to establish standards for discrediting society. What this meant for the majority of workers was a pragmatic acceptance of the status quo. For the skilled laborers, the labor aristocrats, the 'flattened-out' values of the working-class community provided legitimation for an acceptance of middle-class aspirations.

In the absence of transcendental, critical categories, the articulation of collective needs was severely impeded. Qualitative demands were converted to quantitative demands, and communal aspirations were transformed into individual ones. Crucial to this instrumentalization of social relationships and quantification of exchange—which were necessary for the establishment of a reliable, methodical, and free-floating labor force—was the coerced acceptance of the linear, mechanical conception of time. Time was defined by the dynamics of the machine, no longer by its experienced content. Severed from a sense of historical continuity, the image of society associated with the linear conception of time regarded reality as a temporal process, meaningful only in terms of sustained and self-regulating industrial and economic growth; progress was coterminous with an increased domination of nature. From this image of society arose attributional rather than relational explanations of poverty, misery, and powerlessness. Reality was reified as people perceived themselves as objects of their self-activity. Just as play was clearly demarcated from work, so the performing self was separated from the emotional self, and the needs of the latter found no expression in public discourse.[2]

With the mystification of social processes, the worker became confined to the immediacy of the present. The critical thrust of remembrance was mitigated. No longer fantasized as a 'Golden Age,' the past was now viewed from quantitative standards as far inferior to the present. The past was not a *remembered* past. No longer able to participate in the transmission of the past through their distinctive values and practices, the workers came to regard the past as meaningless and invalid.[3] Consequently, the reflexive animus of working-class ideological consciousness was constrained; the worker was isolated in history as well as in society.

The one-dimensionality reflected in these circumstances presupposed the separation of economy and society, and the eventual subordination of the latter to the former. Where previously economic activity received its legitimacy from the social, after 1850 the system of work was approaching a position of being capable of legitimating itself. Increasingly, the only available standards of legitimacy were those—such as the self-help ethic—provided by and intended for the furtherance of industrial capitalism. Domination occurred behind these seemingly impersonal, neutral, and unaccountable standards, and was thereby concealed. The dominated expressed their felt domination as personal inadequacies. And, although protest continued, it was a protest guided by objectives consistent with the established order, never superseding the fundamental presuppositions of industrial capitalism.

This explanation differs considerably from the prevailing explanations of working-class incorporation into English society. Discussed below are four major alternative explanations. After outlining the basics of all four, each will be assessed with reference to the available data and contrasted with the explanation derived from critical theory. In this last regard, particular attention is devoted to the Marxian explanation, since it is from a critical appreciation of the Marxian framework that critical theory emerges.

The Optimistic Explanation

The optimistic explanation is rooted in the economic history of Clapham, Ashton, and Hartwell.[4] According to this position, the early history of industrial capitalism, specifically from 1800 to 1850, is best characterized by the steady improvement of living conditions: per capita income and per capita consumer goods consumption increased while prices fell; and, it is suggested, "the increase in average life over these years is further proof of increasing well-being."[5] The material benefits and living conditions available to the worker of the 1850s were far superior to those existing before 1790. These improvements translated into an increasing emancipation—especially of women—and were reflected in the growing belief that "ills should be identified, examined, analyzed, publicized and remedied, either by voluntary or legislative action."[6]

The decline of working-class social protest, and the subsequent acceptance of industrial capitalism, is attributed by the 'optimists' to the rising standard of living and the better treatment of workers which accompanied it. Following this line of reasoning, Mather contends that the harmonious class relations which developed "must be ascribed to the fact that the English industrial working class was on the whole better housed, better fed, better educated, and far less degraded than in preceding years."[7] In short, the assumption underlying the optimistic explanation is that economic grievances alone were the motivating force behind working-class social protest; and as soon as it became possible to allocate sufficient economic resources to satisfy these grievances, opposition was supplanted by affirmation.

The optimistic explanation has been called into serious question by E. J. Hobsbawm. Noting that the technical facilities available to mid-nineteenth century English society were insufficiently developed to allow extensive distribution of resources, Hobsbawm suggests "that industrialization under the prevailing conditions almost certainly required a more burdensome diversion of resources from consumption . . . because the investment mechanism was inefficient."[8] Throughout this period, then, there was no significant increase in per capita consumption. Furthermore, there was an apparent decline in the quality of foodstuffs consumed. The growing adulteration of foodstuffs is indicated in an 1855 study cited by Hobsbawm:

> (i) *all* bread tested in two separate samples was adulterated
> (ii) over half of oatmeal was adulterated
> (iii) *all* but the highest-quality teas were invariably adulterated
> (iv) a little under half the milk and
> (v) *all* butter was watered.[9]

The debased living conditions of the workers, profusely described in parliamentary reports of the day, corresponded to the polluted food which workers were compelled to eat.

While there was a substantial rise in real wages after 1850, its impact was rather limited. For all but the skilled laborers, unemployment and, more importantly, underemployment were commonplace in a cyclical economy. Harrison estimates that between 1850 and 1875 real wages increased by about one-third. Despite this, however, "the standard of living of the working class had not risen in [this] time of unprecedented prosperity. If the real wages of some workmen rose, the share of wages in the national income declined."[10] With the exception of the labor aristocracy, then, there is no conclusive evidence—from either consumption or wage figures—of the material improvement of the working class.

While there was little, if any, improvement in the material standard of living for most English workers, there certainly was an increase in human misery and uncertainty, and a dehumanization of social relationships.[11] When living standards are examined with reference to the quality of life they engender as well as the quantified, material advances they reflect, the optimistic view is further weakened. Growing insecurity and impersonality combined with an extensive exploitation to strip the workers of their pride, and of their hope for a society built on social responsibility.

The optimistic view of the economic historians has a parallel on a more sociological level of analysis in Neil Smelser's *Social Change in the Industrial Revolution.*[12] Employing the principles and categories of Parsonsian social action theory, to suggest an explanation of the incorporation of the English working class, Smelser rests his optimism not upon an increased standard of living but upon the development of mechanisms which permitted a socially acceptable expression of workers' grievances.

According to Smelser's scheme, working-class discontent and the activities which flowed from it were generated by certain "system-disturbing" factors. Briefly, the argument is presented that, in the process of social change, incongruities arose between the integrative mechanisms and differentiated properties of society. These incongruities created a series of strains which had their greatest impact on the institutions of the working class (e.g., the family economy). Incapable of accounting for these strains and their consequences in terms of traditional beliefs, workers experienced a sense of dissatisfaction which was eventually expressed in social protest activities. But their outbursts were appropriate—that is, functional—since they called forth new "social units" capable of minimizing system strains by bringing the integrative and differentiated properties of the system into line with one another. Through these social units, which were designed to "handle and channel" its grievances, the working class gradually came to accept its position in society to the benefit of the social system at large.

Smelser's account, while conceptually tight and logically rigorous, is not very compelling. In the first place, the English workers were able to understand and critically evaluate their social position with reference to traditional values. They recognized quite clearly that the objects of their opposition were not system strains but factory owners, corrupt legislators, and an 'unproductive class' of landed aristocrats. It was only after the destruction of working-class culture that system needs gained in predominance over human needs, that the well-being of the system became more important than the well-being of workers.

This becomes apparent after examining the social units—the Friendly and cooperative societies and trades unions—which Smelser finds so conducive to the decline of social protest. Initially, these associations were rooted in the working-class community and were expressive of the workers' antagonism toward the prevailing arrangements. In the early 1830s, as we have seen, these associations were in the forefront of radical working-class activity. Only the revived cooperation and unionism of the 1840s and 1850s exhibited the negotiating posture that Smelser describes. These associations developed in the aftermath of the attack of working-class culture, and by no means extended to the whole of the working class. Even after 1850, when the system was supposedly functioning unimpeded by strains and disturbances, the majority of workers continued to live in the most miserable ways, and,

moreover, lacked access to the meliorating "social units" which Smelser
stresses so much. Smelser's major argument, that working-class violence
and protest was generally a mechanical response to stress, is quite incongruous
with the evidence.[13]

Both the economic and sociological variants of the optimistic explanation
are inadequate. Where the former hinges almost exclusively on the economic
and material needs of man, the latter rests entirely on the needs of the social
system. Even if their reading of the data was accurate—and it is not—their
interpretations would still be suspect. For in neither is there a consideration
of human potential or an appreciation of symbol-creating activity and imagination. Man is reduced to an impoverished state—a container of material
resources or a passive object bounced around in a pervasive network of
system exchanges. It is upon such debased assumptions about the nature of
man that the optimistic explanation rests and falls.

The Civic Incorporation Explanation

Following T. H. Marshall, Reinhard Bendix argues that the discontent of
a recently politicized working class derives from its second-class citizenship.[14]
The political movements that such a working class engenders are primarily
directed toward the establishment of universal suffrage which is regarded as
identical to equality. "[T]he extension of civil rights," Bendix contends,
"benefits the inarticulate sections of the popultion, giving a positive libertarian
meaning to the legal recognition of individuality."[15] Accordingly, once the
working class of a given society is incorporated into the civic structures of
the national community, its threatening stance gives way to an acceptance
of the 'rules of the game.'

Although the Bendix-Marshall thesis recognizes that the enlargement of
the electoral system, resulting from the extension of the franchise, establishes mechanisms (the party organization and the secret ballot) designed to
neutralize the impact of the working class vote, it insists that the acquisition
of the franchise enables the workers to enhance their civil and social rights.
Universal suffrage, by giving workers an equal share in the decision-making
process of society, undermines revolutionary or insurrectionary inclinations.
Conflict, like equality, becomes institutionalized. In the case of England this
explanation must be examined with reference to the Reform Act of 1867, to
the working-class agitation which preceded it, and to the political consequences which followed its passage.

With the demise of Chartism, working-class interest in the vote dissipated.[16]
Both modern cooperation and new model unionism were politically neutral.
Labor aristocrats were convinced that equality presupposed initiative and
determination, not the franchise; and the mass of common laborers was
more concerned with meeting daily subsistence requirements than with the

ballot. This situation changed in 1865. The centralized administrators of the various trade unions—the Junta—had worked closely with middle-class sympathizers and Liberal legislators since 1860. Through this alliance a concern with political matters was introduced into union deliberations.

The National Reform League was established in London in 1865 by trade union interests and their middle-class supporters. The objectives of the Reform League were limited:

> 1. To procure the extension of the elective franchise to every resident and registered adult male person of sound mind, and unconvicted of crime.
> 2. To obtain for the voter the protection of the Ballot.[17]

Presenting itself as a working-class organization seeking to remedy labor's grievances—which it attributed to absence of working-class representation in Parliament, the Reform League was actually controlled by the Liberal Party. From the beginning, the Reform League received extensive financial assistance from prosperous Liberal manufacturers and businessmen.[18] In return for such financial and political support, the Reform League agreed to organize the workers as a pressure group behind the banner of the Liberal party.[19] With the Reform League, then, we have the formal beginnings of Lib-Lab politics.

The Reform League's agitation, if it can be called that, consisted of mobilizing workers in support of Liberal policies. Organizing exclusively within the labor aristocracy, the Reform League demanded the franchise—less as a matter of right and more as a matter of just reward. The arguments presented in defense of the extension of the franchise rested on the successes of cooperation and unionism, and emphasized that

> the working classes themselves are deeply interested in the preservation of law and order, of the rights of capital and property; of the honour and power and wealth of our country. They are as members of co-operatives, building and other societies, daily becoming themselves capitalists and landowners; there are among them men of large intellectual capacity, and earnest unaffected Christian principle.[20]

As is apparent, the working-class agitation for universal suffrage was in fact an attempt by representatives of skilled laborers to negotiate improved conditions and protections for trade unions and their members.[21] Through civic incorporation, the skilled laborers sought not a greater share of political power but further status distinctions.

As the strength of the Reform League-Liberal Party alliance grew, Parliament regarded at least the limited extension of franchise as inevitable. The Conservative party in Parliament, headed by Benjamin Disraeli, sought to neutralize the existing working-class support of the Liberals by taking the initiative in electoral reform. After the rejection of Disraeli's initial plan, which stipulated that each class would be awarded parliamentary representation in accordance with its social worth, not its size, the Conservatives submitted another proposal which in August, 1867, became the Second Reform Act.[22] The Reform Act of 1867 extended the franchise to adult males who were "£10 householders (or) lodgers paying £10 rent in the towns . . . [or] householders of houses rented at £12 in the countries."[23] The Act did not affect a significant redistribution of seats; and, despite the fact that it entailed an enlargement of the electorate by about 100 percent, no important shifts in power occurred.[24] The Reform Act did have an immediate impact, however, on the form of politics. The doubling of the electorate necessitated that both parties develop techniques which would allow them to retain traditional bases of support and to successfully recruit among the newly enfranchised. In this regard, the Liberal party had the advantage. First, the majority of workers who received the franchise worked and lived in the manufacturing towns dominated by Liberal manufacturers. Secondly, and most importantly, the Liberals' control of the Reform League gave them clear access to its nationwide network of associations. Eventually, this advantage was transformed into a liability, as the Conservatives continued to perfect their party organizations while the Liberals remained content for many years with the original setup. Through its party organizations, the Conservative party was able to eventually spread its base of support from the countries to the middle-size boroughs and industrial towns and Tory Democracy, the Conservative equivalent of Lib-Lab politics, was born.[25]

The 1868 election was regarded as important primarily because it offered an opportunity for testing the effectiveness of party organizations. As Hanham remarks, the "election was more a matter of establishing or consolidating the position of the parties in the new constituencies created by the Reform Act than a choice between alternative governments, since everybody knew in advance that the Liberals were going to win."[26] The political organizations, especially those of the Conservatives, developed rather rapidly and served as the major link between the recently created citizens and the political process. Voter registration, for example, was done through these political organizations. As a result, participation in the electoral system virtually required affiliation with these organizations. As Clarke observes,

> The elaborate business of claims and objections was the party
> agent's forte; without the agent's help many men could never

have upheld their rights in the revision courts—which suggests that, lacking such aid, many unaffiliated workingmen were disenfranchised.[27]

This state of affairs helps to explain why there was no substantial realignment of power following the 1867 Act.

Although the political system remained stable, the increasing activity of political organizations subjected the newly enfranchised workers to a variety of potentially disruptive cross-pressures. Designed to minimize these cross-pressures and thereby protect the stability of the polity, the Ballot Act, which provided for secret voting, was passed in 1872.[28] Justified as a measure which would release the voter from the sanctions of his employer or landlord, the Ballot Act further contributed to the privatization of the worker, for it also released him from the sanctions of his fellow workers.

The Reform Act only provided a limited extension of the franchise. Only those who were 'Registered and Residential'—and this excluded just about all but the skilled laborers—were qualified to vote. The common laborers, the 'residuum' as they were collectively called, had, by popular opinion, yet to earn such a privilege. However, with an open system of balloting it would have been theoretically possible for the 'residuum' to exercise an influence on the political process, by sanctioning those enfranchised workers who refused to vote in accordance with its position.[29] With the secret ballot the possibility of 'residuum' intervention would be undermined and 'politics as usual' would be assured. After 1872 the importance of political organizations increased, and, as they became more bureaucratic in structure, the isolation of the worker as citizen became more severe.

The Reform Act of 1867, then, was not brought about by a politicized working-class movement. Rather, the Act was engineered by representatives of the labor aristocracy in conjunction with the Liberal party; and it provided civic incorporation to a group of workers, the skilled laborers, who had for years been incorporated into Victorian culture. The 1867 Act should be regarded, not as a victory for the working class, but as an indication of the dominant powers' view that it was then safe to extend the franchise.

The evidence also repudiates the Bendix-Marshall suggestion that, with the franchise, the workers proceeded to enlarge their civil and social rights. The Liberal party won the election of 1868 largely on the basis of its support from working-class voters. But these voters were mobilized by the Reform League in return for the vast financial rewards it had received from middle-class Liberals. The consequence of this agreement between the Reform League and the Liberals, Harrison notes, was that "the Liberal Party derived immense benefits at very little cost [and] the Labour Movement derived no obvious benefit at all.''[30] Furthermore, as a number of observers have found, after 1867 political activity among the working-class enfranchised remained indifferent; there were no attempts—not even in the large boroughs and industrial areas where the skilled laborers tended to congregate—to articulate and support a distinctive program which differed from those traditionally promoted by the Liberals and Whigs.[31] The 1868 election was a sellout by the Reform League; and there is much reason to speculate that the extension of the franchise in 1867 had less to do with working-class agitation than it did with the Liberal strategy to oust the Conservatives from office.

The real working-class agitation for the franchise ended with the demise of Chartism, twenty years before the passage of the Second Reform Act. In contrast to the Reform League, the Chartist Movement was not exclusionary, seeking as it did to enlist the participation of all workers. And, occurring during a period when the values and practices of working-class culture had yet to be fully emptied of their meaning, Chartism claimed independence from the middle class. Thus, where the Chartists

> had appealed to Trade Unionists on the grounds that universal suffrage was an additional means of 'striking property on the head,' the Reform League asked them to support it as a dependable means of their 'rising in the social scale.'[32]

In other words, the Chartist demand for the franchise was a demand for broader civil and social rights. In meeting this demand, the dominant powers would have been undermining their own position. Here, civic incorporation would have spelled societal reconstruction. The Reform League, on the other hand, demanded the franchise in order to further elevate the status of the labor aristocracy. Unlike the workers represented by Chartism, the labor aristocrats had validated themselves through their performance in self-help activities: they had proved trustworthy, and they accepted the presuppositions of industrial capitalism and Victorian morality. In short, the labor aristocracy had legitimated society before it was incorporated into its civic institutions. Indeed, this was why civic incorporation occurred.

A third Reform Act, which reduced the qualifications for the franchise, was passed in 1884. Following this, in 1894, an independent Labour Party was established in general accord with the ground rules of the existing electoral system. Structurally, the Labour Party did not significantly diverge from the Liberal and Conservative party organizations, and ideologically, its objectives did not transcend the established universe of discourse. Thus, as Giddens suggests, "it seems reasonable to conclude that these changes (i.e., the growth of citizenship rights) represent more of a 'completion' or consolidation of capitalist development rather than an undermining of it."[33]

Through the franchise, the workers committed their struggle to the electoral process. But the goals and intensity of this struggle were already muted by the time the franchise was extended. To argue, as Bendix and Marshall do, that the decline of working-class political struggle was a consequence of the extension of suffrage, is to reverse the actual events. For universal suffrage resulted from the decline of working-class opposition.

The Coexistence Explanation

In *The Making of the English Working Class,* E. P. Thompson suggests a third explanation of the accommodation of the working class. It is Thompson's contention that between the years 1780 and 1832 the majority of English working people came to experience a close identity of interests among themselves, and in opposition to their employers and rulers. On the basis of this consciousness, they created a class which actively generated constant and, at times, violent opposition to the people and structures responsible for its mistreatment in society. This opposition was not curtailed by the reestablishment of 'system-equilibrium' or by 'civic incorporation.' Rather, this opposition was mitigated by extensive repression meted out by those groups who had a vested interest in the maintenance of the existing arrangements—namely, by the landed aristocracy and the then rising middle class. Thompson states the matter this way:

> Had events taken their 'natural' course we might expect there to have been some showdown long before 1832, between the oligarchy of land and commerce and the manufacturers and petty gentry, with working people in the tail of the middle class agitation. . . . But, after the success of *Rights of Man,* the radicalization and terror of the French Revolution, and the onset of Pitt's repression . . . the aristocracy and the manufacturers made common cause.[34]

However, Thompson is quick to emphasize that, while this collusion between the landed aristocracy and the entrepreneurial class prevented the working class from making any real inroads on the power structure of society, it did not disable the workers from achieving a 'spiritual gain'—namely, a collective self-consciousness comprised of a moral passion which allowed the workers "to *resist* being turned into a proletariat."[35]

Although Thompson ends his detailed analysis at 1832, he does suggest that the collective working-class consciousness which had developed by 1832 remained a distinctive feature of the working class throughout the nineteenth century. Indeed, it was through this collective consciousness that English workers were able to retain both a sense of solidarity and a basic antipathy toward industrial capitalist society and the other classes which comprised the society. The decline of radical working-class protest was essentially a response to the huge concentration of force at the disposal of the aristocracy and middle class. Confronted by such overwhelming strength, the workers had no choice but to reluctantly accept the established order. What ensued, therefore, was not the integration of the working class, but a detente, a policy of coexistence, whereby the workers begrudgingly accepted the prevailing arrangements. Within those arrangements, however, the workers continued to identify with and receive gratification from their distinctive culture and communities.

While Thompson manages to avoid the pitfalls encountered by the previous two explanations, his analysis is not entirely convincing. The major weakness of Thompson's analysis resides in his overreaction to the kind of sociologism apparent in Smelser's work. Thus, while Thompson is able to add a necessary emphasis on the active and creative elements of the working people, he simultaneously and unfortunately neglects an adequate consideration of the structural and organizational factors involved. As Nigel Young remarks about Thompson's work, "there is a lack of that 'totalizing' sense or sense of system, which can create frames in which macro-societal connections can be made over time."[36] In the absence of a macro-framework, Thompson misreads the 'collective self-consciousness' of the working class as constituting a 'great spiritual gain.' The limitations and consequences of this consciousness he fails to present. Indeed, as one critic observes,

> the 'apartness' of working class consciousness . . . *implies* a kind of deference—for it reigns everything else, the power and secret of society at large, to others, to 'estates' possessing authority or wealth. [It] turns aside from everything not the 'natural' or 'proper affair of the . . . class, all that does not belong to 'its' own world.[37]

While this reaction to Thompson overstates the deferential aspects of the post-1832 ideological consciousness, Thompson's view of the ideological consciousness is an overstatement in the opposite direction. A communal consciousness was retained by England's workers throughout the nineteenth century; but it was one emptied of political meaning. Far from fostering deference, it emphasized class distinctions and inequalities. But it cannot be regarded as constituting a spiritual gain, for by virtue of its lack of alternatives, the prevailing ideological consciousness only allowed for a pragmatic reconciliation with the established order.

Expressed through this pragmatic acceptance is the beginning of one-dimensionality. For Marcuse, one-dimensional thought and behavior occur in a context in which ideas, aspirations, and objectives that, by their content, transcend the established universe of discourse and action are either repeiled or reduced to terms of this universe. They are redefined by the rationality of the given system and of its quantitative extension.[38]

Marcuse's analysis of one-dimensionality is made with reference to advanced industrial society and an accompanying mass culture. In these circumstances human needs are privatized, and the dynamics of domination become incomprehensible. What results is mimesis: "an immediate identification of the individual with *his* society and, through it, with the society as a whole."[39] The critical thrust of reason and the ability to publically articulate collective, transcendental needs are thereby canceled.

One-dimensionality rooted in mass culture is a more advanced phase of the one-dimensionality which emerged in Victorian England. Although this earlier form of one-dimensionality rested on the suppression of imagination, the reification of authority, and the mystification of domination, it did not entail a complete homogenization of culture. As we have seen, a distinct working-class culture and consciousness was maintained after 1850. But it was a culture and consciousness which had been flattened out, leveled down. The communal features of working class life, stripped of their political dynamic, were sustained only in the interpersonal relationships of the workers.[40] The worker was isolated, not from other workers, but from his past and, as well, his future. The integration that occurred at this time was less a matter of mimesis and more a result of the absence of evaluative criteria with which the worker could, first, discredit the established arrangements and, second, articulate viable alternatives. Thus, the English worker in the third quarter of the nineteenth century did not identify completely with society. Rather, he was unable to question the presuppositions of this society. The prevailing ideological consciousness can be considered as a spiritual gain only insofar as it provided the workers with a sense of order. More generally considered, however, this consciousness was becoming increasingly inward-looking; it reflected political estrangement and a culture of consolidation. Charles Booth's extensive, turn-of-the-century surveys of English life portrayed a working-class culture "which was both impermeable to outsiders, and yet predominantly conservative in character; a culture in which the central focus was not 'trade unions and friendly societies, cooperative effort, temperance propaganda and politics (including socialism)' but 'pleasure, amusement, hospitality, and sport.' "[41]

An adequate explanation of the apparent integration of the English working class into the larger society must be capable of accounting for, not only structural oppression and inequality, but also the images of oppression and inequality held by the oppressed. Such an explanation must deal, not exclusively with the constraints and potentialities imposed by technology; but, in addition, there must be a concern with limitations and anticipations embodied by people's cultural achievements. While this explanation would have to focus upon the structural and ideological properties of the working class as a whole and of particular working-class organizations and movements, it must also be capable of going beyond this concern to demonstrate the relationships between these features of the working class and the fundamental social processes underlying English society. The Marxian account of the deradicalization of the English working class claims to do just that.

THE MARXIAN EXPLANATION

It is ironic that the theoretical analysis of social change which has guided the major social revolutions of modern history was developed in no small way with reference to a society which, from 1850 on, was comparatively free of rebellious and revolutionary movements. The theory, of course, is Karl Marx's, and the society is England. Upon his arrival in London in 1849, Marx became a keen observer of all aspects of English life—its history, economic system, political institutions, values, and, above all, its class structure and social movements. On the basis of his observations, and by an immanent critique of classical political economy, Owenite socialism, and, to a lesser extent, Chartism, Marx specified his theory of societal development and social revolution. Through immanent critique, Marx did not abandon completely the intellectual and ideological products of English society; rather, he expanded, reworked, and, in some places, modified his theory in accordance with some of the insights of Ricardo, Mill, Owen, and O'Brien. The influence of English society on Marx's formulations is also found in his extensive use of Parliamentary reports, journalistic observations, and historical accounts on the condition of English workers in his later works, especially in *Capital.* In this regard, Marx was following a course established by Engels in his 1844 study. Moreover, Marx's relation with the English working class—or, more particularly, the English labor movement— was an important source of many ideas and observations which were eventually incorporated into his framework. In short, the structures, ideologies, institutions, movements, and events of nineteenth century England had a profound influence on the formulation of the Marxian framework.[42]

Marx's involvement with the English Labor movement, his close association with Ernest Jones and Brontere O'Brien, the Chartist leaders, and with Edward Beesley, the radical labor organizer, are too well known to warrant more than summary treatment here.[43] Central to Marx's participation was his conviction, expressed as early as 1849, that England provided the major obstacles to, as well as the essential preconditions for, the development of socialism.[44] Marx's initial participation in the working-class movement, postponed by the period of counter-revolution which emerged throughout

Europe in 1848 and 1849, began in 1864 with the formation of the International Working Men's Association in London. The I.W.M.A.—later known as the First International—had as its primary goals the reestablishment of working-class political organizations throughout Europe and the creation of viable links between these organizations. Attracted by the prospects of a working-class organization on a trans-national level, Marx unhesitantly devoted his energies to the development of the International, and was appointed to the Central Council.

Given his prominent position, Marx played an effective role in shaping the policies and programs of the International. Although these policies and programs were geared toward the establishment of a European-wide (and, in turn, worldwide) movement, they focused on England and the English working class. Thus, in a letter written to Engels, dated May 1, 1865, Marx favorably recounted the accomplishments of the recently formed International, and concluded by stating: "If we succeed in reelectrifying the political movement of the English working class, our Association, without making any fuss, will have done more for the working class of Europe than has been possible in any other way. And there is every prospect for success."[45] In the addresses and reports prepared by Marx, the centrality of the English working class to the unification of the European working-class movement received considerable attention. England represented the clearest expression of capitalist development and the renewal of political organization and radicalism here would have international ramifications.

In the divisive atmosphere which began to permeate the International in the late 1860s, Marx retained his position that the attainment of the Association's goal required steadfast concentration on the English movement. Responding to one of several proposals that the General Council (formerly the Central Council) be relocated and formally separated from the Federal Council for England, Marx wrote:

> The English have at their disposal all necessary preconditions for a social revolution. What they lack is the spirit of generalization and revolutionary passion. Only the General Council can provide them with this, and thus accelerate a truly revolutionary movement here, and in consequence, *everywhere*.[46]

Thus, in 1870—in the midst of a growing reliance on arbitration and conciliation measures to settle industrial disputes, twenty years after the disastrous failure of Chartism, and three years after the extension of the franchise to a large number of workers—Marx saw the English working class standing on the threshold of revolution. His view derived from an explanation of the deradicalization of the English working class which differs in many substantial respects from the explanation presented in the previous chapters.

According to the Marxian dialectic, discussed in greater detail below, the working-class revolution will be a necessary revolution, one necessarily arising out of the contradictions internally generated by the dynamics of capitalism. Since capitalism had developed most fully in England, Marx expected that the irreducible structural antagonisms between capital and labor which accompanied this development would ultimately ignite class struggle. But class struggle did not erupt in England.

Marx, and later Engels, suggested a number of factors which contributed to the apparent failure of a working-class revolution in England. First, many of the conditions which aggravated the workers during the early stages of capitalist development had been somewhat minimized, largely as a result of the system's increased ability to produce consumer goods. Second, through constant expansion English capitalism had gained a foothold on the world market, and distributed some of the achieved benefits to the domestic working class. Accompanying this was the rise of factions between English and colonial workers (especially the Irish). Vertical conflict between labor and capital was consequently transformed into horizontal conflict between various segments of the working class. A fourth factor was the cooptation of trade union leaders and political representatives. Together, these four developments impeded the formation of class consciousness.

Marx and Engels emphasized that these developments merely delayed the revolution; they could not prevent it. The deradicalization of the English working class and, more particularly, the adaptation of the labor movement to the principles and institutions of industrial capitalism, were regarded as temporary. The structural antagonisms between capital and labor—between private appropriation and social production, between the interests of the ruling class and the interests of the working class—still existed; indeed, they would become more intense as the process of capital accumulation continued. "Here is the vulnerable place, the heel of Achilles, for capitalistic production," Engels wrote in the 1892 preface to his study of the English working class. "Its very basis is in the necessity of constant expansion, and this constant expansion now becomes impossible. It ends in a deadlock. Every year England is brought nearer face to face with the question: either the country must go to pieces, or capitalist production must. Which is it to be?"[47]

The answer to Engels' question, of course, was "neither." Indeed, as we have already seen, the most enduring and intense class struggle in England occurred not in the later but in the earlier stages of capitalism. They took place, not when capital accumulation was at its highest or when exploitation was most severe, but in the early years of the convergence between industrialization and capitalism. This situation cannot be explained solely in terms of a historical necessity rooted in structural conditions. An additional factor—namely, the interpretation of necessity afforded by symbolic forms—must be employed to properly understand the dynamics of rebellion and revolution.

If Thompson demonstrates anything in his massive history, it is that the English working class was as much a cultural formation as it was an economic formation. By regarding the cultural realm as a reflection of—and thereby reducing it to—material foundations, Marx and Engels removed one-half of the problem from the scope of their investigation. The weaknesses contained in their approach can be directly traced to this neglect of the cultural dimension.

Bertell Ollman notes that, in many places in *Capital,* Marx vividly recounts the widespread suffering silently borne by the English laborers. Marx recognized, *but he did not draw any conclusions from,* the workers' quiet, almost fatalistic, resignation to the degrading conditions. Ollman writes: "Despite his angry retort, his purpose in relating [these] incident[s] was to show the conditions in which the workers were forced to live and work, and not how uncomplainingly they had submitted to these conditions."[48] The apathy with which the workers responded to these degrading conditions was not—could not be—a problem for Marx. For these miserable conditions and, to some extent, the inhuman suffering they produced, would eventually serve as an impetus to revolutionary activity. Apathy and resignation were regarded as a temporary historical phase; as the contradictions in capitalist society worsen, resignation will give way to hope, apathy to class consciousness.

It is here that Marx's explanation differs most drastically from the one we have proposed. Economic conditions and, more generally, society at large may indeed possess certain structural necessities. But for necessity to be actualized, it must first be made meaningful with reference to critical categories which enable the dominated to discredit the legitimacy of—legitimate opposition against, and anticipate future alternatives to—the present order. Remembrance, play, imagination and fantasy are important sources of these critical categories and, moreover, are central elements in the creation of culture itself. By restricting the concern with these factors to the domain of idealism, Marx not only misread the situation of the English working class; he also set the groundwork for the incorporation of passive materialism into the dialectic.

THE MARXIAN DIALECTIC

To fully appreciate the Marxian dialectic, it is first necessary to briefly examine the assumptions concerning the nature of man, history, and society upon which it is constructed. The constitutive categories and the logic of explanation which comprise the dialectic, as well as Marx's substantive treatment of cultural matters, are consistently derived from these assumptions. For Marx the reality of the individual is a social reality. Responding to Feuerbach's abstract conceptualization of man, he writes "the human essence is no abstraction inherent in each single individual. In its reality it is the ensemble of social relations."[49] In a practical manner, man makes society and, in turn, society shapes the character of man. Linking the individual and society in this way is productive activity. "[T]he first premise of all human existence and, therefore of all history [is] . . . that men must be in a position to live in order to be able to 'make history.' But life involves before everything else, eating and drinking, a habitation, clothing and many other things. The first historical act is thus the production of means to satisfy these needs, the production of material life itself."[50]

It is Marx's position, then, that material production is both a natural and a social relationship and, as such, constitutes man's being. Through labor, man makes himself, his society, and his history. "What [individuals] are . . . coincides with their production, both with *what* they produce and *how* they produce."[51] In productive activity, man interacts with nature, and from this dynamic interaction society emerges. History—the progressive development of productive forces and relations—is made as needs are constantly created, satisfied, and re-created.[52] The development of man, the advancement of society, and the progressive transformation of nature occur through human labor.

By confining the process of human self-realization to the category of labor, Marx directs his attention, as Fleischer notes, "to 'how' history works rather than to the meaning of history to men."[53] In the context of this materialist view of history, Marx directly connects the issue of human freedom with productive activity, and in so doing effectively removes from serious consideration the symbolical apparatus which man brings to bear on his productive activity. People win freedom for themselves, Marx and Engels maintain, "to the extent that [is] dictated and permitted not by their ideal of man, but by the existing productive forces."[54] In a more explicit way, they argue that

> it is only possible to achieve real liberation in the real world and by employing real means. . . . 'Liberation' is an historical and not a mental act, and it is brought about by historical conditions, the development of industry, commerce, agriculture, the conditions of intercourse.[55]

Thus is the realm of freedom created out of the realm of necessity by man's labor.

Freedom results from a dialectical process; it is an empirical, not a metaphysical, matter. In order to properly grasp this real dialectical process, philosophical approaches must be abandoned, and replaced with science. The science of society which Marx promulgates is designed in accordance with the dialectical principles operating in reality and it has as its fundamental component the category of labor.

Marx suggests a distinction between real man who actually exists and true man who, on the basis of his 'species-powers,' had the potential to exist.[56] Embedded in concrete social relations and conditions, the distinction between actuality and potentiality constitutes an internal contradiction. Internal contradictions provide reality with its negative character and its dynamic thrust. Potentiality, which is contained in and simultaneously suppressed by the prevailing arrangements, is a negation of these arrangements. Through this struggle of opposites, reality is always in the process of becoming; actuality is always in the process of becoming its opposite, potentiality. Change, then, is inherent in reality; it is not external and arbitrary, but internal and necessary. Each society necessarily begets its own negation.

Internal contradictions, the struggle of opposites resulting in new social forms overcoming the old, are the driving force behind social change. To explain how these contradictions are worked out, Marx relies on the category of historical necessity. In the context of the materialist view of history, the category of historical necessity has been the source of much confusion within Marxist thought. Commonly, necessity has been equated with 'inevitability'; but more recent interpretations of Marx suggest that necessity refers to "urgent desirability.' Where the first interpretation regards social change as an objective inevitability (as inevitable as sunrise and sunset), the second views social change as an ambiguous process, one requiring human choice.[57] Marx, to be sure, recognized the importance of will and consciousness to the making of social change and social revolution. There is, however, much reason to believe that he tended to adopt the more objectivistic rendering of historical necessity.[58] Existence determines consciousness; therefore, ontological necessity, not moral imperative, guides the direction of social change.

The necessary resolution of inner contradictions occurs as a process of negation whereby outmoded relations give way to new, more appropriate arrangements. The process of negation is inherently progressive and rational. "No social order is ever destroyed," Marx writes, "before all the productive forces for which it is sufficient have been developed, and new superior relations of productions never replace older ones before the material conditions for their existence have matured within the framework of the old society."[59] Thus, the material conditions necessary for the supersedence of existing society are supplied by that society (in the process of becoming its opposite). Just as the features of this society once negated previous social relations, so now it is negated by social conditions which it simultaneously sustains and suppresses. The negation is negated; and through the negation of the negation—which, like all dialectical laws, is necessary law—progressive development occurs.

With the Marxian dialectic, concepts are not arbitrarily constructed; they are discovered. More concretely, they are discovered with particular reference to man's productive activity. On this basis, Marx's dialectic is a dialectic between the forces and relations of production. By the 'relations of production' Marx refers essentially to property-relations, those socially established laws which regulate access to the productive facilities. Alongside property relations is another set of relations which emerges from the interaction of men in productive activity. Directly determined by technology and the division of labor, these work relations are central elements of the productive forces of society. Productive forces, or a given society's capabilities to produce, encompass the labor power of workers, the level of technology and science the society has achieved, and the degree of specialization exhibited by the division of labor. Together, the forces and relations of production constitute society's mode of production, the substructure upon which a superstructure—forms of consciousness—is built.

Major social contradictions have their source in the mode of production, in the dialectical interaction between the force and relations of production. For a time, property relations determine what is produced, how it is produced, and how it is distributed. Property relations, however, are more or less static, and they eventually come into conflict with the dynamic character of the productive forces. On another level, this conflict appears as a tension between the interests of those groups or classes which benefit from the existing property relations and those interests which are denied by these relations. As the contradiction between property relations and productive forces intensifies, these interests become more clearly distinguished from each other; and a revolutionary class consciousness, one which recognizes the necessity of change, develops.[60] Thus the process of social change, although carried out by conscious, active people, is initially fueled by the contradictions generated within the mode of production. Just as the individual realizes himself through the category of labor, so society realizes itself through the mode of production. Human and social potentialities are expressed through— liberation is made possible by—productive activity.

Derived from this dialectical perspective, Marx's critique of capitalist society concentrates on the alienation of labor. Under capitalist social relations, production, consumption, distribution, and exchange are organized on the principle of private property. In this context, labor is turned against man; it no longer serves as a medium through which self-fulfillment occurs. With the shift from labor to wage labor (labor power as a commodity), work becomes purely instrumental; it is emptied of its creative thrust. Man's productive activity no longer belongs to him; rather, his productive activity is unfree, enforced, fragmented, and, as a result, expressive only of natural powers. In capitalism, then, labor is not an objectification of human life activity, but a negation of human potentiality. Man's 'species-powers' are not brought any closer to realization; they are crippled. In short, the worker is alienated from his labor: he is alienated from his productive activity, the products he creates, the species as a whole, and himself. Existing social relations become reified: they appear as independent of real social activity; and man comes to view himself as a passive object, incapable of acting upon and changing the external world.

The alienation of labor constitutes the negativity of capitalist society. Only when private property (and this includes wage labor) is abolished will alienation and false consciousness be overcome and social production brought back under conscious, rational control. The conditions necessary for the abolition of private property are shaped by the capitalist mode of production, and receive expression in the basic contradiction between the private mode of appropriation and the social nature of production. Summarizing Marx's position on this matter, Marcuse writes,

> Capitalist society is a union of contradictions. It gets freedom through exploitation, wealth through impoverishment, advance in production through restriction of consumption. The very structure of capitalism is a dialectical one: every form and institution of the economic process begets its determinate negation, and the crisis is the extreme form in which the contradictions are expressed.[61]

As capitalism inexorably and necessarily moves toward this crisis, class lines are more clearly drawn, and structural contradictions become translated into class struggle. The question for Marx is not if the working class revolution will occur, but when.

In light of this brief discussion of the Marxian dialectic, Marx's sustained belief in the imminence of working-class revolution in England becomes readily understandable. From Marx's vantage point, England, as the epitome of capitalist society, contained the objective conditions necessary for revolutionary activity; it only lacked the subjective factor—revolutionary consciousness—which would transform the working class into a 'class-for-itself.' Marx maintained, as we have seen, that this subjective factor could be brought to the workers by politically organized trade unions and, more particularly, by the International Working Men's Association. As it turned out, the Marxian dialectic was incapable of adequately dealing with this most important matter of consciousness. By not completely specifying the relation between the mode of the production and the superstructure, by refusing to seriously examine the autonomy of the cultural realm, Marx was unable to assess the significant impact which the suppression of imagination had on the curtailment of revolutionary dispositions. His treatment of culture, then, constitutes an important shortcoming in his dialectical analysis.

The Marxian view of culture

In discussing the relation between substructure and superstructure—or, in other words, structure and culture—Marx argues that the superstructure is determined by, influenced by, conditioned by, and reflective of the sub-structure. The various uses of the relational terms indicate a certain am-biguity on Marx's part toward cultural phenomena. 'Determined' and 'con-ditioned,' 'influenced by' and 'reflective of' have rather significant dif-ferences in their meaning. Are cognitive systems—is culture in general—merely a function of a particular form of productive activity? Is consciousness, which is 'determined' by existence, consubstantial with prevailing economic conditions? Are symbolic forms mutually dependent with—or are they reducible to—the existing material foundations of society? In an effort to clarify this matter, Engels offers the following remarks:

> We all laid, and *were bound* to lay, the main emphasis, in the first place, on the *derivation* of political, juridicial and other ideological notions, and of actions arising through the medium of these notions, from basic economic facts. But in so doing we neglected the formal side—the ways and means by which these notions, etc., come about—for the sake of content. This has given our adversaries a welcome opportunity for mis-understandings and distortions. . . . [There] is the fatuous notion of the ideologists that because we deny an independent historical development to the various ideological spheres which play a part in history we also deny them any *effect upon history.* The basis of this is the common undialectical con-ception of cause and effect as rigidly opposite poles, the total disregarding of interaction. These gentlemen often almost deliberately forget that once a historic element has been brought into the world by other, ultimately economic causes, it reacts, can react on its environment and even on the causes that have given rise to it.[62]

Consciousness, Engels suggests, emerges from the interaction between sub-structure and superstructure. The process is one of *praxis,* not economic de-terminism. In the context of praxis, a system of symbols can effect the struc-ture generated by productive activity. However, the symbolic forms through which people understand structure, and give meaning to their social activity, have been predetermined, in the last analysis, by the structure itself.[63] Cul-tural and institutional forms, Engels stresses, have no independent logic of historical development. What creative powers they contain derive from and can be explained by the category of labor.

Man develops society and secures knowledge of this society in his interaction with nature. Cognition and, in a larger sense, culture result from this interaction which is essentially productive activity. Cognitive facilities, and the symbolic forms through which they are mediated, allow man to know the external world as it is; that is, they enable appearances but not essences to be grasped.[64] The reality underlying existing social relations can be discovered only with "sober eyes"—detailed, rigorous, scientific investigation. Thus, the cultural apparatus which man creates to order and give meaning to his everyday activities is incapable of generating revolutionary consciousness. It is Marx's position, then, as Wellmer points out, that "the 'correct' proletarian consciousness can ultimately be none other than the consciousness of positive science," for only in this manner can historical necessity be discerned.[65] With the sober eyes of science, Marx does not surrender his commitment to a particular set of values; but he does demand that the association of the dialectic with proletarian interests be justified in terms of scientific analysis. In this way, the Marxian dialectic is imbued with a strong sense of rationality, in terms of which traditional cultural beliefs and practices are viewed as irrational and inhibitory of progressive change. As a consequence, the Marxian dialectic cannot properly appreciate the integral role of nonrational phenomena in the culture-formation process. This is most evident in Marx's treatment of the past, imagination, and play.

With reference to England in the period during which Marx wrote his major works, Zygmunt Bauman writes: "In an age of unshaken faith in the clearly superior rationality of industrial modernity—as well as the innate rationality of human choice—it was taken for granted that, given the chance, people would opt without hesitation for the type of living heralded by the new system."[66] In many respects, Marx shared this view and with it the Victorian abhorrence of the past. "The tradition of all dead generations," Marx comments, "weighs like a nightmare on the brain of the living."[67] With the category of historical necessity, Marx imputes a rationality, a sense of irrevocable and irresistable progress, to the process of sociohistorical change. The future is immanent, it is contained in and suppressed by the present; and eventually conditions will emerge which will make its actualization necessary. If these conditions are to be recognized, however, traditional structures and value orientations must be undermined. Social revolution, Marx continues, "cannot draw its poetry from the past but only from the future. It cannot begin with itself before it has stripped off all superstition in regard to the past."[68] Preserved in institutions and memories, the past has a paralyzing effect on people's capacity for action; it confines them to outmoded relationships, compels them to repeat those activities and uphold those structures which sustain oppression, and promotes a fear of novelty, a sense of uncertainty concerning the future. Only when social action is guided by the progressive rationality of history can rebellious or revolutionary activity ensue. And this presupposes a rejection of the past.

On the basis of these views Marx was lead to misread the machine-wrecking riots of the eighteenth and early nineteenth centuries. Marx regards these riots almost exclusively in economic terms, suggesting that the rioters' activity was motivated by their perception of the machine as a competitor. These retrogressive outbursts occurred because the workers were prevented by their outmoded values from recognizing that the machine served as a basis for a better society.[69] In fact, however, machine-wrecking riots did not constitute a denial of machinery; rather, they were an affirmation of the moral categories contained in traditional standards. Traditional standards guided this rebellious activity, and they did so, as we have seen, in a progressive way. To grasp this, Marx would have had to come to grips with the nonrational in a way that his rational dialectic prevented. As a consequence, the critical implications arising out of the fusion of the factual and the evaluative, the emotional and the cognitive, in nonrational categories is neglected, and the past is written off as superstition.

By insisting that the proletarian revolution will be a rational revolution and, further, by equating the nonrational with the irrational, Marx justifies his contention that revolutionary poetry must abandon reference to the past and draw its content from the future. At the same time, however, he restricts imagination to the domain of rational activity. For Marx the anticipatory powers of imagination derive not from a reconstruction of past but from the direct connection between imagination and the labor process.[70] That is, imagination anticipates the future to the extent that it is instrumental, that it plans a course of action and establishes certain goals which are then implemented through productive activity. In this sense, labor is a process through which 'concretizations' of imagination take place.[71] Imagination, then, allows conscious, rational planning and, in so doing, distinguishes the labor of man from the labor of lower animals.[72] Thus correct anticipations of the future arise only when imagination is harnessed to productive activity. Dissociated from the labor process, imagination results in the creation of self-deceptive utopias which have more in common with myth than science.[73] Scientific socialism, in short, regards imagination as an important element of sociohistorical change to the extent that it is constricted by the rationality inherent in the category of labor.

Marx's position differed in many important respects from the Victorian his reliance on the instrumental notion of rationality. In his critique of Fourier's utopia wherein work becomes play, Marx accuses Fourier of being naïve for even considering that labor might be made a 'joke' or an 'amusement.'

> Really free labour, the composing of music for example, is at the same time damned serious and demands the greatest effort. . . . Work cannot become a game, as Fourier would

like it to be; his great merit was that he declared that the ultimate object must be to raise to a higher level not distribution
but the mode of production. Free-time—which includes leisure
time as well as time for higher activities—naturally transforms anyone who enjoys it into a different person, and it is
this different person who then enters the direct process of
production.[74]

In short, even in free society socially necessary labor predetermines the
organization of non-work activities. The realm of freedom, the sphere in
which the forces of play are developed, is contingent upon necessity.[75] Beyond necessity "begins that development of human power, which is its own
end, the true realm of freedom, which, however, can flourish only upon
that realm of necessity as its basis. *The shortening of the working day is its
fundamental premise.*"[76] The realm of freedom and, accordingly, play
activity, exist beyond, not in, the realm of necessity. Work—labor as the
only mode of activity through which man fulfills himself—is and always
will remain distinct from play. Play is possible, in the last analysis, only
after the productive forces have been sufficiently developed and rationally
organized so that the time and energy required for necessary labor is reduced.

The implication of Marx's position is that the culture-creating process as
a free activity is possible only in post-revolutionary society; and even then it
operates within the limits established by necessity. Prior to this situation,
man exists in a state of prehistory, subordinated to 'blind' historical laws.
In elaborating this theory—or, more appropriately, this approach—to cultural matters, Marx employed categories strongly influenced by contemporary
Victorian values. The rationality which permeated his dialectic was in many
ways consistent with Victorian emphases, and similarly derived from an
adamant belief in the gospel of work. Progress—technological advancement
and the development of productive forces—is directly tied to work; and for
both Marx and his Victorian counterparts, this connection received expression in and was to be analyzed by the natural science approach. Moreover,
Marx shared the Victorian repudiation of the past; and although he did not
neglect imagination, he instrumentalized it, examining imagination only in
terms of rational planning and the labor process. The distinction between
work time and free time, the conceptualization of play as leisure, as less
significant than work, is also apparent in the Marxian theory. To be sure,
Marx's position differed in many important respects from the Victorian
ideology; but to say that his categories superseded the existing social relations
is, perhaps, saying too much.

In the last analysis, the deemphasis of culture and the stress on the rationality contained in the Marxian dialectic closely reflected the changes occurring
in English society after the mid-nineteenth century. Instrumental reason

and the self-legitimating economy are incorporated into Marx's theory in the form of scientific socialism and a dialectic confined to the mode of production. Hence, the critique we have previously applied to English society must now be brought to bear on the Marxian dialectic.

CRITIQUE OF THE MARXIAN DIALECTIC

The critique of the Marxian dialectic must concentrate on the category of labor. Habermas argues, as discussed in Chapter 1, that Marx's use of the category of labor contains a 'latent positivism' which contributes to objectivistic interpretations of the dialectical process of social change. In these interpretations, practical activity and the active process of reflection it embodies are reduced to technical activity defined in terms of a passive materialism. The implications of this are found in the Marxian treatment of ideology.

The critical theorists point out two different conceptions of ideology which appear in Marx's work. The first, which permeates his earlier writings, recognizes the utopian anticipations embodied by the prevailing consciousness, and implies that false consciousness can only be resolved through an emancipatory process mediated by critical self-reflection. In this sense, ideology is reason in its nonrational form: "as conscious being it was *praxis* apprehended in thought, illustions ensuring domination and uncomprehended utopia simultaneously."[77] Whereas this conception of ideology is not amenable to natural-scientific techniques, the conception found in Marx's later works is. According to this second conception, ideology is merely the mental expression of class domination, a direct function of—and therefore reducible to—the substructure. Here the dissolution of false consciousness is seen as a consequence of the tensions created by technological advancement. Underlying this shift was Marx's failure to maintain the distinction between critique and positive science. As Habermas notes:

> Before the authority of scientific consciousness, the dialectical relation of an idea alienated from its interest, and therefore subjected to it, was transformed only too readily into the dependence of consciousness on its historical existence; . . . And later Marx never explicitly rejected the naturalistic version of the doctrine of ideology which Engels supplied.[78]

As historical materialism—that is, as positive science—the Marxian critique cannot locate itself as part of that situation which it intends to supersede. Such critique seeks to ascertain the concrete determinations of freedom, not by a critical and reflective analysis of prevailing traditions, but by rigorous, scientific investigation.[79]

The positivistic aspects of Marx's critique are most evident in the theory of surplus value. Were the theory of surplus value peripheral to Marx's larger work, this positivistic bent would hardly be worth mentioning. But this is not the case. For with reference to the theory of surplus value, Marx develops his critique of the class structure of and alienation in capitalistic society. Domination, as it occurs through the organization and distribution of surplus product, and as it is hypostatized through the reified relations of exchange, is an objective process. Similarly, Marx regards resistance to domination and the demand for emancipation as having their roots in real— that is, empirical and objective—processes. Revolutionary consciousness, to be sure, involves a subjective moment; but from this view the subjective moment is made possible by the system of production. For instance, the task of maintaining the increasing powers of surplus-value extraction, within the boundaries determined by the necessity of converting the surplus value into exchange value, creates irreconcilable contradictions as the capitalist system advances.[80] As economic crises intensify, the proletariat, as an objective class, is compelled to assume a posture of solidarity which is the basis for the formulation of revolutionary consciousness.

In his writings Marx never denied the practical side of revolutionary activity; indeed he was quick to dissociate himself from those 'Marxists' who did. However, in the crisis theory he developed from his critique as positive science, revolutionary consciousness is mechanically linked to structural and necessary contradictions generated by the capitalist mode of production. One consequence of this, as Schroyer notes, is that in the Marxian dialectic "there is no systematic explanation of why man *needs* to overcome domination."[81] With the category of historical necessity, Marx can adequately deal with the matter of why social relations 'need' to progressively change. But how does this structural necessity become meaningfully translated into human needs? What role do symbolic categories play in making the struggle against domination *imperative*? Marx is prevented from considering these problems and the related issue of cultural domination whereby people are prohibited from interpreting their own needs. In his haste to turn Hegel on his head, Marx propounded a theory of work in opposition to, rather than in conjunction with, a theory of culture. Historical necessity as the dynamic of social change was counterposed to, not joined with, symbolical necessity—moral imperatives. By concentrating on the objective determinants of social action, Marx had forged a dialectic which is only capable of incomplete interpretation of the dynamics of domination and emancipation. To complete the interpretation, the cultural dimension, its nonrational aspects and its impact on the cognitive system, must be incorporated into the dialectic and conceptualized, not as a reflection, but as a denial of material constraints. In this sense, as Birnbaum suggests, culture cannot be regarded as "entirely a matter of consciousness, since human consciousness in culture responds to the unconscious communication of meaning through symbols, and conscious reflection or analysis often rests on a deeper stratus of experience not always immediately accessible to consciousness itself.''[82] With this conception of culture, the category of historical necessity is somewhat and conscious reflection or analysis often rests on a deeper stratus of experience not always immediately accessible to consciousness itslef.''[82] With this conception of culture, the category of historical necessity is somewhat weakened as the element of ambivalence is introduced. What is important about this notion of culture is that it allows the search for the sources of domination to go beyond external determinants. Why is it that people decide to discredit the legitimacy of the existing order? How is it that people legitimate their opposition to this order and formulate and choose between future alternatives? Positive science and the assumption of rationality will not fully account for these activities. The nonrational—remembrance, imagination, and play—must also be examined.

In the previous chapters, a case has been made for the importance of the remembered past to the discrediting, legitimating, and anticipating process essential to revolutionary activity. We have found that the poetry which animated rebellious and revolutionary activity does not draw its content from the future, but from the past—the past, not as historical fact, but the remembered past, the idealized, glorified, mythical past. Although guided by the past, these revolutions and rebellions are not retrogressive; for in myth the past is portrayed, not as it actually was, but as it ought to have been. In this way, the future is anticipated with reference to a past which never was. However, conceptions of the future are not merely drawn from the remembered past; rather, they emerge from the interaction between the past remembered in myth, and the present. Accordingly, images of the future constitute, not a denial of the present, but a restructuring of the present in accordance with the organizing principles exhibited in the idealized portrayal of the past. Thus the future society, the society which 'ought to be,' represents a playful synthesis of the mythical past and those features of the present society which are necessary for the actualization of the 'good life.' In other words, for that which is historically necessary to be realized, it must first be made meaningful in terms of the critical categories supplied by the mythical past. A sense of integrated experience—moral imperatives and structural necessity, fantasy and reality, the nonrational and the rational, the past and the future—is important to rebellious and revolutionary activity.

Remembrance, imagination, and play are essential to the development of this integrated experience; they are modes through which people fulfill themselves, create their culture, give meaning to their lives, and interpret their needs. When they are written off as 'weighted nightmares,' when they are confined to the straightjacket of rational planning, or when they are regarded as being subsidiary in importance to work, the result is highly distorted notions of integrated experience, of totality, and of 'true man'—

notions which restrict self-realization to conscious productive activity. What Jacques Ehrmann has to say about play in this regard holds equally well for imagination and remembrance. He writes, "if play as the capacity for symbolization and ritualization is consubstantial with culture, it cannot fail to be present wherever there is culture. We realize then that play cannot be defined as a luxury. Whether their stomachs are full or empty, men play because they are men."[83] Marx did not recognize this; and as a consequence, he remained unconcerned with the attack on working-class traditions, the constriction of imagination, and the suppression of play. In the midst of these developments, Marx's critique never strayed from the focus on the appropriation of surplus value. Thus, the critique of political economy sustained Marx's hope for a revolutionary working class in England; but this hope came at the expense of inaccurate analysis. What I am suggesting here is that the Marxian dialectic is too narrowly defined: it must be expanded to include a critique of the instrumentalization of culture (instrumental reason) as well as a critique of political economy; it must be capable of examining cultural domination as well as economic and political domination, and it must pay consideration to moral imperatives as well as historical necessity.

THE RECONSTRUCTED DIALECTIC

In his reconstruction of the dialectic, Habermas revives 'superstructure'— culture as an institutional and normative framework—as a dimension of the dialectic. By releasing the dynamics of the dialectic from the confines of the category of labor, he invites exploration into the suppression and alienation of man's symbolical as well as productive activity, and thus permits the critique of political economy to be joined with the critique of instrumental reason. In this way, the 'work and interaction' dialectic has the important merit of allowing a comprehensive consideration of sociocultural forms and of the relation between domination and the distortion and manipulation of symbols. In the last analysis, however, the reconstructed dialectic does not go far enough to anticipate future alternatives: it is not comprehensive enough to point to the negation of its own negativity. In the present analysis we have tried to overcome this limitation (and to round out Habermas' critical theory) by including remembrance, imagination, and play as elements of symbolic communication. All three are essential to the process of culture formation, and each constitutes a significant mode of symbolic representation.[84] While a theory of communication inclusive of remembrance, imagination, and play remains to be developed, the incorporation of these factors into the symbolic interaction dimension of Habermas' scheme does allow us to account for the construction of conceptions of the future or utopian anticipations. Moreover, with the category of the remembered past, Habermas' dialectic can be expanded to include both the category of 'ought' (moral imperatives) and the category of historical necessity.

The current dispute between those who contend that transcendence is contained in ontological necessity and those who maintain that transcendence has an epistemological basis and appears as a moral imperative (an 'ought'), reflects the basic dividing line between materialistic and idealistic conceptions of the dialectic. Habermas' 'work and interaction' dialectic is constructed in such a way that it can be used to bring about a useful resolution of this dispute. The category of historical necessity focuses on structural conditions, and is consistent with the critique of political economy. However, since that which is historically necessary can only be brought about by people to whom this necessity is meaningful, a second dimension must be investigated. It is with this second dimension—the dimension of meaning—that the system of symbolic interaction is concerned. Thus the critique of political economy (with reference to the system of work) is accompanied by the critique of instrumental reason (with reference to the system of symbolic interaction). Where the critique of political economy attends to the problem of the supersedence of prevailing social relations, the critique of instrumental reason is concerned with identifying the symbolic conditions under which this supersedence can be actualized. Taken together in a dialectical framework, the interaction of the two initiates a synthesis of objective and subject possibility.

From this viewpoint, the dialectic intends to comprehend noninstrumental relations as well as instrumental (exchange) relations. Fleischer's comments on this matter are highly signficant:

> Men in society make demands on each other and are ready to grant each other things going beyond concrete exchange relations; that is, mutual respect and aid. A definite amount of this is always required by the social code, and underlying the codification is the potential of demand and ability to put through the demand reached at the particular stage of history. *Unfulfilled moral demand becomes the starting-point for a new codification.*[85]

Once this is accepted, the dialectical analysis of social change must come to grips with how these moral demands are constructed. From our perspective, this process is accounted for in the following way: As the system of work advances, traditional moral obligations are abridged. With the abrogation of traditional standards, new codifications are created with reference to the remembered, imaginatively and playfully reconstructed past, not to the future which has no content of its own. Conceptions of the future, in terms of which the discrediting, legitimating, and anticipating processes occur, emerge from the tension between the idea of the remembered past and the actual material conditions and social relationships of the present.

The 'villages of cooperation,' for instance, connoted a future society where industrialization (as a matter of historical necessity) was brought under the control of the moral and communal principles which characterized the imaginatively reconstructed past. Thus, in this creation of conceptions of the future, structural necessity becomes translated into moral necessity: societal requirements and human needs converge. In short, the reconstructed dialectic is capable of offering a critique which, like Marx's, is geared to to ascertaining structurally emergent alternatives while remaining sensitive to the problems of meaning and symbolic forms.[86]

Conclusion

The findings of this study call attention to the many weaknesses associated with the commonly held assumption that rebellion and revolution presuppose a rejection of the past and the development of a rational course of action. Beyond this, they indicate that social revolutions are not merely revolutions of the belly but revolutions of the imagination as well. A number of implications concerning the study and practice of social change arise from these conclusions. First, analysis of revolution and rebellion must take into consideration the role of imagination and play and the category of remembrance. This is especially applicable to those Marxist analyses which attribute the failure or postponement of working-class revolutions in advanced capitalist societies to economic changes flowing out of technology, increasing specialization, governmental intervention, or imperialism. While these factors have undoubtedly been crucial in impeding the development of a revolutionary consciousness, it is apparent that the suppression of play, imagination, and remembrance have had a similar, equally influential, impact. Accordingly, the political role of symbolic communication in the establishment of legitimacy must be systematically examined. On an organizational level, this requires a consideration of the ways by which suppressed modes of symbolic communication can be reactivated. Organization around bread-and-butter issues will emerge only after the negative experience generated by the prevailing class structure (and this negative experience is perhaps more emotional in character than it is material) is made meaningful in some sociohistorical sense.

NOTES

1. *The Life of Thomas Cooper, Written by Himself,* 1872, as quoted in E. J. Hobsbawm, *Industry and Empire* (New York, 1968), p. 103.
2. See John Gunnell, *Political Philosophy and Time* (Middletown, Conn., 1968), p. 254; and Trent Schroyer, *The Critique of Domination* (New York, 1973), p. 25. The distinction between the performing and emotional self is proposed in Richard

Sennett and Jonathan Cobb, *The Hidden Injuries of Class* (New York, 1973).

3. On the importance of remembered past see M. T. Clanchy, "Remembering the Past and the Good Old Law," *History* 55, 184 (1970): 165-176.

4. J. H. Clapham, *An Economic History of Modern Britain* (Cambridge, 1926); T. S. Ashton, "The Standard of Life of the Workers in England, 1790-1850," *Journal of Economic History* 9 (1949): 19-38; and R. M. Hartwell, "The Standard of Living during the Industrial Revolution: A Discussion," *Economic History Review* 16, 1 (1963): 134-146; and *The Industrial Revolution and Economic Growth* (London, 1971).

5. Hartwell, *The Industrial Revolution and Economic Growth,* pp. 338, 314.

6. Ibid., p. 343.

7. F. C. Mather, *Public Order in the Age of the Chartists* (Manchester, 1959), pp. 12-13.

8. E. J. Hobsbawm, "The British Standard of Living, 1790-1850," in *Labouring Men* (London, 1964), p. 65.

9. Ibid., p. 87.

10. Royden Harrison, *Before the Socialists* (London, 1965), p. 22.

11. See, for instance, E. J. Hobsbawm, "The Standard of Living Debate: a Postscript," in *Labouring Men,* p. 122.

12. Neil Smelser, *Social Change in the Industrial Revolution* (Chicago, 1959).

13. For some of the conceptual and empirical weaknesses of this position see Frank Munger, "Participation and Militancy in Industrial Revolution England" (paper presented at Annual Meeting of the American Sociological Association, Montreal, August, 1974), pp. 3-4.

14. T. H. Marshall, *Social Class and Citizenship* (Cambridge, 1950) and Reinhard Bendix, *Work and Authority in Industry* (New York, 1956) and *Nation-Building and Citizenship* (New York, 1964).

15. Bendix, *Nation-Building and Citizenship,* p. 93.

16. Interest in extending the franchise did remain strong in several middle-class circles after 1850. See Francis Herrick, "The Second Reform Movement in Britain, 1850-1865," *The Journal of the History of Ideas,* 9, 2 (1948): 174-192. Also see T. J. Nossiter, "Aspects of Electoral Behavior in English Constituencies, 1832-1868," in *Mass Politics* (New York, 1970), pp. 160-189.

17. "Rules of the Reform League, 1856," reprinted in Cole and Filson, *British Working Class Movements* (New York, 1967), p. 532.

18. See Harrison, *Before the Socialists,* p. 142.

19. See Frances Gillespie, *Labor and Politics in England* (New York, 1967), p. 255.

20. As quoted in Harrison, *Before the Socialists,* p. 114.

21. See H. J. Hanham, *Elections and Party Management: Politics in the Time of Disraeli and Gladstone* (London, 1959), p. 323.

22. Moisei Ostrogowski, *Democracy and the Organization of Political Parties* (New York: 1964), p. 54. Also see Gertrude Himmelfarb, *Victorian Minds* (New York, 1968), pp. 350-391.

23. Cole and Filson, *British Working Class Movements,* p. 544.

24. See Hanham, *Elections and Party Managements,* pp. x-xi; and Harrison, *Before the Socialists,* p. 122.

25. See Hanham, *Elections and Party Management,* Part I.

26. Ibid., p. 209.

27. P. F. Clarke, "Electoral Sociology of Modern Britain," *History,* 57, 189 (1972): 33.

28. See Stein Rokkan, "Mass Suffrage, Secret Voting, and Political Participation," in *Political Sociology* (New York, 1966), p. 118.

29. See Harrison, *Before the Socialists,* pp. 116-119; and Clarke, "Electoral Sociology," p. 40.

30. Harrison, *Before the Sociologists,* p. 208.

31. See ibid., p. 160 and Hanham, *Elections and Party Management,* p. 324.

32. Harrison, *Before the Socialists,* p. 21.

33. Anthony Giddens, *The Class Structure of Advanced Societies* (London, 1973), p. 158.

34. Thompson, *The Making of the English Working Class,* p. 197. A variant of the coexistence explanation is found in G. Bingham Powell, "Incremental Democratization: The British Reform Act of 1832," in *Crisis, Choice, and Change* (Boston, 1973). Conceptualizing coexistence in terms of coalition theory, Powell attributes incorporation less to repression than to the mechanisms of compromise which arose from the interaction of the coalitions.

35. Thompson, *The Making of the English Working Class,* p. 831.

36. Nigel Young, "Prometheans or Troglodytes? The English Working Class and the Dialectics of Incorporation," *Berkeley Journal of Sociology* 12 (1967): 2.

37. Tom Nairn, "The English Working Class," in *Ideology in Social Science* (New York, 1973), p. 201.

38. Herbert Marcuse, *One-Dimensional Man* (Boston, 1964), p. 12.

39. Ibid., p. 10.

40. See Frank Parkin, *Class Inequality and Political Order* (New York, 1971), p. 89.

41. Gareth Stedman Jones, "Working-Class Culture and Working Politics in London," *Journal of Social History* 7 (Summer, 1974): 479.

42. Of course, Marx had an equally significant effect on the emergence of the Left in England. See Stanley Pierson, *Marxism and the Origins of British Socialism* (Ithaca, 1973),

43. The details of Marx's involvement with the English labor movement appear in Saul Padover, "Introduction: Marx's Role in the First International," in *Karl Marx on the First International* (New York, 1973); Henry Collins and Chimen Abramsky, *Karl Marx and the British Labour Movement* (London, 1965); Royden Harrison, "E. S. Beesly and Karl Marx," *International Review of Social History* 4, 1 (1959): 22-58.

44. See Karl Marx, "Speech at the Anniversary of the People's Paper," reprinted in *Articles on Britain* (Moscow, 1971), pp. 262-264.

45. Karl Marx, letter to Engels, May 1, 1865, reprinted in *Karl Marx on the First International,* p. 388.

46. Karl Marx, "Circular to the Swiss Romansh Federal Council," ibid., pp. 171-172.

47. Frederick Engels, "1892, Preface," *The Condition of the Working Class in England* (Stanford, 1958), pp. 369-370.

48. Bertell Ollman, "Toward Class Consciousness Next Time: Marx and the Working Class," *Politics and Society* 3, 1 (1972): 9.

49. Karl Marx, "Theses on Feuerbach," in *The German Ideology* (New York, 1970), p. 122.

50. Karl Marx and Frederick Engels, *The German Ideology,* p. 48.

51. Ibid., p. 42.

52. Karl Marx, *Capital,* vol. I (New York: 1967), p. 127.

53. Helmut Fleischer, *Marxism and History* (New York, 1973), p. 21.

54. Marx and Engels, *The German Ideology,* p. 116.

55. Ibid., p. 61.

56. See Adam Schaff, *Marxism and the Human Individual* (New York, 1970), pp. 87-91.

57. See Fleischer, *Marxism and History,* pp. 118-124.

58. In "Afterward to the German Edition," *Capital,* vol. I, p. 18, Marx gives his imprimatur to a review of the book which strongly emphasizes the natural history—the historical necessity—of revolution in contrast to the subjective or conscious moment.

59. Karl Marx, *A Contribution to the Critique of Political Economy* (New York, 1970), p. 21.

60. See Marx and Engels, *The German Ideology,* p. 94.

61. Herbert Marcuse, *Reason and Revolution* (Boston, 1941), pp. 311-312.

62. Frederick Engels, letter to Franz Mehring, July 14, 1893, reprinted in R. Tucker, ed., *The Marx-Engels Reader* (New York, 1972), p. 648.

63. See Zygmunt Bauman, "Marxism and the Contemporary Theory of Culture," *Co-existence* 5, 2 (1968): 168.

64. See Bertell Ollman, *Alienation: Marx's Conception of Man in Capitalist Society* (New York, 1971), pp. 87-90.

65. Albrecht Wellmer, *Critical Theory of Society* (New York, 1971), pp. 71-72.

66. Zygmunt Bauman, *Between Class and Elite* (Manchester, 1972), p. 3.

67. Karl Marx, *The 18th Brumaire of Louis Bonaparte* (New York, 1963), p. 15.

68. Ibid., p. 18.

69. See Marx, *Capital,* vol. I, pp. 427-437; and Vernon Venable, *Human Nature, The Marxian View* (New York, 1945), pp. 164-166.

70. Marx regards the use of the past in previous revolutions as resulting in the creation of self-deceptions—self-deceptions which the proletarian revolution will not require. See *The 18th Brumaire of Louis Bonaparte,* pp. 15-18.

71. See Maynard Solomon, "Marx and Bloch: Reflections on Utopia and Art," *Telos* 13 (Fall, 1972): 76.

72. See Marx, *Capital,* vol. I, p. 178.

73. The critique of 'utopian socialism' is presented in Karl Marx and Frederick Engels, *The Communist Manifesto* (Peking, 1970), pp. 69-73 and Frederick Engels, *Socialism: Utopian and Scientific* (New York, 1972).

74. Karl Marx, *The Grundrisse* (New York, 1971), pp. 124, 148.

75. See Herbert Marcuse, "The End of Utopia," in *Five Lectures* (Boston, 1970), p. 68.

76. Karl Marx as quoted in Howard Selsam and Harry Martel, *Reader in Marxist Philosophy* (New York, 1963), p. 269 (emphasis added).

77. Wellmer, *Critical Theory of Society,* p. 99.

78. Jürgen Habermas, *Theory and Practice* (Boston, 1973), p. 238.

79. See Wellmer, *Critical Theory of Society,* pp. 100-101 and Lloyd Easton, "Alienation and Empiricism in Marx's Thought," *Social Research,* 37, 3 (1970): 402-427.

80. The contradictions which Marx saw this process giving rise to are examined in Martin Nicolaus, "The Unknown Marx," in *The New Left Reader* (New York, 1969), p. 104.

81. Trent Schroyer, *The Critique of Domination* (New York, 1973), p. 93.

82. Norman Birnbaum, "The Crisis in Marxist Sociology," in *Recent Sociology,* 1 (New York, 1969), p. 29.

83. Jacques Ehrmann, "Homo Ludens Revisited," in *Game, Play, and Literature* (Boston, 1968), p. 46.

84. See Eugen Fink, "The Oasis of Happiness: Toward an Ontology of Play," in *Game, Play, and Literature,* pp. 19-30; Mary Reilly, "An Explanation of Play," in *Play As Exploratory Learning* (Beverly Hills, 1974), pp. 117-149; and John Lukcas, *Historical Consciousness* (New York, 1968). This issue and its broader implications are examined in greater detail in Chapter 7.

85. Fleischer, *Marxism and History,* pp. 95-96 (emphasis added).

86. The nature of the critique suggested by this reconstructed dialectic is described in some detail in Francis Hearn, "The Dialectical Uses of Ideal-Types," *Theory and Society* 2, 4 (1975): 531-561.

CHAPTER 7
One-Dimensionality
in Contemporary Society

Substantively, this study has been concerned with the analysis of social change, in particular the conditions under which rebellions and revolutionary activity are likely to occur, and the various forms that such activities are likely to assume. This study is primarily an interpretive one, applying the much neglected categories of critical theory to a wealth of information which has been previously and extensively examined by the contending schools within the social sciences. In this sense, the study represents a beginning, a preliminary attempt to demonstrate the value of critical categories for the understanding, explanation, and evaluation of social structure, culture, and social change. The purpose of this chapter is to explore the implications of our analysis as they relate to the manner of sociological analysis and to the current problems of legitimation, domination, and social protest in industrial and industrializing societies. This latter concern is most important, for this study has been guided by the assumption that an understanding of why and how the workers in advanced industrial society accept their position and treatment requires information pertaining to the historical incorporation of the working class into the established structures and institutions. Before making this connection between the incorporation of the English working class and the contemporary situation, it is necessary to first briefly summarize our analysis and, in so doing, set the groundwork for generalizing the findings.

ONE-DIMENSIONALITY

The matter of legitimacy is at the heart of challenges to established authority-relations. Protest movements, if they are to be more than short-lived, vengeful responses, must be able to legitimate their activities as well as discredit the legitimacy of the prevailing arrangements. This requires access to an alternative set of standards which constitutes a view of the world transcendent and critical of the existing order. Such an alternative view, with its categories of critical thought, provides meaning, guidance, and goals, as well as legitimacy to protesting groups and movements. Groups and movements guided by alternative standards of legitimacy are much more likely to engage in rebellious and revolutionary activities than are those protest movements which either lack such alternative standards or employ the prevailing standards to assess the effectiveness or justice of the current social order. Unlike the latter, the former does not equate legitimacy with legality; and as a consequence, the legal repression of what they regard to be legitimate activities intensifies the radical disposition.[1]

Critical thought is indispensable to the process of human rebellion. Without it, man—as he has proven so often in past—will either resign himself to, or accept as normal, material deprivation, economic deterioration, and the continued denial of self-fulfillment. That this has been and is the case, strongly repudiates the common and unreflective argument that critical thought is forged in economic crisis. Albert Camus makes this point as he writes, "Poverty and degeneration have never ceased to be what they were before Marx's time, and what he did not want to admit they were despite all his observations: factors contributing to servitude not to revolution."[2] James O'Connor, in a recent critique of modern socialist theory and practice, concurs with Camus' remarks:

> Crisis and depression soften and temporarily reconcile class antagonisms. Capitalist breakdown in the developed poles of the world capitalist system has led to, first, the survival of both capital and proletariat; second, the political containment of the proletariat; and, third, the consolidation of the bourgeois social order as a whole.[3]

Material deprivation, economic exploitation, and unnecessary domination serve to stimulate rebellious tendencies only when the negative experience they engender is meaningfully comprehended, and this presupposes the presence of critical thought. The source of critical thought—or, more specifically, critical reason—must be sought in the nonrational and noninstrumental, in man's culture-creating, as distinguished from structure-creating capacities. In this regard, play, imagination, and tradition (in the form of the remembered past) are of crucial importance. With the suppression of these culture-creating capacities, systematic resistance to deprivation, exploitation, and domination becomes impossible. In this situation of one-dimensionality, where critical thought is suppressed, subordinated to instrumental reason, man's ability to rebel, to participate in the 'Great Refusal,' is expressed in a sporadic, disjointed, and distorted fashion.

The one-dimensionality which permeates advanced industrial society today is expressed in the bland homogeneity of an artificially created mass culture, which prohibits the development of critical alternative standards by confining thought to the established universe of discourse. As we have seen, this stage of one-dimensionality was preceded by an earlier one where cultural heterogeneity persisted. In England, working-class communities, with their distinctive traditions and identities, were maintained well after the mid-nineteenth century; but the critical categories they had once generated and nourished were flattened out. As a consequence, working people were unable to formulate meaningful anticipations of the future: they either criticized the established social order in the terms supplied by that order (thereby allowing their struggles to be institutionalized) or they reluctantly accepted the status quo as inescapable. In the latter case, working-class communities became exclusively defensive in character, merely providing an escape from the hostile, uncaring world. They no longer constituted a viable alternative to and a basis for resistance against the denial of social responsibility. Identification with the established society was rare for most workers during this initial period of one-dimensionality. But, for purposes of maintaining social stability, it was sufficient that these workers lacked access to critical categories with which they could formulate and discover transcendent criteria of social action.

The emergence of one-dimensionality was reflected in the separation of the economy from society, the private from the public, work from play, reality from fantasy, and the present from the past. Resulting from this compartmentalizing of the rational and the nonrational, facts and values, was the gradual development of a self-legitimating economy and, more broadly, the instrumentalization of culture whereby "means (technological innovations) [came] to govern the ends (values and norms); men [became] the 'objects' rather than the 'subjects' of their own activity."[4] In these circumstances, the alternative sources of legitimacy and meaning, once available to the working people in their traditions and imaginings, quickly deteriorated. Conceptions of the future could no longer be adequately elaborated, and collective needs received no public articulation. Qualitative, social demands were transformed into quantitative, individual demands; and, as the system of industrial capitalism reduced the level of material scarcity, the present became regarded not only as inescapable but as constitutive of the good society as well.

The constriction of imagination to the dimension of work placed social interactions under purposive-rational constraints. The number and extent of spontaneously defined interactions correspondingly declined.[5] As spontaneity was significantly reduced, so also was the capacity to resist the infringements of industrial capitalism. Eventually a reconciliation—both in pragmatic and normative terms—with industrial capitalist society was effected by the workers. When the established order was accepted, either because there were no demonstrable alternatives to it or because it was perceived as good, questions pertaining to the fundamental nature of society were replaced with questions which presupposed the validity or inevitability of that society. As a result, the reflective animus of the working-class ideological consciousness was repelled; the worker was isolated in history and in society. For the skilled laborers, this situation entailed the institutionalization of social protest, while, for the 'common people, it engendered a defensive, completely innocuous escape to their now denuded communities. The critical, challenging thrust, the rebellious disposition, which once infused working-class social protest was slowly and effectively drained away.

Similar patterns of protest by and repression of the working class is evident in nineteenth century America. From the 1840s, American society, then commencing to join the market economy with the forces of industrialization, began to exhibit the denial of social responsibility which had been present in England since the turn of the century. The American workers initially responded to this situation in a way similar to their English counterparts, by forming protective communities wherein the principles and practices of mutual responsibility were maintained in opposition to the larger society.[6] Within these communities, traditional customs, beliefs, rituals and play activities were nourished; and they provided a standpoint, independent of the one consubstantial with the needs of industrial capitalism, with which the workers guided their activities. The collective protest activity of these workers, both in form and content, reflected the influence of tradition, imagination and play. As Herbert Gutman remarks, "[c]ustom and tradition that reached far back in historical time gave a coherence to their rage. . . . [Traditional rituals] had a deep symbolic meaning, and, rooted in a shared culture, they sustained disputes."[7] Rooted in the institutions and structures of the American working-class communities, these traditions underlay the class solidarity which did develop, and—by supplying an alternative and meaningful set of legitimating standards—justified the resistance against all efforts designed to deny social responsibility.

As in England, the American government and middle class reacted to working-class social protest by banning, destroying, or suppressing those features of working-class life which enabled both the discrediting of the present and the legitimation of riots, strikes, and insurrections. "Their short-run response," Bruce Johnson observes, "was ruthless repression, and their long-run response was the destruction of the class community in which the challenge was based."[8] With the weakening of the community structures and institutions which had sustained the solidary traditions of the working class, class antagonism became severely muted, and hostility gave way to acceptance. The class components of the workers' communities were subordinated to the ethnic features which, because they provided a more restrictive basis for economic and political protest, could be incorporated into the established order with comparative ease. In America, as in England, the suppression of the community's capacities to create and elaborate categories of critical thought was essential to the constricting of working-class social protest to socially acceptable forms and demands.

In all societies, formal organizations which significantly threaten the stability of the existing arrangements are, if not directly banned, subject to legal sanctions which restrict the scope of their activities. For this reason the informal, often opaque, structures and institutions of the viable community are indispensable to sustained collective action.[9] Through the informal organization of the community, preparation for and the mobilization of resources required by collective action can continue despite repression of the more formal apparatus. Basic resources—size, communication, finances, knowledge and skills, and moral support—can quickly and effectively be mobilized through the informal mechanisms of the established community. An equally important, although much neglected, resource which can be mobilized on this level for purposes of social protest is the remembered past, broadly defined to include play and imagination. The intellectual traditions, the shared beliefs and practices, the ceremony, play, and festival of the community not only contribute to a critical consciousness and enhance solidarity, but also infuse collective action with enthusiasm and excitement: they supply protest with its explosive content, its meaning, and its compassion. Rebellious and revolutionary activity become morally imperative only to the extent that the remembered past, as a community resource, is successfully mobilized. The rebellious impulse, which is after all an expression of compassion, is not delivered by economic crisis or disaffected intellectuals; it has its roots in man's inherent interest in autonomy and responsibility, freedom and community.

When the factors which contribute to this explosive and compassionate content are suppressed, the ability of the community to participate as an actor in social protest is significantly damaged. Accordingly, protest becomes increasingly geared to improving the individuals' lot within the present system. As the community loses its capacity to sustain alternative meaning-systems, the incorporation of its members into the larger society occurs. With incorporation, the dominated are allowed to form and participate in formal organizations, as long as they perform in accordance with the rules of the game. The mobilization of resources through formal mechanisms alone cannot tap those underlying structures and beliefs which animate collective action. The communal and the qualitative are lost to the individual and the quantitative; and the result is instrumental collectivism whereby organizations are no longer regarded as ends-in-themselves, but are treated as means for securing individual advancement.

In this light, new meaning is imparted to the fact that in fully industrial societies the rebellious disposition receives less distorted expression in those groups, such as blacks and students, which have maintained viable communities—open spaces in which to play, remember, and imagine.[10] That we also find society-wide revolutions occurring primarily in those societies where the instrumentalization of culture is not fully accomplished is also completely understandable in these terms. As Eric Wolf documents, it is "not so much the growth of an industrial proletariat as such which produces revolutionary activity, as the development of an industrial work force still closely geared to life in the villages."[11] Tenaciously guarded by the village community, the remembered past supplies alternative standards and engenders a sense of integrated experience, which together provide the moral justification for revolutionary activity. The viable community is essential in more industrialized settings as well. The Irish insurrection of 1916, as William Irving Thompson notes, was prompted and guided by the traditions and imaginative reconstructions of the protective communities.[12] The revolutions described by Wolf and Thompson were not—as history has proven—blind attempts to forbid social transformation and change. Rather, they emerged in response to the denial of social responsibility. They represent instances of man's urge to sustain compassionate communities. That this rebellious disposition has not yet been fully expressed in advanced industrial society cannot be attributed to the eradication of social injustice. The capacity to formulate meaningful critical categories has been blocked in this kind of society; and, as a result, the concept of revolution is—for the moment at least—only applicable to the societies which preceded it.

To understand the human condition is to participate in its transcendence. Sociology, as a reflection and product of one-dimensionality, has surrendered its concern with this task in order to become methodologically sophisticated. That which defies quantification has, for the most part, not only been neglected but also written off as unimportant.[13] There is no adequate theory of social revolution; and this results in large measure from sociology's obsession with staking out a specialized field of study which can be subjected to scientific analysis.[14] If sociology is to overcome this restricted focus and instrumental emphasis to be capable of critical analysis, sociologists must have access to the integrated experience attained in community. As tradition is essential to integrated experience, the theoretical communities formed by sociologists must follow the critical theorists in incorporating the category of remembrance. Sociological theory which has its roots in tradition and membership is simultaneously 'critique.'[15]

A reconstructed and revitalized sociology will not only better understand the human condition; it will also contribute to the improvement of people and society. For to understand, sociology will have to create new communities and cultures; and in so doing, it will learn how to free play, imagination, and remembrance from the constraints of instrumentalization. In this way, sociological theory will manifest an emancipatory intent. Gouldner provides one example of this when he suggests that

> [a]t decisive points, the ordinary language and understanding fails and must be transcended It is essentially the task of social theory, and the social sciences more generally, to create new and 'extraordinary' languages, to help men learn to speak them; to mediate between the deficient understandings of ordinary language and the different and liberating perspectives of social theory.[16]

What makes sociology, as opposed to the other social sciences, most suitable for this revitalization is its irrelevance to modern society. Sociology makes little contribution to the maintenance of the prevailing arrangements; and this has permitted sociology, in comparison to the other social sciences and many of the humanities, a greater range of flexibility in which play, imagination, and remembrance is possible. Although this flexibility has caused sociology to be attacked as a 'hippie cult' by the other social sciences, and to be castigated as a den of permissiveness by opponents of the student movement, it has also allowed sociology to approximate many features of an open social location. Within this open space, the imaginative and playful surmounting of narrow specialization and even narrower empiricism can begin. In turn, it may be possible to apprehend (to know and to change) the system of domination and legitimation as it exists in advanced industrial society.

IMPLICATIONS FOR THE CONTEMPORARY SITUATION

The analysis of the past is essential for critically understanding the present and anticipating the future. The historical analysis we have provided must be assessed with reference to how well it has contributed to these two tasks. To what extent can the system of legitimation prevailing in advanced industrial society be traced to the erosion of community traditions and the suppression of play, imagination, and remembrance? What is the connection between the one-dimensionality of mass culture and the one-dimensionality forged with the separation of economy and society? What is the relationship between the constriction of critical thought and the widespread apathy and political inactivity of modern society's workers and poor? Although this project, like any based on an objective reconstruction of the past, cannot establish meaningful conceptions of the future, it should be capable of identifying the conditions under which such meaningful alternatives are anticipated. Accordingly, this study should also contribute to an understanding of the possibilities of delegitimation and change in contemporary society. In the remainder of this chapter these issues are systematically taken up in an effort to explicate the connections between the incorporation of the nineteenth-century working class and the contemporary problems of legitimacy, domination, resistance, and change.

Legitimacy in Modern Society

Accurately reflecting the contemporary situation, recent definitions of legitimacy focus on effectiveness and efficiency. These definitions stand in sharp contrast to earlier conceptions which equated the legitimate society with the just and fair society; and they aptly, if inadvertently, suggest some of the significant changes undergone by the process of legitimation. In the England of the eighteenth and early nineteenth centuries, as we have seen, the effort to impart legitimacy to power required that decisions and their implementation be justified with reference to standards of authority or right, over and beyond the powerful themselves. Thus the source of legitimacy was independent of the established order, and, as a result, the standards of authority were capable of discrediting, as well as legitimating, the prevailing arrangements. These standards, John Schaar reminds us, "consist[ed] of a more or less coherent body of shared memories, images, and ideals that [gave] to those who shared it an orientation in and toward time and space. [They] link past, present, and future into a meaningful whole, and tie means and ends into a continuum that transcends a merely pragmatic or expediential calculation."[17] While authority of this kind established limits on liberty, it also, as Schaar rightly suggests, fulfilled and gave meaning to liberty. An experiential basis underlay this earlier form of legitimacy, and it infused the system of domination with responsiveness and social responsibility. In short, legitimacy rested on a moral and normative foundation which sustained alternatives to the established social relations and patterns.

Separated from this normative anchor, legitimacy in advanced industrial society involves, as S. M. Lipset notes, "the capacity of the system to engender and maintain the belief that the existing political institutions are the most appropriate ones for the society."[18] Legitimacy and, more concretely, obedience and compliance result from the system's effectiveness in performing these tasks; legitimacy is no longer "a matter of reason and principle, of deepest sentiment and conviction."[19] In the absence of any meaningful external standards of authority, legitimacy is dissolved into public opinion which assesses the prevailing arrangements in terms of how effectively they allow the acquisition of established goals and the satisfaction of established needs. In other words, the exisitng order is evaluated by standards which it supplies. As Mueller writes, "[D]eprived of moral and consensual referents, technocratic legitimation is completely 'secularized' and establishes legitimacy either (1) through the manipulation of public opinion or (2) through the provision of material compensations."[20] As long as the system reproduces itself, acquiescense is virtually guaranteed. The element of consent is detached from the process of legitimation. Compliance results, not from a critical assessment of two or more alternatives, but from the lack of alternatives.

The reduction of legitimacy to public opinion and effectiveness is possible only in conjunction with the depolitization of social life. In the early period of one-dimensionality, political considerations were confined to the public realm, and were prohibited from arbitrarily intruding on the private sphere. In advanced industrial society, with the public sphere—the state—compelled to assume a larger role in maintaining economic stability, political legitimacy, like economic legitimacy before it, had to be made value-free. Under these conditions bureaucracy, technology, and science become politically as well as economically important; and political support—that is, compliance with the state—becomes a free-floating resource. Habermas provides a simplified, though useful, approach for understanding the changes in legitimacy brought about by the increased state intervention in the economy:

> [The state's] output consists in sovereignly executing administrative decisions. To this end, it needs an input of mass loyalty that is as unspecific as possible. . . . Output crises have the form of the efficiency crisis. . . . Input crises have the form of the legitimation crisis. The legitimation system fails to maintain the necessary level of mass loyalty.[21]

Input or legitimation crises can be avoided or significantly minimized to the extent that the administrative functions of the state are separated from political participation. A legitimation process that attracts mass loyalty (e.g, by symbolic manipulation and/or the provision of material goods) while simultaneously encouraging political passivity or apathy is highly suitable to this task. Upon the basis of such a legitimation process, a depoliticized public or a civil privatism marked by "strong interests in the administrative system's output and minor participation in the process of will-formation," is created.[22]

The depoliticization of the public sphere is a major feature of advanced industrial society. Focusing on political participation in the United States, Lester Milbrath, for one, has found:

> About one-third of the American adult population can be characterized as politically apathetic or passive; in most cases, they are unaware, literally, of the political part of the world

around them. Another 60 percent play largely spectator roles in the political process. . . . In the purest sense of the word, probably only 1 or 2 per cent could be called gladiators.[23]

These findings partially reflect the fact that the basic values and ends, as well as the fundamental procedural assumptions, of society are unreflectively accepted in society at large.[24] As long as the system works—that is, as long as the administrative functions remain effective, loyalty, not participation, is warranted.

A legitimation process contingent upon political apathy and passivity replaces consent with acquiescence. Legitimacy as acquiescence has its roots in the pervasive inability to formulate meaningful alternatives to the existing order. The constriction of critical thought and the accompanying instrumentalization of culture, which was earlier accomplished by the dismantling of traditions and the destruction of communities, is now continued with the suppression of language and the consequent distortion of communication. Claus Mueller, who has examined the relation between communication and legitimacy in England and the United States, suggests that distorted communication—that is, communication either restricted by a particular linguistic environment or constrained by political intervention—undercuts the capacity to rationally and symbolically engage in political discourse.[25] Not only does distorted communication inhibit the perception of political interests and needs (which must be perceived before they can be acted on), it also renders communities and classes incapable "of articulating experienced deprivations and . . . generat[ing] from its own base symbols and ideas alternative to the dominant ones."[26] Lacking access to a normative framework which would allow experienced deprivations to be meaningfully apprehended, people are unable to critically and comprehensively analyze society. As a consequence, people can either resign themselves to or accept, more or less positively, the established arrangements. When collective, qualitative needs receive no public expressions, when, through distorted communication, people are confined to the here and now, organized dissent becomes virtually impossible. As Mueller remarks,

> Articulated dissent presupposes that political symbols (terms, concepts, and ideological interpretations) be attached to subjectively experienced conditions that do not correspond to expectations or needs. Political consciousness is perforce bound to a symbolic interpretation of sociopolitical experience.[27]

The repression of the capacity to formulate and sustain such symbolic interpretations, combined with the many obstacles preventing the recognition of qualitative needs and the elaboration of collective expectations, has allowed the social roots of deprivation and misery to go unchallenged. If material and cultural impoverishment are attributed to personal inadequacies rather than to the system of domination, legitimation crises are unlikely to occur.

Advanced industrial society is best characterized by its inauthenticity rather than by its alienating features, resting as it does more on cultural than material impoverishment.[29] The inauthentic society is responsive to certain needs—for instance, needs which have been artificially established or needs whose satisfaction will not violate the operating principles of the prevailing arrangements. Needs which cannot be so satisfied—collective, qualitative needs—are incapable of articulation and, therefore, of recognition in the inauthentic society. With the expression of these needs blocked, the formulation of and exposure to alternatives is difficult. Thus, in the inauthentic society an apparent responsiveness exists—for those needs which are expressed are responded to—while those needs which society cannot satisfy are suppressed. This situation does much to foster instrumental collectivism or civil privatism, to undermine collective membership and participation as a value in and of itself. As Etzioni observes, "the great concern with marginal increments over peers, and comparisons to remote groups, rather than attention to the extent to which one's basic needs are responded to," are good indications of the inauthentic society.[29]

Those needs which are not articulated, and remain unsatisfied, create a tension which is reflected in the ways people, especially working people, acquiesce to and legitmate society. Underneath the outward signs of adaptation to modern industrial society lie indications of resentment and reconciliation. Ambiguity and contradiction characterize the perspectives which people bring to bear on their society and their lives. Those incoherent and meaningless perspectives impede rather than guide social action. The connection between inauthenticity and the legitimation process will be illustrated with reference to the United States and England. Richard Sennett and Jonathan Cobb's recent examination of American workers, Richard Hoggart's earlier and more impressionistic study of English working class communities, and Michael Mann's compilation and analysis of numerous studies concerned with attitudes and activities of American and British workers, all have central bearing on this problem.[30]

The working-class community, with its distinctive features and close-knit relations, continues to prevail in English society. However, as Hoggart finds, it bears only superficial resemblance to the workers' communities created a century and a half ago. A combined sense of mutual responsibility and independence is still evident in the modern community; but it produces a static, almost exclusively defensive, posture. Now the working-class community is overly protective; and this reduces its capacity for action. Class identity, in terms of a rigid distinction between 'Them' and 'Us,' is keenly developed, but it coexists with a basic acceptance of the presuppositions of the existing order. The community is integrated into society even though it does not share the dominant values: integration is less a matter of adaptation and acceptance and more a matter of reconciliation. While this restricts the extent and intensity of mass loyalty that the state can rely on, it also deflects challenge. Frustrations, Hoggart observes, are minimized by a stress on the need to 'keep cheerful' which "is derived . . . from the assumption that life is bound to be materially unrewarding and difficult."[31]

Less critical and rebellious than the communities which preceded them, the contemporary working-class community in England is also less playful and less attached to the past. Festivals and recreational activities no longer constitute a celebration of the past or an affirmation of the community itself. Rather, they have been transformed into mechanisms which make present experiences and conditions more tolerable. Without a meaningful attachment to the past, these communities possess no conception of the future. They tend to encourage among their members

> the temptation to live in a constant present. If the temptation succeeds, a condition may be induced in which time has been lost: yet time dominates, because the present is for ever changing, but changing meaninglessly . . . with no informing pattern. Each innovation is assumed to be better than its predecessors, simply because it comes after them: any change is a change for the better so long as it is in chronological succession.[32]

History, the remembered past, provides the worker with no informing perspective from which he can locate himself and others in society. The only available perspective is the simplistic division between 'Them' and 'Us,' where 'Them'—the outside world—is hostile and untrustworthy. Unable to depend on society, the working-class community distances itself from it: it assumes a stance of indifference which, in the last analysis, contributes to a pragmatic acceptance of the existing arrangements.[33]

Investigators have found that deep commitment and strong informal bonds similarly characterize the contemporary American working-class community. A sense of mutual responsibility, reinforced by a nostalgic concern with the past, underlies this commitment and these bonds.[34] The American working-class community fosters a distinctive class identity for its members which, very much like the one generated by its English counterparts, leaves the predominant value-orientations of society untouched. What results, in Sennett and Cobb's words, is a "painful paradox" wherein the larger culture, by according respect and worth on the basis of individual achievement, is incongruous with the community which allocates respects and worth in terms of one's commitment to the fraternal bond.[35]

Unable to critically assess the dominant value-orientations of society, and incapable of disengaging from the fraternal bond of the community, the worker attributes his inability to act, to make decisions, to personal inadequacy and failure. While a pervasive sense of powerlessness is generated, its social roots are not discernible. Power, like respect and worth, must be achieved. With this achievement, one enters the middle class and gains a greater independence; but this first requires a repudiation of the fraternal bond. Caught in this bind, the worker regards himself as being in no position to challenge the existing relationships.

Feelings of powerlessness combine with low esteem and feelings of guilt to effectively prevent the workers from acting on the world.[36] By assuming personal responsibility for his failure to become respectful and worthy, the worker finds himself in a situation where authority is passive, constitutive of an established set of standards in terms of which he must prove himself. Legitimacy becomes intricately bound up in self-validation. Advanced industrial society, as Sennett and Cobb observe,

> injures human dignity in order to weaken people's ability to fight against the limits class imposes on their freedom. . . . [The purpose] is to divert men from challenging the limits on their freedom by convincing them that they must *first* become legitimate, must achieve dignity on a class society's terms, in order to have the right to challenge the terms themselves.[37]

Legitimacy rests, then, on calling people's dignity into question. One must be certified 'worthy' by the prevailing standards of legitimacy if he is to criticize these standards. Oppression, accordingly, is less a matter of economic exploitation and more a matter of undermining confidence and instilling self-doubt. Self-doubt impedes action, and eventually results in the development of that indifference which presupposes pragmatic acceptance.[38]

From Hoggart's descriptive study of English workers, and Sennett and Cobb's more analytical treatment of American workers, a similar picture emerges of a frustrated yet passive group of people chained by paradoxes and contradictions to inactivity. Unable to establish a consistent commitment to a general set of values which would allow them to meaningfully interpret the reality they experience, these people accept society on its own terms. This portrayal receives substantial support from Mann's wide-ranging analysis of worker attitudes in England and the United States. Mann's central and strongly documented finding is that it "is not value-consensus which keeps the working class compliant, but rather a lack of consensus in the crucial area where concrete experiences and vague popularism might be translated into radical politics."[39] The ideological *dissensus* which Mann taps is rooted in a simultaneous acceptance and rejection of the existing arrangements. For instance, a widespread agreement that the opportunity structure in society is a fair and just one coexists with a distrust and consequent repudiation of those who have risen in that structure.[40] Thus, being successful requires becoming like the people you distrust. This dilemma underscores the creation of self-doubt noted by Sennett and Cobb, and further intensifies feelings of self-derogation. These tensions and paradoxes are firmly entrenched in working-class attitudes which, as Marc Fried finds, "indicate an underlying conflict between a deep, if inchoate, sense of class differences and common interests and the blandishments of potential success."[41]

The confusion which permeates working-class attitudes and consciousness is marked by a significant incongruity between general values and concrete experience, an incongruity which permits society to be challenged only from a simplistic and narrow—as opposed to an abstract and comprehensive— perspective.[42] The compartmentalization of social reality into 'Them' and 'Us' and, on a more experiential level, the separation of the performing self (achievement) from the emotional self (the fraternal bond) not only makes the disjunction between dominant values and everyday experience more tolerable, but also inhibits the formulation of a logically consistent, more exhaustive approach which is necessary for understanding the complexities of advanced industrial society. Unable to transcend immediate experience and the situational boundaries in which it occurs, the worker, because he cannot discover what is wrong with society, is incapable of initiating change. "It is this sense of impotence, of defeat, and the futility of efforts to change unsatisfying situations," Fried observes, "that is more distinctively characteristic of working-class people than any specific attitudes toward political and social events."[43] Society, from this view, is regarded as beyond control.[44]

Social relations, authority relations in particular, are experienced by workers in advanced industrial society as impoverished. A set of values has been perpetrated which prevents these workers from drawing the connection between personal deprivation and the structural basis of power. Compliance with the role behavior required by society, and acceptance of political decisions and practices, rest both on material incentives and, more importantly, on the ethos of the expert—the doctrine that those people who have proven themselves worthy of decision making should not be challenged by those who have failed. The incentives to compliance are, however, shaped in an apparently inescapable present. Pragmatic acceptance—compliance where there are no alternatives—is really at the bottom of the legitimation process in an advanced industrial society.

Qualitative, collective needs can be suppressed, and man's capacity to create future alternatives can be constricted, but these needs and capacities can never be completely abolished. "They persist," Andre Gorz remarks, "although the possibility of expressing themselves is denied to them by the falsification, misinterpretation and commercialization of the language and the objects (literature, songs, works of art, subversive behavior) through which they seek to assert themselves."[45] If a process of delegitimation is to be initiated, modes suitable to the free expression of these needs and capacities must be discovered. "A crisis of legitimation," Habermas notes, "arises as soon as . . . expectations come about that are different and cannot be satisfied by those categories of reward conforming with the present system."[46] Once the currently suppressed needs and capacities receive articulation and recognition, it is likely that new demands, ones incompatible with the prevailing arrangements, will be forthcoming. Delegitimation would involve a drastic change in the motivational structure, a more appropriate assessment of societal resources and distribution processes, and the anticipation of a better society; it would require the 're-politicization' of the public. Collective needs and capacities cannot be expressed through economic categories; the demands associated with economic struggle very rarely transcend the established boundaries of society. Accordingly, our search for those modes of expression which presuppose a legitimation crisis in advanced industrial society must be directed to other areas of social life.

Resistance, Challenge, and Change

The task at hand is to identify those areas in advanced industrial society which are potentially conducive to the expression of a rebellious disposition and, in conjunction with this, to specify possible strategies for overcoming one-dimensionality. Pursuant to our earlier findings, attention will be focused on play (and its relation to imagination) and forms of community.

Play In advanced industrial society, play, in the form of recreation and leisure-time activity, is shaped with specific reference to work. As a recess from and a compensation for the repetitive, burdensome tasks of the work world, play is regarded as tangential to social life, as a reward that must be earned through work. In this form, play is truncated: the alienation of play in modern society is as real and as pervasive as the alienation of labor. Imagination becomes, in Jurgen Moltmann's words, reproductive imagination restricted by the parameters of mass culture to the reproduction of the work world in play.[47] Yet it is possible to distinguish potentially liberating play— play that rebels against the structure of domination and rigid hierarchy— from commercialized, reproductive play. In the imaginary universe engendered by play, political aspirations denied by society are preserved. Indeed, through the senses of freedom and equality which play evokes, these aspirations may be enhanced.

A concise and vivid example of liberating play is presented in Bill Watson's study of "Counter-planning on the Shop Floor."[48] The workers employed in the automobile plant examined by Watson were engaged in a prolonged struggle aimed at obtaining a greater say in decisions pertaining to the productive process. This struggle was motivated not by 'bread-and-butter' concerns but by the continual production of poor-quality goods and the regimentation of plant life. Outbursts, usually in the form of sabotage, slowdowns, and work stoppages, occurred regularly. What is important about this year-long protest is that it was organized exclusively about informal channels of cooperation among the various groups of workers. The union's role throughout the year was inconsequential. As a result, participation in the struggle against the rationalization of time was widespread, and the specific actions of protest were highly festive in nature. Play, amusement, and, sometimes, spontaneous parties would develop out of the slowdowns and stoppages. As Watson noted at the time, "Beer in coolers stored in trunks is not uncommon and leads to spontaneous parties, wrestling, brawling, and laughter that spills over into the parks and streets round the factory."[49] As the workers dissolved the barriers between work and play, they not only attained a heightened sense of enjoyment, but their rejection of the plant's structure of domination—which the management equated with a repudiation of efficiency—was intensified as well.

The spirit of festival, of celebration, and of reaffirmation that Watson and others observe in liberated play awakens the rebellions disposition, invites cooperation and solidarity, and prepares people to challenge.[50] Through play, protest becomes more than task: it becomes rejoicing; and in play, imagination can contribute to the forging of critical perspectives. What makes play a potentially promising source of rebellion is its relatively tangential status in advanced societies. In other words, to the extent that play is defined, in contradistinction to work, as '*free*-time,' the alienation of play can be more easily overcome than the alienation of labor. Stanley Aronowitz is one of the few to recognize this: "Capitalism forces children to regard play and most adults to regard their leisure as the core of their self-controlled lives. *It is here alone that the chance remains to escape domination.*"[51] Strategies concerned with developing a liberating consciousness must not be designed with exclusive reference to the organizational structure of labor. Moltmann concurs with this view, and he contends that

> to accomplish a *humanizing emancipation* of man in a society, it makes more sense to wrest control of the alienated games of that society from the ruling interests and to change them into games of freedom which prepare men for a more liberated society.[52]

Games of freedom, by liberating people at least temporarily from the coercion of the 'real' world, provide a vision and experience of autonomy and community which, when sustained, make the unresponsiveness of society unbearable. The ensuring tension between the active rejoicing involved in play and the passive resignation entailed by work is one not easily resolved. The celebration of freedom in play may lead to the realization of freedom in work.

In examining the various studies of American and English workers we have found evidence of the existence of a fairly solid class identity or awareness which enables the worker of each society to distinguish between 'Them' and 'Us,' between the achievement emphases of middle-class values and the emotional components stressed in the fraternal bond. This class awareness, however, is encased in an inconsistent and ambiguous framework which immobilizes rather than activates. For class awareness to become an action-guiding consciousness, a meaningful culture must first be formulated; and this cannot be accomplished, as Gorz comments, "until the barrier dividing the world of work from the world of leisure has been broken down."[53] The playful rebellion against domination and rationalization is often invisible and, by itself, always uncritical. Nevertheless, the rebellion of liberated play is real; and, at the moment, it offers one of the few significant means for discrediting society. The way people play—as much as, if not more than, the way people work—affects the nature of legitimacy and domination in advanced industrial society.

Class Community   Within the interstices of advanced industrial society there exists an uncritical, usually invisible, rebellious movement comprised of groups and people who sustain, in a more or less unreflective manner, an orientation which enables them to disobey, to say no. In liberated play we saw one of these orientations. A second, perhaps more important, orientation is found in the working-class community. The contemporary working-class community, as previously discussed, is much more a static than a dynamic entity: it protects but does not act. Nevertheless, these communities do contain a set of images and practices which are incongruent with the dominant tendencies of the larger society. If imaginatively translated into political terms, these images and practices may permit the formulation of an alternative set of standards and, in so doing, effect the transformation of class awareness to class consciousness.

As in play, the interactions which occur in the working-class community are characterized by a sense of equality. Just as one plays with equals, in the working-class community one interacts with equals. In the dichotomy of work and life, the working-class community exists alongside play in contradiction to work. The working-class community is not, of course, a fantasy world; but like the imaginary universe generated in play it constitutes a place that is less burdensome and hostile, more personal and authentic than the world of work. The working-class community is, as Gans so aptly describes it, a peer group society where relationships are more personal and satisfying, and where, in Sennett and Cobb's terms, people receive respect for who they are, not what they do.[54]

The working-class community, however powerless it has become over the years, exhibits a relatively high degree of residential stability, which is importantly reflected in the viable and pervasive informal structures around which community life revolves. The informal network constitutes the backbone of the working-class community; and it, rather than more formal agencies, provides the organization for community activities.[55] The lack of significant working-class participation in voluntary associations has been widely recorded in the sociological literature.[56] While some, like Lipset, attribute this to the workers' inability to reason or to deal adequately with the complexities of democratic life, it seems that a more appropriate explanation must recognize that the workers avoid participation in voluntary associations because, first, they realistically discern the unresponsiveness of society, and, second, they acquire greater meaning from the informal structures of their community.[57]

Within the informal structures of the working-clas community, social relationships are more affective, less instrumental, than those engaged in at work. The striking emphasis on mutual responsibility derives not so much from a concern with dependency as it does from a concern with comfort, pleasure, and security. Interpersonal relationships are, by and large, ends in themselves. According to Fried,

> Working-class people reveal a marked concern about social relationships, sociability, social facility, and the approval of others, a concern that goes to the very core of their personalities. The working-class social orientation involves a sense of being part of the group, of being taken for granted and assuming that one can take others for granted, of being among the same kind of people.[58]

These value orientations, and the practices they give rise to, provide the major source of emotional satisfaction for the community members. At the same time, however, they tend to induce an intolerant particularism which isolates and further enfeebles the community. The violent and vile features of the working-class community should not be overlooked; nor, however, should they divert from our attention the very humane and compassionate qualities they sustain. The features of social responsibility maintained in the working-class community constitute a significant alternative to the impersonal domination of advanced industrial society. The problem is to translate these features into political categories and, in so doing, to separate them from the more narrow and intolerant orientations which currently accompany them. Such translation would have to entail, as well, the mini-mization of ethnic variations which often becloud the institutional and structural similarities which underlie working class communities.[59]

The institutional features of the working-class community, in both their positive and negative forms, are reflected in the working-class language code. Basil Bernstein, who has done extensive work on the relationship between language patterns and social class, labels the working-class language code "restricted," and contrasts it to the "elaborated" code characteristic of the middle class.[60] While the elaborated code—by drawing upon rationality and allowing access to relatively context-independent meanings—is linked to an abstract mode of reasoning, the restricted code draws upon metaphor and more context-bound meanings, and provides an essentially unreflective and descriptive mode of reasoning. The restricted code, like the working-class community, supplies a sense of security, as well as a sense of identity—inasmuch as underlying assumptions and meanings are limited to the speakers. At the same time, however, the restricted code limits the autonomy of its speakers and confines them to the here and now. Unlike elaborated codes, "[r]estricted codes are . . . tied to a local social structure and have a reduced potential for change in principles."[61] As a consequence, Bernstein suggests, the restricted code encourages more authoritarian and conformist relation-ships; the elaborated code, more democratic and autonomous relationships. Mueller has extended Bernstein's views to argue that the middle class, on the basis of its elaborated language code, is more reflective, analytic, and democratic and, therefore, a more likely agency of rebellious or revolu-tionary change than is the working class.[62]

While the restricted code does have a tendency to confine speakers to the present situation, it also embodies a suppressed yet potentially liberating thrust which Bernstein and Mueller are unable to recognize. In the first place, as William Labov has demonstrated, the restricted code is not any less intelli-gent, logical, and capable of dealing with abstract issues than the elaborated code.[63] In the second place, in contrast to the instrumental, free-floating features of the elaborated code, the restricted code expresses a commitment to community, a stress on person-oriented relationships rather than object goals. Thus, where the elaborated code is value-free—that is, independent of any specific value system—the restricted code, as Bernstein himself notes, "gives access to a vast potential of meanings, of delicacy, subtlety and diversity of cultural forms, to a unique aesthetic whose basis in condensed symbols may influence the form of imagining."[64] The symbolic form of the communication influenced by the restricted code "is condensed, *yet the specific cultural history of the relationship is alive in its form.* We can say that the roles of the speakers are communalized roles."[65] The restricted code, in short, ties speakers not only to the community but also to the past. Under certain conditions the restricted code, because it draws more on metaphor than on rationality, may enable the articulation of meaningful alternatives to the existing order. The ties to the past, the emphasis on community relationships, and the importance of mutual responsibility in the community institutions, constitute a solid, if latent, basis for discrediting society and legitimating social protest.

"[T]he capacity to anticipate new solutions—new social and economic relations and a new way of life," writes Andre Gorz, "is a necessary element in mobilizing and liberating repressed aspirations and energies."[66] Although the working-class community has been seriously weakened as a basis for collective action, it possesses in its informal structures and restricted language code the fundamental components of a capacity to anticipate new solutions. Strategies concerned with tapping this capacity must be built upon the recognition that workers are likely to express their grievances in concrete terms which have direct bearing on their everyday reality. This descriptive and metaphoric orientation contains analytic and rational qualities, and the latter should not be sacrificed for the former; rather, a way must be found to allow the two modes to reciprocally interpret each other. The metaphoric content, based on a commitment to community values of responsibility and compassion, embodies a sense of what is possible; the analytic-rational content is essential for determining appropriate courses of action in pursuit of the possible. The task is to initiate a dialogue between the metaphoric and the analytic.

Apparent in the set of working-class attitudes and beliefs examined earlier in this chapter, is a pervasive ambiguity which has its roots in the incongruity between concrete experiences and generalized, predominant values. Reflected in these beliefs is an emotional awareness of problems and frustrations, which exists without theoretical understanding. If a dialogue between the metaphoric and analytic can be established, it may be possible to synthesize emotional awareness with theoretical understanding.[67] Only in this way can the 'new' conceptions of man, society, and life submerged in the working-class community and in liberated play gain meaningful expression. What is required, then, is the creation of a new culture and a new public. As Wilbert Moore notes with reference to Latin America, the gist of acculturation studies is that the young, the women, and the lower classes—in short, the oppressed—are quickly attracted to new cultures introduced in society.[68] There is no reason to doubt that workers in advanced industrial society will similarly find new cultures appealing. The task of the new culture would be to mediate between the deficient understandings which currently prevail and the theoretical understandings available through more comprehensive perspectives. In this regard, the social sciences and, for reasons outlined earlier, sociology in particular, are crucial. For, as Gouldner suggests, "to say social theorists are concept-creators means that they are not merely in *knowledge*-creating business but, above all, in the *language*-reform and

language-creating business. In other words, they are from the beginning
involved in creating a new culture.''[69] In this context social theory can
supplement emotional awareness with theoretical understanding and, in so
doing, can translate concrete experience into political categories. In conjunction with social theory, emotional awareness can animate the workers
to struggle for those goals which are within their reach—that is, those which
are ascertainable by their own actions. Once expressed, the elements of
human community now buried in the patterns, institutions, and relationships
of working-class life will not only justify resistance; they will also normatively
guide social protest.

The supersession of one-dimensionality does not entail a 'return to a
wild,' the dismantlement of the industrial apparatus and the disparagement
of science and technology. It involves, rather, a restructuring of industrialization, science, and technology so that they become responsive to basic
human needs. In one sense this requires that men "re-learn some of the arts
of living lost in the industrial revolution; how to fill the interstices of days
with enriched, more leisurely, personal and social relations; how to break
down once more the barriers between work and life."[70] This rediscovery of
the lost—or, more appropriately, the submerged—arts of living must take
place in conjunction with the realities of advanced industrial society, where
people, as Thompson points out,

> must somehow combine in a new synthesis elements of the old
> and of the new, finding an imagery based neither upon the
> seasons nor upon the market but upon human occasions.
> Punctuality in working hours would express respect for one's
> fellow workmen. And unpurposive passing of time would
> be behavior which the culture approved.[71]

In terms of industrialized societies, this requires a dialectic between work
and play, between the world of the factory and the world of the community.
In terms of industrializing societies, this entails a model of development
which does not subordinate the traditional to the modern, the emotions to
the achievement motivation, or the informal structures of community to the
formal and bureaucratic structures of the nation-state. The synthesis of the
old and the new, the fantasy and the real, the nonrational and the rational,
creates the integrated experience which humanizes space and time.

CONCLUSION

The analysis of the English working class proffered in this study has been
guided by a concern with the sources of and obstacles to rebellious and revolutionary activity. In this chapter, this concern continues to be evident both

in our examination of the nature of legitimacy in modern society and in the effort to further identify the conditions under which people are likely to demand that their society become more responsive and more responsible. The interpretive scheme which we have brought to bear on the issues of rebellion and revolt derives from a social theory which incorporates a conception of autonomous human interests. As a consequence, this scheme conjoins analysis with a critical assessment of societies in terms of how effectively they allow for the satisfaction of basic human interests and needs. At the same time, such a theory and interpretive framework provide the expectation that societies and cultures will be under constant, though varying, pressure to assume more responsive orientations.[72] The issue of standards of legitimacy—both as it relates to the confirmation and/or discrediting of existing arrangements and to the justification of challenges to these arrangements—is tied to and defined in terms of this expectation.

When the capacity to express human interests and needs is suppressed, and when critical categories are, in turn, precluded from the standards of legitimacy, the pressure applied to make society and culture more responsive substantially declines. In situations of one-dimensionality, instances of overt rebellion are rare. For the English workers of the nineteenth century, one-dimensionality rested on the physical destruction of community traditions, values, and customs. For the workers of advanced industrial society, one-dimensionality is rooted in less harsh but no less debilitating measures. The advance of industrialization has made domination, in most cases, materially less uncomfortable but spiritually more debasing. In suggesting, as we have, the need to release the liberating tendencies currently locked in play and in the institutions of the working-class community, we are not dismissing the importance of industrial advances to human well-being; nor are we calling for their abolition. One-dimensionality will be overcome by abandoning, not industrialization, but the techniques of cultural impoverishment which have accompanied it.[73]

Social theory—more specifically, social theory that remains critical of itself—can contribute much to the cultural development and growth that presupposes both the reemergence of the rebellious disposition and the reintroduction of critical categories into standards of legitimacy. This statement does not constitute a renewal of Comte's vision of the sociologist as the high priest of society; nor is it an attempt to sneak sociologists into the leadership positions of Lenin's vanguard party. Workers may bear the brunt of domination in modern society, but they are not dumb and ignorant. To be sure, their knowledge of the impact of domination far surpasses anything sociology can make available. However, this knowledge receives inappropriate articulation: it is not comprehensively connected to the social totality. Sociology is capable of providing the theoretical understandings through which these connections can be made. It is essential, if not imperative, for sociologists to shed their unwillingness to supply these theoretical understandings and to "instruct the world in the very things they have learned from the world."[74] This does not mean that sociologists can or should lead social movements critical of the established order. What it does mean is that sociology should be committed to the establishment of the true human community.

NOTES

1. See Georg Lukacs, *History and Class Consciousness* (Cambridge, 1971), pp. 265-271.

2. Albert Camus, *The Rebel* (New York, 1956), p. 214.

3. James O'Connor, "Merging Thought with Feeling," in *The Revival of American Socialism* (New York, 1971), p. 23.

4. William Leiss quoted in Trent Schroyer, *The Critique of Domination* (New York, 1973), p. 25.

5. See Victor Gioscia, "On Social Time," in *The Future of Time* (New York, 1972), p. 77.

6. See Herbert Gutman, "Work, Culture, and Society in Industrializing America," *American Historical Review* 78, 3 (1973): 556-557.

7. Ibid., pp. 576-577.

8. Bruce Johnson, "The Democratic Mirage: Notes Toward a Theory of American Politics," *Berkeley Journal of Sociology* 13 (1968): 17.

9. For the specific case of England see Munger, "Participation and Militancy in Industrial Revolution England," pp. 6-8 and for the general implications see Charles Tilly, "Do Communities Act?" *Sociological Inquiry* 43, 3-4 (1973): 209-240.

10. See Harvey Cox, *The Feast of Fools* (Cambridge, 1969), p. 64.

11. Eric Wolf, *Peasant Wars of the Twentieth Century* (New York, 1969), p. 292.

12. See William Irwin Thompson, *The Imagination of an Insurrection* (New York, 1967). The role of play in the French upheaval of 1968 is documented clearly in Angelo Quattrochhi and Tom Nairn, *The Beginning of the End* (London, 1968); and Sherry Turkle, "Symbol and Festival in the French Student Uprising," *Symbol and Politics in Communal Ideology* (Ithaca, 1975), pp. 68-100.

13. On the sociological mistreatment of past and play see, respectively, John O'Neill, *Making Sense Together* (New York, 1974); and Edward Norbeck, "Man at Play," *Natural History* 80 (December, 1971): 48-53.

14. See Thompson, *The Imagination of an Insurrection,* pp. 232-233.

15. See John O'Neill, "The Responsibility of Reason and the Critique of Political Economy," *Phenomenology and the Social Sciences,* vol. II (Evanston, 1973), p. 309.

16. Alvin Gouldner, "The Politics of Mind," in *For Sociology* (New York, 1973), p. 103.

17. John Schaar, "Legitimacy in the Modern State," in *Criminal Justice in America* (Boston, 1974), p. 74.

18. Seymour Martin Lipset, *Political Man* (New York, 1960), p. 64.

19. Schaar, "Legitimacy in the Modern State," p. 64.

20. Claus Mueller, *The Politics of Communication* (New York, 1973), p. 135. The relation between this and Habermas' position is examined in Dick Howard, "A Politics in Search of the Political," *Theory and Society* 1, 3 (1974): 271-306.

21. Jürgen Habermas, "What Does a Crisis Mean Today? Legitimation Problems in Late Capitalism," *Social Research* 40, 4 (1973): 655. A more extensive development of this argument is found in Habermas' *Legitimation Crisis* (Boston, 1975).

22. Habermas, "What Does a Crisis Mean Today?" p. 661.

23. Lester Milbrath, *Political Participation* (Chicago: 1967), p. 21.

24. See Schaar, "Legitimacy in the Modern State," pp. 80-83.

25. See Mueller, *The Politics of Communication,* p. 19.

26. Ibid., p. 43.

27. Ibid., p. 113.

28. See Amitai Etzioni, "Basic Human Needs, Alienation, and Inauthenticity," *American Sociological Review* 33, 6 (1968): 881.

29. Ibid., p. 880.

30. Richard Sennett and Jonathan Cobb, *The Hidden Injuries of Class* (New York, 1973); Richard Hoggart, *The Uses of Literary* (New York: 1957); Michael Mann, "The Social Cohesion of Liberal Democracy," *American Sociological Review* 35, 3 (1970), reprinted in *Contemporary Analytical Theory* (New York: 1972), pp. 210-229.

31. Hoggart, *The Uses of Literacy,* p. 110.

32. Ibid., p. 159.

33. Ibid., p. 161. For some similarities between this and the working-class community in the United States, see Herbert Gans, *The Urban Villagers* (New York: 1962), p. 265.

34. See Gains, *The Urban Villagers,* pp. 223-224 and Marc Fried, *The World of the Urban Working Class* (Cambridge, 1973), pp. 94-95.

35. See Sennett and Cobb, *The Hidden Injuries of Class,* p. 117.

36. See ibid., p. 95; and Fried, *The World of the Urban Working Class,* p. 208.

37. Sennett and Cobb, *The Hidden Injuries of Class,* p. 153.

38. See Fried, *The World of the Urban Working Class,* p. 207. Some of the psychological consequences of this situation are insightfully examined by Ernest Becker in *The Revolution in Psychiatry* (New York, 1964) and *The Structure of Evil* (New York, 1968), pp. 327-346.

39. Mann, "The Social Cohesion of Liberal Democracy," p. 225.

40. Ibid., p. 215; and Richard Hamilton, *Class and Politics in the United States* (New York, 1972), p. 519.

41. Fried, *The World of the Urban Working Class,* p. 228.

42. See Mann, "The Social Cohesion of LIberal Democracy," pp. 217-225. These simplistic challenges to society should not be taken as indications of working-class authoritarianism. See Sennett and Cobb, *The Hidden Injuries of Class,* pp. 119-150; and Hamilton, *Class and Politics in the United States,* pp. 399-506.

43. Fried, *The World of the Urban Working Class,* pp. 195-196.

44. This sense of impotence is reflected in and reinforced by the regular use of the passive voice. See Sennett and Cobb, *The Hidden Injuries of Class,* p. 193.

45. Andre Gorz, *Socialism and Revolution* (New York, 1973), pp. 26-27.

46. Habermas, "What Does a Crisis Mean Today?," p. 659.

47. See Jürgen Moltmann, *Theology of Play* (New York, 1971), pp. 69-70. Moltmann's argument receives support in Eric Klinger, "Development of Imaginative Behavior: Implications of Play for a Theory of Fantasy," *Psychological Bulletin* 72, 4 (1969): 284-285.

48. Bill Watson, "Counter-Planning on the Shop Floor," *Radical America* 5, 3 (1971).

49. Ibid., p. 7.

50. Support for Watson's observations is found in: Jeremy Brecher, *Strike!* (Greenwich, Conn., 1974), p. 304; Stanley Aronowitz, *False Promises* (New York, 1973), pp. 21-50, and Gorz, *Socialism and Revolution,* pp. 27-37.

51. Aronowitz, *False Promises,* pp. 82-83.

52. Moltmann, *Theology of Play,* p. 12.

53. Gorz, *Socialism and Revolution,* p. 202.

54. See Gans, *Urban Villagers,* pp. 36-37.

55. See Fried, *The World of the Urban Working Class,* pp. 94-95 and Gans, *Urban Villagers,* p. 303.

56. See, for instance, Morris Axelrod, "Urban Structure and Social Participation," *American Sociological Review* 21 (February, 1956): 13-18 and Floyd Dotson, "Patterns of Voluntary Associations Among Working Class Families," *American Sociological Review* 16 (October, 1951): 687-693.

57. See Lipset, *Political Man,* pp. 87-126.

58. Fried, *The World of the Urban Working Class,* pp. 201-202.

59. See ibid., p. 230; and Gans, *Urban Villagers,* pp. 229-230.

60. See Basil Bernstein, "Social Class, Language, and Socialization," *Language and Social Context* (Baltimore: 1972), pp. 157-178 and *Class, Codes, and Control* (London: 1971).

61. Berstein, "Social Class, Language, and Socialization," p. 164.

62. See Mueller, *The Politics of Communication,* pp. 160, 73.

63. See William Labov, "The Logic of Nonstandard English," *Language and Social Context,* pp. 179-215.

64. Bernstein, "Social Class, Language, and Socialization," p. 176.

65. Ibid., p. 165 (emphasis added).

66. Gorz, *Socialism and Revolution,* p. 30.

67. See O'Connor, "Merging Thought with Feeling," p. 36. This distinction between emotional awareness and theoretical understanding parallels the distinction made in Chapter 6 between moral imperatives and structural necessity. The linguistic background of this distinction is brilliantly assessed by Alvin Gouldner, "Prologue to a Theory of Revolutionary Intellectuals," *Telos* 26 (Winter, 1976): 3-36.

68. See Wilbert Moore, *Industrialization and Labor: Some Aspects of Economic Development* (Ithaca, 1951), p. 41.

69. Gouldner, *For Sociology,* p. 105. The relationship between this position and Habermas', and the broader relation between language and play, is examined in Francis Hearn, "Toward a Critical Theory of Play," *Telos* 33 (Winter, 1977).

70. E. P. Thompson, "Time, Work-Discipline, and Industrial Capitalism," *Past and Present* 38 (December, 1967): 95.

71. Ibid., p. 96.

72. See Etzioni, "Basic Needs, Alienation, and Inauthenticity," p. 878.

73. See Andre Gorz, *Strategy for Labor* (Boston, 1964), p. 126; and William Leiss, *The Domination of Nature* (Boston, 1974), p. 203.

74. O'Neill, *Making Sense Together,* p. 61.

Bibliography

BOOKS

Anderson, Michael. *Family Structure in Nineteenth Century Lancashire.* Cambridge: Cambridge University Press, 1971.

Annan, Noel. *Leslie Stephen.* Cambridge: Harvard University Press, 1952.

Arendt, Hannah. *The Human Condition.* Chicago: University of Chicago Press, 1958.

Aronowitz, Stanley. *False Promises.* New York: McGraw-Hill, 1973.

Ashton, T. S. *An Economic History of England: The Eighteenth Century.* London: Methuen, 1955.

Aspinall, A., ed. *The Early English Trade Unions.* London: Batchworth Press, 1949.

Bailyn, Bernard. *The Ideological Origins of the American Revolution.* Cambridge: Harvard University Press, 1967.

Bauman, Zygmunt. *Towards a Critical Sociology.* Boston: Routledge and Kegan Paul, 1976.

Bauman, Zygmunt. *Culture as Praxis.* Boston: Routledge and Kegan Paul, 1973.

Bauman, Zygmunt. *Between Class and Elite.* Translated by S. Patterson. Manchester: Manchester University Press, 1972.

Bendix, Reinhard. *Nation Building and Citizenship.* New York: Doubleday, 1969.

Bendix, Reinhard. *Work and Authority in Industry.* New York: Harper and Row, 1956.

Bernot, Lucien, and Blançard, Rene. *Nouville, Un Village Francais.* Paris: Institut d'Ethologie, 1953.

Bernstein, Basil. *Class, Codes, and Control.* London: Routledge and Kegan Paul, 1971.

Birnbaum, Norman. *The Crisis of Industrial Society.* New York: Oxford University Press, 1969.

Bland, A. E.; Brown, P. A.; and Tawney, R. H., eds. *English Economic History, Select Documents.* London: G. Bell and Sons, 1914.

Blau, Peter. *Exchange and Power in Social Life.* New York: Wiley and Sons, 1967.

Blumberg, Paul. *Industrial Democracy.* New York: Schocken Books, 1974.

Brecher, Jeremy. *Strike!* Greenwich, Conn.: Fawcett Publications, 1974.

Briggs, Asa. *Victorian Cities.* New York: Harper and Row, 1965.

Briggs, Asa. *The Making of Modern England, 1783-1867.* New York: Harper and Row, 1959.

Brown, Ford K. *Fathers of the Victorians.* Cambridge: Cambridge University Press, 1961.

Browning, Don. *Generative Man.* New York: Dell, 1975.

Buckley, Jerome. *The Triumph of Time.* Cambridge: Belknap Press, 1966.

Bythell, Duncan. *The Handloom Weavers.* Cambridge: Cambridge University Press, 1969.

Camus, Albert. *The Rebel.* New York: Vintage, 1956.

Carpenter, Kenneth, ed. *The Rising of the Agricultural Labourers.* New York: Arno Press, 1972.

Challinor, Raymond, and Ripley, Brian. *The Miners' Association—A Trade Union in the Age of the Chartists.* London: Lawrence and Wishart, 1968.

Checkland, S. G. *The Rise of Industrial Society in England, 1815-1885.* London: Longmans, 1964.

Clapham, J. H. *An Economic History of Modern Britain.* Cambridge: Cambridge University Press, 1926.

Clark, G. Kitson. *The Making of Victorian England.* New York: Atheneum, 1971.

Cole, G. D. H. *Attempts at General Union.* London: Macmillan & Co., 1953.

Cole, G. D. H. *A Century of Co-operation.* London: Allen and Unwin, 1944.

Cole, G. D. H. *British Working Class Politics, 1832-1914.* London: Routledge and Sons, 1941.

Cole, G. D. H. *A Short History of the British Working Class Movement.* (2 vols.) New York: Macmillan Co., 1930.

Cole, G. D. H., and Filson, A. W. *British Working Class Movements: Select Documents, 1789-1875.* New York: St. Martin's Press, 1967.

Cole, G. D. H., and Postgate, Raymond. *The British Common People.* New York: Barnes and Noble, 1961.

Collins, Henry, and Abramsky, Chimen. *Karl Marx and the British Labour Movement.* London: Macmillan & Co., 1965.

Connelly, James. *Labor in Irish History.* New York: Donnelly Press, 1919.

Cottle, Thomas, and Klineberg, Stephen. *The Present of Things Future.* New York: The Free Press, 1974.

Cox, Harvey. *The Feast of Fools.* Cambridge: Harvard University Press, 1969.

Curtis, L. P. *Apes and Angels.* Washington, D.C.: Smithsonian Institute Press, 1971.

Curtis, L. P. *Anglo-Saxons and Celts.* Bridgeport, Conn.: University of Bridgeport Press, 1968.

Darvall, Frank. *Popular Disturbances and Public Order in Regency England.* London: Oxford University Press, 1934.

Deane, Phyllis. *The First Industrial Revolution.* Cambridge: Cambridge University Press, 1965.

Deane, Phyllis, and Cole, W. A. *British Economic Growth, 1688-1959, Trends and Structures.* Cambridge: Cambridge University Press, 1962.

de Grazia, Sebastian. *Of Time, Work, and Leisure.* New York: The Twentieth Century Fund, 1962.

Dobb, Maurice. *Studies in the Development of Capitalism.* New York: International Publishers, 1947.

Douglas, Mary. *Natural Symbols.* New York: Random House, 1973.

Duncan, Hugh. *Communication and Social Order.* New York: Oxford University Press, 1962.

Eisenstadt, S. M. *The Political System of Empires.* New York: Free Press, 1964.

Ellis, P. B. *A History of the Irish Working Class.* London: Victor Gollancz, 1972.

Engels, Frederick. *Socialism: Utopian and Scientific.* Translated by E. Aveling. New York: International Publishers, 1972.

Engels, Frederick. *The Condition of the Working Class in England, 1844.* Stanford: Stanford University Press, 1958.

Faulkner, Harold. *Chartism and the Churches.* New York: Columbia University Press, 1916.

Fleischer, Helmut. *Marxism and History.* New York: Harper and Row, 1973.

Frankfurt Institute of Social Research. *Aspects of Sociology.* Translated by John Viertel. Boston: Beacon Press, 1972.

Freeman, T. W. *The Conurbations of Great Britain.* Manchester: Manchester University Press, 1959.

Fried, Marc. *The World of the Urban Working Class.* Cambridge: Harvard University Press, 1973.

Furniss, Edgar. *The Position of the Labourer in a System of Nationalism.* New York: Kelly and Millman, 1957.

Gans, Herbert. *The Urban Villagers.* New York: Free Press, 1962.

Gayer, Arthur D.; Rostow, W. W.; and Schwartz, Anna. *The Growth and Fluctuation of the British Economy, 1790-1850.* New York: Oxford University Press, 1953.

Giiddens, Anthony. *The Class Structure of Advanced Societies.* London: Hutchinson University Library, 1973.

Giddens, Anthony. *Capitalism and Modern Social Theory.* London: Cambridge University Press, 1971.

Gillespie, Frances. *Labor and Politics in England, 1850-1867.* New York: Octagon Books, 1966.

Gorz, Andre. *Socialism and Revolution.* Translated by M. Nicolaus and V. Ortiz. New York: Doubleday, 1973.

Gorz, Andre. *Strategy for Labor.* Translated by N. Denny. Boston: Beacon Press, 1964.

Gouldner, Alvin. *For Sociology.* New York: Basic Books, 1973.

Gunnell, John. *Political Philosophy and Time.* Middletown, Conn.: Wesleyan University Press, 1968.

Habermas, Jürgen. *Legitimation Crisis.* Translated by J. McCarthy. Boston: Beacon Press, 1975.

Habermas, Jürgen. *Theory and Practice.* Translated by J. Viertel. Boston: Beacon Press, 1973.

Habermas, Jürgen. *Knowledge and Human Interests.* Translated by J. Shapiro. Boston: Beacon Press, 1971.

Habermas, Jürgen. *Toward a Rational Society.* Translated by J. Shapiro. Boston: Beacon Press, 1970.

Halevy, Elie. *The Birth of Methodism.* Chicago: University of Chicago Press, 1971.

Halevy, Elie. *A History of the English People in the Nineteenth Century.* Vol. I. London: Peter Smith, 1949.

Halevy, Elie. *The Age of Peel and Cobden.* New York: Peter Smith, 1948.

Halevy, Elie. *The Growth of Philosophic Radicalism.* New York: Macmillan Co., 1928.

Hamilton, Richard. *Class and Politics in the United States.* New York: Wiley and Sons, 1972.

Hammond, J. L. and Barbara. *The Skilled Labourer.* London: Longmans, 1936.

Hammond, J. L. and Barbara. *The Village Labourer.* London: Longmans, 1936.

Hanham, H. J. *Elections and Party Management: Politics in the Time of Disraeli and Gladstone.* London: Longmans, 1959.

Harrison, J. F. C. *The Early Victorians, 1832-1851.* New York: Praeger, 1971.

Harrison, Royden. *Before the Socialists.* London: Routledge and Kegan Paul, 1965.

Hartwell, R. M. *The Industrial Revolution and Economic Growth.* London: Methuen, 1971.

Hibbert, Christopher. *King Mob.* New York: World Publishing Company, 1958.

Himmelfarb, Gertrude. *Victorian Minds.* New York: Knopf, 1968.

Hobsbawn, E. J. *Industry and Empire.* New York: Pantheon, 1968.

Hobsbawn, E. J. *Labouring Men.* London: Weidenfeld and Nicolson, 1964.

Hobsbawn, E. J. *Primitive Rebels.* New York: Norton and Company, 1959.

Hobsbawn, E. J. and Rudé, George. *Captain Swing.* New York: Pantheon, 1969.

Hodgskin, Thomas. *Labor Defended Against the Claims of Capitalism.* London: Labour Publishing Co., 1922.

Hoggart, Richard. *The Uses of Literacy.* New York: Oxford University Press, 1957.

Hollis, Patricia, ed. *Class and Conflict in Nineteenth-Century England, 1815-1850.* London: Routledge and Kegan Paul, 1973.

Hollis, Patricia. *The Pauper Press.* London: Oxford University Press, 1970.

Horkheimer, Max. *Eclipse of Reason.* New York: Seabury Press, 1974.

Horkheimer, Max, and Adorno, Theodor. *Dialectic of Enlightenment.* Translated by J. Cumming. New York: Herder and Herder, 1972.

Houghton, Walter. *The Victorian Frame of Mind.* New Haven: Yale University Press, 1957.

Huizinga, Johan. *Homo Ludens.* Boston: Beacon Press, 1950.

Hurlburt, E. P. *Essays on Human Rights and Their Political Guaranties.* New York: Fowles and Wells, 1853.

Inglis, K. S. *Churches and the Working Class in Victorian England.* London: Routledge and Kegan Paul, 1963.

Israel, Joachim. *Alienation: From Marx to Modern Sociology.* Boston: Allyn and Bacon, 1971.

Jackson, John. *The Irish in Britain.* London: Routledge and Kegan Paul, 1963.

Jay, Martin. *The Dialectical Imagination.* Boston: Little, Brown, and Co., 1973.

Jones, Gareth Stedman. *Outcast London.* New York: Oxford University Press, 1971.

Kelsen, Hans. *What is Justice?* Berkeley: University of California Press, 1957.

Leff, Gordon. *History and Social Theory.* New York: Doubleday, 1971.

Leiss, William. *The Domination of Nature.* Boston: Beacon Press, 1974.

Lipset, Seymour Martin. *Political Man.* New York: Doubleday, 1960.

Lubenow, William. *The Politics of Government Growth.* Hamden, Conn.: Archon Books, 1971.

Lukacs, Georg. *History and Class Consciousness.* Cambridge: M.I.T. Press, 1971.

Lukcas, John. *Historical Consciousness.* New York: Harper and Row, 1968.

Lynd, Staughton. *Intellectual Origins of American Radicalism.* New York: Random House, 1968.

Maccoby, S. *English Radicalism, 1762-1785.* London: Allen and Unwin, 1955.

Macpherson, C. B. *The Political Theory of Possessive Individualism.* New York: Oxford University Press, 1962.

Malcolmson, Robert. *Popular Recreations in English Society, 1700-1850.* London: Cambridge University Press, 1973.

Malthus, Thomas. *An Essay on the Principle of Population and its Effects on Human Happiness*. London: Ward, Lock, and Co., 1890.

Mannheim, Karl. *Man and Society in an Age of Reconstruction*. New York: Harcourt, Brace, and World, 1940.

Mantoux, Paul. *The Industrial Revolution in the Eighteenth Century*. London: Jonathan Cape, 1961.

Marcus, Stephen. *Engels, Manchester, and the Working Class*. New York: Random House, 1974.

Marcuse, Herbert. *Studies in Critical Philosophy*. Translated by J. deBres. Boston: Beacon Press, 1973.

Marcuse, Herbert. *Five Lectures*. Boston: Beacon Press, 1970.

Marcuse, Herbert. *One-Dimensional Man*. Boston: Beacon Press, 1964.

Marcuse, Herbert. *Eros and Civilization*. New York: Random House, 1955.

Marcuse, Herbert. *Reason and Revolution*. Boston: Beacon Press, 1941.

Marris, Peter. *Loss and Change*. New York: Pantheon, 1974.

Marshall, Dorothy. *Industrial England, 1776-1851*. New York: Scribner's, 1973.

Marshall, T. H. *Social Class and Citizenship*. Cambridge: Cambridge University Press, 1950.

Marx, Karl. *The Grundrisse*. Translated and edited by D. McLellan. New York: Harper and Row, 1971.

Marx, Karl. *A Contribution to the Critique of Political Economy*. Edited by M. Dobb. Translated by S. W. Ryazanskaya. New York: International Publishers, 1970.

Marx, Karl. *Capital*. Vol. I. New York: International Publishers, 1967.

Marx, Karl. *The 18th Brumaire of Louis Bonaparte*. New York: International Publishers, 1963.

Marx, Karl. *Wage-Labour and Capital*. New York: International Publishers, 1933.

Marx, Karl, and Engels, Frederick. *Articles on Britain*. Moscow: Progress Publishers, 1971.

Marx, Karl, and Engels, Frederick. *The Communist Manifesto*. Peking: Foreign Language Press, 1970.

Marx, Karl, and Engels, Frederick. *The German Ideology*. Edited and translated by C. J. Arthur. New York: International Publishers, 1970.

Mather, F. C. *Public Order in the Age of the Chartists*. Manchester: Manchester University Press, 1959.

McAlister, John, and Mus, Paul. *The Vietnamese and Their Revolution*. New York: Harper and Row, 1969.

McCord, Norman. *The Anti-Corn Law League, 1838-1846*. London: Allen and Unwin, 1958.

Milbrath, Lester. *Political Participation*. Chicago: Rand McNally, 1965.

Mill, John Stuart. *Principles of Political Economy*. New York: D. Appleton and Co., 1895.

Moltmann, Jürgen. *Theology of Play*. Translated by R. Ulrich. New York: Harper and Row, 1971.

Moore, Barrington. *Reflections on the Causes of Human Misery*. Boston: Beacon Press, 1973.

Moore, Barrington. *Social Origins of Dictatorship and Democracy*. Boston: Beacon Press, 1966.

Moore, Barrington. *Political Power and Social Theory*. New York: Harper and Row, 1958.

Morton, A. L., and Tate, George. *The British Labour Movement, 1770-1920*. London: Lawrence and Wishart, 1956.

Mueller, Claus. *The Politics of Communication*. New York: Oxford University Press, 1973.

Neale, Robert. *In Praise of Play*. New York: Harper and Row, 1969.

Neumann, Franz. *The Democratic and Authoritarian State*. New York: Free Press, 1957.

Nisbet, Robert. *The Social Bond*. New York: Knopf, 1970.

Ollman, Bertell. *Alienation: Marx's Conception of Man in Capitalist Society*. New York: Cambridge University Press, 1971.

O'Neill, John. *Making Sense Together*. New York: Harper and Row, 1974.

O'Neill, John. *Sociology as a Skin Trade*. New York: Harper and Row, 1972.

Ostrogrowski, Moisei. *Democracy and the Organization of Political Parties*. Vol. I. New York: Doubleday, 1964.

Padover, Saul, ed. *Karl Marx on the First International*. New York: McGraw-Hill, 1973.

Paine, Thomas. *The Rights of Man*. New York: Parke & Co., 1908.

Park, George. *The Idea of Social Structure*. New York: Doubleday, 1974.

Parkin, Frank. *Class Inequality and Political Order*. New York: Praeger, 1971.

Parsons, Talcott. *The Structure of Social Action*. New York: McGraw-Hill, 1937.

Peacock, A. J. *Bread or Blood*. London: Gollancz, 1965.

Peel, Frank. *The Risings of the Luddites*. London: Frank Cass and Co., 1968.

Pelling, Henry. *Popular Politics and Society in Late Victorian Britain*. New York: St. Martin's Press, 1968.

Pelling, Henry. *A History of British Trade Unionism*. London: Macmillan & Co., 1963.

Perkin, Harold. *The Origins of Modern English Society, 1780-1880*. Toronto: University of Toronto Press, 1969.

Perry, Thomas. *Public Opinion, Propaganda, and Politics in Eighteenth-Century England*. Cambridge: Harvard University Press, 1962.

Piaget, Jean. *Play, Dreams, and Imitation in Childhood*. New York: Norton and Company, 1962.

Pierson, Stanley. *Marxism and the Origins of British Socialism*. Ithaca, New York: Cornell University Press, 1973.

Pocock, J. G. A. *Politics, Language, and Time*. New York: Atheneum, 1971.

Pocock, J. G. A. *The Ancient Constitution and the Feudal Law*. Cambridge: Cambridge University Press, 1957.

Polanyi, Karl. *Primitive, Archaic, and Modern Economics: Essays of Karl Polanyi*. Edited by G. Dalton. New York: Doubleday, 1968.

Polanyi, Karl. *The Great Transformation*. Boston: Beacon Press, 1944.

Pollard, Sydney. *The Genesis of Modern Management*. Baltimore: Penguin, 1965.

Redford, Arthur. *Labour Migration in England, 1800-1850*. Manchester: Manchester University Press, 1964.

Reilly, Mary. *Play As Exploratory Learning*. Beverly Hills: Sage Publications, 1974.

Reith, Charles. *British Police and the Democratic Ideal.* London: Oxford University Press, 1943.

Ricardo, David. *Principles of Political Economy and Taxation.* London: Bell and Sons, 1891.

Richter, Melvin. *The Politics of Conscience.* Cambridge: Harvard University Press, 1964.

Robbins, Caroline. *The Eighteenth Century Commonwealthman.* Cambridge: Harvard University Press, 1959.

Rudé, George. *Hanoverian London, 1714-1808.* Berkeley: University of California, 1971.

Rudé, George. *Paris and London in the Eighteenth Century.* New York: Viking Press, 1970.

Rudé, George. *The Crowd in History.* New York: Wiley and Sons, 1964.

Rudé, George. *Wilkes and Liberty.* New York: Oxford University Press, 1962.

Schaff, Adam. *Marxism and the Human Individual.* Translated by O. Wojtasiewicz. Edited by R. Cohen. New York: McGraw-Hill, 1970.

Schroyer, Trent. *The Critique of Domination.* New York: George Braziller, 1973.

Selsam, Howard, and Martel, Harry, eds. *Reader in Marxist Philosophy.* New York: International Publishers, 1963.

Semmel, Bernard. *The Methodist Revolution.* New York: Basic Books, 1973.

Sennett, Richard, and Cobb, Jonathan. *The Hidden Injuries of Class.* New York: Knopf, 1973.

Shelton, Walter. *English Hunger and Industrial Disorders.* Toronto: University of Toronto Press, 1973.

Smelser, Neil. *Social Change in the Industrial Revolution.* Chicago: University of Chicago Press, 1959.

Simmel, Georg. *The Sociology of Georg Simmel.* Translated by K. Wolff. New York: The Free Press, 1950.

Sombart, Werner. *Socialism and the Social Movement.* New York: Augustus M. Kelly, 1968.

Stone, Julius. *Human Law and Human Justice.* Stanford: Stanford University Press, 1965.

Strauss, Leo. *Natural Right and History.* Chicago: University of Chicago Press, 1953.

Sweezy, Paul. *The Theory of Capitalist Development.* New York: Monthly Review Press, 1942.

Taylor, E. R. *Methodism and Politics, 1791-1851.* Cambridge: Cambridge University Press, 1935.

Thomas, Maurice. *The Early Factory Legislation.* Westport, Conn.: Greenwood Press, 1970.

Thomis, Malcolm. *The Luddites.* New York: Schocken, 1972.

Thompson, Dorothy. *The Early Chartists.* Columbia, S.C.: University of South Carolina Press, 1971.

Thompson, E. P. *The Making of the English Working Class.* New York: Random House, 1963.

Thompson, William Irwin. *The Imagination of an Insurrection.* New York: Oxford University Press, 1967.

Tobias, J. J., ed. *Nineteenth-Century Crime in England*. New York: Barnes and Noble, 1972.

Tobias, J. J. *Crime and Industrial Society in the 19th Century*. Oxford Alden Press, 1967.

Tucker, Robert, ed. *The Marx-Engels Reader*. New York: Norton and Company, 1972.

Turner, H. A. *Trade Union Growth, Structure, and Policy*. Toronto: University of Toronto Press, 1962.

Turner, Victor. *The Ritual Process*. Chicago: University of Chicago Press, 1969.

Udy, Stanley. *Work in Traditional and Modern Society*. Englewood Cliffs, N. J.: Prentice-Hall, 1970.

Veitch, George. *The Genesis of Parliamentary Reform*. London: Constable, 1913.

Venable, Vernon. *Human Nature, the Marxian View*. New York: World Publishing Company, 1945.

Ward, W. R. *Religion and Society in England, 1790-1850*. New York: Schocken, 1973.

Wearmouth, Robert. *Some Working Class Movements of the Nineteenth Century*. London: Epworth Press, 1948.

Wearmouth, Robert. *Methodism and the Working-Class Movements of England, 1800-1850*. London: Epworth Press, 1937.

Webb, R. K. *The British Working Class Reader*. New York: Augustus M. Kelley, 1955.

Webb, Sidney and Beatrice. *The History of Trade Unionism*. London: Longmans, 1935.

Weisskopf, Walter. *Alienation and Economics*. New York: Dell Publishers, 1971.

Wellmer, Albrecht. *Critical Theory of Society*. Translated by J. Cumming. New York: Herder and Herder, 1971.

Wickham, E. R. *Church and People in an Industrial City*. London: Lutterworth Press, 1957.

Wiener, Joel. *The War of the Unstamped*. Ithaca: Cornell University Press, 1969.

Williams, Gwyn. *Artisans and Sans-Culottes*. New York: Norton and Co., 1969.

Williams, Raymond. *The Long Revolution*. New York: Columbia University Press, 1961.

Wilson, Charles. *England's Apprenticeship, 1603-1763*. London: Longsmans, 1965.

Wolf, Eric. *Peasant Wars of the Twentieth Century*. New York: Harper and Row, 1969.

Wright, Thomas. *Some Habits and Customs of the Working Classes*. Original edition, 1867. New York: Augustus M. Kelley, 1967.

ARTICLES

Allen, V. L. "The Origins of Industrial Conciliation and Arbitration." *International Review of Social History* 9, 2 (1964): 237-254.

Ashton, T. S. "The Standard of Life of the Workers in England, 1790-1850." *Journal of Economic History* 9 (supplement, 1949): 19-38.

Axelrod, Morris. "Urban Structure and Social Participation." *American Sociological Review* 21 (February, 1956): 13-18.

Bauman, Zygmunt. "Marxism and the Contemporary Theory of Culture." *Co-existence* 5 (July, 1968): 161-171.

Beales, H. L. "The Historical Context of the Essay on Population" in *Introduction to Malthus.* Edited by D. V. Glass. London: Watts and Co., 1953.

Bernstein, Basil. "Social Class, Language, and Socialization." *Language and Social Context.* Edited by P. Giglioli. Baltimore: Penguin Books, 1972.

Birnbaum, Norman. "The Crisis in Marxist Sociology" in *Recent Sociology, 1.* Edited by H. P. Dreitzel. New York: Macmillan Co., 1969.

Briggs, Asa. "The Language of 'Class' in Early Nineteenth Century England" in *Essays in Labour History.* Edited by A. Briggs and J. Saville. London: Macmillan & Co., 1960.

Briggs, Asa, ed. "The Local Background of Chartism." *Chartist Studies.* New York: Macmillan Co., 1959.

Briggs, Asa, ed. "National Bearings." *Chartist Studies.* New York: Macmillan Co., 1959.

Briggs, Asa. "Middle-Class Consciousness in English Politics, 1780-1846." *Past and Present* 9 (April, 1956): 65-74.

Briggs, Asa. "Social Structure and Politics in Birmingham and Lyons." *British Journal of Sociology* 1 (March, 1950): 67-80.

Brown, Lucy. "The Chartists and the Anti-Corn Law League" in *Chartist Studies.* Edited by A. Briggs. New York: Macmillan Co., 1959.

Burke, Richard. " 'Work' and 'Play.' " *Ethics* 82, 1 (1971): 33-47.

Bythell, Duncan. "The Handloom Weavers in the English Cotton Industry during the Industrial Revolution: Some Problems." *Economic History Review* 17, no. 2 (1964): 339-353.

Clanchy, M. T. "Remembering the Past and the Good Old Law." *History* 55 (June, 1970): 165-176.

Clark, G. Kitson. "The Repeal of the Corn Laws and the Politics of the Forties." *Economic History Review* 4, no. 1 (1951): 1-13.

Clarke, P. F. "Electoral Sociology of Modern Britain." *History* 57 (February, 1972): 31-55.

Clements, R. V. "British Trade Unions and Popular Political Economy, 1850-1875." *Economic History Review* 14, no. 1 (1961): 93-104.

Coats, A. W. "Economic Thought and Poor Law Policy in the Eighteenth Century." *Economic History Review* 13, no. 1 (1960): 39-51.

Coats, A. W. "Changing Attitudes to Labour in the Mid-Eighteenth Century." *Economic History Review* 11, no. 1 (1958): 35-51.

Collins, Henry. "The London Corresponding Society" in *Democracy and the Labour Movement.* Edited by J. Saville. London: Lawrence and Wishart, 1954.

Cousins, J. M., and Davis, R. L. " 'Working Class Incorporation'—A Historical Approach with Reference to the Mining Communities of S. E. Northumberland, 1840-1890." *The Social Analysis of Class Structure.* Edited by F. Parkin. London: Tavistock Publications, 1974.

Deane, Phyllis. "Capital Formation in Britain Before the Railway Age." *Economic Development and Cultural Change* 10, 3 (April, 1961).

Derry, T. K. "The Repeal of the Apprenticeship Clauses and the Statute of Artificers." *Economic History Review* 3 (January, 1931): 67-87.

Dotson, Floyd. "Patterns of Voluntary Associations Among Working Class Families." *American Sociological Review* 16 (October, 1951): 687-693.

Easton, Lloyd. "Alienation and Empiricism in Marx's Thought." *Social Research* 37 (Autumn, 1970): 402-427.

Ehrmann, Jacques. "Homo Ludens Revisited" in *Game, Play, and Literature.* Edited by J. Ehrmann. Boston: Beacon Press, 1968.

Etzioni, Amatai. "Basic Human Needs, Alienation, and Inauthenticity." *American Sociological Review* 33 (December, 1968): 870-885.

Fink, Eugen. "The Oasis of Happiness: Toward an Ontology of Play" in *Game, Play, and Literature.* Edited by J. Ehrnamm. Boston: Beacon Press, 1968.

Floisted, Guttörn. "Social Concepts of Action." *Inquiry,* 13 (Summer, 1970): 175-198.

Foster, John. "Nineteenth-Century Towns—A Class Dimension." *The Study of Urban History.* Edited by H. J. Dyos. New York: St. Martin's Press, 1968.

Giddens, Anthony. "Notes on the Concepts of Play and Leisure." *The Sociological Review* 12 (1964): 73-89.

Gioscia, Victor. "On Social Time" in *The Future of Time.* Edited by H. Yaker, H. Osmond, and F. Cheek. New York: Doubleday, 1972.

Gouldner, Alvin. "Prologue to a Theory of Revolutionary Intellectuals." *Telos* 26 (Winter, 1976): 3-36.

Gouldner, Alvin. "The Norm of Reciprocity: A Preliminary Statement." *American Sociological Review* 25 (April, 1960): 161-178.

Grampp, William. "On Manufacturing and Development." *Economic Development and Cultural Change* 18 (April, 1970): 451-463.

Grampp, William. "The Liberal Elements in English Mercantilism." *Quarterly Journal of Economics* 66 (November, 1952): 465-501.

Grampp, William. "On the Politics of the Classical Economists." *Quarterly Journal of Economics* 62 (November, 1948): 714-747.

Gray, R. Q. "Styles of Life, The 'Labour Aristocracy' and Class Relations in Later Nineteenth Century Edinburgh." *International Review of Social History* 18, 3 (1973): 428-452.

Gutman, Herbert. "Work, Culture, and Society in Industrializing America." *American Historical Review* 78 (June, 1973): 531-588.

Habermas, Jürgen. "What Does a Crisis Mean Today? Legitimation Problems in Late Capitalism." *Social Research* 40 (Winter, 1973): 643-667.

Habermas, Jürgen. "Summation and Response." *Continuum* 8 (Spring/Summer, 1970): 123-133.

Habermas, Jürgen. "Toward A Theory of Communicative Competence." *Recent Sociology,* 2. Edited by H. P. Dreitzel. New York: Macmillan Co., 1970.

Hammond, J. L. "The Industrial Revolution and Discontent." *Economic History Review* 2, no. 2 (1930): 215-228.

Harrison, Brian. "Teetotal Chartism." *History* 58 (June, 1973): 193-217.

Harrison, Brian. "Religion and Recreation in Nineteenth-Century England." *Past and Present* 38 (December, 1967): 98-125.

Harrison, J. F. C. "Chartism in Leeds" in *Chartist Studies.* Edited by A. Briggs, New York: Macmillan Co., 1959.

Harrison, J. F. C. "Chartism in Leicester" in *Chartist Studies.* Edited by A. Briggs. New York: Macmillan Co., 1959.

Harrison, Royden. "The British Working Class and the General Election of 1868." *International Review of Social History* 5, 4 (1960): 424-455.

Harrison, Royden. "Professor Beesly and the Working Class Movement" in *Essays in Labour History.* Edited by A. Briggs and J. Saville. London: Macmillan & Co., 1960.

Harrison, Royden, "E. S. Beesly and Karl Marx." *International Review of Social History* 4 1 (1959): 22-58.

Hartwell, R. M. "The Standard of Living During the Industrial Revolution: A Discussion." *Economic History Review* 16, no. 1 (1963): 134-146.

Hearn, Francis. "The Dialectical Uses of Ideal-Types." *Theory and Society* 2, 4 (1975): 531-561.

Hearn, Francis. "The Implications of Critical Theory for Critical Sociology." *Berkeley Journal of Sociology.* 18 (Fall, 1973), 127-158.

Herrick, Francis. "The Second Reform Movement in Britain, 1850-1865." *Journal of the History of Ideas* 9 (April, 1948): 174-192.

Hobsbawm, E. J. "The Social Functions of the Past." *Past and Present* 55 (May, 1972): 3-17.

Hobsbawm, E. J. "The Standard of Living During the Industrial Revolution: A Discussion." *Economic History Review* 16, no. 1 (1963): 120-134.

Hobsbawm, E. J. "Custom, Wages, and Work-Load in Nineteenth-Century Industry" in *Essays in Labour History.* Edited by A. Briggs and J. Saville. London: Macmillan, 1960.

Hobsbawm, E. J. "Methodism and the Threat of Revolution in Britain." *History Today* (February, 1957): 115-124.

Hobsbawm, E. J. "Machine-Breakers." *Past and Present* 1 (February, 1952): 57-70.

Howard, Dick. "A Politics in Search of the Political" in *Theory and Society* 1 (Fall, 1974): 271-306.

Huch, Kurt Jürgen. "Interest in Emancipation." *Continuum* 8 (Spring/Summer, 1970): 27-39.

Huzel, James. "Malthus, the Poor Law, and Population in Early Nineteenth-Century England." *Economic History Review* 22 (December, 1969): 430-452.

Jaeger, Gertrude and Selzmick, Philip. "A Normative Theory of Culture" in *The Study of Society.* Edited by P. Rose. New York: Random House, 1970.

Jay, Martin. "Some Recent Developments in Critical Theory." *Berkeley Journal of Sociology* 18 (Fall, 1973): 27-44.

Johnson, Bruce. "The Democratic Mirage: Notes Toward a Theory of American Politics." *Berkeley Journal of Sociology* 13 (1968) [reprinted as Warner Module no. 315].

Johnson, Richard. "Educational Policy and Social Control in Early Victorian England." *Past and Present* 49 (November, 1970): 96-119.

Jones, Gareth Stedman. "Working-Class Culture and Working-Class Politics in London, 1870-1900: Notes on the Remaking of a Working Class." *Journal of Social History* 7 (Summer, 1974): 460-508.

Klinger, Eric. "Development of Imaginative Behavior: Implications of Play for a Theory of Fantasy." *Psychological Bulletin* 72 (Fall, 1969): 277-298.

Lane, Roger. "Crime and the Industrial Revolution: British and American Views." *Journal of Social History* 7 (Spring, 1974): 287-303.

Lifton, Robert. "Individual Patterns in Historical Change: Imagery of Japanese Youth." *Comparative Studies in Society and History* 6 (Winter, 1964): 369-383.

Lockwood, David. "Sources of Variation in Working Class Images of Society." *Sociological Review* 14 (May, 1966): 249-267.

MacAskill, Joy. "The Chartist Land Plan" in *Chartist Studies*. Edited by A. Briggs. New York: Macmillan Co., 1959.

Macpherson, C. B. "Democratic Theory: Ontology and Technology" in *Political Theory and Social Change*. Edited by D. Spitz. New York: Atherton Press, 1967.

Maehl, William. "Chartist Disturbances in Northeastern England, 1839." *International Review of Social History* 8, 4 (1963): 389-414.

Mandle, W. F. "Games People Played: Cricket and Football in England and Victoria in the Late Nineteenth Century." *Historical Studies 15 (April, 1973): 511-535.*

Mann, Michael. "The Social Cohesion of Liberal Democracy." *Contemporary Analytical Theory*. Edited by D. Apter and C. Andrain. New York: Prentice-Hall, 1972.

Marcuse, Herbert. "Remarks on a Redefinition of Culture." *Daedalus* 94 (Winter, 1965): 190-207.

Mathias, Peter. "Social Structure in the Eighteenth Century: A Comparison by Joseph Maisse." *Economic History Review,* 10, no. 1 (1957): 30-45.

Miller, Stephen. "Ends, Means, and Galumphing: Some Leitmotifs of Play." *American Anthropologist* 75 (February, 1973): 87-98.

Mueller, Claus. "Notes on the Repression of Communicative Behavior." *Recent Sociology,* 2nd ed. Edited by H. P. Drietzel. New York: Macmillan, 1970.

Nairn, Tom. "The English Working Class." *Ideology in Social Science*. Edited by R. Blackburn. New York: Vintage Books, 1973.

Nettles, Curtis. "British Mercantilism and the Economic Development of the Thirteen Colonies." *Journal of Economic History* 12 (Spring, 1952): 105-114.

Nicolaus, Martin. "The Unknown Marx" in *The New Left Reader*. Edited by Carl Oglesby. New York: Grove Press, 1969.

Norbeck, Edward. "Man at Play." *Natural History* 80 (December 1971): 48-53.

Norris, J. M. "Samuel Garbett and the Early Development of Industrial Lobbying in Great Britain." *Economic History Review* 10, no. 3 (1958): 450-460.

Nossiter, T. J. "Aspects of Electoral Behavior in English Constituencies, 1832-1868" in *Mass Politics*. Edited by E. Allardt and S. Rokkan. New York: Free Press, 1970.

O'Connor, James. "Merging Thought with Feeling" in *The Revival of American Socialism*. Edited by George Fischer. New York: Oxford University Press, 1971.

O'Higgins, Rachel. "The Irish Influence in the Chartist Movement." *Past and Present* (November, 1961): 83-96.

Oliver, W. H. "Robert Owen and the English Working-Class Movements." *History Today* 8 (November, 1958): 787-796.

Ollman, Bertell. "Toward Class Consciousness Next Time: Marx and the Working Class." *Politics and Society* 3 (Fall, 1972): 1-24.

O'Neill, John. "The Responsibility of Reason and the Critique of Poitical Economy." *Phenomenology and the Social Sciences.* Vol. 2. Edited by M. Nathanson. Evanston, Ill.: Northeastern University Press, 1973.

Plumb, J. H. "Political Man." *Man versus Society in 18th-Century Britain.* Edited by J. Clifford. New York: Norton and Company, 1968.

Pollard, Sydney. "Factory Discipline in the Industrial Revolution," *Economic History Review* 16, 2 (1963): 260-269.

Pollard, Sydney. "Nineteenth-Century Cooperation: From Community Building to Shopkeeping" in *Essays in Labour History.* Edited by A. Briggs and J. Saville. London: Macmillan, 1960.

Porter, J. H. "Wage Bargaining Under Conciliation Agreements, 1860-1914." *Economic History Review* 33 (December 1970): 460-475.

Powell, G. Bingham. "Incremental Democratiziation: The British Reform Act of 1832" in *Crisis, Choice, and Change.* Edited by G. Almond and R. Mundt. Boston: Little, Brown, and Co., 1973.

Prothero, I. J. "London Chartism and the Trades." *Economic History Review* 24 (May, 1971): 202-219.

Prothero, I. J. "Chartism in London." *Past and Present* 44 (August, 1969): 76-105.

Read, Donald. "Chartism in Manchester" in *Chartist Studies.* Edited by A. Briggs. New York: Macmillan Co., 1959.

Reid, Herbert. "American Social Science in the Politics of Time and the Crisis of Technocorporate Society: Toward A Critical Phenomenology" in *Politics and Society,* 3 (Winter, 1973): 201-244.

Rokkan, Stein. "Mass Suffrage, Secret Voting, and Political Participation" in *Political Sociology.* Edited by Lewis Coser. New York: Harper and Row, 1966.

Rose, R. B. "Eighteenth Century Price Riots and Public Policy in England." *International Review of Social History* 6, no. 2 (1961): 227-292.

Rose, R. B. "The Priestley Riots of 1791." *Past and Present* 18 (November, 1960): 68-88.

Rosenberg, Nathan. "The Direction of Technological Change." *Economic Development and Cultural Change* 18 (October, 1969): 1-24.

Rowe, D. J. "The Chartist Convention and the Regions." *Economic History Review* 22 (April, 1969): 58-74.

Rowe, D. J. "The Failure of London Chartism." *The Historical Journal* 11, 3 (1968): 472-487.

Rowe, D. J. "Chartism and the Spitalfields Silk-Weavers." *Economic History Review* 20 (December, 1967): 482-493.

Rudé, George. "Protest and Punishment in Nineteenth-Century Britain." *Albion* 5 (Spring, 1973): 1-23.

Rudé, George. "Review of *The Early Victorians.*" *American Journal of Sociology* 78 (March, 1973): 1325-1326.

Rudé, George. "English Rural and Urban Disturbances on the Eve of the First Reform Bill, 1830-1831." *Past and Present* 37 (July, 1967): 87-102.

Rudé, George. "The London 'Mob' of the Eighteenth Century." *The Historical Journal,* 2, no. 1 (1959): 1-18.

Rudé, George. "The Gordon Riots." *History Today* 5 (July, 1955): 429-437.

Rudé, George. "The Gordon Riots: A Study of the Rioters and Their Victims." *Transactions of the Royal Historical Society,* 5th series, no. 6 (1955): 93-114.

Saville, John. "The Christian Socialists of 1848" in *Democracy and the Labour Movement.* Edited by J. Saville. London: Lawrence and Wishart, 1954.

Schaar, John. "Legitimacy in the Modern State" in *Criminal Justice in America.* Edited by R. Quinney. Boston: Little, Brown and Co., 1974.

Schroyer, Trent. "The Dialectical Foundations of Critical Theory: Jürgen Habermas' Metatheoretical Investigations." *Telos* 12 (Summer, 1972): 93-114.

Schroyer, Trent. "Marx and Habermas." *Continuum,* 8, (Spring/Summer, 1970), 52-61.

Schroyer, Trent. "Toward a Critical Theory of Advanced Industrial Society." *Recent Sociology,* 2. Edited by H. P. Dreitzel. New York: Macmillan Co., 1970.

Sennett, Richard. "Charismatic De-Legitimation: A Case Study." *Theory and Society* 2 (Summer, 1975): 171-181.

Shapiro, Jeremy. "One-Dimensionality: The Universal Semiotic of Technological Experience" in *Critical Interruptions.* Edited by P. Breines. New York: Herder and Herder, 1970.

Shiman, Lillian. "The Band of Hope Movement: Respectable Recreation for Working-Class Children." *Victorian Studies* 17 (September, 1973): 49-74.

Silver, Allan. "The Demand for Order in Civil Society" in *Criminal Justice in America.* Edited by R. Quinney. Boston: Little, Brown, and Co., 1974.

Simon, Daphne. "Master and Servant" in *Essays in Labour History.* Edited by A. Briggs and J. Saville. London: Macmillan & Co., 1960.

Solomon, Maynard. "Marx and Bloch: Reflections on Utopia and Art." *Telos* 13 (Fall, 1972): 68-85.

Thackery, Arnold. "Natural Knowledge in a Cultural Context: The Manchester Model." *American Historical Review* 79 (June, 1974): 672-709.

Tholfsen, Trygve. "The Intellectual Origins of Mid-Victorian Stability." *Political Science Quarterly* 86 (March, 1971): 57-91.

Tholfsen, Trygve, "The Transition of Democracy in Victorian England." *International Review of Social History* 6, 2 (1961): 226-248.

Tholfsen, Trygve. "The Origins of the Birmingham Caucus." *Historical Journal* 2 (1959): 161-184.

Tholfsen, Trygve. "The Chartist Crisis in Birmingham." *International Review of Social History* (1958): 461-480.

Thomas, Keith. "Work and Leisure in Pre-Industrial Society." *Past and Present* 29 (December, 1964): 50-62.

Thompson, E. P. "Patrician Society, Plebian Culture." *Journal of Social History* 7 (Summer, 1974): 382-405.

Thompson, E. P. "The Moral Economy of the English Crowd in the Eighteenth Century." *Past and Present* 50 (February, 1971): 76-136.

Thompson, E. P. "Time, Work-Discipline and Industrial Capitalism." *Past and Present* 38 (December, 1967): 56-97.

Tilly, Charles. "The Modernization of Political Conflict in France." in *Perspectives on Modernization.* Edited by E. Harvey. Toronto: University of Toronto Press, 1973.

Treble, J. H. "O'Connor, O'Connell and the Attitudes of the Irish Immigrants Towards Chartism in the North of England, 1838-48." *The Victorians and Social Protest.* Hamden, Conn.: Archon Books, 1973.

Treble, J. H. "The Irish Agitation" in *Popular Movements.* New York: St. Martin's Press, 1970.

Turkle, Sherry. "Symbol and Festival in the French Student Uprising" in *Symbols and Politics in Communal Ideology.* Edited by S. Moore and B. Myerhoff. Ithaca: Cornell University Press, 1975.

Vicinus, Martha. "The Study of Nineteenth-Century British Working-Class Poetry" in *The Politics of Literature.* Edited by L. Kampf and P. Lawter. New York: Random House, 1972.

Walker, Kenneth. "The Classical Economists and the Factory Acts." *Journal of Economic History* 1 (November, 1941): 168-177.

Wallace, Anthony. "Revitalization Movements." *American Anthropologist* 58 (April, 1956): 264-281.

Watson, Bill. "Counter-Planning on the Shop Floor." *Radical America* 5 (May/June, 1971): 1-12.

Werly, John. "The Irish in Manchester, 1832-1849." *Irish Historical Studies* 18 (March, 1973): 345-358.

White, Robert. "Motivation Reconsidered: The Concept of Competence." *Psychological Review* 66 (September, 1959): 297-334.

Williams, David. "Chartism in Wales." *Chartist Studes.* Edited by A. Briggs. New York: Macmillan Co., 1959.

Wrigley, E. A. "The Process of Modernization and the Industrial Revolution in England." *The Journal of Interdisciplinary History* 3 (Autumn, 1972), 215-259.

Young, Nigel. "Prometheans or Troglodytes? The English Working Class and the Dialectics of Incorporation." *Berkeley Journal of Sociology* 12 (Summer, 1967): 1-43.

UNPUBLISHED PAPERS AND DISSERTATIONS

Bickford, Christopher. "The Improving Principle: Changing Attitudes Toward Social Mobility in England, 1700-1860." Dissertation, University of Connecticut, 1971.

Lemert, Charles, and Rossel, Richard. "Cultural Revolution and the Definition of Reality." Paper read at the Annual Meeting of the American Sociological Association; New York, August, 1973.

Marglin, Stephen. "What Do Bosses Do? The Origins and Functions of Hierarchy in Capitalist Development." Research Paper, Harvard University. May, 1971.

Munger, Frank. "Participation and Militancy in Industrial Revolution England." Paper presented at Annual Meeting of the American Sociological Association, Montreal, August, 1974.

Vicinus, Martha. "The Lowly Harp: Nineteenth Century Working Class Poetry." Dissertation, University of Wisconsin, 1969.

Index

ABOUT THE AUTHOR

FRANCIS HEARN, a specialist in social theory, political sociology, and social organization, is assistant professor of sociology at State University College, Cortland, New York. He has previously published articles in the *Berkeley Journal of Sociology, Theory and Society, Politics and Society, Telos,* and *The Sociology Quarterly.*